UNCONDITIONAL DEMOCRACY

www.hoover.org

Hoover Institution Press Publication No. 244

First printing, 1982
First paperback printing, 2004
14 13 12 11 10   9 8 7 6 5 4 3

Manufactured in the United States of America
The paper used in this publication meets the minimum requirements
of American National Standard for Information Sciences—Permanence
of Paper for Printed Library Materials, ANSI Z39.48-1984. ∞

Excerpted with permission:

Reminiscences by General of the Army Douglas MacArthur,
McGraw-Hill Book Company. Copyright © 1964 by Time Inc.

The Yoshida Memoirs by Shigeru Yoshida. Translated by Kenichi Yoshida.
First American edition, 1962. Copyright © 1962 by Shigeru and Kenichi Yoshida.
Reprinted by permission of Houghton Mifflin Company.

Japan's American Interlude by Kazuo Kawai. Copyright © 1960 by
University of Chicago Press.

Sources of Japanese Tradition by Ryusaka Tsunoda, William Theodore de Barry,
and Donald Keene. Copyright © 1964 by Columbia University Press.

ISBN 978-0-8179-7441-1 cloth
ISBN 978-0-8179-7442-8 pbk
ISBN 978-0-8179-7443-5 ebook
Library of Congress Catalog Card Number: 80-8328

To my mother and late father

Contents

PART ONE: FROM EMPIRE TO DEMOCRACY

Preface to
Paperback Edition

        In every man's life, in every nation's existence, there is
an extraordinary moment of revelation when faith in certitude vanishes
like dewdrops in the summer sun, leaving in its wake a mirage of unrecoverable splendor.

        On the bright horrific morning of September 11, 2001, America's
hearts and souls united for justice. The American flag colored the land.
The United States had no choice but to search and destroy the guilty. The
battle cry "regime change for democracy" echoed the rightful rage and
hopes of the American people.

        Islamic Iraq, one of the oldest civilizations on earth with the world's
second-largest oil reserves, had emerged as a hotbed of terrorism. Confronted by U.S. soldiers, the Iraqi leaders and troops who had presented
themselves as formidable combatants proved with dazzling swiftness to be
skillful at hiding among civilians. Baghdad fell in only three weeks. Then,
the whole world witnessed looting, plundering, pillaging, and shooting by
and among the Iraqi people themselves.

        Can a ravaged and anarchistic Iraq in the interminably volatile
region be guided to democracy and prosperity? Can the United States
transform the ethnocentric fervor of Islam to a sustainable energy for

democracy? Is there even a glimmer of hope for Afghanistan, the poverty-stricken and relentlessly warring ancient land?

History favors the fortunate, indeed. The United States has a brilliant track record of effecting a "regime change": witness Imperial Japan.

Imperial Japan, fiercely proud, had fought to the last soldier against the strongest nation in the world and lost. Then, undergoing a spectacle of extraordinary metamorphosis, Imperial Japan was transformed into a prosperous democracy and the best friend of the United States in the Asia-Pacific region.

Five days before I was born in Osaka, Imperial Japan, presuming an imminent attack from the United States and underestimating the enemy, bombed beautiful Pearl Harbor. Japan called it "the preemptive first strike." America retaliated with a vengeance by firebombing all the major cities in the Japanese archipelago.

In burning Tokyo, in the heart of the empire ablaze, the Japanese, who had survived the massive blanket bombings by the feared "flying fortress" B29s and the two atomic bombs, waited for the dishonor of surrender. The exhausted and hungry Japanese could no longer recall the roars of victory of December 7, 1941, on the streets of Tokyo. Throngs of women and children inspiring the soldiers to kill every enemy had also died for the promise of eternal glory. Four horrible years. The Empire of the Rising Sun sacrificed everything, even its own soul, but could not repel the American forces. In the collective Japanese mind, being alive in the aftermath of battle was tantamount to unbearable shame.

I remember leaving Osaka with my mother for the mountainous countryside, where she, a wealthy landowner, held a large agricultural piece of land and employed many tenant farmers. The train we took had all its windows painted black to hide from the B29s, which rained incendiary firebombs on everything visible or moving. Even with that precaution our train crawled in the darkness of the night. I was four years old. Soon afterward, Osaka was reduced to a smoldering heap of charcoal. I heard adults whispering that the smoke smelled of decay. Perhaps it was the pungent odor of a dying empire.

President Harry S. Truman assigned the illustrious U.S. Army general Douglas MacArthur to the unprecedented task of changing militant Japan to a peace-loving nation. We, conquered and starving, thought the tall, handsome, and charismatic MacArthur was "the missionary of democracy." He told us he was. My mother would lose her land because MacArthur said that the absentee landlord was feudalistic, hence a hindrance to democracy, and ordered her land, which her family had owned for hundreds of years, to be handed over free of charge to the tenants. She believed for a long time that MacArthur was a communist.

The United States occupied Japan for seven years and changed the regime. Japan has become a shining showcase for U.S. foreign policy, a great success by any standard anywhere in the world. *Unconditional Democracy* is a detailed account of the massive regime change from the perspective of a Japanese boy, who grew up in devastated postwar Japan and went to America to graduate school.

The American success in Japan, however, has raised some serious questions for the Japanese people; that is, for democracy and prosperity have we traded something precious and unrecoverable that we should have kept at all costs?

Let me describe my encounter with American soldiers in Japan.

On a hot, humid afternoon in late August 1946, I was almost five when I saw for the first time American GIs in the famous Jeep driving fast on a dirt road between the rice paddies of my little farming village. I had never seen foreigners or automobiles running on gasoline. This village, nourished by a narrow meandering river and embraced by soft evergreen mountains, was a paradise of wildflowers everywhere, black fighting beetles, iridescent butterflies and carnivorous dragonflies and bumblebees, large nonpoisonous snakes, the largest salamander in the world, and haunting fireflies. The well-cared-for tiers of lush rice paddies blanketed the village. Overlooking the village from the highest mountain was a samurai castle in its dilapidated glory. The village was idyllic like a French impressionist painting. Men of the village went to war, and most did not come home.

On the Jeep, now moving slowly, the GIs, laughing happily, waved at us three boys, barefooted in tattered shorts, bare-chested, and deeply tanned. In a small creek along the paddies we had been catching delicious catfish and big black carp. Throwing away a bucket with a few catches, we dashed after the Jeep and GIs in khaki uniforms. They threw handfuls of chocolates, chewing gum, and cigarettes up in the air repeatedly. We screamed with joy. Scrambling on the dusty road for the treasures from heaven, we stuffed our mouths first with gum and chocolates and then filled our pockets with the cigarettes and more gum and chocolates. The Jeep stopped, and the GIs took our picture as we appreciatively posed for them. They smiled and said something, then waved and drove away fast. A bluish exhaust fume smelled magical, like the perfume of an advanced civilization.

Carrying the rare harvest cradled in my arms, I went home and showed the gift from America to my father. "You shameless beggar!" was his indictment. But I caught a flash of immense sadness over his lean features, a handsome face that revealed the want of food yet undying pride. I would learn later that this pride of the Japanese men and women helped

Japan maintain grace and dignity even in colossal defeat. There was no looting, no plundering, no pillaging, or shooting by and among the Japanese. There was not one incident of Japanese attack on American soldiers, ever, in the seven years of the Occupation.

In the summer of 1945, Douglas MacArthur landed on Japanese soil to teach the Japanese the virtues of peace and democracy. Standing on the pinnacle of devastated Japan, MacArthur said that Japanese society was "four hundred years behind the West." The Japanese did not argue with the American Shogun, for they understood that Japan had lost, and thus in accord with their martial culture they must silently endure the consequences of defeat. MacArthur's devoted staff interpreted the Japanese acquiescence as a natural result of the general's "brilliant appraisal of the Oriental mind."

As a precondition for democracy, MacArthur ordered the Japanese government to search out all militarists and jingoists, those who were once called "true patriots." All conspicuous promoters of the war, who had not yet committed honorable suicide, were easily caught (they did not hide) and, after the Tokyo Military Tribunal, hanged or imprisoned. Is this cleansing not Japan's ultimate reparation for the war?

MacArthur's term for the treatment of the undesirable Japanese was "moral disarmament." "Armament" or "military preparedness" became immoral, a dirty word in the defeated nation. But it was an alien concept in the land of martial arts.

MacArthur's most urgent task was to make sure that Japan would never again become a threat to the United States: future Japan must remain physically incapable of fighting, as MacArthur put it, "even for preserving its own security." His determination resulted in the famous (and notorious) Article Nine of the Japanese Constitution, the document his staff wrote in six days in English.

Article Nine reads, "Aspiring sincerely to an international peace based on justice and order, the Japanese people forever renounce war as a sovereign right of the nation and the threat or use of force as a means of settling international dispute." To accomplish this lofty ideal, "land, sea, and air forces, as well as other war potential, will never be maintained. The right of belligerency of the state will not be recognized."

MacArthur expounded on the difficult art of utopia-building to every Japanese pupil (me included). His staff censored all textbook manuscripts and deleted such unacceptable words as *patriotism*. MacArthur, a great American patriot, preached to the Japanese that one's patriotism implied a propensity to fight for his country and thus contradicted Japan's new "pacifism."

His lecture worked miracles. Even now the word *patriotism* is taboo in Japan. The Japanese have become addicted to the purest grade of pacifism, feeling superior to the rest of warring nations, like an idealist who ignores reality. Yet postwar Japan cannot defend itself. Japan, an island nation smaller than California yet the second-largest economic power in the world, has been behaving like "a big chicken of the Pacific" in the face of immediate and imminent threats in Asia and the Middle East. A rich but insecure Japan kowtows to the world to survive.

The world has changed since 1945. Japan, at last, has begun changing. Although the Japanese still want to hibernate in a cocoon of peace, an increasingly loud call for self-defense is emerging from our little archipelago in the sea of lethal dangers.

We Japanese must break out of the narcotic self-deception that any crisis can be solved by "peaceful means" or more dialogue. Indeed, it is dangerous to assume that just because we have no territorial ambitions, other neighboring nations, some of which own nuclear arms and are openly predatory, would not invade our country. Would the 40,000 American soldiers stationed in Japan, costing us $5 billion dollars a year, come to our rescue? Yes, they would. Should they? No, they should not because we must not rely on American goodwill for our own survival. For the sake of our pride and dignity, which I believe are more important than anything we possess, we ought to fight for our land. I do not want to see even a drop of young American soldiers' blood shed on our shore defending us. If and when there is a battle for our lives, it should be our own blood on our shores.

The reissued *Unconditional Democracy* (originally published in 1982) I hope will illustrate the difficult mission of a regime change, of a successful metamorphosis that amalgamates incompatible cultures and religions, conflicting memories of hopes and disappointments, and then gives birth to something greater than the past.

TOSHIO NISHI
Summer 2003
Japan

Editor's Foreword

In *Unconditional Democracy*, the first publication in the Education and Society series, Toshio Nishi presents a powerful account of how, between 1945 and 1952, the American occupation forces deliberately used education as an instrument to transform Japanese culture from an imperialistic society into a democratic nation.

Few examples from history equal the Japanese experience in the intentional use of education to change a people's basic values and behavior. In the mid-nineteenth century the Meiji Emperor designed an educational system to catapult Japan into the modern world. A generation ago General Douglas MacArthur, during the American occupation of Japan, employed education to inculcate democratic values and institutions.

Unconditional Democracy is a carefully documented study by a Japanese scholar of 1) the nature of his society before World War II; 2) the war and the defeat of his nation, which then was occupied by General MacArthur and the American military; 3) the sweeping changes in social, economic, and political goals and activities directed by General MacArthur; 4) the fundamental reforms made in education in order to teach the people new values and institutions appropriate to a democratic society; and 5) the price Japan has paid for these changes.

In a unique introduction to the main thesis of this book, Dr. Nishi recalls his personal experiences as a school and college student at the time of the reforms and his responses to the changes in educational content and methods that the school authorities were introducing to foster the new democratic society. In the conflict between the traditional and the new, the older stress on discipline, morals and manners, and rote memorization competed with the new emphases on the individual freedom to initiate, create, and challenge. The traditional values of worship of and loyalty to the emperor and of conformity to one's group became intermingled with the democratic idea of freedom from restraint. The final synthesis of traditional pedagogy and the occupation's imposed schooling in the author's personality forms the background of this book.

The purpose of this treatise is to document how the Japanese were led to accept democracy unconditionally. The Allies had won the war. The Americans under General MacArthur's command were in charge of pacification and reconstruction. The Japanese had accepted defeat and the occupation and assumed that the conqueror must have won because of superior values and institutions. Most were ready to learn what they imagined were the better goals and methods of the Americans and to integrate those lessons with the best from their ancient society. Their acquiescence and the strong drive of individual Japanese to excel through learning were significant prerequisites for the American effort to change Japan.

The three parts of this book constitute a logical framework within which Dr. Nishi shows how the occupying forces conceived the task of pacifying Japan and joining it to the community of Western democracies. Part One sets the stage by describing Japanese society and Japanese education before World War II. It is clear that the indoctrination of that period powerfully reinforced the goals and means of the oligarchy that ruled Japan in the name of the emperor. Part Two relates the war, the defeat of Japan's military forces, and the efforts of the American military to pacify the warlike nation, including General MacArthur's retention of the emperor as a symbol of the nation and the Japanese acceptance of the general and his imposed constitution as the new authority. Part Three documents the struggle to create new educational content and methods to help develop a democratic nation. The old military and economic oligarchy thwarted efforts to change the curriculum and teaching and learning. Through the teachers' union the Communists exploited every opportunity to obstruct the planned changes. The determination of MacArthur and his educational advisers was sufficient to win most of the conflicts.

The author has rendered an important service by the depth of his archival research. His presentation of failures and successes is balanced.

While revering MacArthur for his use of his power to force democratic institutions and values on the nation, Dr. Nishi does not hesitate to criticize the general and his Washington superiors for blunders and confused judgments. Dr. Nishi seems to say that the world is a safer and better place because of the vision and wisdom that directed the occupation of Japan. And the book demonstrates once again that education plays a powerful role in war and peace.

PAUL R. HANNA

Hoover Institution

Acknowledgments

My indebtedness to individuals and institutions is substantial. I received a generous grant in aid of research from the Hoover Institution on War, Revolution and Peace at Stanford University. The Harry S. Truman Library Institute offered me a grant to read the Truman papers.

I am most grateful to Ramon H. Myers of the Hoover Institution for his vigorous encouragement and generous hospitality. Paul R. Hanna, Charles G. Palm, Richard Burress, and Richard T. Staar of the Hoover Institution facilitated my research at the Hoover Library and Archives.

The title of the book sprang from Charles Burgess's mouth during one late summer night conversation at his house on Puget Sound. It sounded right and accurately depicted the American intention in 1945.

Brian Molmen, my tolerant and demanding friend, read the entire manuscript as many times as I did.

To J. M. B. Edwards of Berkeley, California, I would like to express my deep appreciation for his meticulous attention to detail and sharp editorial judgment.

For their valuable advice and assistance I would like to express my appreciation to Dennis Bilger, Edward J. Boone Jr., William G. Carr,

Arthur Coladarci, Robert Cope, George S. Counts, John K. Emmerson, Jean S. Hanna, Donald Hellmann, Earnest R. Hilgard, James R. Huntley, Kazuo and Natsuki Ihara, Marius B. Jansen, Christine Jayne, Emiko Moffit, Edna Myers, George D. Stoddard, Takemae Eiji, John Taylor, Robert E. Ward, Donald T. Williams Jr., and Benedict K. Zobrist.

To John Raisian, director of the Hoover Institution, and Richard Sousa, senior associate director, I thank you deeply for reissuing *Unconditional Democracy*.

Mototaka Hiroike, chairman of the Hiroike Academy and the Institute of Moralogy in Chiba, Japan, is a man of exemplary courage, rare in contemporary Japan. I try to emulate him.

Maria, my wife, you are my beautiful muse. To my two children growing up wholesome near Tokyo and Stanford, I hope you will become the bridge over the Pacific.

Personal
Introduction

After the Americans left Japan and after the avalanche of American reforms had swept through the Japanese school yards, indigenous Japanese forms remained. Conspicuously, at that. From 1948 to 1954, when I was in primary school, every morning before class began all the pupils from the first to the sixth grades stood in the school yard in straight lines by grade, class, and height. It was called the *chorei,* or "morning greeting." We stood facing a row of our teachers, who wore their "serious faces" for the occasion. The head of each class (always the brightest academically) recorded the roll and handed the roll book to our teacher. In front of us there was a four-foot platform, upon which our principal stood to give us his morning talk. It was the most solemn moment of the day when even the usual mischief makers remained voluntarily quiet.

The principal talked about virtuous deeds and habits that we should emulate. And he announced all important school events and decisions, which our own teacher further explained to us later, in our classroom. When the principal had finished his talk, we marched back to our classrooms to marching music from a loudspeaker. The first grade marched first, always most vigorously and with abnormally straightened backs, overswung arms and overraised legs, but still in a neat line.

Also standing in front of us in the school yard was a famous statue of Ninomiya Sontoku (1787–1856). Known to all Japanese, the statue depicted him carrying a heavy load of firewood on his back and at the same time reading a book. Orphaned at fifteen, he was a devoted reader of the classics but forbidden by his foster family to read at night because of the high cost of lamp oil. He lived a frugal life and worked extraordinarily hard. And he showed a brilliant talent, especially in the subject of agricultural economy, which caught the Tokugawa Shogun's attention. The Shogun asked for his services. Ninomiya symbolized hard work, passion for knowledge, high moral standards, humility, frugality, and self-elevation from poverty to enlightenment. Virtually all Japanese schools had his statue in their school yards.

For the sake of example, it may be appropriate here to describe my personal experiences in postwar schools. I was born in Osaka one week after the Japanese attack on Pearl Harbor in December 1941. The Japanese Empire could not sustain the initial euphoria of having devastated the US Pacific Fleet. Soon metropolitan Osaka, like all other major cities, became an easy and frequent target of massive incendiary bombings by American B-29s. In late 1944 my family moved to the mountainous countryside near Takahashi, in Okayama Prefecture, southwest of Osaka. My maternal grandmother lived there until her death in 1980.

Through the middle of this small, picturesque town runs a river of clear water. Overlooking the town, on top of the highest mountain in the region, is an ancient warrior castle; it is the only remaining mountain castle in Japan. The mountains that encircle the town change color with the seasons. Autumn transforms the summer greens into a many-hued tapestry.

At that time, however, the war was visible everywhere: the white plaster walls of the houses were painted black to hide them from the feared B-29s. Also, across a street from my house, there was an underground neighborhood bomb shelter, which later became our favorite playground. It was dug into the ground about five feet deep, ten feet wide, and fifteen feet long. Its roof, at the ground level, was covered by sheets of lumber and layers of dirt. No concrete was used anywhere, probably because none was available for civilian use. One incendiary bomb would have penetrated the roof. Fortunately, the town was tiny enough for the mighty B-29s to ignore. I never saw any American war planes until the Occupation began; American pilots flying Grumman fighters occasionally used the narrow, winding river for their training. The war ended when I was almost four years old.

My parents lost the land they owned, for they did not cultivate it themselves; under the new law they were absentee landlords. MacArthur called his hastily accomplished land reform a step towards economic democracy. Though not quite convinced of his wisdom, my parents bowed to harsh reality; Japan had lost the war, and it could not be helped. My father was a primary school teacher before and during the war, and became a junior high school English teacher under the new postwar educational system. A teacher's salary was wretched beyond belief. My mother, who came from a wealthy farmer's family, complained bitterly about Mac-Arthur's land reform. She called the reform a fraud. She said, "We never stole our land from anybody. Why do they steal it from us?" My father, the direct descendant of a minor but proud warrior fief lord, never complained about the loss. He liked to repeat the old saying, "Material things come and go. Your education and knowledge stay with you." He seemed to believe that material austerity was a clear sign of one's irreproachable honesty, and that austerity cultivated the spiritual profundity and simplicity that formed the crux of Japanese aesthetics.

"Real hardship began with the end of the stupid war," my mother told me. During the war and the Occupation everything was rationed. To me "real hardship" was the normal state of affairs. Every recyclable item was collected throughout the town: glass bottles, broken glass, all kinds of paper, scrap iron, wire, nails, torn rubber shoes and slippers, rags, and clothes beyond repair. I learned early the seven wild edible spring herbs, which many people in the town collected in baskets. I sensed we were becoming poor, rapidly. For example, we had four houses in the town, and one by one my parents sold three of them. Also sold were three large rocks and a century-old Japanese maple tree from a beautiful garden of our house. My parents borrowed a patch of land from our grandmother (who was by tradition a farmer and had a large holding of fertile land) and cultivated sweet potatoes, pumpkins, tomatoes, cucumbers, onions, snow peas, egg plants, and other things that grew rapidly. They collected firewood in my grandmother's mountains for cooking. Feeling as if I was on a picnic, I followed them whenever they went into the field. My elder brother and two elder sisters also worked hard in the borrowed patch of land. My mother later told me that she exchanged all of her silk kimonos for food and that near the end of the war, when the government had appealed to people to donate precious stones and metals to help the empire launch the last glorious attack on the beastly Americans and change the course of the war, she donated all she had. Of course, so did many other Japanese people. After that appeal the war abruptly ended. Nothing was returned to anybody. The militarists who "lost the war" and who "stole" from the people were not very popular anywhere.

I was a first grader when I saw American soldiers in the town for the first time. About five GIs in a jeep drove through the town throwing chocolates, chewing gum and cigarettes in the air. My friends and I ran after the jeep and frantically collected anything they threw at us, while they were taking our pictures. We kept the chocolates and gum and gave the cigarettes away to neighborhood adults. I proudly told my parents about the day's haul and my father sternly warned me never to repeat it. Those Americans were my first encounter with the aliens, and they all looked alike.

In 1946, at the age of four, I went to the first postwar kindergarten—first, that is, under the new education law. All activities were group-oriented. We danced in a group, sang in a chorus, napped together, and cleaned our room in a group, as there was no janitor. I stayed there two years.

In April 1948 I became a first grader. I vividly remember the fear and excitement of going to "a real school." It was a big event for all first graders and their parents. The first graders' parents attending the entrance ceremony were all mothers. (In Japan it does seem to be a mother's primary task to take full charge of her child's education.) All of us wore our best clothes and shoes and our whitest handkerchief with our names, grade, and class name handwritten on it with black India ink. Mine read: "Nishi Toshio, First Grade, Class—Cherry Blossom." Our fingernails were clean and cut short, our ears had been cleaned out the night before, and our hair was trimmed short. My best clothes and best shoes were those of my seven-years-older brother.

We were introduced to our first real school teacher, Mr. Itoh. He said smilingly, "Welcome to the School! Your first task is to study hard." I did not understand the meaning of "study hard," but it did excite me, for I had already heard the phrase many times and each time it echoed something very serious. Then, a shocking thing happened. Mr. Itoh asked the class if any among us could write our own names and read a book. All of our mothers were standing at the back of the classroom. Immediately about ten of my classmates (there were sixty altogether) raised their hands straight up with convincing shouts of *hai* ("Yes!"). Not only frustrated, I was embarrassed because I could not read and write. Had I played too much in kindergarten? No question about it. The teacher reassured our mothers that they should not worry and that everybody in the class would be able to read and write very soon. After this shattering experience on the first day, my memory of the rest of the day still remains blank.

From the second day onward, all of us wore our usual clothes of rags. They were well washed but had patches all over. In fact, we boys looked like a quilt of subdued colors. Subdued, because schoolboys in Japan did not and still do not wear bright colors; those were and still are for girls. And the girls looked like a colorful quilt. I rarely saw leather shoes among us. Regardless of the seasons most of us wore rubber slip-pers, rice-straw slippers, or *geta* (wooden clogs). Occasionally a rich kid wore a pair of tennis shoes without any holes.

The way we looked in rags and straw sandals did not convince the occupation authorities that we took a daily bath, although we did. About four times a year our heads were blasted by a DDT sprayer. Our black hair turned temporarily white. All fleas and lice died from the overdose, I'm sure. A few girls wept when their long thick hair became a messy tangle. Also, during the primary school years all of us received smallpox vaccinations, twice—each time, six incisions on an arm. I thought I was going to die from the resulting "infections."

At lunch time we were treated to a cup of lukewarm American skim milk, and fresh bread made of American flour. Even though all of us were hungry all the time, most of my friends found drinking the skim milk a form of self-immolation at high noon. I managed to like it—very much, in fact—and gladly drank their share. In addition to the skim milk and some fluffy, airy bread (which was called *koppe* for a reason I still do not know), we sometimes had a cup of vegetable soup, which was very unpopular. Too infrequently we had strawberry jam for the bread, and a half-dozen roasted almonds, or dried apple strips. We all ate those favorites slowly. To supplement our nutritional needs, once a week the school forced us to swallow a large spoonful of cod-liver oil. A few of my classmates used to cry when faced by the spoon the teacher held. Their tears were wasted: everybody had to swallow this very nourishing fish extract.

All of our primary school activities were organized by class and grade. For instance, every autumn there was (and still is) a schoolwide athletic competition, the "Undokai." The entire town attended the event. The school's preparations were intense and elaborate. All teachers and pupils participated both in the preparations and in the actual events. Special practice began two months prior to the Undokai. Two hours a day were spent on a grade-wide mass gymnastics practice, and many hours a week on various athletic exercises. There were dozens of competitions that tested individual skill and agility. But the most exciting events were those in which our class competed against all other classes. A coed relay race—two girls and three boys in a team—was an obsession among all boys and girls who thought themselves fast runners. To make a class team was a big honor in itself. Those of us who made the team practiced hard, as we clearly understood that the fate of our class was at stake. Those who did not make the team (55 of them) would become a team of fanatic cheer-leaders. Our teacher, neighbors, parents, brothers and sisters, and their friends contributed their advice generously on how to run faster, on how to handle a relay baton efficiently, and even on whether we should run barefoot or with a pair of special "racing" rice-straw sandals. Again, none of us wore tennis shoes. Only teachers wore them. Somehow a runner wearing shoes in this serious race would commit a sacrilegious, and worse, a cowardly act. The shoes would add unnecessary weight and slow you down, wouldn't they? But they would protect your little toes from losing nails, wouldn't they? Would you protect your insignificant toenails and risk the fate of your class? We all ran barefoot, gladly, in full expectation of losing a few toenails.

The day before the Undokai all pupils made the school spotless. The arena of competition, an oval track 100 meters in circumference, was prepared with a wet lime line in the center of the school yard. Around the course a rope demarcated a large area for the general audience, and one tent-covered area was reserved for the town notables, such as the mayor, fire chief, police chief, and PTA chairman. The night before the Undokai the whole town prayed for a morning of clear blue autumn sky. When a myriad of gods answered our prayers, virtually all able-bodied persons, including many babies and grandparents, came out. All families cooked and packed the special meal for lunch and came early to get the seats closest to the track. They brought their own straw mats and *zabuton* ("floor cushions").

All pupils wore a uniform at the Undokai: for the boys, white shorts and half-sleeve T-shirts; for the girls, short black bloomers and white half-sleeve blouses. Most of us were barefooted. At the opening ceremony at nine o'clock the mayor, our principal, and the PTA chairman spoke, briefly. They were followed by an academically bright and athletically gifted sixth grader who, with the oath of sportsmanship, declared the Undokai formally open.

The nerve-wracking relay race—our favorite—undoubtedly excited the audience, and the pupils, the most. The relay was the last event before sunset, and by that time people were really worked up about it. The race among the first graders began first. Each of the runners wore a cotton *hachimaki* ("headband") of the designated color for his or her class. My first grade class wore the white *hachimaki*. The more tightly we wore it, the more determined we felt, and the better sprinters we felt we surely became. We devised a secret way to keep the *hachimaki* knot behind our heads tight throughout the race: we put a generous amount of our own saliva on the knot. The *hachimaki* on our forehead (or any Japanese forehead) was a public declaration that we were absolutely and irreversibly committed to our mission; all kamikaze pilots had worn their white *hachimaki* with the crimson rising sun.

The entire audience went wild cheering for their favorite class. Parents whose son or daughter was in the race grew progressively more incoherent. Those of us running in the race were stoically but desperately praying "*Kamisama! Hotokesame!*" ("Shinto gods and Merciful Buddha!") that we would not stumble and fall. A heart-breaking scene of stumbling and falling took place every time, especially among the first, second, and third graders, because of the hyperanxiety that the screaming audience naturally caused them. When I ran as a first grader, my feet were bare but I seemed to have lost all feeling in them; it seemed to me that the deafening waves of cheers were pushing me forward. Luckily, I lost only one toenail. It was not until my sixth Undokai that I could recognize, while sprinting, some faces and voices in the audience and feel the pain of ripped toenails.

After the Undokai was over, the pupils and teachers took a while to get out of the lethargy the excitement had caused. The school, however, had a series of organized events on line. For example, an *ensoku* (literally, "long walk") or "study tour" restored our energy. The first graders went to a nearby riverside park, and the second and third graders up to the castle on the top of the mountain. On the *ensoku* day we came very early to school with a special lunch in a small backpack. We walked to our destination in two neat lines, one for boys and the other for girls, with the shortest one at the head of each line. Our teacher walked in front of us with a class flag and a whistle (it was more like marching than walking). All pupils loved this day, and frequently mothers accompanied the lower grades.

The sixth graders took a "graduation tour" of three nights and four days. It was the most expensive tour of the primary school and since most families could not come up with the large sum of money at the time of the tour, a savings account was established for each pupil by the school and each family put a small amount in the account each month. In twelve months most pupils had the necessary money. The pocket money we were allowed on the tour was 200 yen. At that time one US dollar was 360 yen. A few pupils of wealthy families complained about the amount but our teacher harshly reprimanded them in class. Their complaints, he said, were not only inconsequential but also detrimental to the happiness of everybody. He lectured them that they ought to think harder of those among us who could barely afford the tour itself, and that an additional 200 yen would incur a burden upon these pupils' parents. None of those complaining opened their mouths again, and in fact looked extremely ashamed.

When I was a sixth grader, we went to Yashima on the Island of Shikoku. Yashima was one of the most famous naval battlegrounds. In the late twelfth century two rival clans were striving for hegemony and left many enduring tales of chivalry and tragedy. The Minamoto clan,

which was victorious, ended the imperial regime and began the first Shogunate (warrior regime) in 1192. (The clan that controlled the Shogunate
changed several times, but the imperial regime was not revived until the
1868 Meiji Restoration.) Before we left for the tour, we studied the history
of the two rival clans and especially the emerging code of samurai warriors. At the actual battleground our tour guide told the story of the twelfth-
century combat with great emotional force. We were spellbound. We knew
all the names she was citing and we could see the scene. We kept a minute
diary of our journey and upon our return wrote the longest composition
of our primary school years.

There were several other schoolwide activities. A theater arts festival (*gakugeikai*) was a popular annual winter event that involved every
pupil in one act or another. I was selected to sing a solo in some act. The
reason our music teacher chose me was that I had a voice loud enough for
anybody in our auditorium to hear. In spring and autumn the school conducted a major house cleanup. These were biannual additions to our daily
cleaning of our classroom. We actually used toothpicks to get at the dirt
in the cracks of our wooden floor. Naturally we competed for the honor of
having the shiniest and cleanest classroom in the school. In six years our
class never won it.

Study was, above all, of utmost concern to our parents and to the
pupils. The Japanese school days were (and still are) from Monday through
Saturday; Saturday was a half-day class. Our teacher was the center of
classroom learning. He presented the facts through repeated dictation
and the use of the blackboard. We copied everything on the blackboard.
We chanted the multiplication tables in rhythmic chorus. Not every pupil
in the class could afford to buy textbooks; indeed, most of us shared one
textbook between two pupils and we treated our textbooks with reverence.
Tests were frequent. Homework was assigned every day and had to be
handed in the next day: if one forgot to bring it, he was inevitably sent
home to get it. Few forgot. And on Saturday an extra load of homework
was given to us, because playing all day Sunday might damage our study
habits. Our teacher had a high stake in our achievement: his reputation
as an effective and demanding teacher.

An enormous emphasis on memorization began in the first grade, as
if no decent "thinking" would take place without a vast amount of facts
in one's brain. In fact, the demand to memorize intensified as the grades
progressed. Among our friends the amount one could memorize became
one sure sign of intelligence; a few of my friends showed extraordinary
capacities in this direction.

Throughout primary school our quarterly grades were published in
the main hallway of the school with our names not alphabetically ordered,

but academically. A constellation of the top ten stars remained permanent, while the rest of us migrated back and forth. To all of us the day of judgment caused intense anticipation as well as trepidation. Even those near the end of the list found the day an emotional occasion; they went home and courageously told their eagerly waiting parents that their class standing had once more failed to show signs of mobility. It took courage, I know.

Postwar schools lack any special honor program for the academically gifted, because GHQ thought it would be utterly undemocratic to have one. Prewar imperial Japan had one, and so does the contemporary United States.

I was a fourth grader in 1951, when I took my first course in Romaji. It fascinated most of us for a month or so. Not only I but several of my classmates asked our teacher if we were learning "English" (and wished we were). "No," he replied, "you are studying the Japanese language written in the English alphabet." When an examination came, we used to memorize an entire chapter from the Romaji textbook without being able to read the Romaji. This kind of memorization was not what we generally called "memorization"; rather, it was a blind chanting of a short story written in Romaji. When our teacher asked us to read a section from some other chapter, our eyes became teary and our mouths dry. Writing Romaji was not emphasized, however. We learned how to write the English alphabet in a junior high school English course.

From the first grade our social manners were also an important aspect of our education. A few examples:

1. When our teacher entered the class, we jumped to our feet, bowing and greeting him in unison; only with his permission did we sit down.
2. When an individual pupil was asked a question by the teacher, he swiftly stood up and answered; if he could not answer, he had to say, "I am sorry, but I do not know the correct answer," and remain standing until another pupil could answer correctly.
3. When the teacher asked a question in class, those who knew the answer raised their hands with enthusiastic shouts of *hai*.
4. Perhaps the most difficult thing expected of us was that we keep our fingernails, hands, and faces clean, and our white handkerchiefs white. Our teacher's lectures were frequent but we failed him on this request.

Corporal punishment was meted out unhesitantly by our teacher. It was taken as a natural corrective measure against bad behavior. Punishment ranged from a crisp slap on the face, to standing in a hallway for an hour or two, to a gentle lecture in the faculty office. In my experience the last one was the worst. I never saw the girls receiving any corporal punishment. Did they always behave? Perhaps. Or perhaps, in the Japanese culture of pristine male chauvinism, it was beneath the dignity of a male teacher to punish a female pupil. As for female teachers, they used to take me to the faculty office for a lecture.

The Japanese word for "democracy" is *minshushugi* (literally, "an ideology of people first"). I heard the word daily, especially in the classroom during the primary and secondary school days. One of the most frequent practical examples of democracy at my primary school was a home-room *hanseikai,* or "self-reflection hour," at the end of the day. Our "self-reflection" was a euphemism for public confession. We confessed how bad we were today and vowed that tomorrow we would try harder to be good. After our voluntary confession ended, real "democracy" began. We openly accused each other of this or that, adding that such behavior left a lot to be desired. We did not think we were squealing. A couple of bullies remained suspiciously quiet during this hour of public scrutiny in front of our teacher. I cite this example of democracy in action at my primary school because that was the closest thing there to an open expression of our feelings. The rest of the class activities were carried out efficiently according to the traditional disciplined Japanese style of teaching and learning. And the virtue most consistently encouraged in and out of the classroom was our willingness and ability to behave and work harmoniously in a group. Our best efforts at excellence on our own behalf and for the group's reputation and welfare were openly expected and inconspicuously monitored by all the group members.

While we were taught the idea and practice of democracy, we also learned that the Emperor was the symbol of the State. We did not understand this state symbol at all until, one day in the early elementary school year (perhaps when I was a second grader), its practical meaning was made clear to us. The special train with the Emperor was going to come through the town. One of my neighbors was a steam locomotive operator, and great good fortune befell him: he was chosen to run the imperial train from our station to the next town. According to neighborhood gossip, for a whole month he took a bath twice a day and prayed morning and night at a Shinto shrine that he would not make a mistake and that his locomotive would run perfectly. The day before the train's arrival, our teacher instructed us how to bow most reverently; our heads practically touched our knees. The entire primary school and secondary school population and everybody in the town went to the train station and lined up along the track. The imperial train very slowly sailed before us; from the way we bowed the only thing we could see was the train's wheels. That memorable occasion was our first concrete meeting with the symbol. My second encounter was during my senior high school year in Osaka. This time the wife of the Emperor's brother visited our school. All of the students and faculty lined up along the road leading to our school. It was a hot early summer day. Her scheduled arrival was delayed. We kept standing, which served to enhance our discipline. Her motorcade appeared finally, and while we were bowing, swiftly disappeared out of our view.

Symbols like this one do not stand up well to the test of reality; to preserve their credibility, they must be isolated from the vicissitudes of daily life. Precisely because of their otherworldly character, however, they can retain the spellbinding, surrealistic quality that we Japanese correctly regard as divine.

Our junior high school was newly built in 1953 to accommodate the expansion of compulsory education by three more years. No statue of Ninomiya Sontoku was built in the new school, but the style of our learning hardly changed from primary school except that the volume of learning materials dramatically increased, and we were taught each subject by a specialized subject teacher. Our grades were published in the hallway, and we knew who was the smartest and who was that most unfortunate but courageous one at the end of the list.

Most schoolwide activities in primary school were repeated in junior high school, including the *chorei* ("morning greeting"). The most exciting event was still the Undokai. Again, everybody involved himself in the preparation and actual games. Like the primary school Undokai, the function was attended by the whole town. Also popular with us were games in which our class competed against other classes. When I was a seventh grader, I saw a shocking thing in a relay race: one team of the ninth graders wore spiked running shoes. They looked formidably professional. We seventh graders, who came from the primary school convinced that we were the fastest sprinters the town had ever seen, were intimidated. They carried themselves with an air of controlled pomposity, which we mistook as the aura of superiority. We emulated them. Humility was the hardest quality to achieve and, according to the samurai code, only those who were truly accomplished acquired authentic humility. Most of us ran barefoot, in a kind of frenzy. Humility was nowhere in sight.

The junior high school introduced me to my first athletic club. I should briefly mention the culture peculiar to the Japanese athletic club, as it retains the best and the worst of the Japanese style of discipline in the service of the collectivity. I picked volleyball as my extracurricular activity. It quickly threatened to become my main curriculum. The regular classes ended about three o'clock in the afternoon, and immediately after that our practice began in the school yard and lasted until six o'clock, every day. When it rained, we jogged for an hour or two through the town. On Sunday all club members were required to come to practice.

The hierarchy among the seventh, eighth, and ninth graders was well defined and strictly enforced. We were trained by the ninth graders, who also made the rules of the club. When we were seventh graders, those among us who did not know how to speak properly to a senior (which should have been a part of family education) learned it very fast after being physically chastised a few times for our bad manners.

One day during the training the seniors decided that we seventh graders were not hustling hard enough and our lazy attitude was demoralizing the entire club. We needed immediate and thorough correction, they said. Their corrective measures were that we lined up in a neat line in front of them. They told us to clench our teeth so that we would not lose them. They asked us then if we had any excuse. No, sir, we had no excuse. When the first fist struck my cheek, I saw for the first time in my life a spectacular show of tiny sparks before my darkening eyes. All the seniors, seven of them, struck all the seventh graders, ten of us, with equal ferocity. A few hours after this necessary talk our faces changed hue to bluish-purple and swelled rather grotesquely, while our eyes became nearly closed.

None of us told the real reason to our parents. My parents certainly asked whatever had happened to me. "I ran into the door at the school while playing rough." An obvious lie, and my parents knew exactly who had rearranged my face. They did not press for the truth from my lips. They did not complain to the school. My father was a teacher and vice-principal of the same school. If he had chosen to call in those volleyball club seniors and punish them, what would I have become? The squealer of the century. The crushing dishonor would have prevented me from ever going back to school. Our temporarily disfigured faces shone as badges of courage among the other boys, and even attracted the prettiest faces in the school, temporarily. And none of the other parents complained. It is understood by all that any serious athletic club sometimes goes to extremes in its passionate and youthful pursuit of excellence. Although I do not think I am a masochist, I felt then that the ninth graders' determination to make our team better was genuine; that we seventh graders were not good enough and hence needed to put forth our extraordinary efforts every day; and that when we did not push ourselves we deserved to be punished for harming our own team. And, of course, if any one of us inferiors had politely dared to inform our superiors that they were not very democratic, not only they but the rest of us would have instantly concluded that he had gone insane and was not responsible for his babblings—unless he wanted to die. Our volleyball team was by no means an exception to what was generally done in all the other athletic clubs.

The word for democracy, *minshushugi*, appeared everywhere in our junior high school textbooks. We learned about the concepts of popular sovereignty, parliamentary deliberation, basic human rights, the symbol of the State, the evils of war, the virtues of peace, and the inhumanity of the atomic bombs. We learned little about World War II: Japan had started it by invading China and lost it to the Allied Powers. Militarists were responsible for it. When we learned so much about Japanese history, we felt cheated by the brief paragraphs on the war. We nagged our teachers to tell us more about the war but they were uniformly reluctant to talk.

Our junior high school graduation *ensoku* was a five-night, six-day excursion to the two ancient imperial capitals, Nara and Kyoto. Before we left for the trip, we studied the history of the two cities and learned about their numerous temples and shrines. Study was now our most serious preoccupation, because all of us had to take an entrance examination to a noncompulsory senior high school of our choice. "All of us" is incorrect; approximately eighty percent of my class took the examination. The rest went to work. The exam covered all the subjects that the junior high school taught us. We studied hard, knowing full well that nobody could help us on the day of the exam. Our teachers were also keenly aware of our parents' aspirations for us and their accompanying anxiety. The pressure was on everybody involved in school education. Our fear of the exam was used, though infrequently, as the most effective means to restore law and order in the classroom. A usual line of our teacher was, "I do so hope your fun and games now will not hinder your performance on the day of the exam, which you know is approaching faster than you wish." His remarks, made with a smile, drenched us in cold sweat.

In our town there was one senior high school, which was the only one in the larger vicinity of the town. My brother went to this school during the war, when it was still the noncompulsory "middle school," and stayed there when it became the senior high school. He and his friends told me and my friends many stories about their fierce pursuit of academic excellence and the rigorous physical discipline they had to endure. The more blatantly their stories were inflated with half-truths and outright fictions, the more we desired to get in there. The high school buildings, built entirely of wood, stood at the foot of the castle mountain; they were encircled by white earth-and-stone walls, and had received loving attention as they aged. The school looked impressive and exclusive.

As the examination day in early March approached to within a few weeks away, our junior high school slid into a peculiar mood of calmness. So calm, it was unnatural. Our teachers told us to sleep well and eat right; they even insisted that we play hard. Similar advice came from our parents. To show our parents and teachers that we were in top form, a few of my classmates and I went to see a movie. I cannot recollect now what movie it was because we were so nervous in the theater that we were doing math problems or memorizing some more English vocabulary. Mental paralysis did not ensue, but intense anxiety pervaded us. Perhaps this anxiety, heightened by our desire to learn, existed from the seventh grade onwards and served to instill in us the habit of concentrated study.

The night before the exam day I ritualistically sharpened a dozen medium-soft pencils with my pocket knife and put them with a large rubber eraser and a ruler.

On the day of the exam I woke up around five o'clock; the exam was to start at eight o'clock. One of the bright kids in my neighborhood had earlier confided in me that the human brain functioned best in the two or three hours after waking. Many unfamiliar faces were on the high school campus; they came from other junior high schools. All of us looked, in spite of ourselves, very nervous; we knew there were too many of us here and that half of us would not make it. Some were accompanied by their parents, who looked more worried than their children.

The exam began at eight o'clock sharp, broke at noon for lunch for one hour, resumed at one o'clock, and lasted until five o'clock. We were exhausted.

The next day our junior high school circulated the official answer sheet of the exam. Our trembling fingers counted the correct and incorrect scores.

A month later in early April the official announcement was made in the high school yard, where many pupils and their parents congregated early. School officials pinned a large long white sheet on the wall of the building to display the names of those who had passed. And my eyes raced for my name. My name in the thick black ink looked so big. My exclamation was drowned by others' simultaneous cries of joy. And there were those pupils who quietly left the school yard, tears streaming down their cheeks. This scene of joy and sorrow is repeated every spring in Japan.

Soon after the entrance ceremony at the high school our home-room teacher reminded us that our minds should be fixed on the university entrance examination. He said that the three years of high school would fly past, and that we should not miss a day of hard study.

Our senior high school, like any other high school in Japan, had a strict uniform code. All students wore black in autumn, winter, and spring; and in summer we wore black pants and white shirts, and the girls black skirts and white blouses. All wore white socks and white tennis shoes. We boys wore a black cap with two white lines around it. Everybody in the town and vicinity knew by our uniforms that we were in the senior high school and we wore them with pride.

Three months after I began senior high school, my family moved back to Osaka. I was disappointed to be leaving a school that was so well thought of, but excited to be returning to metropolitan Osaka. To my surprise, no transfer was allowed from my public high school to any other in Osaka. I had to take another entrance exam to another public high school, an exam especially tailored for a transfer student. I took one and completely failed it. It seemed unusually difficult to me, perhaps because I was not at all ready for another major exam so soon. After failing this, I took another exam at a private boys' high school. I passed it.

Once I was inside the high school the ethos of vigorous study controlled my daily thought and behavior. All of us knew the college entrance exam counted most. One's primary school score, one's academic or athletic performance in junior high school, one's brilliance and social grace in senior high school, did not matter at all if he did not pass the college entrance exam. The life and death of a senior high school student literally hinged on the college entrance exam. The traditional Japanese designation of the days and nights preceding the college entrance exam has been very accurately labeled the "examination hell." One example will perhaps suffice to illustrate how hard we studied for it. Our school expected all of us who wanted to go to college to memorize a pocket English dictionary in three years. There was a weekly test on English vocabulary, besides many other tests on many other subjects. Most of us did not sleep as much as seven hours a day; and even our teachers warned that if we slept too much (i.e., for seven to eight hours a day), we might as well not wake up. My athletic propensity was controlled to the maximum; I swam for the school swimming team, but my heart was not in it. An Undokai was held at senior high school, too. It was exciting for the tenth graders, but for the rest of the students the examination hell was too close for us to be carried away. Also there was, for the twelfth graders, a graduation *ensoku*, which took us on a grand tour of the Island of Kyushu (where Nagasaki is located), the southernmost island of Japan proper, for seven nights and eight days. We visited many historical sites and shrines and a chain of hot springs and volcanoes. I remember the latter most vividly.

Our high school began officially at 8:30 in the morning, and unofficially at 7:00. This unofficial hour-and-a-half was used by eager students who wanted to prepare better for the entrance exam. Our teachers were there to tutor us. And the school closed at 3:30 in the afternoon. Some of my classmates went immediately to one of the many commercially run study centers for more specialized "advanced" courses. After the regular classes our school, too, offered several self-study courses in math, English, chemistry, physics, Japanese language, and Japanese classics. Again, our teachers were there to answer our questions.

Discipline in the classroom was maintained by a combination of corporal punishment and our own pervasive fear of the entrance exam. At our all-boy high school this combination was used frequently and very effectively. The most authoritarian teacher in the school was also the most respected. He taught social studies, which emphasized the virtues of the new democracy. He was, school rumor had it, a black belt in karate. The rumor was quickly confirmed before our own eyes when he discovered, while he was lecturing, that one of my classmates was chewing gum. The teacher ordered the student to stand up and walk to the front of the class, which he swiftly did. The next thing we saw was our classmate, literally flying through the air and colliding with the wall. The gross impropriety of chewing gum in front of our teacher, as this student had done, was now clear to us, and it was with a definitely physical sense of conviction that we turned to the teacher as an authority who demanded our absolute attention. He said calmly that the student's casual attitude toward study would cause him to fail the exam. We resumed our study of democratic governance.

The examination hell gives rise to many manuals by self-styled experts on how to survive it. Survival is undoubtedly an issue: suicides among high school seniors are frequent. Some of the manuals deal with special brain energy diets. Bookstores pack their shelves with those manuals, and senior high school students buy them up, as I did.

The examination hell even creates sacred retreats. Some shrines and temples are known throughout the nation as residences of the lucky exam gods and spirits; many students and their parents (if not every one of the applicants) make a pilgrimage and most sincerely pray. I, of course, did so at one shrine near our house.

All of us who aspired to higher education had to choose a college and file an application with our major field of study specified. Although I did not have any ideas about "college subjects," I persuaded myself that I wanted to study English literature or linguistics. I applied to Kwansei Gakuin University in Nishinomiya, located between Osaka and Kobe. It is a private university.

Finally, in early February, the exam day came. My friend and I arrived early with our usual exam paraphernalia—a dozen sharpened medium-soft pencils, a large eraser, and a ruler. The beautiful university campus was jam-packed with applicants and their parents. Too many of us here again, we thought, and a rumor circulated that only one in ten would pass. Well, it could be worse. The exam began at eight o'clock, broke at noon for one hour, and resumed to last until half past four. When I came home, my parents asked how I had done. I said okay. They asked no further questions.

A high school graduation ceremony was held in early March before any official announcement of the exam at any university had been made, so that none of us would feel embarrassed by failure.

Spring arrived with the cherry blossom. On the university campus a long white sheet of paper displayed the names of those who had passed the exam. Again, my eyes raced for my name, and found it. My friend found his, too. We jumped up and down screaming happily. Some applicants silently left the campus; despite their obvious efforts at self-control, excruciating disappointment was visible on their faces.

Passing through the examination hell was liberation—no more menacing exam in sight! My life as a freshman seemed as carefree and triumphant as the flowers of spring. College classes, compared with the high school classes, impressed me as slow—too much dialogue without facts. Most of my classmates on the campus shared this impression. College examinations were open-textbook, open-notebook, and open-reference-book. But then the professors asked us to write elaborate essays on one or two questions; there were no multiple-choice exams. Indeed, in four years of college education I never had a multiple-choice exam; all exams were essay tests. So it did not matter how many reference books I brought with me to take a test: I always had to read the question and start writing my own thoughts. Memorization, once the kingpin of our intelligence, came close to being outlawed from campus life. The general unspoken understanding was that anyone who had passed the entrance exam was capable of memorizing essential facts and utilizing them; hence there was no need to test this capacity again. Perhaps, because of this sudden, conspicuous absence of compulsive memorization from our student lives, college education seemed deceptively easy.

My happy freshman year was 1960. The same year brought a traumatic issue to Japan: the mutual defense treaty, which Japan and the United States had signed in San Francisco at the conclusion of the Occupation. The issue was whether or not Japan should renew it. Popular sentiment in Japan was overwhelmingly against renewal. Massive street demonstrations, one after another, day after day, kept Japan on the edge of open revolt. University students, led by the Zengakuren, staged many violent confrontations with the special riot police force. My friends and I joined in massive street demonstrations, for we felt Japan did not need this defense treaty and that the United States was making a convenience of us for the sake of its own hegemony in Asia. We felt that if war started between the United States and the Soviet Union, the Soviets would attack us first, and worse yet, the war would be fought upon our soil. "Yankee, Go Home!" was a slogan spontaneously inspired by Japanese nationalism.

Concurrently with the mutual security issue, the Japanese government was engaged in another heated debate over Japan's obligation for reparation to Vietnam. Vietnam was divided. The Japanese government (i.e., the Kishi cabinet) insisted that Japan pay reparations only to South Vietnam. The opposition, led by the Japanese Socialist Party, countered that Kishi's real intention was to strengthen the military power of South Vietnam, and it demanded that the Japanese government wait until North and South Vietnam united. But the Kishi government, to the people's astonishment, rammed the Vietnam reparation bill through the Diet.

Flushed with confidence after his triumph on the sensitive reparations issue, Prime Minister Kishi, though formerly a war criminal, decided to visit President Eisenhower for the signing of the mutual security treaty in Washington. The Japanese Ministry of Foreign Affairs advised Kishi that as the US government had assigned the secretary of state as head of its delegation, Japan should send its minister of foreign affairs, not the prime minister. Kishi ignored this advice and planned to leave Tokyo on January 16, 1960. The night before his departure the Zengakuren students forcefully occupied the Tokyo Airport lobby. On the morning of his departure the road leading to the Tokyo Airport was guarded by an unprecedentedly massive force of police. The Japanese people derided his morning flight as "a flight by night." Kishi was welcomed in the United States, and he in turn invited Eisenhower to Japan for a ratification exchange ceremony.

The situation in Japan became ugly. On May 1, 1960, an American U-2 spy plane was shot down over the Soviet Union. The news made the Japanese people even angrier than before. The rebellious national mood was kept at fever pitch by the mass media. On national television we saw our Diet members engaging in fisticuffs. Their brawls were not on the street but on the floor of the Diet Building, which our primary and secondary schools had carefully taught us was the sacred forum of democracy. I wept in angry despair; my outrage stemmed from the excessively idealistic democracy that our schools had inculcated in us postwar generations. Or perhaps our national culture of pacifism, the germ of which the US Occupation had planted deeply, was too vigorous to accept any foreign militaristic elements.

Though the Japanese people heard many ideologically motivated arguments for and against the mutual security treaty, they were split early in the game into two warring camps. There were very few in the middle. The camp against the treaty included a majority of the people, Socialists, Communists, various labor union members and other liberal breeds, and the nation's student and faculty population. The other camp was spearheaded by the nation's most powerful political club, the Liberal Democratic Party, which controlled the Japanese government.

Prime Minister Kishi was obsessed with the successful renewal of the security treaty, and began ignoring the opposition parties. For the first time in Japanese history the chairman of the Diet called 500 policemen into the Diet chambers to control the behavior of the opposition members, who were holding a sit-in strike. In May 1960 approximately 170,000 people surrounded the Diet Building in protest. The transportation unions called a general strike. The Kishi government warned it was illegal. The warning was ignored. On June 10 Eisenhower's press secretary came to Tokyo to assess the mood of Japan. Before he could begin his assignment, his motorcade from the Tokyo Airport to the US Embassy was trapped on a highway by the Zengakuren students; he had to be rescued by a US Marine helicopter. On June 15 in front of the Diet Building 20,000 Zengakuren students clashed with the police force, and one woman student was trampled to death. Furious demonstrators set cars and trucks on fire. Prime Minister Kishi blamed international communism for the national disaster. But he was forced to announce a cancellation of his invitation to President Eisenhower. Kishi's humiliation was visible on his face.

The opposition parties proposed a slow and careful deliberation on the defense treaty. Nearly 330,000 people encircled the Diet Building as if keeping a silent vigil. At midnight on the night of June 19–20 the government, ignoring the opposition, decided to end the debate and force passage of the treaty. On June 20 the government, again without the opposition present, rammed the treaty through the Diet. The nation boiled in indignation at the government's repeated, blatant abuse of the most basic premise of parliamentary process. On June 23 the United States and Japan exchanged a ratification note; the same day Kishi announced his resignation.

The violent national mood did not subside, however. On July 14 an elderly assassin stabbed Kishi's thigh while he was at his official residence. He recovered well. On October 12 the chairman of the Japanese Socialist Party, the very popular Asamuma Inejiro who was the most vocal opponent of the mutual security treaty, was assassinated by the dagger of a right-wing youth. This fatal attack was carried out while he was delivering a public speech in Tokyo before television cameras. It was government by assassination—as the nation watched.[1]

The year 1960 was to me both euphoric and catastrophic. To my inexperienced and idealistic mind, politics in the real world appeared dirty, insane, and inhumane. The politicians' lust for power was repulsive to me. Democracy, the new postwar political religion that we were taught to cherish and defend, appeared to crumble so easily. The most appalling thing was that the Japanese people, who were being so callously abused by the Liberal Democratic Party, could not and did not kick it out of power. The people acquiesced in the government that was violating them. Was that the extent of Japanese democracy? I hoped not. But my hope, pitted against the devastating reality, did not last long. I remember, after the mutual security treaty came into effect, a painful apathy engulfed me. I told myself that apathy in politics was the most dangerous course, dangerous because it encouraged the "bad guys." My apathy did not go away, however. Perhaps it was all that remained of my shattered dreams of democracy.

My apathy in politics fanned my energy in athletics. Our university, like any other, offered a wide choice of extracurricular cultural and athletic activities. I decided to join the University Fencing Club. The hierarchy of authority within the club was strictly and visibly defined. Within the first week of our club life, the seniors (who rarely talked to us), juniors, and sophomores told us freshmen (all twenty-five of us) that we were worthless. Our true worth, they informed us, lay in our willingness to perform the club's chores such as cleaning the club room, washing uniforms, polishing swords, or massaging the sore muscles of our masters—them. We griped aloud about this injustice, not to them, but among ourselves. Our griping did not last, for there were too many things to gripe about.

A daily practice (seven days a week) began at 3:00 P M and ended at 6:30, with a ten-minute break at 5:00. From 3:00 to 6:30 we could not drink a drop of water, even in summer. The reason for no water, we were told, was to conquer ourselves. Every day for the first year I wanted to defeat myself with just a cup of water. An example of a typical exercise will illustrate the ethos that ruled club life. Our campus was located at the foot of a steep mountain. The upper echelons of the club found the mountain eminently suitable for training our legs. We ran up and down it in desperation because the sophomores, with cheerful grins, encouraged us with their green bamboo sticks. Around the middle of the mountain a Shinto shrine stood with its usual granite stone stairs, which we were sure reached to heaven. When the sophomores grinned benevolently, we knew we had to risk our lives by running upstairs. Going downstairs was worse: so steep, and each step so narrow, and our legs so shaky, we all felt we were plunging into Dead Man's Gulch. We quickly learned that fear was a great motivator for survival.

We discussed quitting en masse, but never got around to actually doing so. There were reasons. We could not take the public shame of being exposed as "quitters." If one did quit without a reasonable excuse, such as family financial difficulties, the club would post a large white sheet of paper on the campus describing in thick black ink that so-and-so was expelled for the gutless nonsense that he spewed out during easy daily exercise, and for his gross disregard for his club's morale. This public announcement would also ask other university clubs for coopera- tion; if this person applied, he was to be rejected. While I was a freshman I saw a couple of cases of this sort of devastating social ostracism. So all of us freshmen stuck together for mutual survival. We grew very close; we knew each other's strengths and weaknesses; we studied together; we frequently ate together; indeed, we moved in one homogeneous pack of underdogs. And other students on the campus and the public, too, viewed us as such.

This social perception of ourselves as budding athletes was a very strong social reinforcement for overcoming the often excruciating pain of our physical exercises. About ten of us commuted from Osaka to our university in Nishinomiya by changing from the subway to above-ground rapid transit. Climbing subway stairs was a difficult task during that first year, due to our aching muscles. In the midst of the rush hour, ten of us slowly climbed up and down the stairs by clinging to the stair rails. None of the other commuters complained or pushed us; we could tell from their smiles of pity and sympathy that they understood we were freshmen athletes under intensive training. This scene is an annual occurrence.

Not only physical training did we receive, but also extensive lessons on social manners and decorum, especially toward our seniors. We were taught how to speak with proper reverence. Fortunately, some of us knew and practiced this proper speech; others, less fortunate, received sharp slaps on their faces. In Japan propriety of speech is considered the public sign of one's intelligence, education, family upbringing, and character. A rumor among college athletes had it that the business world would hire students from the athletic clubs first for their proper behavior in any social and business hierarchy and their ability to work effectively within a group. Also, if a student (man or woman) has lasted for four years in an athletic club, the Japanese tend to believe that student would and could endure any hard task without ever giving up.

During the first year we freshmen hardly held a sword because, as our trainers told us, we were not good enough to use one. They were right. So off we went for more running up and down the mountain roads and shrine steps. Intensive, disciplined training went on for four years. During my senior year my team realized its dream and mine by winning the All-Japan Intercollegiate Sabre Championship—a first for our uni- versity. It was 1964, the year of the Tokyo Summer Olympic Games. As an extension of my dream I thought I would make the Japanese Olympic team. I was invited to try out twice. Twice I was thoroughly defeated.

Throughout this description of my education in Japan I deliberately cite examples of athletics. Deliberately, because the institution of athletics in Japan has retained many traditional Japanese values such as the loyalty of the individual to the collectivity, his obedience to and reverence for his seniors and superiors, paternalistic benevolence, and conspicuous absence of demarcation between the individual and the group. The US occupation authority viewed these values as utterly undemocratic and attempted to eliminate them from Japanese society. The Japanese people, while paying lip service to the victorious foreign military government, were not fully convinced that the values were necessarily bad. In the abstract, they may well be undemocratic if not downright feudalistic. But in practice they function as a social lubricant. The harmonious social interactions that result can still enhance an individual's motivation to achieve excellence. That is the secret of the Japanese people's ability.

As my last comment on education I should like to talk about a chronic debate over comparative levels of academic excellence as between the prewar and postwar educational systems. My brother went to the prewar primary school, prewar "middle school," and postwar senior high school, and then graduated from a postwar university. I went through the postwar schools and university. My late father taught in the two educational systems, prewar and postwar.

While I was growing up I listened to frequent discussions about the prewar and postwar schools among my father's colleagues and within my family. A dominant theme in their talks was whether the postwar mass education system lowered the standard of academic excellence. The outcome of the comparison was predictable: the American-initiated mass secondary education diluted academic excellence. In light of my brother's obvious intelligence and motivation to excel, this sounded convincing.

The level of academic excellence did not go down, however. What happened was this. The prewar middle schools, which were not compulsory, had far fewer students, and these had early shown their academic proclivity. The discrepancy between the gifted and the less gifted was narrow; and the pupils had to climb a steep academic pyramid to reach the heights of academic excellence. Indeed, the pyramid, so steep, resembled a tower. Only a few pupils were able to climb it. So steep a climb induced an illusion of height that was higher than the reality. As they climbed higher, their number grew even less. The smallness of this number, moreover, gave them an elitist mentality, so that they took it for granted that they were certified to rule the nation.

In the postwar decades all the pupils in primary schools have gone to junior high schools. It is compulsory, and the Japanese people observe the law and take pride in education. Because a greater number of pupils are mixing, discrepancy in academic achievement is conspicuous. In the postwar educational reconstruction, however, the base of the pyramid has been broadened and its middle section thickened; it is therefore more stable. But the height remains the same. The postwar academic pyramid, by comparison, offers a gentler climb to reach the same heights of excellence; and because far more pupils are climbing, the climb itself looks deceptively easier.

Those who decry the postwar academic standard do not fully appreciate how greatly the ordinary Japanese people's educational standards have been raised. Hardly any pockets of ignorance are left anywhere. The American-initiated mass educational reforms have revitalized the Japanese passion for learning and offered the people a broader horizon to explore. Also, the substance of learning has changed for the better. I say "better" because the substance is no longer monolithic. Unquestionably, postwar education offers all pupils a great opportunity for equal education.

Throughout the national discussion on the academic merits and demerits of the prewar and postwar educational systems, I sensed a strong undercurrent of romantic longing for the orderly, "clean" working of prewar teaching and learning. In the prewar days the goals of education were fewer, and they were well defined by the government in Tokyo. The hierarchy of authority among teachers and students was faithfully observed. The teachers, though modestly paid then, enjoyed high social prestige. A tightly regimented small group of teachers and students working towards well-defined goals radiated an atmosphere of discipline and efficiency. The atmosphere in the schools perfectly matched that of society. The nation appeared purposeful, coherent, free of extravagance, solid, and strong. But such straining after virtue induced a dangerous rigidity.

The goals of postwar education are many and diverse. Democracy, popular sovereignty, individual human rights, freedom of the press—these are not easy subjects to teach and learn. The government in Tokyo cannot set absolute standards for these elusive concepts and practices. Absence of such absoluteness is the essence of democratic governance. The postwar teachers, still not famous for high salaries, do not enjoy the same high social prestige that their prewar counterparts did. This status change may be due to the sheer numerical increase of teachers in postwar Japan. Also, in the postwar society the people appear to have less reverence for authority. Appearances, however, do not tell the full story. The Japanese are still great respecters of authority and hierarchy, and are willing to obey the government's policies insofar as they are defined as national. But they want clear explanations of the policies and they demand to participate in making them. Their often vocal and sometimes violent demand for participation is popular sovereignty in action. Those in higher authority, accustomed to a symphony of obedience, find the new political culture a cacophony of disobedience. Blind obedience, once hailed as true loyalty, no longer commands open respect. It commands secret respect, however, as various subgroups of the Japanese society (including the athletic clubs I belonged to) can continue to demand and receive loyalty to the will of the collectivity.

This book consists of three parts. Part One discusses political affairs with emphasis on how the Japanese, while living in a subsistence economy, were taught about their liberties. Part Two analyzes the American use of Japanese education to teach Japanese pupils the virtues of democracy and the wisdom of pacifism. Parts One and Two are closely related, for ideological reforms and reforms in education are interdependent. Finally, Part Three covers events up to and including the American peace treaty with Japan.

It was the Americans who made the policies and ordered the Japanese government to implement them. It was the American perceptions and assessments of Japanese affairs that provided the concrete basis for American policies. As a matter of emphasis, therefore, the American official and personal documents, written during the Occupation, are the primary source for this study. Contained in it are numerous recently declassified American documents from the US National Archives (Washington, DC), the MacArthur Archives (Norfolk, Virginia), the Truman Library (Independence, Missouri), and the Hoover Institution of Stanford University (Stanford, California).

The so-called official language during the Occupation was English. All policy statements originated by the Japanese government and all articles in the Japanese mass media were required to be translated into English, so that GHQ could evaluate them according to its scale of democracy. Translations from the Japanese in American documents are therefore quoted as they appear in the original. All other translations of Japanese-language sources are by the author, except when otherwise noted.

PART ONE
FROM
EMPIRE
TO
DEMOCRACY

On August 6, 1945, an atomic bomb reduced Hiroshima to debris. Fifteen minutes after dropping the bomb, an American pilot cabled to the White House Map Room: "Results clear cut successful in all respects. Visible effects greater than in any test. Conditions normal in airplane following delivery."[1] Thirty minutes later rain fell heavily upon the dying city; the closer to the core of the explosion, the greater the downpour. But it quickly evaporated. To cool their melting skins and burning lungs, many people in Hiroshima crawled to the river that ran through the middle of the city. The river eased their last pain and then carried their bodies to the sea. Two hundred thousand died.

On August 9 picturesque Nagasaki burned in a second scorching wind. One hundred twenty thousand died.

Absolute pacifism, once unthinkable and unmentionable, now became Japan's highest ideal, while nationalism and patriotism, once awe-inspiring imperial slogans, fell from grace. Japan surrendered—unconditionally. When the Americans landed in Japan under the command of General Douglas MacArthur, the Japanese people were ready to do what they were told. This readiness facilitated American efforts to convert the Japanese politically.

American policies in Japan were not isolated from the broader American postwar strategy in Asia, which closely influenced Mac-Arthur's behavior. When the Japanese Empire collapsed, there was no indigenous power immediately capable of bringing back order and prosperity to Asia. The United States, by defeating Japan, appeared to be the only nation that could restore things to normal and lay the foundations for economic progress. The vacuum left by the fall of the Japanese Empire attracted the United States. Asians, anticipating total freedom from the slavery of both European and Japanese colonialism, welcomed the United States as a champion of human rights and fighter for liberty. The United States in turn believed that all nations could blossom into political independence and economic self-sufficiency under the aegis of American goodwill. Such idealism was inseparable from the euphoria of victory. "American goodwill," throughout Asia, was a euphemism for American hegemony. The ever-present American military garrisons in Asia represented, in the face of equally numerous Soviet forces, the determination of the United States to protect its interests, if necessary at the cost of military confrontation.

During the nearly seven years of the Occupation the United States attempted to write into Japanese daily life such ideals as "individuality," "liberty," "freedom," and "equality." The US occupation authorities labeled this attempt the "political reorientation of Japan." The program was directed by General MacArthur. Armed with awesome executive powers and surrounded by his devoted entourage, MacArthur from his general headquarters (GHQ) in Tokyo, tried to lead the Japanese people to the threshold of democracy. His title "Supreme Commander for the Allied Powers" (SCAP) accurately depicted the absolute supremacy with which he administered the entire Occupation. His words and whims were mightier than laws. His ideological posture, as much as any political objectives of the US government, dictated the new direction that Japan had to follow without question. Any apparent doubt in the Japanese mind about MacArthur's policies bordered on insubordination; vocal support or silent acquiescence was the safest rule of survival.

The fervor of the victor's idealistic reforms during the early stage of the Occupation mirrored the policy of unconditional surrender; the victor's ideology, it naturally followed, should now prevail just as his arms had prevailed. In MacArthur's eyes no nation, especially the defeated totalitarian Japan, had the right to negotiate such fundamental principles as "liberty" and "justice." The new Constitution of Japan embodied MacArthur's vision of ideal parliamentary democracy and pure pacifism.

American policymakers at GHQ believed that democracy

would come only after a sweeping purge of the undesirable element among the Japanese people. The undesirables were the "right wing," the militarists and ultranationalists who had "caused and lost" the war. The magnitude of the purge caused intense fear among Japanese conservatives and serious doubts in Washington. But MacArthur was satisfied. The vacuum the purge created was readily filled by young, less experienced but enthusiastic people, including members of the "left wing"—Liberals, Socialists, and Communists. In the postwar Japanese political landscape, "war" became associated with the right wing, and "peace" with the left wing. To be sure, GHQ did not openly encourage the Japanese leftists; but it did condone their vigorous political activity. This policy of non-interference complemented the public freedom of thought and action that was one of the most cherished American means of teaching the Japanese people democracy. Despite all the rhetoric, however, it was only a guided democracy, as American press censorship showed.

     Soon after the US Occupation began, communism began to make rapid gains throughout the world. Japan's new public slogans—"liberty," "democracy," "freedom of speech"—were sadly diluted for the sake of strategic expediency. When leftist Japanese critics accused GHQ of practicing "rationed democracy" or "American imperialism," they were silenced. Together with the conservative Japanese government, GHQ initiated the Red Purge. The purge swept the nation, frightening the intellectuals, who were habitually on the left. It was a great success. The Japanese conservatives, with GHQ's blessing, quickly filled the vacuum that the purge created. Reinforcing the conservatives' firm grip on Japan, MacArthur permitted the Japanese government to welcome the ultranationalists and militarists back to society. Power had swiftly moved from the conservatives to the liberals and back again to the conservatives.

     Japanese education was reformed along the same lines as Japanese politics. John Locke conceived the child's mind as a tabula rasa upon which a teacher could make any kind of beneficial impression; the US government nurtured similar expectations toward defeated Japan. MacArthur tried his best to mold Japanese thought and behavior; proper education, he believed, would make his dream come true. He clearly understood the classic interdependence between political indoctrination and compulsory education. The survival of democracy, he believed, could not be guaranteed without effective control of the nation's educational system. He therefore invited the US Education Mission to Japan to make recommendations for reform. "We do not come in the spirit of conquerors," proclaimed the mission in March 1946; it went on to make various recommendations and its report became the blueprint for Japanese educational reform. Among the suggestions offered was that Japan should develop "the consciousness of a worthy national culture."

The Japanese Ministry of Education was hard pressed to find any such thing, but nonetheless published a *Guide to New Education in Japan*, one of the most embarrassing documents that it had ever offered to Japanese teachers and pupils. The reason was the ministry's continuing loyalty to the definitive 1890 Imperial Rescript on Education, a personal message from the Emperor that commanded absolute loyalty on the part of subjects to the throne. The Ministry of Education as well as the entire bureaucracy of the conservative Japanese government could not abandon the rescript, with its restrictive message, and it soon became a rallying point. GHQ, seeing the Japanese government struggle to keep the rescript alive, decided it was dangerous and moved to kill it.

Though the Japanese government tried to retain as much of the ancient regime as possible, MacArthur would not tolerate such maneuvers. The government was forced to realize that the only way to secure a withdrawal of the occupation forces was full cooperation with GHQ. The Japanese government accordingly began issuing numerous instructions on democracy to Japanese teachers and pupils. Delighted, GHQ encouraged the Japanese government to become a fanatical advocate of democracy, until both GHQ and the Government were trapped in a rush to get the ideal democracy on paper. Teachers and pupils, surprised by the government's sudden about-face, now understood that a victorious America now ruled Japan, and that "democracy" was the new guidebook for their future behavior and welfare.

The quick transfer of power in Japanese politics, from the conservatives to the liberals to the conservatives, occurred in Japanese education as well. At the beginning of the Occupation, GHQ purged the ultranationalists and militarists—a move welcomed by the liberals in Japanese education, who saw it as an effective cleansing of Japan's past sins. The liberals then began to push hard for their own ideological reforms. Some of their programs were identical with those proposed by GHQ; others infuriated GHQ.

The quick and easy success of the Red Purge in Japanese politics and education convinced GHQ and the US government that Japan, cured of communism and pregnant with industrial growth potential, would remain a loyal ally in the Pacific. The American hunch proved right. Continental American reality and ideals were transfused into the island nation; occupied Japan became a microcosm of the United States.

The fall of imperial Japan in the summer of 1945 was as stunning a spectacle as its rise to world power. The United States was not blind to the Japanese people's extraordinary talents. As Secretary of

War Henry Stimson informed President Truman a few weeks before the Japanese surrender, the Japanese were an "extremely intelligent people" and their nation building during the last seventy years had been "one of the most astounding feats of national progress in history."[2] Something, no doubt, went terribly wrong. An overview of imperial Japan (1868–1945), which follows this introduction, will serve as background for my lengthier account of the dramatic American experiment in Japan.

1
An Overview of Prewar Japan

The British industrial revolution of the eighteenth century precipitated the blossoming of state-supported capitalism in Europe. The American Revolution and the French Revolution triggered a profound ideological reorientation toward the governance of a nation state. But Japan under the Tokugawa Shoguns (1604–1867) chose to remain isolated from changes so drastic—and so hazardous.

The western industrial nations, believing themselves enlightened, considered it their humanitarian obligation to propagate their new perspectives throughout the world. Although their intentions may have been virtuous, their behavior in Asia and Africa degenerated into European cultural chauvinism. The Western cultural superiority complex, supported by Western military superiority, served to justify imperialistic expansion. Aggressive Western mercantile activity along the Asian coastline disfigured the face of Asia. Many Japanese intellectuals were well aware of the British exploitation of India and China. The Japanese knew that they had no choice but to physically resist the West in order to avoid a debacle similar to the one their neighbors had suffered.

The End of Isolation

As early as 1844 King William II of the Netherlands (the only Western nation with which Japan traded during the nearly two hundred fifty years of isolation) warned of imminent Western gunboat diplomacy. He urged the Tokugawa Bakufu (Warrior Administration) to open the country. The Bakufu refused. In 1844, 1845, and 1846, British and French warships visited Nagasaki and requested commercial relations; so, too, did Commodore James Biddle of the American East Indian Fleet when he came to Uraga in 1846. Each time the Bakufu refused. Finally, in July 1853, Commodore Matthew C. Perry, special envoy of US president Millard Fillmore, arrived at Uraga with his imposing naval squadron. At gunpoint he demanded trade concessions from the Tokugawa Bakufu.[1] The Bakufu, frightened by its own inability to fight back, asked Perry to return in a year for a formal reply, and then for the first time solicited opinions from local lords and officials.[2] This action suggested the Bakufu's serious lack of confidence in its own ability to govern.

Perry returned in January 1854 and successfully concluded the Treaty of Peace and Amity. Two ports were made accessible to American ships for fuel and provisions; and England, Russia, and the Netherlands soon acquired the same privileges. Four years later Townsend Harris, the first American consul, skillfully concluded the Treaty of Amity and Commerce with the Bakufu. This treaty introduced the concept of extraterritoriality to the Japanese people. England, the Netherlands, as well as this time France, and Russia, followed suit and concluded similar treaties.[3] The Bakufu did not fully comprehend the practice of extraterritoriality. The differential treatment of foreigners, who were now immune from Japanese laws, and the resulting conflicts between Japanese and Westerners, soon caused bitter resentment among the Japanese. Extraterritoriality smacked of colonization. The Bakufu felt that the Western powers, by capitalizing upon Japanese ignorance of foreign affairs, had cheated.

The series of concessions to the foreign powers revealed the Bakufu hegemony at bay. Such signs of weakness in turn encouraged the rebellious activities of young low-ranking samurai (the warrior class) who advocated the "restoration" of imperial rule. The rebels regarded the treaties as a national disgrace. They recognized, however, the frightening difference in military might between Japan and the West. The difference compelled them to appreciate the paramount importance of military strength for national defense and foreign expansion. The Japanese rebels insisted that only a new imperial regime could remedy the disgraceful situation. However, the Imperial House during the efficient Bakufu administration possessed no political power; rather, it retained the "sacredness" associated with the continuity of "the original Japanese family."

In 1860 the desperate Bakufu arranged the marriage of the presiding Shogun Iemochi and Princess Kazunomiya of the Imperial House. The Bakufu's reason for the marriage was to "unite the hearts of all the country" and to "clear the barbarians (Westerners) out of the country."[4] The marriage did not enhance the position of the Bakufu; instead, the Imperial House gained power, prestige, and authority at the Bakufu's expense. The marriage confirmed for the Japanese people the ultimate legitimacy of imperial governance.

While the Bakufu was compelled by crushing Western pressure to abrogate its isolationist policy, the young samurai rebels demanded the continued maintenance of national isolation. The rebels' frustration at their unanswered demands frequently exploded in the murder of foreign officials and merchants. Western naval forces retaliated by bombarding cities. While these sensational incidents publicized its impotence, the Bakufu sat paralyzed. To finalize the transition of power, the Bakufu and the rebels waged a civil war. The Bakufu's surrender, to the Imperial House, signified the "restoration" of imperial governance. The new regime was named "Meiji" or Enlightened Reign. The year was 1868.

The New Order

The fundamentally authoritarian style of national governance hardly changed after the transition from the Tokugawa Bakufu to the imperial oligarchy. The Japanese people experienced little need to alter their basic attitude toward hierarchical authority. The stability of their attitude was due to the Bakufu's successful development of a vertical class structure based upon Confucian ethics. A harmonious vertical integration, without an antagonistic dichotomy between superior and inferior, constituted the ideal order of the family, the fief, and the nation. In this society an individual independent of his group, like a farmer without his rice field, a samurai without a fief lord, or "a Japanese without Japan," was meaningless. A superior expected loyalty and obedience from a subordinate, and his benevolence toward the subordinate implied his compassion and wisdom. This traditional homogeneity coalesced in the face of Western colonialism.

To the Japanese imperial oligarchs, industrialization was a pressing national objective. They believed that it could be accomplished by adopting Western technological skills. The imperial government constructed new industrial plants and sold them to a few private merchants. Government protection, no competition, and great opportunities for expansion enabled those merchants to develop their firms into huge conglomerates, commonly called *zaibatsu* (literally, "financial cliques"), that dominated the market through oligopoly. At the same time Japanese leaders suspected that the culture of the West might contain some vital secrets that were responsible for its superior technology. Various missions and many bright students were sent abroad to search them out. Anything that suggested Western civilization was imported under the banner of "modernization," which—especially during the early Meiji period of Imperial Japan—was confused with westernization.

It was appropriate that imperial Japan's national slogans were *Fukoku Kyohei* ("Enrich the Nation! Strengthen Its Arms!"), which mirrored Japanese perception of superior Western industrial and military technology, and *Bunmei Kaika* ("Civilization and Enlightenment"), which reflected Japanese admiration for the seemingly advanced culture of the West. The regime neither questioned nor resisted the imperialistic propensity that was inherent in these idealistic slogans. With remarkable solidarity, the Japanese leaders dreamed of a civilized and mighty utopia. They wanted to combine harmoniously the best of the West (its technique) with the best of the East (its spirit). Ito Hirobumi, a rebellious young samurai who later became Japan's first prime minister, proclaimed confidently in 1909 that *bushido* ("the warrior's code") offered the nation "splendid" moral standards that were "rigorously enforced" among the educated classes. The result of *bushido,* he said, was

> an education which aspired to the attainment of Stoic heroism, a rustic simplicity and a self-sacrificing spirit unsurpassed in Sparta, and the aesthetic culture and intellectual refinement of Athens. Art, delicacy of sentiment, higher ideals of morality and of philosophy, as well as the highest types of valor and chivalry—all these we have tried to combine in the man as he ought to be. We laid great stress on the harmonious combination of all the known accomplishments of a developed human being, and it is only since the introduction of modern technical sciences that we have been obliged to pay more attention to specialized technical attainments than to the harmonious development of the whole.[5]

In its determined endeavor to build a paradise with "splendid standards of morality" and "modern technical sciences," insular Japan grew into imperial Japan. The glorious empire expanded with every war. In the game of conquest, peace became a misfortune.

Imperial Expansion

Imperial Japan wished to lead the other Eastern nations in its own right, not by the default of its cultural ancestor, China. In 1895

China was thoroughly defeated by a Japanese army. Japan's umbilical cord had finally been severed. Japan's new position was confirmed when, in 1905, its troops went on to humiliate Czarist Russia. US president Theodore Roosevelt rejoiced and declared that Japan had truly become one of the great world powers.

Japanese confidence, supported by world recognition, nurtured further ambition. Japan's participation on the victorious side in World War I placed the Japanese Empire firmly among the top-ranking nations of the world. Victory after victory created a self-fulfilling prophecy: uncivilized Asia was only waiting to be civilized by a fellow nation, civilized Japan. The Japanese sense of imperial destiny—and corresponding aptitude for imperial exploitation—began to surpass anything currently seen in the West.

Imperial Japan, because of its xenophobic fascination with the West, was extraordinarily sensitive to the military and political movements of the Western powers. This sensitivity found expression in a fervent and uncompromising nationalism; the Japanese oligarchs of the late nineteenth century had "rectified" the nation's indulgent dependence upon the West and restored the "real Japan." Militarism began to pervade Japanese domestic and foreign policies. Imperial Japan, winning all its wars, grew arrogant. The stronger it became internationally, the more apprehensive were the other imperialistic nations. Japan's annexation of Korea and obvious territorial appetite for China and Southeast Asia frightened the Western colonizers.

The 1921–22 Washington Naval Conference was called primarily to limit the naval strength of imperial Japan. Japan grudgingly accepted an inferior ratio of three to the American and British navies' five each. This imposition left a lasting bitterness in the minds of the Japanese people. Concurrently, a further national humiliation, perhaps more painful than anything Japan had yet experienced, continued unabated in the United States: racist treatment of Japanese immigrants. The crowning insult to the Japanese race came in 1924, when the US Congress passed a law declaring Japan an unacceptable source of immigrants. Ironically, the American treatment of Japanese immigrants matched the Japanese treatment of Koreans and Chinese people in Japan as well as in their native countries. Imperial Japan abused its far superior military force to create a new pecking order in Asia. Equal treatment of those people did not form part of the Japanese sense of justice; the measure of a nation's worth was overt military strength. Perhaps because of this "might is right" mentality, and because imperial Japan did not at all feel militarily "inferior" to the United States, American treatment of Japanese immigrants critically upset the Japanese sense of equity.

In 1930 Japan took part in the London Naval Conference with the United States and Britain. Although Japan reluctantly agreed to slow down its military buildup, it did not hesitate to express its abhorrence of the American and British demands. Then, in September 1931, the Japanese Army invaded Manchuria and quickly and completely occupied it. When, in February 1933, the League of Nations harshly condemned the invasion, the Japanese delegates walked out of the league meeting. One month later Japan withdrew from the league.

Japanese leaders felt that they were humiliated every time they succeeded in the very game that the West had introduced to Asia. Their humiliation aggravated their suspicion that the West was always conspiring against Japan. The ubiquitous Japanese militarists collectively interpreted the civility of one nation toward another as a clear sign of weakness. They were sure that foreign policy was not a matter of diplomacy but of conspiracy. Some Japanese openly asserted that the difficulties between Japan and the West would eventually lead to interracial war. Young military officers, frustrated by domestic and foreign affairs, frequently planned coups d'état and actually assassinated several cabinet members and a prime minister who, they thought, were detracting from the glory of the Imperial Household. Though they always failed to gain power, their bloody violence silenced other domestic dissidents, especially those who would question the military's predominance in the Japanese government.

The increasing political power of the Japanese military was well reflected in budget allocations. In 1933, 39.9 percent of Japan's gross national product went to military expenditures; in 1934, this rose to 43.7 percent; in 1935, to 46.1 percent; and in 1937, to 68.9 percent.[6] Nazi Germany's spectacular successes in Central Europe enchanted the Japanese military and their civilian cohorts. With mutual antipathy against communism, Germany and Japan signed the 1936 Anti-Comintern Pact which, by including Italy in 1940, became the infamous Tripartite Pact. The Japanese government abrogated the Washington Naval Agreement in December 1934 and the London Naval Agreement in January 1936. Japan was physically and psychologically prepared for war. In October 1934 the Ministry of the Army printed 1.3 million copies of *Kokubo no hongi to sono kyoka no teisho* (Principle of national defense and proposal for its reinforcement), the well-known "army pamphlet." Its first sentence read, "War is the father of creation and the mother of culture."[7]

Education

When one national hegemony replaces another, new political slogans determine not only the nation's educational orientation but also the shape and content of its learning. With the emergence of imperialistic Japan, the question was, What role should the national educational system perform for the new imperial regime committed to building a new Japan?

NATIONAL IDENTITY

Education in Japan was never isolated from government ideological objectives. For the imperial government, compulsory education was the most effective means of generating nationalism, and was especially important while the nation was struggling to stabilize its still fragile government and cope with its ambivalence—a mixture of admiration and fear—toward the West.

The new national identity had ancient connotations. It activated the Japanese people's faith in their Emperor's sanctity and omnipotence—a faith that had never wavered. Domestic governance for the imperial oligarchs was thereby simplified, as was their task of presenting, to an unfamiliar world of superior powers, the spectacle of a unified Japan. In this respect, the oligarchs demonstrated their extraordinary talent for governing. They swiftly issued a series of laws and ordinances that, they claimed, were based upon sacred imperial wishes. The laws and ordinances reflected the prevailing values and mood of the nation; at the same time, they projected the wishes and ideals of the government in power. The oligarchs proclaimed that the national slogan of Civilization and Enlightenment would be best reflected in law and order. It followed that the people—especially displaced samurai—should have their weapons confiscated.

The basic ideological position of imperial Japan became clear at the birth of the new imperial regime in 1868. The young Emperor Meiji proclaimed the Charter Oath:

1. Deliberative assemblies shall be widely established and all matters decided by public discussion.
2. All classes, high and low, shall unite in vigorously carrying out the administration of affairs of state.
3. The common man, no less than the civil and military officials, shall each be allowed to pursue his own calling so that there may be no discontent.
4. Evil customs of the past shall be broken off and everything based upon the just laws of Nature.
5. Knowledge shall be sought throughout the world so as to strengthen the foundation of imperial rule.[8]

COMPULSORY EDUCATION AND
PRACTICAL LEARNING

To implement the spirit of the Charter Oath, the imperial government issued its first *gakusei* ("education law"), the Education Act of 1872. The preamble conveyed the Japanese infatuation with practical learning: "Language [reading], writing, and arithmetic, to begin with, are daily necessities in military affairs, government, agriculture, trade arts, law, politics, astronomy, and medicine; there is not, in short, a single phase of human activity which is not based on learning . . . . Learning is the key to success in life, and no man can afford to neglect it." The preamble denounced the useless learning of the samurai, because they "indulged in poetry, empty reasoning, and idle discussions, and their dissertations, while not lacking in elegance, were seldom applicable in life." That sort of learning "hampered the development of talent and accomplishments, and sowed the seeds of poverty, bankruptcy, and disrupted homes." Thus, "a guardian who fails to send a young child, whether a boy or girl, to primary school shall be deemed negligent of his duty."[9] By the act, issued just four years after the violent civil war, the imperial government wished to stabilize its new national aspirations through compulsory education. The government's sense of urgency came from uncertainty about its own future in the face of both domestic and foreign threats.

Practical learning (i.e., vocational education) and material success in life now became a popular equation that appealed to ambitious young men. The virtue of hard work was concurrently supported by various Western social philosophers such as Samuel Smiles, whose best seller *Self-Help* nourished the new Japanese shibboleth, "Heaven helps those who help themselves." High academic achievement was considered a guarantee of wealth, which engendered social status and prestige. Since wealth implied virtue, poverty connoted either a social ill or an individual's unworthiness.

The Japanese emphasis on material wealth was an ideological necessity for nation building. The Japanese oligarchs' crash program for compulsory education and practical learning reflected their keen appreciation that a modern nation-state must have a radically more efficient production system than the traditional one based on handicrafts and apprenticeship to a guild. Intensive government-sponsored industrialization was the natural course of action. Practical knowledge and useful learning mirrored the oligarchs' deliberate policy to mass-produce a literate and skillful labor force.

There was opposition to the 1872 Education Act. Particularly unhappy with it were the poor who could not spare even the small expense for schooling. Their opposition was not aimed at learning as such; rather, it reflected their intense frustration that, because of their poverty, they were missing great opportunities for acquiring higher status and wealth. To the oligarchs, however, this opposition proved only the poorest classes' frightening lack of Civilization and Enlightenment.

The discontent of the poor over their inability to pay school expenses was aggravated by their concurrent apprehension of the mandatory draft law. In a few prefectures there were open revolts. Although the imperial government swiftly suppressed them, the revolts compelled it to be even more aware of the need for a tighter and more uniform educational administration. The most intense focus was on the manifest symbol of national solidarity, the Emperor. Despite sporadic resistance, compulsory education spread quickly. In 1873, the year following the promulgation of the Education Act, 12,500 primary schools were established. Within five years the number of schools doubled, bringing a total almost equal to that of the 1970s.[10] The percentage of elementary school attendance rose from only 28 percent of school-age children in 1873 to over 50 percent in 1883, and has exceeded 96 percent since 1906.[11]

DANGEROUS THOUGHTS
AND THE PUBLIC PEACE

"Knowledge" in the 1868 Charter Oath as well as during the early Meiji period (1860s–1880s) meant practical knowledge from the West. The best and brightest Japanese students were sent abroad to acquire technical and institutional knowledge. They brought back as well "the political world of Rousseau and the French Revolution, of British liberalism and the statism of Prussia . . . the economic world of Malthus, Smith, Mill and List . . . the intellectual world of Kant, Hegel, Darwin, Huxley, and Spencer."[12] Waves of Western philosophy seemed to wash over the entire Japanese archipelago. Japanese intellectuals and students were enchanted by their ever-growing domain of inquiry.

That development, however, did not please the Japanese oligarchs. Ito Hirobumi, for instance, found Western political thoughts downright dangerous. In September 1879 he warned the Emperor of the influence upon students, especially, of "the radical schools of European thought." So much talk about politics was undermining Japanese society.

Deceit is praised and profit pursued without shame. Benevolence is forgotten and rivalries and conflict prevail. Manners have collapsed and ethics declined. . . . Strange ideas are warmly taken up and inflammatory thoughts casually advocated. Pleasure is found in stirring people's minds, destroying the national polity [kokutai], and brewing disorder. That we have so many politically minded people is no blessing to the nation.[13]

To remedy this situation Ito urged the Emperor to encourage the industrial arts; candidates for higher education should "unlearn the habits of shallow excitement" and devote themselves to practical aims. Above all the government should keep in mind that the framework of the national polity was the national culture.

Ito's desire to make higher education noncritical of the government was well expressed in article I of the 1886 Ordinance on the Imperial University. It read: "The Imperial University regards as its aim the teaching and research of subjects and skills according to the needs of the State."[14] The continuous flow of Western thought, however, kept Japanese intellectuals busy and adventurous in their public utterances. The imperial government found them a serious threat to public peace and tranquility and Ito saw the more outspoken ones as treading a precarious path between legitimate political opposition and treason.[15] Because these two domains were so hard to distinguish, the imperial government now moved to eliminate the possibility of "treason," which did in fact include "political opposition" of many kinds. The Law of Libel and Slander, and the Newspaper Law, both issued on June 28, 1875, conveyed the government's earliest intention to control public freedom of speech. The Law of Libel and Slander, in part, warned the public to be extremely reverent toward the Imperial Throne and members of the Imperial Family. It also protected "any official" from contempt. The Newspaper Law demanded that "with the exception of the ordinary paragraphs of news, the writers of articles in newspapers or magazines must sign their names and residences in every case where the discussion turns up domestic or foreign politics, finance, the feelings [of the people], the aspects of the times, learning or religion, or matters affecting the rights of officials and people." Advocates of revolution, rebellion, or subversion, it warned, would be liable to imprisonment for up to three years.[16] The imperial government, because of its own troubled birth, feared that to give the people freedom of speech without a concrete contextual framework would at best create anarchy. Although Japanese leaders repeatedly endorsed freedom of speech in principle, their wish for internal solidarity and public tranquility determined their actual behavior.

The imperial government continued to issue numerous thought-control laws, of which the most restrictive was the Public Peace Preservation Law (*Chian iji ho*) of April 1925. Two months later the law was revised to include the death penalty for anyone advocating constitutional change or questioning imperial sovereignty in public. The succession of tight regulations on freedom of speech revealed that sizable public discontent existed. Indeed, the feverish national stampede for industrialization had created various social malfunctions. The economic depression that followed the Russo-Japanese War offered favorable conditions for socialist movements among Japanese laborers. In 1906 the Japanese Socialist Party was formed. The imperial government banned it instantly. Japanese involvement in World War I provided the government with an excellent reason for silencing disruptive ideas and people. The war also brought an economic boom. In 1918, while imperial Japan basked in the prestige of being a first-class world power, "rice riots" sprang up throughout the nation and precipitated the fall of the cabinet. The price of rice quadrupled in 1918, because of the domestic rice crop failure and extensive hoarding of rice brokers; they wrongly anticipated that the Japanese army would again advance into Russia in a war of territorial expansion. Not only the police but also the military forces were mobilized to suppress the rice riots. Thirty people were killed and more than eight thousand arrested, of whom more than two thousand were punished, some with death sentences.[17]

The successful Russian Revolution of 1917 provided impetus for Japanese laborers to organize under a more coherent ideology. Japanese dissidents saw the historical validity of Marxism confirmed by the success of the Russian Revolution. Indeed, *Das Kapital* seemed to explain everything for Japanese intellectuals, who began to claim that Japan should emulate the Soviet Union in order to save itself from the chronic ills of capitalist society. But such arguments, which evoked brutal government repression, were too theoretical for common laborers, and Japanese reality continued to elude the Japanese Marxists' rigid formulae.

As imperial Japan invaded Asia under the banner of the "New Asian Order," official intolerance of dangerous thoughts—thoughts very popular among students and other intellectuals—grew increasingly severe on the domestic front. The global depression of 1929–30 aggravated Japan's already precarious economic situation. The Japanese government had to relieve the worsening economic situation. A prospect of external wars appeared inviting. But the United States in the Pacific and China, and England and France in Southeast Asia, remained extremely alert against any possibilities of Japanese military expansion.

Not surprisingly, the Japanese government's control of soldiers' public speech began as early as that of the civilians'. In 1878 Yamagata Aritomo, another of the young samurai rebels and the one who became the chief architect of the powerful Japanese armed forces, expounded on the virtues of loyalty, courage, and obedience. "If one is not loyal," he said, "how can he serve His Majesty, who is our Supreme Commander, and our country? If one is not courageous, how can he engage in battle, brave danger and perform glorious deeds? If obedience is not valued, how can the armed forces be maintained and troops made to behave like

one person?" Yamagata, like his contemporary Ito, feared the politicization of the military; he therefore warned the soldiers against criticizing
imperial policies, going in for "noisy argumentation" or "frequent indignation at current events," openly supporting "such things as civil rights,"
and "imitating the irresponsible disputations of private men and the crazy
attitudes of students." He even cautioned against writing anonymous letters to newspapers and magazines on current events. The soldiers' duty
was "to support His Imperial Majesty and be loyal to his Court."[18] The
1882 Imperial Rescript to Soldiers and Sailors codified Yamagata's
warnings.[19]

THE 1889 IMPERIAL CONSTITUTION

The Emperor filled an important symbolic role for the
new and insecure regime. Japan's anxiety over its identity would have
been too painful to endure without the idea of an exalted Emperor. The
symbol further nurtured faith in an enlightened tomorrow for Japan. The
Emperor, at once the most personal and the most transcendent institution,
became the ultimate political instrument that the imperial oligarchy used
to solidify and legitimize its power. Through the Emperor the oligarchs
assumed authority to rule the nation purposefully and then to expand the
Japanese enlightenment in Asia.

The 1889 Imperial Constitution (commonly called the "Meiji Constitution") stated that the Japanese Empire should be ruled "by a line of
Emperors unbroken for ages eternal." The Emperor was called "sacred
and inviolable"; he combined in himself the rights of sovereignty, which
he exercised according to the Constitution. The ministers of the state
were responsible only to the Emperor, as were all military forces; the
Emperor's Privy Council, however, was extraconstitutional. These three
bodies made the crucial policies of imperial Japan. The Imperial Diet
remained a vigorous debating society.

The Constitution affirmed itself as "an immutable fundamental law,"
granted to the people by virtue of "the supreme prerogative inherited
from our imperial ancestors." Only the Emperor could initiate amendments. Not a single amendment was made until Douglas MacArthur summarily terminated the letter and spirit of the Meiji Constitution in 1946.

THE 1890 IMPERIAL RESCRIPT
ON EDUCATION

To further inculcate popular devotion to the sacred and
inviolable Emperor, the imperial government, on October 30, 1890, is-

sued the Imperial Rescript on Education. Because of its uniquely impressive influence upon all subsequent educational policy, full quotation of the rescript is in order.

> KNOW YE, OUR SUBJECTS:
> Our Imperial Ancestors have founded Our Empire on a basis broad and everlasting and have deeply and firmly implanted virtue; Our subjects ever united in loyalty and filial piety have from generation to generation illustrated the beauty thereof. This is the glory of the fundamental character of Our Empire, and herein also lies the source of Our education. Ye, Our subjects, be filial to your parents, affectionate to your brothers and sisters; as husbands and wives be harmonious, as friends true; bear yourselves in modesty and moderation; extend your benevolence to all; pursue learning and cultivate arts, and thereby develop intellectual faculties and perfect moral powers; furthermore advance public good and promote common interests; always respect the Constitution and observe the laws; should emergency arise, offer yourselves courageously to the State; and thus guard and maintain the prosperity of Our Imperial Throne coeval with heaven and earth. So shall ye not only be Our good and faithful subjects, but render illustrious the best traditions of your forefathers. The Way here set forth is indeed the teaching bequeathed by Our Imperial Ancestors, to be observed alike by Their Descendants and the subjects, infallible for all ages and true in all places. It is Our wish to lay it to heart in all reverence, in common with you, Our subjects, that we may all thus attain to the same virtue.[20]

Through the rescript the imperial will became the Japanese national will that all loyal subjects were expected to share. The rescript revealed to the people the visible collective soul, which was taking on a life of its own. Coercion to reinforce the solidarity of the collective soul was regrettable, but the government used it whenever it deemed necessary. Moral or physical coercion, if an individual needed it, was considered a necessary response to weakness. The more passionately one strove to contribute to the state, the better he looked in the eyes of the public.

The rescript reflected the confidence of the imperial oligarchs in their ability to rule the nation. It also assured the people that Japanese values were superior to Western technological knowledge. With the rescript the initial national emphasis on practical knowledge shifted more toward moral education. The purpose of "right education" was now to cultivate not the dexterity of one's hands but one's unshakable loyalty to and worshipful respect for the Emperor.

The 1890 Rescript on Education and the 1882 Rescript to Soldiers and Sailors harmoniously unified the nation's "mind" and "body." The harmony that culminated in the person of the Emperor was, as the 1889 Imperial Constitution put it, "sacred and inviolable" for ages eternal. The Constitution provided the nation's metaphysical contour. The task for the Japanese people was to find their primordial identity within it and remain prepared to defend the nation willingly to the death.

The imperial government and its intellectual cohorts kept embellishing Japanese traditions and myths. Such embellishment was not difficult. Japan's indigenous ancient religion, *Shinto* ("The Way of Gods"), provided sufficient material for their historical imagination. Among the prominent deities in Shinto happened to be deceased emperors and empresses, some of whom lived a purely mythical existence. Indeed, Japanese history began to read like a chronology of the Imperial Household. The regime instituted a cult of antiquity. Anything old (the older the better) was believed to possess an invisible but profound wisdom, which the new society had to emulate in order to grow sagacious and strong. This regressive nationalism worked well for Japan and helped the nation unite ferociously in a show of strength for the rest of the world. The imperial government believed that national solidarity under the flag of the rising sun would overcome both Japan's critical lack of natural resources and its geographic vulnerability. But the same nationalism, supremely ethnocentric, narrowed the spectrum of choices that a less limited discourse with the West could have offered.

Since the nation's crisis, given these choices, was a permanent one, the imperial government ruled on the assumption that dissent was treason. Suppression of civil liberties grew so habitual that the Government stopped justifying its actions. It interpreted the public fear, silence, and acquiescense as public tranquility.

The government's control of the academic world was equally effective. To be sure, the majority of professors supported the prevailing political ideology. Disobedience or disloyalty was rewarded with permanent banishment from university teaching. Most professors, though they extensively debated various social, economic, and political ideas, shared the fundamental national goals as defined by the imperial government. There were, of course, a few professors—and a large number of students— who failed to distinguish between "political" and "nonpolitical" scholarly inquiry. One example will suffice to convey the Japanese government's intolerance of scholarly divagation: the case of law professor Takigawa Yukitatsu of Kyoto Imperial University. He lectured on criminology; his thesis was that society should analyze the roots of crime rather than merely punish criminals in a vengeful manner. In October 1932 an informant alerted the Ministry of Justice that Takigawa was indirectly defending persons detained in prisons for being Communists. Minister of Education Hatoyama Ichiro ordered the president of Kyoto Imperial University to scrutinize Takigawa's thoughts—and proceeded to ban his books. The law department of Kyoto Imperial University protested that the ministry's action would surely kill the spirit of learning. The ministry replied that the issue at stake was not freedom of inquiry but the frightening social consequences of his thought. The law department retorted that the government suppressed scholarly views that questioned its policy.

To correct this "misunderstanding" of freedom among scholars, the Ministry of Education came up with a definition of academic freedom that divided it into three components: (1) freedom of instruction, (2) freedom of research, and (3) freedom of expression. When freedom of instruction did not match the needs of the state, the ministry said, article I of the Ordinance on the Imperial University was violated. Freedom of research was always granted, the ministry added, but freedom of expression was a different matter when it threatened to cause public chaos.

In May 1933 Minister of Education Hatoyama suspended Professor Takigawa. Immediately all thirty-six faculty members of the law department submitted their resignations. The Ministry of Education accepted the resignations of only twenty-one professors. More than 1,700 law students withdrew. Students and professors of other departments suspended their classes in protest. The president of Kyoto Imperial University resigned. Students of Tokyo Imperial University demonstrated in the streets, and 362 of them were arrested by the police.[21] In September 1933 Kyoto Imperial University opened with no students in the department of law.[22]

The Japanese imperial government believed that political debate, especially on the campuses, would instigate public discontent against the imperial regime. The consensus of the oligarchs was expressed by Prime Minister Ito when he informed the Emperor that "politics" was detrimental to the glory of the empire. The imperial government accordingly tried to depoliticize present and future generations of students and soldiers by means of "right education." It was in this context that Japanese schools began emphasizing the importance of Japanese history in the curriculum. History provided the students with a sense of the Imperial Household's continuity. *Shushin* ("morals") was a compulsory subject taught at all primary schools to develop the virtues of loyalty, obedience, and filial piety. The Ministry of Education, perhaps the most skillfully authoritarian educational administration in the contemporary world, scrutinized all textbooks. The government presumed that a uniform curriculum would nurture societal homogeneity, while diverse curricula would lead straight to societal disintegration. Such monolithic regimentation was tragic for freedom of inquiry and creativity. The imperial universities suffered while trying to satisfy the government, which was never satisfied. The government, to make sure that the universities would stay within its control, codified their duty: to teach and research in accordance with state needs, interpreted as the strengthening of imperial sovereignty and the *kokutai* ("imperial national polity"). Further, the government established only a few imperial universities, thus effectively controlling the flow of bright recruits into the central bureaucracy. Tokyo Imperial University stood at the apex of Japan's academic pyramid; graduates of this university monopolized the highest echelons of government and the intellectual establishment. By this mechanism the imperial system perpetuated itself the more securely. The imperial government, however, failed to appreciate the paradox inherent in using education as the tool of indoctrination. No doubt, education reinforced the dominant sociopolitical system. But it also compelled the bright students, from whom the government expected intellectual confirmation of imperial legitimacy, to question the sacred system itself. Doubts, if expressed in public, constituted blasphemy and treachery. Yet, students and professors realized that, in order to make meaningful contributions to the state, they had to exercise a greater degree of independence from the government. They assured the government that the only way they could contribute more to the prosperity of the empire would be if the government granted them a little more freedom. The government refused to consider such aberrant promises; instead, it established rigid rules and narrow guidelines for scholarly inquiry and ordered academicians to observe them faithfully.

However, conflict between the government and the universities continued, as each sought for more autonomy in its affairs. Their relationship was imbued with mutual antipathy. The intellectuals' frustrations and dilemmas emerged, in the government's eyes, as "dangerous thoughts"—Marxism, socialism, and their Japanese derivatives. The government suppressed literally all of these thoughts and their exponents as well. By so doing, it simultaneously destroyed a vital intellectual environment that might have nourished the nucleus for social and political improvement. When the government refused to grant independence of inquiry, the universities became incapable of improving the empire's "Civilization and Enlightenment." Rather, they became self-righteous and even enthusiastic advocates of imperialism. Once this spiral had begun, the very system that the government was desperately attempting to sustain began disintegrating from within.

The Japanese government's quest for the perfect and pure form of *kokutai* suggests that an ideology, like fire, is a good servant but a bad master. The creation of an organic unity for Japan under the human god-emperor undoubtedly provided the Japanese Empire with powerful psychological security. For the vast majority of the Japanese people, the sacred Emperor, the 1889 Constitution, and the 1890 Imperial Rescript on Education formed an organic trinity. For the oligarchs, translating the trinity into actual national and international policies was a matter of noblesse oblige, with the Imperial Household as the touchstone of political wisdom. At the same time, Japan had nothing but contempt for Asian nations that happened to be "unenlightened"—and militarily weak. Japanese liberation of these nations invariably meant annexation.

The Emperor encouraged the people to work hard in accordance with the national slogans, "Enrich the Nation! Strengthen Its Arms!" and "Civilization and Enlightenment." The Emperor's repeated encouragement and appreciation of his subjects' industriousness was very gratifying to them. They knew that they were building a powerful empire out of the rocky archipelago. They knew they were bright and talented. The nation's spectacular growth, nourished by the blood of its soldiers, inspired their devotion. In such an atmosphere the people could endure immense sacrifice.

Every aspect of Japanese life was now dominated by war. It was war that reinforced the total fusion of the individual with the Emperor. Without war or the perpetual prospect of it, the very expensive military establishment had little reason to exist. Neo-Shintoism, the government-sponsored national religion, spread the doctrine of *hakko ichiu* ("the world under the roof of one family"—with Japan as family head). To prove imperial Japan sacred and superior, a series of wars followed, beginning with the Manchurian Incident of 1931 and not ending until Hiroshima and Nagasaki in 1945.

Internal solidarity had been engineered at the expense of freedom of thought and action—freedoms that might have grown, as Japanese intellectuals of both left and right had once thought, to be inherent byproducts of modernization and industrialization. With the same slogans of modernization and industrialization the young oligarchic revolutionaries dreamed of building an enduring utopia. Major domestic opposition to the imperial regime came from the Japanese Communists and Socialists, who had their own utopian dream: a classless society. But the regime had no trouble in controlling them. Intellectually if not physically suppressed, Japanese Marxists had no chance to reach the mass of the people. Imperial persecution of the Marxists and other undesirables resembled religious witch hunting, in which brutality was seen as strength of faith.

The breathtaking speed and efficiency with which Japan expanded its empire did not permit ideological pluralism; there was no variety of ideas among which the Japanese mind could roam and reflect. The gap between the real and the ideal kept widening. The ethnocentric idolatry of the Emperor failed to fill the gap.

2
Unconditional Surrender

On June 15, 1944, US forces began the invasion of Saipan Island in the South Pacific. Every Japanese soldier on Saipan died. Many civilians committed suicide. Children died with their mothers. On October 24 the legendary Japanese Pacific Fleet, which had executed the brilliant attack on Pearl Harbor, was sunk by American air power. The next day the first kamikaze attackers left for their last mission.

Massive American forces kept advancing. On April 1, 1945, they began landing on Okinawa. This was an unthinkable development for the Japanese government. The Japanese forces on Okinawa were determined to die fighting, without thought of surrender; Japanese civilians, both men and women, joined in waves of banzai attacks to defend the sacred archipelago where the Emperor resided. Despite this ferocious resistance, on June 23, 1945, Okinawa fell.

The situation on the home islands was bleak. Charles S. Cheston, acting director of the Office of Strategic Services (OSS), reported to President Truman:

> Allied air attacks on Tokyo have demolished 500,000 houses and killed 300,000 people. Although there is no sign of civil strife, civilian morale is

low. Some angry civilians stoned former Premier Tojo's residence, causing him to leave Tokyo. There is no talk of victory. Rumors of peace are rampant in Tokyo, and the civilians believe that the war will be over in the winter.[1]

On May 8, 1945, the once formidable Nazi Germany was conquered. Frightened by the catastrophic collapse of its only ally in Europe, the Japanese imperial government in desperation urged Japanese ambassadors in neutral nations to begin soliciting any assistance they could get for negotiating a quick end to the war.

Prelude to Potsdam

On May 11, 1945, William J. Donovan, director of the OSS, reported to President Truman that the Japanese ambassador in Switzerland, Kase Shunichi, had "expressed a wish to help arrange for a cessation of hostilities between the Japanese and the Allies," and that Kase considered "direct talks with the Americans and the British preferable to negotiations through the USSR, because the latter eventually would increase Soviet prestige so much that the whole Far East would become Communist." The condition Ambassador Kase wished to present was "the retention of the Emperor as the only safeguard against Japan's conversion to Communism." "Kase feels," added Donovan, "that Undersecretary of State Grew [Joseph C. Grew, ambassador to Japan from February 1932 to December 1941], whom he considers the best US authority on Japan, shares this opinion."[2]

OSS representatives in Europe were increasingly contacted by intermediaries with Japanese peace feelers. On May 31 Cheston again informed the President that this time the counselor of the Japanese Legation in Portugal, Inoue Masutaro, wanted to contact US representatives because "the Japanese are ready to cease hostilities." Counselor Inoue emphasized that the United States and Japan shared " 'common interests' against the USSR."[3] Then on June 4, G. Edward Buxton of the OSS reported to the president that Fujimura Yoshikazu, one of the principal Japanese navy representatives in Europe and a former assistant navy attaché in Berlin, said "the Japanese government would be willing to surrender but wish, if possible, to save some face from the present wreckage." Fujimura, too, said that the Japanese navy believed in "the necessity of preserving the Emperor in order to avoid communism and chaos."[4]

Meanwhile the Japanese ambassador to the Soviet Union, Sato Naotake, was trying hard to meet Stalin or Foreign Minister Molotov. Neither of them was available because of other, more pressing business—

preparing for the Potsdam Conference scheduled in mid-July 1945. Both Ambassador Sato and the Japanese government in Tokyo remained ignorant of the Yalta Declaration, made on February 11, 1945, by Roosevelt, Stalin, and Churchill. It insured that "in two or three months after Germany has surrendered and the war in Europe has terminated the Soviet Union shall enter into the war against Japan."[5] To lure Soviet commitment at Yalta, Roosevelt and Churchill offered Stalin a generous postwar territorial arrangement. In the declaration the 1904–1905 Russo-Japanese War was characterized as "the treacherous attack of Japan." Stalin wanted to recover everything that Czarist Russia had lost to Japan and take more. He was not interested in peace with Japan without first fighting a little.

Roosevelt died in April, but Truman dispatched Harry Hopkins, Roosevelt's personal advisor, to Moscow with instructions to discover exactly what Marshal Stalin wanted. The Hopkins-Stalin conference lasted from May 26 to June 6, 1945. US ambassador W. A. Harriman and Soviet foreign minister Molotov were also present. Hopkins kept Truman informed by a daily top-secret cable headed "For the Eyes of the President Only." When Hopkins asked Stalin "whether the Japanese would surrender unconditionally before they were utterly destroyed," Stalin replied in the negative. Hopkins then asked for his views on the Emperor. Stalin opined that "it would be better to do away with the post of Emperor since while the present incumbent was not an energetic leader and presented no great problem he might be succeeded at some time in the future by an energetic and vigorous figure who could cause trouble."[6] Stalin also told Hopkins that Japan was "doomed and they know it."[7] "The marshal expects," Hopkins cabled to Truman, "that Russia will share in the actual occupation of Japan and wants an agreement with the British and us as to occupation zones."[8]

After Hopkins returned to Washington, Secretary of War Henry L. Stimson wrote a perceptive memorandum for President Truman. Stimson appears to have been the first one to propose the Potsdam Declaration. He suggested to the president that "a carefully timed warning be given to Japan by the chief representative of the United States, Great Britain, China, and if then a belligerent, Russia, calling upon Japan to surrender and permit the occupation of her country in order to insure its complete demilitarization for the sake of the future peace." He even listed preliminary items to be included in the "carefully timed warning." The Allied reasons for inviting Japanese surrender were presented by Stimson as follows:

1. American landing and subsequent forced occupation of Japan might be "a very long, costly and arduous struggle on our part." The Japanese terrain

was perfect for "a last-ditch defense" for the Japanese, but it would be
"much more favorable with regard to tank maneuvering than either the
Philippines or Germany."
2. The Japanese were "highly patriotic and certainly susceptible to calling for
   fanatical resistance to repel an invasion." When this happened, the Americans would have to "leave the Japanese islands even more thoroughly destroyed than was the case with Germany."

At the same time there were "enormously favorable factors" on the
American side. Stimson listed them:

1. Japan had no allies.
2. The Japanese navy was "nearly destroyed" and Japan was vulnerable to "a
   surface and underwater blockade which can deprive her of sufficient food
   and supplies for her population."
3. Japan was "terribly vulnerable to our concentrated air attack upon her
   crowded cities, industrial and food resources."
4. Japan was confronted not only by the United States and Britain but "the
   rising forces of China and the ominous threat of Russia."
5. The United States had "inexhaustible and untouched industrial resources
   to bring to bear against her diminishing potential."
6. The United States enjoyed "great moral superiority through being the victim of her first sneak attack."

The problem as Stimson saw it was to translate these advantages
into a quick and economical victory. Japan, he believed, was far more
susceptible to reason than most current observers would concede. His
own appraisal was remarkably accurate.

Japan is not a nation composed wholly of mad fanatics of an entirely different mentality from ours. On the contrary, she has within the past century
shown herself to possess extremely intelligent people, capable in an unprecedentedly short time of adopting not only the complicated technique of
Occidental civilization but to a substantial extent their culture and their
political and social ideas. Her advance in all these respects during the short
period of sixty or seventy years has been one of the most astounding feats
of national progress in history.[9]

He therefore suggested "a carefully timed warning" to the bright and
reasonable Japanese that they should surrender.

An Ambiguous Declaration

On July 16, 1945, the Potsdam Conference began.[10] The
same day at Alamogordo Air Base, 120 miles from Albuquerque, New
Mexico, the first atomic bomb was tested—with complete success. Presi-

dent Truman was immediately informed at Potsdam of the devastating new weapon at his disposal.

At Potsdam Truman had voluminous memoranda that the State and War Departments had prepared for him. For instance, the State Department explicitly advised Truman that, if Churchill or Stalin asked who should govern and make policies for occupied Japan, "the President propose the setting up of the Far Eastern Advisory Commission."[11] Later organized as the Far Eastern Commission, it was eventually accepted as a multinational policymaking body by both Stalin and Churchill, and brought serious problems for MacArthur and the State Department when the actual occupation of Japan was under way. It was this commission that MacArthur later derided as "a debating society." The State Department firmly advised Truman that occupied Japan "should be under the jurisdiction of the United States" and that the military occupation of Japan "should be unified and not zonal."[12] Unified military government was especially advisable, the State Department reasoned, because of "the unified character of Japan from an administrative, economic, social and ethnic point of view."[13] The department said (as Harry Hopkins had earlier informed Truman) that the Soviet Union would demand Karafuto (southern Sakhalin), the Kurile Islands, and possibly Hokkaido (the northern island of Japan proper) as its own separate military zone. But the department believed that there were "no valid reasons to allow the Soviet Union to have a separate zone."[14] Rather, the United States might have to "acquiesce" to a separate Soviet zone for Karafuto and the Kuriles.[15] This American acquiescence actually materialized, and Japan lost a part of what it considered its indigenous territory, the Kuriles, to the Soviets. The State Department then suggested to Truman that an Allied commander "who will be an American" should be designated to govern occupied Japan. This American stance meant that Stalin could not easily split Japan as he did Nazi Germany. It also meant that if he wanted to participate in even a partial governance of Japan, he would have to confront MacArthur—certainly a formidable foe to the Soviet Union.

While the Potsdam Conference was deciding how to govern occupied Japan, Japanese cities were being bombed at will by the US air forces.[16] The Japanese, who were left with only a few fast fighter planes, were digging pine roots to extract the rosin as a crude substitute for gasoline, and melting sacred bells from Buddhist temples for scrap iron. At the same time the Japanese government was developing jet- and rocket-engined planes—successfully, but too late. As the Military Intelligence Division of the US War Department later conceded, several of the Japanese designs would in time have become operational and given serious trouble to Allies in the Pacific.[17]

Time was running out on Japan. Foreign Minister Togo Shigenori in Tokyo and Ambassador Sato in Moscow exchanged numerous top-secret telegrams revealing the devastating state of affairs. Sato, in a lengthy telegram on July 20, 1945, lamented that "even if the officers and men and the entire citizenry, who already have been deprived of their fighting ability by the absolute superiority of the enemy's bombing and gunfire, were to fight to the death . . . the state would not be saved. Do you think that the Emperor's safety can be secured by the sacrifice of seventy million citizens?"[18] The US intelligence services intercepted these secret Japanese telegrams. Not only the top American leaders but also Stalin himself knew that Japan was bent on surrender; indeed, Stalin informed Truman at Potsdam that the Japanese government proposed to send Prince Konoe to Moscow "to ask the Soviet government to take part in mediation to end the present war," and that he had rejected the proposal because "there was nothing new" in it.[19] Stalin was preparing for war against the dying Japanese Empire.

Ambassador Sato grew increasingly suspicious of the Soviets' sincerity, although the two nations kept up a facade of neutrality under the terms of their treaty. Meanwhile, the Japanese peace feelers in Western Europe became more insistent and more responsive to Allied demands. Allen Dulles, then chief of the OSS mission in Wiesbaden, West Germany, was contacted through an intermediary by Brigadier General Okamoto Kiyotomi, who was believed to be chief of Japanese intelligence in Europe. Okamoto had been consulting directly with the Japanese chief of staff. They indicated via their intermediary that Japan's unconditional surrender was no longer a matter of question; their primary concerns, it appeared, were the preservation of the Emperor, and the possibility of returning from the present military form of government to a parliamentary government under the Imperial Constitution of 1889.[20] William Donovan reported to President Truman that, in the opinion of Allen Dulles, these two Japanese were insisting on the retention of the Emperor because they felt that he alone could initiate an unconditional surrender, and that he would be unlikely to do so unless his own survival was assured. "The Japanese," Donovan argued, "have taken to heart the consequences which Germany has suffered, including extensive physical destruction and the collapse of all German authority, because it prolonged a futile struggle many months after its hopelessness was wholly apparent."[21]

On July 19, Okamoto sent a long cable to the Japanese chief of staff urging that, as Japan had apparently lost the war, it must accept the consequences. His cable was acknowledged without comment. On or about July 21 Ambassador Kase informed Japanese foreign minister Togo about his activities in Switzerland and his contact with Allen Dulles. "Is that all you have to say?" was Togo's reply. Kase interpreted it as encouragement for continuing to sue for peace.[22]

On July 26, 1945, the Potsdam Declaration was issued. The Soviet Union did not sign the document, perhaps out of diplomatic courtesy (if not conspiracy). The original draft of the declaration (the so-called draft of July 1, 1945) contained the "[USSR]" in brackets in the body of the text with the notation "Delete matters inside brackets if USSR not in war."[23] As of July 26 the USSR was not yet in the war.

At 4:00 P.M. on July 26, the US government began broadcasting the English text of the Potsdam Declaration to Japan. After the State Department language experts had checked and rechecked the Japanese text, the first broadcast in Japanese began at 6:00 P.M. from San Francisco. "Thereafter," an officer in charge reported to the White House Map Room, "Japanese text broadcast repeatedly on our eleven west coast shortwave transmitters, shortwave transmitter at Honolulu and on our medium-wave Saipan transmitter. Carried in twenty languages from west coast. All regular programs were cancelled to permit full and repeated broadcasts of the proclamation."[24] The next day Truman was informed that, although Japanese air resistance in the Pacific continued light, "Japan will ignore surrender ultimatum and fight to bitter end."[25]

The Potsdam Declaration contained explicit Allied objectives for the defeated empire: punishment for "those who have deceived and misled the people of Japan into embarking on world conquest"; complete dismantlement of Japan's war-making powers; and establishment of "freedom of speech, of religion, and of thought, as well as respect for the fundamental human rights" under the Allied military occupation.[26] The Japanese government neither fully comprehended nor accepted these provisions. Would the Emperor himself be one of "those who have deceived and misled the people of Japan"? The declaration never specified the fate of that most important of Japanese institutions; in fact, there was no statement about him. The American omission was deliberate; it was intended to increase the possibility of Japanese acceptance of the declaration.

On August 2 US military intelligence informed Truman that "two important Japanese objections to the Potsdam Proclamation are probably the lack of a definite guarantee regarding the continuation of the Imperial House, and the provision for trial of war criminals."[27] The same day the OSS reported to Truman that the Japanese peace contacts in Bern were emphasizing that "the Allies should not take 'too seriously' what was said over the Tokyo radio about the tripartite [Potsdam] proclamation," because it was merely "propaganda to maintain morale in Japan." The real reply, according to these contacts, would be given "through some 'official channel,' . . . possibly by Minister Kase or General Okamoto, if an official Government reply [were] not made over the Tokyo radio."²⁸ Since Japanese initiatives through Moscow had failed miserably, the Japanese peace contacts in Bern became the most important and only credible such channel of communication with the Allied Powers.

Massacre and Surrender

On August 4 Truman learned that the Twentieth Air Force had mined all major Japanese harbors. The blockade of Japan was now complete.²⁹ President Truman, however, had already decided to use the atomic bomb. By "ignoring" the Allies' invitation to unconditional surrender, the Japanese imperial government unintentionally offered Truman the excuse he needed. On July 30 Secretary of War Stimson prepared for the president a draft of a press release to be issued immediately after the bomb had been dropped on Japan.³⁰ The British government read the draft and made two minor suggestions. Secretary of State James F. Byrnes, however, made an extensive revision.

On August 6 the first atomic bomb incinerated Hiroshima. Sixteen hours later President Truman issued the press release: "The Japanese began the war from the air at Pearl Harbor. They have been repaid many fold. . . . It is an atomic bomb. . . . It is a harnessing of the basic power of the universe. The force from which the sun draws its power has been loosed against those who brought war to the Far East."³¹ The land of the rising sun had been punished by the sun. The Potsdam Declaration, Truman said, had been issued "to spare the Japanese people from utter destruction" but their leaders had "promptly rejected the ultimatum." If they did not accept it now, he warned, they might expect "a rain of ruin from their air, the like of which has never been seen on this earth."³²

On August 8 Ambassador Sato was invited to Molotov's office. According to the Japanese account,

> Molotov cut short Sato's attempts to make the meeting a friendly one and began reading a short note that ended with the following words: "the Soviet Government declares that from tomorrow, that is from August 9, the Soviet Union will consider herself in a state of war against Japan." Within two hours the Red Army had entered Manchuria and begun its systematic annihilation of Japan's once invincible Kwantung Army.³³

For this the Soviet Union managed to acquire a lasting characterization of "insidiousness" from the bitter Japanese people. The feeling of the Japanese was perhaps comparable to that of the Americans toward the Japanese attack on Pearl Harbor.

Meanwhile, on August 7, Truman was urged by Senator Richard B. Russell of Georgia to drop all efforts at persuading the Japanese to make peace and instead to force unconditional surrender on them by military action. "If we do not have available a sufficient number of atomic bombs with which to finish the job immediately," opined the senator, "let us carry on with TNT and fire bombs until we produce them."[34] This was too much even for Truman. "I know," he replied to Russell, "that Japan is a terribly cruel and uncivilized nation in warfare but I can't bring myself to believe that, because they are beasts, we should ourselves act in the same manner." After the Russians had entered the war, he added, the Japanese would "very shortly fold up." Although his objective was "to save as many American lives as possible" he also had "a humane feeling for the women and children in Japan."[35] Despite his prediction of a Japanese collapse, Truman nevertheless decided to drop the second bomb over Nagasaki on August 9, whether as a revengeful coup de grace or a warning to the Russians is not clear.[36]

On August 10 the Japanese government announced via the government of Switzerland that it was ready to accept the Potsdam Declaration "with understanding that the said declaration does not comprise any demand which prejudices the prerogatives of His Majesty as a Sovereign Ruler."[37] The same day, the Japanese government issued its official protest against the American savagery in using such a horrible weapon to "indiscriminately massacre the defenseless civilians." The atomic bomb was compared with poison gas. The Japanese protest had little impact outside Japan. The world's ears, deafened by victory cheers, did not hear the Japanese reminder that the United States had preached to the rest of the world that gas or its equivalent should never be used in any war.[38] The next day Secretary of State Byrnes, after consulting with Truman, replied to the Japanese government:

> From the moment of surrender the authority of the Emperor and the Japanese government to rule the state shall be subject to the Supreme Commander of the Allied Powers who will take such steps as he deems proper to effectuate the surrender terms. The Emperor will be required to authorize and ensure the signature of the government of Japan and the Japanese Imperial General Headquarters of the surrender terms necessary to carry out the provisions of the Potsdam Declaration.[39]

Byrnes's answer implied that the Emperor would remain but did not at all guarantee "the prerogatives of His Majesty as a Sovereign Ruler." The Japanese government's unilateral condition for accepting unconditional surrender was wishful thinking.

On the night of August 11 the Japanese government, despite the army's vigorous opposition, informed the Allied Powers of its acceptance of the Potsdam Declaration. The Japanese letter of surrender went through the Swiss government in Bern.[40] That same day Truman had informed Churchill that he was designating Douglas MacArthur as supreme commander for the Allied Powers (SCAP).[41] On the morning of August 14 the Emperor heard the imperial cabinet debate the lack of Allied guarantees for "the prerogatives of His Majesty as a Sovereign Ruler" and, more immediately, for his physical survival. It was the Emperor himself who terminated the heated debate: "No matter what may happen to me," he declared, "I can no longer bear watching the people's suffering by continuing the hopeless war any further."[42] The Japanese chief of staff sent a telegram to Brigadier General Okamoto, head of Japanese intelligence in Europe, thanking him and his associates in Bern for their most useful work in persuading the imperial war council to reach a final decision.[43] The next day, August 15, the Emperor's proclamation for surrender was broadcast throughout the nation. The same day Okamoto committed suicide. The Japanese chief of staff, in his message of condolence to the Bern office, lauded Okamoto's "patriotic service rendered at our country's most critical moment."[44]

On September 2 the Japanese delegates signed the terms of surrender on the USS *Missouri*. The same day the Emperor issued an imperial rescript to all the Japanese people "to lay down their arms and faithfully to carry out all provisions of instrument of surrender and the general orders issued by the Japanese imperial government."[45] The Emperor's wish was faithfully carried out. But then, the Emperor was following the explicit orders of the US government.[46]

The Japanese imperial government, at this point, was obsessed with preserving the *kokutai*—that is, the Emperor and imperial sovereignty. Japanese leaders did not believe that imperial sovereignty could, or should, disappear merely because of the defeat in one war. At the same time, they trembled in fearful anticipation that the death of the Emperor would surely give birth to communist anarchy. The US occupation forces led by MacArthur would confront this attitude of the Japanese government by introducing radical policies aimed at destroying everything that was even suggestive of Japanese loyalty to the ancient regime.

3
MacArthur's Japan

On the morning of August 30, 1945, troops of the US Eighth Army, under the command of Lieutenant General Robert L. Eichelberger, landed on Atsugi, the most famous training ground for kamikaze pilots.[1] One of this advance group was Arthur Coladarci (presently professor in the School of Education at Stanford University). His recollections of that morning were vivid during an interview in 1977.

> I was one of the very first Americans who landed on Atsugi and the very first who entered the city of Yokohama. I was scared. In fact, terrified. But, my superior ordered me to check the port of Yokohama and see what's there. Somehow we managed to find this really small rickety motor scooter, and I rode it all the way from Atsugi Airport to the port of Yokohama [a distance of 24 kilometers, or 16 miles]. I saw nobody on the road. Absolutely nobody. I could however vividly sense that many Japanese people were watching me from behind the windows. Oh, was I scared! But, somehow I reached Yokohama. I could find nobody on the streets. I did not know where the harbor was. I had to ask, but nobody was in sight. I entered a large building, hoping someone might be there to direct me to the harbor. In a large lobby, which I later learned was a bank, there were so many people packed in it. All of them stared at me in breathless silence. I was extremely uneasy. "Does anyone speak English?" I said, loudly. No answer.

"Does anyone speak English?" A long silence. One man at last said that he did understand a little English. I told him that I was looking for the harbor. He turned toward the Japanese people in the lobby and explained that this American soldier was here just to go to the harbor and not to punish anyone. I could actually hear a simultaneous collective sigh of relief from them. I myself smiled a sigh of relief, and they smiled back.[2]

MacArthur's Authority

At 2:05 P.M. on August 30 MacArthur, supreme commander for the Allied Powers (SCAP), landed, unarmed, on Atsugi. "He is a big man," the *Asahi Shimbun* (a national daily newspaper) said.[3] President Truman had given him powers to match.

1. The authority of the Emperor and the Japanese government to rule the state is subordinate to you as supreme commander for the Allied Powers. You will exercise your authority as you deem proper to carry out your mission. Our relations with Japan do not rest on a contractual basis, but on an unconditional surrender. Since your authority is supreme, you will not entertain any question on the part of the Japanese as to its scope.
2. Control of Japan shall be exercised through the Japanese government to the extent that such an arrangement produces satisfactory results. This does not prejudice your right to act directly if required. You may enforce the orders issued by you by the employment of such measures as you deem necessary, including the use of power.[4]

William Sebald, who succeeded the first US political adviser, George Atcheson, Jr., in 1947, commented: "This was heady authority. Never before in the history of the United States had such enormous and absolute power been placed in the hands of a single individual."[5]

MacArthur's mission in Japan was further defined in two important government documents. *The United States Initial Post-Surrender Policy for Japan* established general politico-philosophical guidelines. Jointly prepared by the Departments of State, War, and Navy, it was transmitted to MacArthur by radio on August 29, 1945.[6] *Basic Directive for Post-Surrender Military Government in Japan Proper* gave him more explicit instructions.[7] It was drafted by the State-War-Navy Coordinating Committee (SWNCC).[8] The Joint Chiefs of Staff approved it on November 3, 1945.

Max W. Bishop, a Foreign Service officer assigned as a political liaison officer to the Office of the US Political Adviser (POLAD), said that the *Basic Directive* was meant "to define the authority which the

Supreme Commander will possess and the policies which will guide in the occupation and control of Japan in the initial period after surrender." The document's authors, he added, apparently expected MacArthur to interpret and revise it "in the light of actual conditions."[9] This flexibility immensely enhanced MacArthur's executive power. His personal discretion was indeed supreme. When US Senator Bourke B. Hickenlooper of Iowa (Committee on Foreign Relations) asked him in May 1951 if he exercised his authority "with the broadest discretion," he replied: "There is no question, a discretion which I have exercised frequently. The various proclamations, the various statements, the various manifestoes which I issued to the Japanese people were under the authority delegated to me. They were not subject to the controls of any higher authority."[10]

MAC ARTHUR AND THE ALLIES
Joint Allied responsibility for the Occupation, a facade at best, was crumbling from its very beginning. The US Initial Policy made it clear to MacArthur that although the principal Allied Powers would be consulted, and "appropriate advisory bodies" set up, any differences of opinion would be settled in favor of US policy.[11] Fortunately for MacArthur, there were always differences of opinion between the United States and the Soviet Union. His order of September 8, 1945, showed his confidence in the propriety of American rule: "Have our country's flag unfurled and in Tokyo's sun let it wave in its full glory as a symbol of hope for the oppressed and as a harbinger of victory for the right."[12] In addition, MacArthur ordered that all contact between official representatives of foreign governments and the Japanese government would be made only through GHQ–SCAP.[13] The other Allied Powers, who had tacitly conceded American primacy in the occupation, naturally resented such American high-handedness. The Soviet Union and Britain requested equal shares in the administration of occupied Japan; and the Soviet Union demanded that it occupy Hokkaido, the northernmost of Japan's home islands, with forces independent of MacArthur.[14]

In mid-October 1945 MacArthur told Edwin A. Locke, Jr., President Truman's emissary on Chinese economic recovery, that Russia's "desire to share in the Supreme Allied Command" resulted in part from its "intention to demoralize Japan so as to create the environment for successful communist revolution." The Far East, he informed Locke, was now "the most important part of the world for America." He was seriously concerned about the Korean Peninsula where, he said, the Russians had assembled large quantities of arms—including the biggest tanks he had ever seen—on the Thirty-Eighth Parallel. Also, he wanted to know "what

the Russians were doing in Manchuria," because "in the event of a clash
between America and Russia in the Far East," he was sure that North
China would be "pretty important."[15]

President Truman and Secretary of State Byrnes, however, began
preparing for a formal accommodation of the Soviet and British demands
for joint control of occupied Japan. On September 4, 1945, two days
after the formal surrender of Japan on the *Missouri,* the War Department
informed MacArthur of the opening of negotiations with China, Great
Britain, and Russia "with regard to convening a far eastern advisory
commission in Washington."[16] On October 11 the department asked Mac-
Arthur four questions to assist American negotiations on the proposed
Commission.[17] On October 13 he answered them.[18] To combine the two
top-secret telegrams:

> WAR DEPARTMENT. Have the representatives of any United Nations gov-
> ernment or military commander raised objections with you as
> to the policies being followed by you in Japan or as to the imple-
> mentations by you of such policies?
> MACARTHUR. Absolutely none.
> WAR DEPARTMENT. Have Allied representatives free access to you and your
> senior staff representatives to discuss occupation problems?
> MACARTHUR. Complete free access both to me and to all members of my
> staff. I and my staff have had long and frequent conferences
> with the foreign liaison groups. Local relationships have been
> completely cordial.
> WAR DEPARTMENT. What restraints, if any, have been imposed by your
> headquarters upon the movement of foreign representatives
> within Japan?
> MACARTHUR. Absolutely no restraints except those imposed by opera-
> tional conditions which apply equally to American forces. Equal
> facilities have been furnished all foreign elements as are avail-
> able to American forces. These include rail, water, motor and
> air transportation.
> WAR DEPARTMENT. Has there been any official indication to you in any other
> way that other governments may be dissatisfied with the way
> in which the Occupation of Japan is being conducted?
> MACARTHUR. None whatsoever.

The Foreign Ministers of the United Kingdom, Soviet Union, and
United States met in Moscow on December 26, 1945. The Far Eastern
Commission and the Allied Council for Japan were created for a joint
control of occupied Japan. The Soviet and the British were supposedly
pacified.[19] But MacArthur was not at all pacified. In fact, he did not want
Secretary of State Byrnes even to begin negotiating with the Soviet Union.
On October 22, 1945, he learned that Secretary Byrnes and Ambassador
W. A. Harriman were about to talk with Stalin.[20] He immediately made

his view clear to the War Department. An Allied military council, he said, would be unsatisfactory because it would contradict "every basic principle of unity of command." Moreover, Byrnes's proposal "would make it not only impossible for SCAP to execute the surrender terms but would only render his control of the military forces doubtful." Any change at this late stage, he warned, would produce "a condition of chaos, the result of which would be unpredictable."[21] Byrnes, after consulting with President Truman, informed MacArthur that his objection was overruled: "There shall be established an Allied military council."[22] MacArthur was deeply disappointed, but he could console himself with the thought that this Allied Council for Japan (ACJ) was only for "the purpose of consulting and advising the supreme commander."[23] And it was stationed in Tokyo, where his control was indeed supreme.

The Far Eastern Commission (FEC) in Washington, DC, had much broader and stronger roles than the ACJ. The FEC's major functions were: (1) "To formulate the policies, principles, and standards" that would conform to the terms of surrender, and (2) "To review, on the request of any member, any directive issued by the supreme commander for the Allied Powers or any action taken by the supreme commander involving policy decisions within the jurisdiction of the commission."[24] It posed a serious threat to MacArthur's authority. Secretary Byrnes confirmed MacArthur's apprehension about the FEC when it met for the first time on February 26, 1946; the US government, Byrnes said, had always desired that the control of Japan should become an Allied responsibility, and "that responsibility" now belonged to the Far Eastern Commission.[25]

MacArthur did not think so. He believed "that responsibility" belonged exclusively to him. On April 13, 1946, he told Major General Frank R. McCoy, the American who was the FEC's chairman, that the FEC, "by its terms of reference," was "a policy-making body with no executive powers, functions or responsibilities." It had no power, he continued, to require that any action taken either by the supreme commander or the Japanese government to administer the surrender be approved by itself in advance.[26] MacArthur's recalcitrance raised some misgivings in Washington. Secretary Byrnes, talking in a closed-door session of one congressional committee, commented that while "that fellow" (MacArthur) had been doing a fine job, he was nonetheless "a prima donna—because I have known him for thirty years," and was "liable to fly the coop and raise a lot of sin."[27] The War Department quickly relayed his remark to MacArthur.

Sinful or not, MacArthur's reason for the American monopoly of Japan was simple. He told Undersecretary of the Army William H. Draper that the United States, having not only contributed most toward victory in the Pacific, but having also carried almost the entire burden of occupying Japan, should insist "formally and openly" upon its right to shape policy.[28] He repeated in his *Reminiscences* that none of the Allied Powers had been able to send troops for the Pacific war when the United States needed them.[29] Such statements were for public consumption. Privately he concluded that "the Far Eastern Commission became little more than a debating society" and that the ACJ's "sole contribution [was] that of nuisance and defamation."[30] But when, in June 1946, there were rumors of a friction between himself and the FEC, he denied them with the words: "It is difficult to visualize any serious disagreement."[31]

ASSESSING THE SOVIET THREAT

The FEC and the ACJ could not effectively compete with MacArthur's absolute monopoly of the administrative powers in Japan. After all, MacArthur was a theater commander in the aftermath of battle, and he made decisions on the spot. The supposedly powerful FEC was in Washington, DC. Not until June 19, 1947, did the FEC adopt the *US Initial Policy*, which President Truman had approved on September 6, 1945, and MacArthur by then had made numerous important decisions. Nonetheless, MacArthur had called the FEC's declaration of policy "one of the great state papers of modern history."[32]

These two multinational policy-making bodies turned out to be a benevolent American gesture to give the public impression that the Occupation was in fact by the Allied Powers. The gesture was without much substance, however, because the US government did not genuinely desire to share the unconditional surrender with any other nation, especially the Soviet Union. As the US government and MacArthur increasingly sensed global communist encroachment, this policy stance stiffened. Indeed, soon after the establishment of the Far Eastern Commission and the Allied Council for Japan in late December 1945, the United States and the Soviet Union began to share an image of mutual antagonism, a vicious one at that. On September 19, 1946, the Military Intelligence Division of the War Department informed President Truman that "Soviet propaganda efforts to undermine United States prestige in Japan" were increasing, and that *Izvestiya,* a Soviet newspaper that often reflected official thinking, had condemned MacArthur's statement on the first anniversary of the Japanese surrender as indicating that the United States wished to turn Japan into a "springboard for war."[33]

Truman wanted to know the basic policy stance of the Soviet Union in relation to the United States. He directed Clark M. Clifford, his special counsel, to prepare a study. On September 24, 1946, Clifford submitted a gloomy summary of Soviet attitudes. The Soviet leaders, he informed the president, appeared to believe that a war with the United States and the other leading capitalistic nations was inevitable. In preparation for this conflict, they were increasing both their military power and the sphere of Soviet influence. In so doing, they were "trying to weaken and subvert their potential opponents by every means at their disposal."[34] The Central Intelligence Agency (CIA) concurred with Clifford that occupied Japan, in Soviet eyes, was being prepared by the United States as a springboard against the Soviet Union.[35]

Although the Soviet Union was rapidly enhancing its military powers, it did not have the atomic bomb. The Military Intelligence Division of the War Department recognized this when it reported to the President that as long as the US enjoyed an atomic monopoly, it was relatively secure from attack. Once the monopoly was broken, however, the United States, in the department's opinion, would be "the first target for any nation desiring to achieve its end through aggressive war."[36] How imminent, then, was the danger of the Soviet Union developing an atomic bomb? Military intelligence, as of October 1946, reported informed estimates of five to ten years.[37]

Thus American national security, in the dawn of the nuclear age, came to be based on the nation's effort to maintain its atomic secrecy and monopoly as long as possible. This American decision marked a clear contrast with Churchill's suggestion to Truman two days after the Hiroshima bomb. Churchill, who was soon to coin the phrase "the Iron Curtain," was surprisingly optimistic on August 8, 1945.

> The attack on Hiroshima has now demonstrated to the world that a new factor pregnant with immense possibility for good or evil has come into existence. . . . you and I, as heads of the governments which have control of this great force, should without delay make a joint declaration of our intentions to utilize the existence of this great power not for our own ends, but as trustees for humanity in the interests of all people in order to promote peace and justice in the world.[38]

Truman did ask each cabinet member to comment in writing on Secretary of War Stimson's proposal for the free and continuous exchange of information on atomic energy among all United Nations members. Opinions varied from monopoly to promiscuity, but in light of the Soviets' aggressive policies Truman's decision to keep an American monopoly was expected.[39]

On September 26, 1947, the National Security Council (NSC) held its first meeting at the White House. The CIA's first report, known as *CIA 1*, was submitted to the NSC. This meeting set a definite tone for

American foreign policy. "From the point of view of containing the USSR and eventually redressing the balance of power," the CIA stated, "the order of priority among the major regions of Europe and Asia is (a) Western Europe, (b) the Near and Middle East, (c) the Far East (but within the region Japan is important as the only area capable of relatively early development as a power center counterbalancing the Soviet Far East)."[40] At the ninth meeting of the National Security Council, on April 2, 1948, its executive secretary, Sidney Sours, reaffirmed that "the ultimate objective of Soviet-directed world communism is the domination of the world."[41]

MacArthur's Political Vision for Japan

Both the GHQ and the Japanese people were now wholly preoccupied with the idea of democracy. All private and public thought and action, especially of prominent Japanese public figures, were retroactively judged from a democratic standpoint. As the public slogan of the moment, "democracy" was expected to liberate the Japanese from past enslavement to lesser ideals.

As a social force democracy seemingly matched the prewar slogans of *Kokutai, Fukoku Kyohei,* and *Bunmei Kaika*; no Japanese dared or even wanted to question its political wisdom. But what did MacArthur mean by "democracy"? In his numerous eloquent—and frequently grandiloquent—public statements it took on a visionary aspect, a dream of what Japan might be. On September 2, 1945, immediately after the Japanese and Allied delegates signed the surrender documents, he broadcast the following message to the American public.

> Today the guns are silent. A great tragedy has ended. A great victory has been won. The skies no longer rain death—the seas bear only commerce—men everywhere walk upright in the sunlight. The entire world lies quietly at Peace. The Holy Mission has been completed.... We stand in Tokyo today reminiscent of our countryman, Commodore Perry, ninety-two years ago. His purpose was to bring to Japan an era of enlightenment and progress by lifting the veil of isolation to the friendship, trade, and commerce of the world. But alas the knowledge thereby gained of Western science was forged into an instrument of oppression and human enslavement. Freedom of expression, freedom of action, even freedom of thought were denied through suppression of liberal education, through appeal to superstition and through the application of force. We are committed by the Potsdam Declaration of Principles to see that the Japanese people are liberated from this condition of slavery. It is my purpose to implement this commitment just as rapidly

as the armed forces are demobilized and other essential steps are taken to neutralize the war potentials. . . . Today, freedom is on the offensive, democracy is on the march. Today, in Asia as well as in Europe, unshackled peoples are tasting the full sweetness of liberty, the relief from fear.[42]

It was significant that MacArthur at the moment of the Japanese surrender paid homage to Commodore Perry, who had epitomized the emerging American interest in the Far East and had opened Japan irrevocably to Western enlightenment and mercantile territorial imperialism. By implication MacArthur was tearing down the last door of Japanese isolationism; he was determined to reorient Japan this time toward "a simple philosophy embodying principles of right and justice and decency."[43]

THE LOVING OCCUPATION

MacArthur believed that Japan represented an extreme fascistic feudalism that had caused "the tragedy of Japan's present," while the United States exemplified his democratic political ideals—ideals that were "responsible for the strength of America's present."[44] He was not saying that might was right; he was saying that Japan was dead wrong. Thus his assessment of Japan was not especially favorable: "Supposedly, the Japanese were a twentieth-century civilization. In reality, they were nearly a feudal society, of the type discarded by Western nations some four centuries ago. There were aspects of Japanese life that went even farther than that."[45] In fact, he said that being in Japan was "almost like reading the pages of mythology," and that the Japanese people "had little or no realization of how the rest of the world lived."[46] Concurring, John K. Emmerson, the second Foreign Service officer who landed in Japan after the surrender, wrote to Secretary of State Byrnes that "in their present state, the Japanese people are not only politically illiterate but politically indifferent."[47] This Japan, in MacArthur's view, "had become the world's great laboratory for an experiment in the liberation of a people from totalitarian military rule and for the liberalization of government from within."[48]

MacArthur had some very definite ideas as to how democracy should be established in Japan:

First destroy the military power. Punish war criminals. Build the structure of representative government. Modernize the constitution. Hold free elections. Enfranchise the women. Release political prisoners. Liberate the farmers. Establish a free labor movement. Encourage a free economy. Abolish police oppression. Develop a free and responsible press. Liberalize education. Decentralize the political power. Separate church from state.[49]

To MacArthur, the Japanese surrender signified something more than a mere military defeat. It symbolized "the collapse of a faith," a collapse that "left a complete vacuum morally, mentally, and physically. And into this vacuum flowed the democratic way of life."[50] By "the democratic way of life," MacArthur meant American democracy, which "for nearly two centuries [had] emerged triumphant through the successive crises of war and peace—and in every test [had] established its soundness in comparison with every other philosophy which governed the lives of men."[51] With unshakable faith in this form of democracy, he continued: "A spiritual force whose purity of purpose is doubted by none, it demonstrated in the American experience of blending men of all races and cultures into a composite whole that it can thrive in any heart, and raise all who embrace it to a higher dignity and more useful purpose."[52] He hoped that "once the process of assimilation has been completed, the Japanese may be expected to adhere to, cherish and preserve this way of life."[53] He prayed with "firm anticipation" that the Japanese people would seize this opportunity to meet the challenge of democracy. "Therein lies Japan's salvation—therein lies the opportunity for future peace and happiness for Japan's people—and therein lies the hope of all of the peoples of the East for a better civilization."[54]

"Democracy is a relative thing. It is a question of the degree of freedom you have," MacArthur informed the reporters at a press conference in March 1947. "If you believe in the Anglo-Saxon idea, you will believe this will stay here," he added. He himself was absolutely certain it was here to stay.[55]

The moral vacuum that MacArthur perceived in the Japanese soul was to be filled by a specific theological doctrine. Christianity, he believed, was imbued with "a spiritual repugnance of war." He therefore tried to create in defeated Japan "a complete spiritual reformation," effective not only now but for generations to come, that would conduct the Japanese people "from feudalistic slavery to human freedom, from the immaturity that comes from mythical teachings and legendary ritualism to the maturity of enlightened knowledge and truth, from the blind fatalism of war to the considered realism of peace."[56] MacArthur proudly explained why his occupation of Japan was the most loving one in history: Allied policy, apart from destroying the Japanese will and the capacity to wage war, was based squarely on the Sermon on the Mount.[57] Japan was therefore "the world's great laboratory for an experiment" in which "a race, long stunted by ancient concepts of mythological teaching," could be uplifted by "practical demonstrations of Christian ideals."[58]

Christianity, to MacArthur, had "a spiritual quality which truly reflected the highest training of the American home."[59] He saw the United

States, with its "advanced spirituality," as the agent of Christianity in the Far East.[60] It was superior by virtue of its superior "moral force."[61] Through this "frail spearhead," he believed, millions of "backward peoples," now sunk in fatalism and therefore warlike, might achieve a new spiritual strength through which they would develop the opposite attributes.[62] In order to propagate Christianity among the completely demoralized Japanese, MacArthur, who himself "had to be . . . a theologian of a sort," put out a call for missionaries.[63] "Whenever possible," he recalled, "I told visiting Christian ministers of the need for their work in Japan. 'The more missionaries we can bring out here, the more occupation troops we can send home, the better.' The Pocket Testament League, at my request, distributed 10 million Bibles translated into Japanese. Gradually, a spiritual regeneration in Japan began to grow."[64] One educational adviser in GHQ concurred that MacArthur "became a name to conjure with— almost a God—and the United States in truth worthy of being called 'God's own country.' The other Allies had no part in this."[65] George Atcheson wrote to Secretary of State Marshall that "more and more Japanese are turning to the Christian faith whose essential precept for the conduct of men is the Golden Rule."[66]

SAVIOR AND CAESAR

MacArthur's desire to personify these ideals, and so act as savior of Japan, was well understood by the majority of the Japanese people. One Japanese letter to "His Excellency, the President of the United States of America" exemplified the Japanese spirit, which combined resignation with a certain opportunism. "It is my firm conviction," it read, "that if you continued to help us by sending to Japan raw materials and Christian guidance, the devastated Japan will be revived in time and will then be able to contribute to world peace."[67] Another Japanese said, "We look to MacArthur as the second Jesus Christ."[68] A large number of Japanese, however, "accepted the Bibles because the paper served as a cheap substitute for the high-priced cigarette paper on the black market."[69] According to the *Handbook on Christian Missions and Missionaries,* which the Civil Information and Education Section (CI & E) of GHQ published in April 1950, Japanese Christians numbered 342,607 as of December 31, 1948.[70] This was only 0.6 percent of the Japanese population—about the same as before MacArthur arrived in Japan.

Despite this unimpressive conversion rate, MacArthur once told an American missionary: "I could make the Emperor and seventy million people Christian overnight, if I wanted to use the power I have." He is also reported to have said to Billy Graham that the Emperor himself had privately "declared his willingness to make Christianity the national religion of Japan but [that] he had rejected the offer because he felt it wrong to impose any religion on a people."[71]

Besides being the savior of Japan, MacArthur was a symbol of sportsmanship and fairness to Japanese pupils. The first MacArthur Cup competitions in lawn tennis, softball, tennis, and ping pong were held near Osaka in August 1947. Various Japanese officials including governors and Ministry of Education representatives attended the opening ceremony, at which a US army band provided music. A physical education officer of GHQ spoke: "It is fortunate that in sports Japan can salvage much from its own past in skills and accomplishments. If freed completely from regimentation and feudalistic notions, sports can contribute tremendously to those practices and ideals which collectively are known as democracy."[72] "Seeing the grand scenes of the ceremony with aid of US Band," one Japanese organizer of the event wrote to the physical education officer, "many participants shed their tears with joy and gratitude." He also stated that if MacArthur permitted Japan to attend the Olympic Games, "our sportsmen will almost go mad with joy and gratitude."[73] Winners received the MacArthur cups and special large MacArthur medals. A small MacArthur medal was given to each participant.

MacArthur of course made full use of the Japanese school system to propagate Christianity. One example of his sensitivity to even a suggestion of blasphemy will suffice here (a fuller discussion of this subject will be found in part II). In late 1947, with CI & E's approval, the Japanese Ministry of Education published *History of the West,* a textbook for an optional course in the upper secondary schools. One paragraph of the book read: "Today we cannot believe in all that is written in the Gospel (the birth of Christ, the miracles he achieved, and his resurrection)."[74] "It is an outrageous insult not only to Christ, but to all Christians of the United States," Miss Marjorie Benson of Macon, Georgia, protested to MacArthur on January 14, 1948.[75]

MacArthur asked Lieutenant Colonel Donald R. Nugent, chief of CI & E, how this kind of statement could appear in a Japanese textbook that CI & E was supposed to carefully inspect and censor. On January 26 Nugent, after making a thorough investigation, wrote a lengthy memorandum to the commander-in-chief. He said that the Japanese author and publisher had made a mistake in not deleting the passage even after CI & E had ordered them to. They had accordingly been "reprimanded by this section." As a remedy he had considered ordering the Ministry of Education to collect all the textbooks throughout Japan but had decided not to, because it would invite "greater attention and public discussion of the issue." Also, "the textbooks would not be used after March 1948."

Nugent then assured MacArthur that there was, in fact, "more Christian content in the Japanese course-of-study and textbooks than ... content relating to any other religion." His explanation, he emphasized, was not presented "as an excuse for the present incident." Well aware of the lengths to which MacArthur's missionary fervor could go, Nugent concluded his memorandum by offering to take full responsibility should the commander-in-chief or his command be thought to have suffered embarrassment.[76] He included within his memorandum a draft letter of reply to Benson, which MacArthur did not use.

On January 28 MacArthur wrote to Benson: "Fortunately, the errors were detected shortly after the first release and corrective action was taken at once"; both author and publisher he added, had been "severely disciplined."[77] He then took this opportunity to expound the philosophy that underlay his missionary work in Japan and his proud record of accomplishment to date:

> We have in our favor the complete spiritual vacuum left in the wake of war and defeat and destruction which obliterated the very foundation to those false concepts on which the Japanese heretofore have depended for guidance, sustenance and protection. Through daily contact with our American men and women who are here engaged in the reshaping of Japan's future, there is penetrating into the Japanese mind the noble influences which find their origin and their inspiration in the American home. These influences are rapidly bearing fruit, and apart from the great numbers who are coming to formally embrace the Christian faith, a whole population is coming to understand, practice and cherish its underlying principles and ideals.[78]

MacArthur's faith in Christianity had become his political doctrine: Christianity equaled democracy. To be sure, military considerations were still uppermost. "Highlighting all else, of course," he declared, "lies the grave responsibility of protecting our national security against future threat to our Pacific coast."[79] Removing this threat was the United States' main object in occupying Japan. Indeed, the *US Initial Policy* instructed MacArthur

> to insure that Japan will not again become a menace to the United States or to the peace and security of the world [and] to bring about the eventual establishment of a peaceful and responsible government which will respect the rights of other states and will support the objectives of the United States as reflected in the ideals and principles of the Charter of the United Nations. The United States desires that this government should conform as closely as may be to the principles of democratic self-government but it is not the responsibility of the Allied Powers to impose upon Japan any form of government not supported by the freely expressed will of the people.[80]

Another aspect of MacArthur's behavior in Japan shows how little he was given to self-doubt. This personality trait was the source of his authority for some, but to others it looked more like arrogance. His behavior during the Occupation suggested that he was afflicted by the same "illusion of a master race" that he himself had warned might be one of the consequences, for Americans, of a prolonged occupation of Japan.[81] For instance, we are told that "except on state business, he almost never mixed with the Japanese. . . . He left Tokyo only twice from September 1945 to June 1950; he never visited Hiroshima or Nagasaki, never inspected outlying American units. . . . He would not even permit a telephone to be installed in his office."[82] This inaccessibility stemmed from MacArthur's belief that he completely understood the oriental mind. The orientals were more effectively controlled, he reasoned, by force, authority, and hierarchy. According to Edwin A. Locke, Jr., President Truman's emissary on the Chinese economy who stopped at Tokyo, MacArthur believed "that Oriental peoples suffer from an inferiority complex which leads them to 'childish brutality' when they conquer in war and to slavish dependence when they lose; and that the conquered Oriental is likely to throw himself completely and fatalistically on the hands of his conqueror, to be killed or taken care of. The general does not want that attitude to become prevalent in Japan."[83] That was October 1945, when the Occupation had just begun.

His opinion of the Japanese did not change during his six-year reign in Tokyo. After President Truman removed him from active duty, MacArthur came home to the United States. Spectacular welcome-home receptions waited for him in San Francisco and New York, and in fact everywhere he went. After basking in the applause he went on to attend joint hearings before the Senate Armed Services and Foreign Relations Committees. There he gave an evaluation of Japanese mental ability.

> If the Anglo-Saxon was say forty-five years of age in his development in the sciences, the arts, divinity, culture, the Germans were quite as mature. The Japanese, however, in spite of their antiquity measured by time, were in a very tuitionary condition. Measured by the standards of modern civilization, they would be like a boy of twelve as compared with our development of forty-five years. Like any tuitionary period, they were susceptible to following new models, new ideas. You can implant basic concepts there. They are still close enough to origin to be elastic and acceptable to new concepts.[84]

MacArthur maintained a paradoxical stance: the more aloof and invisible he remained in order to manipulate the "tuitionary" mechanics of the Japanese mind, the more persuasively he encouraged the traditional Japanese attitude of acquiescence toward authority. His dramatic style and missionary zeal gave a sharper contour to the "illusion of a master race." John Gunther appropriately called him the "Caesar of the Pacific." Indeed, MacArthur compared himself with Alexander, Caesar, and Napoleon and in his personal judgment excelled all of them. MacArthur's lack of self-doubt and his confidence in the purity of his purpose were his strength; they enhanced his charisma and sustained his autocratic administration. He certainly had no doubt about the greatness of his accomplishments in Japan. He told Congress in May 1951 that "a great social revolution [had] taken place there," a revolution in Japan that "could only be compared to the great revolution of our own type, such as the Magna Carta that brought liberty to the English people; or the French Revolution, that brought international freedom to France; our own revolution which brought the concept of local sovereignty."[85]

One form of fanaticism, it appeared, had replaced another, but MacArthur's offered more freedom to the Japanese people. Max W. Bishop, observing Japanese bewilderment, remarked that too little time had passed for the great mass of Japanese to assimilate their newly found freedom, for which nothing in their history had prepared them. "The question remains," he concluded pessimistically, "whether future developments will result finally in the birth of a truly democratic consciousness throughout the masses or a reversion in essence to totalitarian or controlled society under new and perhaps radical leadership." Bishop worried especially about Japanese misgivings about American motives. "They cannot visualize the future which the United States foresees for Japan," he told Secretary of State Byrnes.[86]

THE AMERICAN EXAMPLE

If the Japanese had misgivings about the future being planned for them, they were not likely to find the behavior of American soldiers in Japan a source of reassurance. Howard Bell, an education officer at GHQ, made a field tour of Sapporo, Hokkaido, in September 1947, and reported that the presence there of the 187th Parachute Infantry Regiment of the 11th Airborne Division, under the command of General Swing, amounted to "a mild reign of terror"; the regiment's younger members, he said, appeared "determined to practice their martial arts on the helpless Japanese civilians."

> The most common crimes seem to be vandalism and assault. The soldiers involved go out for blood. They beat up, knife, or otherwise maul Japanese for a trivial or imagined reason, or for no reason at all. They will enter stores, take what they want, and perhaps smash a window or two just for the hell of it. Girls and women are seldom on the street after dark.

The result is that the population which, ironically, it is our business to "inform and educate," is taking its lessons about Americans and the American way of living from a mob of vicious bully boys, who clearly know nothing about what democratic and decent behavior means and care less.[87]

Few such crimes were ever reported to the police—no more than one in five, according to Bell. In the first sixteen days of September 1947, he said, of the sixteen reported crimes that he reviewed, "only one, a case involving some fast driving and the death of a Japanese woman on a county road, showed that the soldier involved had been apprehended. All the other reports ended with the phrase 'MP informed'."[88] Bell himself witnessed one similar accident, an attempt by a US military vehicle "to plow through a cluster of Japanese on a crowded market street." Only at his insistence, Bell implies, was the man it hit removed to a hospital. The driver and passenger, he adds, were military police.[89]

An American civilian lawyer in Tokyo was not very impressed by MacArthur and his entourage, either. Alex Pendleton, who went to Japan as a naval officer and remained there to practice law, confided to Charles S. Murphy, administrative assistant to President Truman, in Washington, about "the intolerable abuses of SCAP." Murphy told Truman that Pendleton "impressed me as a very intelligent man," but one who was "inclined to overstate things considerably." Nevertheless, he added, Pendleton's charges seemed to warrant further investigation.[90] A few samples of these charges form an effective counterpoint to MacArthur's hymns of praise on his own behalf.

1. The attitude of SCAP from the beginning was anything but friendly, and on many occasions the poor Japanese was treated like a dog, regardless of his character, education or standing in the community. There is no provision for a Japanese citizen to appeal for help against the actions of a SCAP employee, no matter how small the employee nor how unjust his action. . . .
2. For the Japanese, freedom of the press and of speech does not exist. . . .
3. The necessity of bribing is so common that it is taken for granted. . . .
4. Needless and extravagant requisitioning of property from an already destitute people is rampant. . . .

"Unless we do something now," Pendleton warned, "Japan will welcome any overtures that the Communists might make"; even an invading army, he thought, would draw substantial support. American abuses, he concluded with marked exaggeration, were driving the Japanese to communism.[91] Pendleton's views were not very popular anywhere, especially in the United States where MacArthur was viewed as the last and finest representative of the self-sacrificing military ideal.

MacArthur himself was perhaps not well informed as to his soldiers' undemocratic and unspiritual behavior. If informed, however, he must have been very good at ignoring it, for he never mentioned any such thing. On the contrary, for on May 5, 1951, at the Senate committee hearings already referred to, he remarked: "I believe that the Japanese admire and respect not only the American way of life, but the American personality." In particular, he claimed, "they were struck enormously by the spirituality of the American home."[92]

4
Housecleaning

"Japan," the *US Initial Policy* demanded, "will be completely disarmed and demilitarized. The authority of the militarists and the influence of militarism will be totally eliminated from her political, economic, and social life. Institutions expressive of the spirit of militarism and aggression will be vigorously suppressed.... Japan is not to have an army, air force, secret police organization, or any civil aviation."[1] To implement this policy, the *Basic Directive* specified which Japanese personnel would be arrested and detained, and organizations that would be abolished.[2] Eager Japanese compliance made such a policy easy to carry out.[3]

An early US concern was for Japanese nuclear capability. The US Scientific Intelligence Mission began inquiries in September 1945. As Karl T. Compton, president of the Massachusetts Institute of Technology and a prominent member of the Manhattan Project, reported to President Truman on October 4, 1945, the Japanese nuclear physicists were well aware of the basic scientific background, but had mistakenly calculated that the reaction rate would be too slow to produce an explosion, and had therefore made no effort to develop an atomic bomb. They did, however, begin work on a pilot plant to produce uranium 235 as a power source.

American bombing raids over Tokyo destroyed the Japanese nuclear research laboratory—the end of Japan's effort in this field.[4]

That was not, however, the end of it as far as the US government was concerned. The fact that the Japanese scientists knew something about nuclear fission was serious enough. On October 31, 1945, the Joint Chiefs of Staff sent MacArthur a top-secret message: "All facilities for research on atomic energy or related matters shall be seized and all persons engaged in such research taken into custody. . . . No research activities on atomic energy or related matters should be permitted in Japan."[5] On November 24, 1945, MacArthur informed the Joint Chiefs that five cyclotrons had been seized on November 20 and their destruction begun on November 24. "Pertinent records" had also been seized.[6] Four days later, MacArthur received another top-secret message, this time from General Dwight D. Eisenhower, chief of staff, US Army, asking him about "the feasibility of shipping intact a cyclotron from Japan for re-erection in the States." They were particularly interested, he added, in "the large one from the Institute for Physical and Chemical Research Tokyo or one of the two at Osaka Imperial University."[7] Alas, there were none left in Japan. On December 3 the War Department, prompted by a United Press query, told MacArthur that "no orders were issued for cyclotron destruction, but rather order was for 'seizure'." What, it asked, were MacArthur's reasons for destroying them?[8]

The same day, MacArthur responded: "There must be some misunderstanding in the War Department. . . . On 9 November I received a specific order from the secretary of war through special security channel . . . which directed the destruction of the cyclotrons. You apparently are not aware of this order. . . . This headquarters was opposed to the destruction of the cyclotrons and had no intention to do so under the general directive. . . . Request clarification."[9] "You are correct," the War Department replied to MacArthur the next day.[10] The same day, Secretary of War Robert P. Patterson admitted at a press conference that the War Department handled the matter "without the thorough consideration that the subject warranted" and that the destruction "was due to an error in judgment." He also said that MacArthur properly followed his order.[11]

On December 15 the Joint Chiefs of Staff ordered MacArthur to release from custody all the Japanese scientists formerly engaged in research on atomic energy and to impound all stocks of uranium and thorium—but without publicity.[12] GHQ in Tokyo remained vigilant. Major General William F. Marquat, chief of the Economic and Scientific Section (ESS), reported to the Department of the Army on April 18, 1949, that GHQ "maintains continuing surveillance of all research work in Japan, and research bordering in any way upon restricted atomic energy research is strictly controlled."[13]

Moral Disarmament

"Demilitarization, in view of Japan's lack of resources and complete disruption of its economy, presents no problem," reported Max W. Bishop to Secretary of State Byrnes as early as December 1945.[14] But he was not sure about "a peace-loving democratic Japan." Bishop was worried about "three major forces working against achievement of our basic aim." They were: "first, the desire of certain elements in all Asiatic countries 'to expel all foreigners'; second, the latent nationalistic ambitious and potentially dangerous urge of the Japanese people ... and, third, the revolutionary drive of militant communism."[15] Bishop conveyed this warning to Secretary Byrnes, because he was convinced that failure of American policy in Japan would probably mean failure of American policy in the Pacific, to the consequent benefit of Soviet Russia, not only in that region but worldwide.[16] It was precisely because of this kind of American apprehension that MacArthur wished to persuade the Japanese people themselves to denounce the fanatical militarism that had pervaded their daily life. Demilitarization was a psychological task of suasion, which the Government Section of GHQ characterized as "moral disarmament."[17]

The Japanese people had to be convinced of the evil of militarism. As "a first logical step," MacArthur swiftly implemented a political purge.[18] His first targets were "those self-willed militaristic advisors whose unintelligent calculations [had] brought the Empire of Japan to the threshold of annihilation"—those, in short, who had "deceived and misled the people of Japan into embarking on world conquest."[19] On September 11, 1945, MacArthur proclaimed that Army General Tojo Hideki, a former prime minister, was Japan's first war criminal. When the American MPs came to arrest him at his residence, Tojo tried to commit suicide not with a sword, as everyone expected, but with a pistol. Unfortunately for him, he did not die. "The ridiculous Tojo," *Newsweek* commented, "could only make a modern mess of his attempt—despite centuries of precedents" of the ancient Japanese ritual of *seppuku*, which the Americans call "harakiri."[20] Tojo's failure to die gracefully deeply disappointed some Japanese and infuriated others. "Tojo" became a dirty word.

Minister of the Army Anami Korechika committed suicide, successfully. The army's chief of staff at the time of Pearl Harbor Gen Sugiyama and his wife committed suicide, as did former education minister Hashida

Kunihiko. Many Japanese people took these suicides as a matter of natural course.

MacArthur's purge was then broadened to take in all Japanese who had been "active exponents of militarism and militant nationalism." They had to be "removed and excluded from public office and from any other position of public or substantial private responsibility."[21] Rumors of the Emperor's abdication began circulating when, on December 2, 1945, MacArthur named three of the Emperor's top aides as suspected war criminals. When Kido Koichi, the Emperor's closest adviser, appeared on MacArthur's war criminal list, the Japanese people feared that the next would be the Emperor himself.[22]

Here the possibility of the Emperor being tried as Japan's leading war criminal should be discussed, as the mere hint of it paralyzed the thinking ability of the Japanese conservatives. To both the Japanese and US governments, the Emperor was the single most important person in Japan. The occupation authorities' initial treatment of him would determine the nature of Japan's reaction to the Occupation.

On July 3, 1945, the State Department recommended to President Truman at the Potsdam Conference that "immediately upon the unconditional surrender or total defeat of Japan, the constitutional power of the Emperor should be suspended" and that "if it is politically practicable and physically possible the Emperor and his immediate family should be placed under protective custody in a detached palace outside of Tokyo." But the State Department did not recommend "to remove the Emperor from Japan." It further advised that if the Emperor escaped from Japan or could not be found, the occupation authorities should notify the Japanese people that any action of the Emperor would carry no validity. Although both the Chinese government and public opinion in the United States seemed to want the imperial system abolished, the State Department believed that such a course would be "ineffective"; the Japanese people continued to show "an almost fanatical devotion to their sovereign."[23] These State Department recommendations did not mean that the Emperor was exonerated from possible war guilt before the Occupation had actually begun. In fact, on October 26, 1945, two months after it did begin, the US government instructed MacArthur that Emperor Hirohito was not immune from trial as a war criminal and that his treatment as such could not be divorced from the American objectives in occupied Japan.

MAC ARTHUR SAVES THE EMPEROR

On December 18, 1945, while potential war criminals were being arrested, Count Tokugawa Narihiro visited the Office of the

US Political Adviser without a previous appointment and asked to speak to George Atcheson. Tokugawa was a member of the Tokugawa Shogun family that ruled Japan for nearly three centuries without interruption until 1867; he was also an intimate friend of Prince Higashikuni Naruhito. Atcheson and Emmerson met him. Tokugawa told them: "The Emperor is prepared to abdicate and will do so in due course." As a replacement Tokugawa recommended Higashikuni.[24] (The latter, born in 1887, was a member of the Imperial Family, studied in France from 1920 through 1927, and married the ninth daughter of Emperor Meiji.) Atcheson did not believe Higashikuni could govern the nation; the Japanese people, he accurately advised MacArthur and Secretary of State Byrnes, were unlikely at this time to "place deep trust" in the prince's leadership.[25] On January 7, 1946, he confessed that what he really wanted, "if at all feasible," was that the Emperor should be tried as a war criminal. "I have not altered my opinion," he stressed, "that the Emperor system must disappear if Japan is ever to be really democratic."[26] Atcheson knew, however, that his ideal solution was too drastic. As he put it: "Trial of the Emperor would cause such a wrench that most people who know Japan believe that it would be impossible to find suitable men to maintain government." He recommended "the most cautious policy," namely, one of using the Emperor, who "manifests sincerity in wishing to aid in the accomplishment of our general objectives and is seemingly more anxious to be democratic than some of the people around him." He was convinced beyond question that the Emperor was "most useful." This usefulness was threatened, however, by the very real prospect that the Emperor might resign for fear of being named a war criminal. "If we decide to continue to use the Emperor indefinitely," urged Atcheson, "he should be given some indication that we regard his continuing on the throne desirable for the carrying out of the surrender conditions."[27] MacArthur, too, clearly understood the Emperor's usefulness: he had to be left alive and untouched. MacArthur also knew that the Soviet Union, China, Britain, and Australia wanted the Emperor tried as a war criminal.

On January 25, 1946, MacArthur, in a lengthy secret cable to the War Department, warned that "[the Emperor's] indictment will unquestionably cause a tremendous convulsion among the Japanese people, the repercussions of which cannot be overestimated. . . . Destroy him and the nation will disintegrate." If the Allied Powers tried the Emperor, "the hatreds and resentments" of the Japanese people, he said, "will unquestionably last for all measurable time. A vendetta for revenge will thereby be initiated whose cycle may well not be complete for centuries if ever." He continued his gloomy prediction: "All government agency will break down, the civilized practices will largely cease, and a condition of underground chaos and disorder amounting to guerrilla warfare in the mountainous and outlying regions result. . . . I believe all hope of introducing modern democratic methods would disappear and that when military control finally ceased some form of intense regimentation probably along communistic line would arise from the mutilated masses." To cope with these potential disasters, he told the War Department, "a minimum of a million troops would be required which would have to be maintained for an indefinite number of years. In addition a complete civil service might have to be recruited and imported, possibly running into a size of several hundred thousand." He concluded: "The decision as to whether the Emperor should be tried as a war criminal involves a policy determination upon such a high level that I would not feel it appropriate for me to make a recommendation."[28]

MacArthur's nightmare description of Japan without the Emperor worked wonders. The State Department and the War Department were convinced that they should leave the Emperor untouched. Other Allied Powers that wanted the Emperor dead were persuaded to be silent, or if still noisy, were ignored. Nevertheless, as the Tokyo Tribunal kept compiling war crimes of the Emperor's senior advisers, rumors of his abdication lingered on. Two weeks prior to the tribunal's verdict, MacArthur and US Political Adviser William J. Sebald discussed the possibility of an abdication.[29] When Sebald asked for MacArthur's opinion on the subject, MacArthur replied that "the Emperor might perhaps contemplate abdication, or under strong emotional strain arising out of the sentences in the major war criminal trial, perhaps even consider committing suicide." But all the rumors of abdication, he added, were "fabrications," and had "no substance whatsoever." It was MacArthur himself who was guilty of fabrication, for the rumors definitely worried him. He needed the Emperor; he told Sebald that "abdication by the Emperor would be politically disastrous" and that he would do what he could to stop it.

Stopping the Emperor was not difficult for MacArthur. The Emperor, he told Sebald, intended to call upon him immediately after the announcement of the major war crimes judgment and at that time, should the subject be raised, he would tell him that any thought of abdication would be not only "ridiculous and preposterous," but would "result in a major disservice to the Japanese people." "I told General MacArthur," Sebald wrote, "that I was very glad to have his views as they agree entirely with my own, and that I furthermore feel that they are also the views of the United States government. The general said that there could be no other views, and agreed with me that abdication by the Emperor would play directly into the hands of communism and chaos in Japan."[30]

MacArthur's remote control or taming of the Emperor was skillful as well as complete. The rumor of his abdication just faded away.

PURGE OF PUBLIC OFFICIALS

The American purge of undesirable Japanese was divided into two phases. The first one began in January 1946. By the end of July its massive extent had become obvious. The Japanese government screened 5,520 holders of important public and corporation offices, 3,384 candidates for the Diet (for the election of April 10, 1946), and all members of and nominees to the House of Peers. The government barred 814 policy-making officials, 9 Diet members, 252 candidates for the Diet, and 6,202 other persons under MacArthur's sweeping civil liberties directive of October 4, 1945. Some 186,000 government employees were removed and all professional military and naval personnel were automatically banned from public office.[31].

While the extensive screening of potential purgees was under way, MacArthur ordered a national election for the House of Representatives on April 10, 1946. He said this election was urgently needed

> (1) to dispel confusion resulting from the failures of discredited political leadership; (2) to eliminate from public life those who were tainted with war guilt; (3) to introduce new political figures; (4) to evaluate political thinking of the Japanese people; (5) to establish executive authority responsible for the people; (6) to provide means for legislative decision to be made by the will of the people; (7) to permit political expression on long-repressed political views; (8) to provide the legislation required for the implementation of SCAP directives; (9) to avoid the use of undemocratic methods of government by imperial rescripts and ordinances. . . .[32]

A total of 2,770 candidates competed for the 466 seats in the House of Representatives; of these candidates, 2,624 were campaigning for the first time. When the results were tallied, it was found that 377 of the new members were freshmen, 39 were re-elected incumbents, and 48 were former members of the House. The remaining two contests had to be decided by runoff elections. For the first time women ran for election, and 39 of the 82 women candidates won. Another unique aspect of the election was that the Communist Party endorsed 143 candidates and 5 won seats in the House. At this election a massive and unprecedented expansion of the electorate took place. In prewar Japan only males above 25 could vote. On April 10, 1946, men and women above 20 voted. The increase in the number of potential voters was phenomenal, from 13.5 million to 37 million.[33]

For MacArthur this was a most important election; indeed, he called it a "plebiscite" on the new Japanese draft Constitution. The new House of Representatives was to deliberate the draft that MacArthur ordered GHQ and the Japanese government to write (see chapter 6).

The results of the election pleased MacArthur. "Given the opportunity for free expression of their popular will," he said, the Japanese people had rejected "the two extremes of the Right and of the Left" and chosen "a wide central course."[34] But the Far Eastern Commission, especially the Soviet Union, denounced the election as dominated by reactionaries.[35] The Soviet worry was inconsequential to MacArthur, who intended, according to John K. Emmerson, to dissolve the Diet if he found it unsatisfactory and call for a new election.[36]

MacArthur's absolute power was obvious to Yoshida Shigeru, Japan's new prime minister.* Nominated because his rival Hatoyama Ichiro had been purged by MacArthur, Yoshida wrote MacArthur a letter that began "My Dear General"—the first of many to be so addressed—and concluded "I wish you will be good enough to let me know of your opinion on the matter."[37] "No objection from SCAP. Best of luck, MacArthur" was his answer.[38] Concurrently, the Military Intelligence Division of the War Department reported on the prime minister: "Labelled a 'liberal' before the war because he desired amicable relations with the United States and Great Britain, Yoshida is considered a conservative in contemporary Japanese politics."[39]

The second phase of the purge was to remove undesirable people from local governments. The Government Section said that it was timed "to coincide with the general elections of April 1947, when for the first time the people voted for their local chief executives and assemblymen as well as for Diet members."[40] Before the election, according to the Government Section report, "some 7,000 persons" of past militaristic and ultranationalistic connection were purged from local governments, "about 600 persons" from the economic field, and "200 from the field of public information."[41]

The Research and Analysis Branch of the State Department concluded that "the immediate effects of the purge in removing militarists from the public scene must be regarded as primarily psychological."[42] Evidence from the political arena, however, indicated that the effect was far more than psychological. Indeed, the purge gave rise to a rare phenomenon in Japanese political history: in May 1947 Katayama Tetsu, a

---

*Graduated from Tokyo Imperial University in political science in 1906, Yoshida (1878–1967) entered the Ministry of Foreign Affairs, served as ambassador to England and Italy, and from the militarist view was considered too liberal, too pro-British, and too pro-American.

devoted Socialist, became Japan's first Socialist prime minister. Mac-
Arthur suspected that the rise of a socialist was an unpleasant consequence of a perhaps too successful purging of conservatives. Socialism
was clearly not MacArthur's favorite political ideology. On May 24, the
day after Katayama became prime minister, MacArthur, an Episcopalian,
told the Japanese people that the political implications of Katayama's
appointment were less important than its spiritual ones. "For the first
time in history, Japan is led by a Christian leader—one who throughout
his life has been a member of the Presbyterian church. It reflects the
complete religious freedom which exists throughout this land."[43] Mac-
Arthur naturally saw the spiritual implications of this event as reaching
far beyond Japan.

> It is significant, too, from a broad international viewpoint that the three
> great oriental countries now have men who embrace the Christian faith at
> the head of their governments, Chiang Kai-shek in China, Manuel Roxas in
> the Philippines and Tetsu Katayama in Japan. It bespeaks the steady ad-
> vance of this sacred concept, establishes with clarity and conviction that
> the peoples of the East and West can find common agreement in the spirit-
> uality of the human mind, and offers hope for the ultimate erection of an
> invincible spiritual barrier against the infiltration of ideologies which seek
> by suppression the way to power and advancement. This is human progress.[44]

On June 1, 1947, Prime Minister Katayama (1887–1978), evidently
buoyed by the same mood of optimism, took up MacArthur's theme. As
befitted one who, in 1919, had opened a law office in the Tokyo YMCA,
the new prime minister declared to the nation that "democratic gover-
ment must be permeated by a spirit of Christian love and humanism"
and that "government in future must be guided by a Christian spirit of
morality." His new cabinet, Katayama said, would make especially sure
"to demarcate a clear line vis-à-vis communism."[45]

In governing the nation the Katayama cabinet, boycotted by the
still-influential conservative Liberal Party (led by Yoshida), suffered
from its own lack of experience and talent. Worse yet, factional infighting
in the midst of the nation's acute food crisis accelerated its downfall.
Four months after the cabinet had been formed only 22 percent of the
people supported the Katayama government while 54 percent opposed
it.[46] The Katayama cabinet resigned on February 10, 1948; and the Japanese Socialist Party has never been able to regain power.

Actually, it did not matter whether the Japanese government was
dominated by Conservatives, Liberals or Socialists during this period.
They were expendable puppets and MacArthur was handling the strings.
The Japanese people knew that; they voted at every election, nonethe-

less, as the novelty of voting for public officials gave them the illusory but instant gratification of seeming to create a popular democracy.

Meanwhile MacArthur watched the Japanese government's every move. When he saw undesirable behavior, he intervened to correct it. He listened to every word the high Japanese officials uttered. When he heard them reminiscing about the prewar imperial regime, he banished them. Some of the puppets played eagerly while others simulated enthusiasm for MacArthur; both groups survived well. MacArthur also had under a tight rein the corps of popularly elected representatives in the Japanese Diet, who were willing to do whatever he told them to do and even made statements similar to his. The Emperor, too, openly supported MacArthur.

Religious Purge

As a natural sequel to "moral disarmament" MacArthur issued an order on "Abolition of Governmental Sponsorship, Support, Perpetuation, Control, and Dissemination of State Shinto (*Kokka Shinto, jinja Shinto*)." By this he intended to destroy the psychological foundation of imperial sovereignty; specifically, he condemned "the doctrine that the Emperor of Japan is superior to the heads of other states because of ancestry, descent, or special origin."[47]

The Japanese government grew nervous at the thought of the glorious past being buried. Japanese conservatives worried that without Shinto and imperial sovereignty Japan would never be strong again. Bishop accurately perceived this mood when he wrote to Atcheson and Byrnes that "emphasis on future strength is found in expressions of both desire and determination to rebuild Japan as a *strong* nation."[48] The Office of Intelligence Research (OIR) of the State Department also sensed the Japanese conservatives' underlying resentment toward American "destruction" of what they believed were the core of Japanese culture and nationhood. Conservative Japanese leadership, in the OIR's assessment, was "ideologically opposed to many occupation-instituted reforms, and there [were] indications that during the tenure of the Liberal-led Yoshida cabinet the government [had] sought to minimize the effects, if not the implementation, of these reforms."[49]

GHQ was well aware of the Japanese government's sentiment but did not show the slightest sign of possible compromise. On November 1, 1946, under MacArthur's order, the Ministries of Education and of Home Affairs jointly told the nation's academic and political communities that public institutions would refrain from memorial ceremonies for war dead. On November 6, 1946, MacArthur ordered the Japanese government to punish violators of freedom of religion (that is, those Japanese who denounced Christianity) and to stop neighborhood fund raising for Shinto.[50] The US military government (the Eighth Army, stationed throughout Japan) issued an order to prohibit all memorial services for Japanese killed in action.[51] One conspicuous reason for the ferocity of GHQ's attack on the former state religion was that the origins of the imperial system and of Shinto were virtually indistinguishable. The Emperor was the object and primary practitioner of Shinto rituals. Another and more practical reason was, as GHQ put it, that "the blighting effect upon the spiritual and intellectual integrity of the Japanese people of complete conformity with the debasing requirements of the Shinto cult can scarcely be overestimated." Secularization of the Japanese state, GHQ continued, had therefore meant much more than depriving Shrine Shinto of financial aid; rather, it had meant "release from an ideological tyranny so insidious and all-pervasive as to reduce to impotence all opposition, whether of individual or of ideas."[52] At the same time, GHQ was extremely anxious to plumb the secrets of Shintoism, which American military men in Tokyo believed to be the driving force behind the Japanese fighting spirit. The Research Unit of CI & E's Religions Division extensively studied the subject and produced numerous lengthy reports.[53]

Japanese conservatives' attempts to retain imperial sovereignty in law and education will be further discussed in chapters 6 and 7.

Economic Purge

American policy for the Japanese economy was clearly spelled out in the State Department's recommendation to President Truman at the Potsdam Conference. "The essential aspects of Japanese economy should be controlled," the department advised, "to meet the needs of the occupation forces and to prevent starvation and such disease and civil unrest as would interfere with the operations of military government." Further, in order to demilitarize Japanese industry, the US occupation authority had to prevent Japan "from again developing an economic war potential." Japan should have no aircraft industry and "should be deprived of its heavy industry capacity."[54]

The *Basic Directive* bluntly told MacArthur: "The plight of Japan is the direct outcome of its own behavior, and the Allies will not undertake the burden of repairing the damage." MacArthur was therefore not to assume any responsibility for the Japanese economy whatsoever, whether to rehabilitate or to strengthen it.

You will make it clear to the Japanese people that: (a) You assume no obligation to maintain or have maintained any particular standard of living. . . . (b) . . . the standard of living will depend upon the thoroughness with which Japan rids itself of all militaristic ambitions, redirects the use of its human and natural resources wholly and solely for purposes of peaceful living, administers adequate economic and financial controls, and cooperates with the occupying forces and the governments they represent.[55]

The US government presumed that a subsistence economy in Japan would accelerate the disintegration of the Japanese Empire and guarantee the future paralysis of any potential Japanese war machines. It also anticipated that the internal disintegration of the Japanese economy would encourage the democratization of Japan. In the State Department's own words: "The development of democratic organizations in labor, industry, and agriculture should be encouraged and a wider distribution of ownership, management and control of the Japanese economy system should be favored."[56] With the same reasoning MacArthur swiftly began dissolving *zaibatsu,* those family-centered financial conglomerates that had played such a part in the development of Japanese business and commerce. On November 6, 1945, MacArthur issued a directive, *Dissolution of Holding Companies*; it was intended, he said, to "permit a wider distribution of income and of ownership of the means of production and trade," and to "encourage the development within Japan of economic ways and institutions of a type that will contribute to the growth of peace and democratic forces."[57]

Max W. Bishop was among those who expressed keen apprehension about such thorough dismantling of the Japanese economic structure. The Japanese economy, he wrote to Atcheson, had been "stripped of its military backbone and deprived of some of its best brains and guiding genius." He saw all Japanese economic activities and even relief measures as characterized by indecision and drift.[58] Atcheson himself reported to President Truman that the Japanese government had miserably failed to supply the people with rice, and that the US government would "have to provide relief supplies, whether we wish to or not, in order to maintain sufficiently solid ground on which to push forward with our political objectives."[59]

THE POLITICS OF HUNGER

The Japanese, to remain alive, scrambled for food. The plight of the urban population was especially acute. Farmers had no faith in paper money. City people had to take jam-packed trains to the countryside to get whatever food they could barter for with silks or jewels. In December 1945 one Japanese informant of the Office of the US Political Adviser rode such trains. "Everyone is for himself," he reported, "and the waiting crowd of passengers simply make a head-on dash to the platform and scramble into the train through windows once the wicket is opened." Petty black-market dealers, he continued, traveled back and forth carrying rice and apples to Tokyo as these commodities brought a good profit on the black market. Political subjects—political parties, women's suffrage, the coming election—were conspicuously absent from the train passengers' conversation.[60] There was indeed practically nothing in the cities except the remnants of successful American B-29 incendiary bombing. Karl T. Compton was surprised at the bombing's effectiveness. "The actual destruction," he reported to President Truman, "considerably exceeded the reports based on reconnaissance photographs." Of Tokyo and its adjacent cities—a total of 210 square miles, or about the area of greater Chicago—some 85 square miles were "nothing but a level ash heap."[61]

Emmerson wrote to Secretary of State Byrnes: "The sense of economic insecurity, the fear of starvation, the frantic day-to-day living by the black market extend through all classes of Japanese society and condition the thinking of every Japanese.... Political parties, elections, democracy, the Emperor: all are of academic importance when the rice bowl is empty."[62] MacArthur was well aware of the situation. "One of the first things I did," he stated in his *Reminiscences*, "was to set up our army kitchens to help feed the people. Had this not been done, they would have died by the thousands."[63] He also made available numerous air fields, which were not required by the occupation forces, for cultivation of food crops. He had to take these emergency measures to reduce the risk of public demonstrations for food. The nation's food situation was clearly reported to him. The Office of Strategic Services (OSS) stated in April 1946 that even the minimum food requirements of the urban population could not be met from indigenous supplies over the next six months; relief would have to come from imports.[64] The Civil Intelligence Section of the US Army filed an even gloomier report: as of July 8, 1946, food stocks in the Tokyo area would run out in 4.2 days. All other major cities faced a similar predicament.[65]

MacArthur began importing food supplies from the United States, especially canned foods, bulk wheat, corn, and bagged flour. He made public announcements whenever food-laden ships were about to arrive at Yokohama or Kobe. This enhanced his power and prestige, besides serving as brilliant public relations with the hungry Japanese people. On May 29, 1946, Prime Minister Yoshida expressed to MacArthur his "sense of profound gratitude" for 2.5 million pounds of flour. Because of Mac-Arthur's generosity, Yoshida said, "we have been able thereby to ease a situation which was fraught with a iminent (sic) danger of violent out-breaks."[66] On July 5, 1946, the House of Representatives of the Japa-nese Diet passed a resolution expressing gratitude to MacArthur: "A famine has overtaken Japan. All her people, suffering privation, are now plunged into the depth of anxieties. At this critical juncture, to the bound-less gratitude of the entire nation, the Supreme Commander of the Allied Powers has come to the rescue, by releasing the foodstuffs imported from the United States in large quantities."[67]

Nevertheless, the Japanese people continued to be preoccupied with food and apathetic toward politics. A vivid example of the public mood was the mayoral election at Fukuoka, declared null and void "be-cause over 75 percent of the voters failed to exercise their franchise."[68] One indication of how serious the food situation had become was its effect on education. Immediately after the surrender the Ministry of Education had encouraged all prefectural governors and school principals "to make the students work for the increase of food production."[69] In November 1945 the ministry again instructed them: "Labor service in food produc-tion and reconstruction to be coordinated [so] as to enhance physical education."[70] Kyoto Imperial University announced that because of the food shortage its literature department would suspend classes two months from late December 1945. Other departments soon followed.[71] The Min-istry of Education in June 1946 told all schools to start the summer vaca-tion early. For elementary school pupils the ministry with GHQ's assis-tance started a lunch program beginning in 1947.[72]

"Food deficiencies are real," Karl C. Leebrick, an American edu-cational observer, reported to Atcheson. His observation continued: "Children show signs of malnutrition. Physical exercises (sic) has of ne-cessity been restricted. Schools have shortened the school day to permit the students to eat at home. In several schools instruction ceases about midday." Malnutrition did not single out only school children; university faculty members, too, were seen to be suffering from it.[73] Because of the rampant inflation, and the sheer lack of goods to buy, the faculty's tra-ditionally low salaries made survival miserable. The monthly salary of most assistant and associate professors seldom exceeded 200 yen, when the monthly cost of living was calculated at about 340 yen.[74] Elementary school teachers, who were paid even less (around 130 yen a month), scraped for food in Tokyo. Elsewhere, salaries were even lower: in one prefecture elementary school teachers were paid 58 yen a month (as of June 1946) and their demand to a governor was for 90 yen a month.[75]

The stunning misery of local school teachers was vividly portrayed in a letter written by one of them to a metropolitan newspaper in December 1945:

> Since great importance is attached to the function of education in new Japan, the prospects are enough to make us shudder. The base salary of a teacher in one of the lower grades [of an elementary school] is 30 yen a month. With an additional 3 yen for good attendance and 10 yen for bonuses his total 43 yen monthly salary is less than a laborer's daily wage.

The same teacher spelled out what his 43 yen a month meant in terms of actual groceries: "The current price of rice is 15 yen per *sho* [1.588 quarts], one sardine, 1 yen; and 1.10 yen per egg." The teacher went on to complain that "society even criticizes our purchase of farm produce which we had raised in cooperation with our students."[76]

While trying to cope with an appalling economic situation which threatened to become yet worse, Japanese teachers had, however, begun organizing themselves into a national labor union. This teachers' movement was soon to become one of the most politically active unions in postwar Japan. Encouragement of the teachers' participation in the political process and unionization was a public policy of GHQ. (The Ministry of Education, which was not accustomed to encouraging teachers' civil and political liberties, later thought differently; indeed, the ministry found it actually "desirable" that they organize to help themselves, and even urged them in 1947 to run as candidates for the National Diet seats.[77]) The teachers, preoccupied with their physical survival, presented their demands to the education minister, home minister, and finance minister on 20 December 1945:

> (1) Increase in pay of 500 percent; (2) allocation of working suits, rubber-soled socks, rain gear, and bicycles which were necessary for teachers to attend schools and perform their services; (3) enlargement of teachers' farms and obtaining of houses for teachers; (4) the position and salaries of all teachers from university professors down to primary teachers should be determined on one scale, and everyone should be given an opportunity for promotion to the highest position, according to his ability and experience; (5) salaries of all teachers should be paid by the State; and (6) teachers should receive education in schools and other agencies to improve themselves while they hold their posts.[78]

The hardships of a teacher's life seemed to evoke sympathy from various prefectural assemblymen. One prefectural assembly in December 1945 offered to every public school teacher in the prefecture a raise in salary of 1 yen a month. Translated into market terms, this amounted to three tangerines. The same prefecture reported that one young teacher had collapsed on the way home from lack of nutrition.[79] What ensued was inevitable. Teacher resignations increased dramatically, a serious national setback in the "building of the new Japan."

University students were also hit hard. Since they did not have much money anyway, they could not buy even necessary food on the black market. "Most students lie in bed on Sundays to save strength," a group of them told Emmerson. "None of them," they said, "eats more than two meals a day. However anxious they may be to read good books, study or to organize themselves in political movements, they have no desire so long as they can think only of their own hunger." The entire Japanese people, they told Emmerson, were preoccupied with food, shelter, and clothing. Hungry people could not be expected to practice democracy or even to take any steps towards it.[80] CI & E concurred. For the present, it reported, student hardships were extreme; many university and technical students had been forced to study at home or give up school entirely.[81] Even as late as June 1949 one graduate student of Tokyo University said in his report to GHQ that "those wishing to receive higher education must groan" and make a painful decision between food or books.[82]

The 1945 crop harvest suffered from typhoon damage and lack of fertilizers. Even with a good harvest MacArthur had anticipated food imports of at least 1.5 million tons would be needed just to assure "bare subsistence for the Japanese people in 1946." With a bad harvest he feared that the food imports might run as high as 4 million tons.[83] On May 1, 1946, the first May Day celebration in eleven years, half a million people gathered in front of the Imperial Palace demanding the immediate establishment of "people's democracy" (whatever that may have meant) and, more seriously, people's administration of food.

On May 6 MacArthur, acutely aware of the still-deteriorating food situation, appealed to Herbert Hoover, chairman of the Famine Emergency Committee, who was then in Japan as head of the United States Food Mission. Mass starvation in Japan, he told Hoover, would defeat the major objectives of the Occupation and seriously harm Allied interests "not only in the Far East but the world over." His request was particularly urgent, he said, "since Japan [could] only be considered a vast concentration camp under the control of the Allies." But he made clear that preferential treatment for the Japanese was out of the question. "[W]hat is requested," he said, "are only those quantities of food required to achieve the objectives of the occupation."[84] MacArthur's request to the War Department was blunter: "Send us food or send us soldiers."[85]

The continuous street demonstrations demanding food severely irritated MacArthur. On May 19 approximately a quarter of a million people once more gathered in front of the Imperial Palace. This time some of them forcibly entered the palace kitchen to examine what His

Majesty ate, while others invaded the official residence of Prime Minister Yoshida. As a matter of personal pride, MacArthur would not tolerate this kind of behavior from the Japanese; it destroyed the appearance of public tranquility during his reign. The next day he issued a public warning that Japan's very future was endangered by what he called "mass violence and physical processes of intimidation, under organized leadership." He reassured the Japanese that "every possible rational freedom of democratic method" had been and would be permitted to them. What would not be permitted, he bluntly told them, was "the physical violence which undisciplined elements [were] now beginning to practice." "They constitute," he reasoned, "a menace not only to orderly government but to the basic purposes and security of the Occupation itself." To such "minor elements of Japanese society" MacArthur issued a clear warning: if they could not restrain themselves, he would "be forced to take the necessary steps to control and remedy such a deplorable situation."[86]

STARVATION AND SUBVERSION

Phrases such as "organized leadership," "undisciplined elements," and "minor elements" meant the aggressive Japanese Communists. This fact did not escape Lieutenant General K. Derevyanko, the only Soviet member of the Allied Council for Japan, who on May 21 requested from MacArthur "more detailed information"; the "concrete reasons" for MacArthur's statement of May 20 were, he said, unknown to him. The political situation, Derevyanko argued, did not present "the appearance of a threat to the occupation regime on the part of the masses of the people" and, if it did, a statement such as the one in question should come under the jurisdiction of the Allied Council.[87] The inquiry offended MacArthur, particularly because it came from the Allied Council which, he believed, should not have existed in the first place. On May 22 Atcheson, as deputy for the supreme commander and chairman of the Allied Council, curtly replied to Derevyanko: "You have apparently misinterpreted his statement. . . . The action of General MacArthur is a security measure for the purpose of protecting the Occupation and its forces."[88]

His reason was hardly convincing, for the American occupation forces, to say the least, enjoyed such physical and psychological supremacy as hardly to be bothered by the Japanese food demonstrators, who did not carry even bamboo spears. The true reason was that Atcheson and MacArthur shared a mutual abhorrence of Derevyanko. Derevyanko and "his staff of more than 400," Atcheson complained to Secretary Byrnes, "has [sic] made it apparent over [a] long period that Soviet government resents predominant American role here." Derevyanko, he continued, "strives to further dissention [sic] and discontent among Japanese, furthers Communist propaganda and in general does not wish this Occupation to achieve announced and agreed-upon Allied objectives." The list of charges against Derevyanko was nothing if not comprehensive.

> He has endeavored to utilize Allied Council as inquisitorial and investigative body by presenting requests for unnecessary detailed information on wide range of subjects and making hypercritical statements.... His agents have encouraged mob violence by discontented elements and he himself has made public defense of demonstrations instigated or led by Japanese Communists and has persistently attacked Japanese government and its members as "reactionaries" both in statements before Allied Council and in written communications to SCAP.[89]

A further aggravation was that the representative of the British Commonwealth, MacMahon Ball, an Australian, appeared to side with Derevyanko. An angry Atcheson told Secretary Byrnes: "He [Ball] almost invariably supports Soviet member and receives from the latter only smiles of approbation."[90]

The Counter-Intelligence Section of GHQ could discover only twenty incidents of actual or threatened food rallies from September 1945 through May 1946. Each one of these incidents, Atcheson told Byrnes, though allegedly spontaneous, had been organized and led by Japanese Communists and their sympathizers, and "showed a progressive tendency towards unruliness and violence." MacArthur's statement of May 20 had therefore been "both timely and advisable," and had influenced the Japanese people in favor of restraint.[91] Unfortunately for the Japanese people, any public demonstration of their hunger was bound to be interpreted by SCAP as politically subversive.

At the same time, the US government had expected more of the Japanese than a few mild food demonstrations. A top-secret telegram from the US chief of staff to MacArthur on September 24, 1945, informed him of a critical addition to the original text of the US Initial Post-Surrender Policy for Japan. The original text read: "Changes in the form of government initiated by the Japanese people or government in the direction of modifying its feudal and authoritarian tendencies are to be permitted and favored." But the Japanese people might have to use physical force to achieve such favorable changes. The chief of staff, in concurrence with President Truman, therefore advised MacArthur: "In the event that the effectuation of such changes involves the use of force by the Japanese people or government against persons opposed thereto, the supreme commander should intervene only where necessary to ensure the security of his forces and the attainment of all objectives of the Occupation."[92]

Japanese weapons, including even ornamental swords, had been swiftly confiscated by the occupation forces. There was not the slightest hint of "the use of force by the Japanese people" against either the imperial regime or the occupation forces. The Japanese people did not feel like fighting at all: they were too hungry. This extraordinary public calmness, GHQ commented, was "nothing short of miraculous." The miracle, according to GHQ, was due to "the simple formula of utilizing the present Japanese government, centered upon the person of the Emperor and the psychic force of tradition." The formula, of course, proceeded from expert intelligence work, on the one hand, and, on the other, from General MacArthur's "brilliant appraisal of the Oriental mind."[93]

As things turned out, MacArthur did not need the "changes in the form of government initiated by the Japanese people"; he himself initiated the changes according to his own plan. Too much change in the form of government would have made his plan useless. MacArthur's initial success at maintaining law and order spoiled him. He did not question his method and wisdom. He thought democracy was an infinitely malleable concept that could easily take on a Japanese form. He chose the reality of political stability under his own autocratic rule over the possible benefits of fundamental social reforms, with their potential for disorder, that the Japanese people might have undertaken if permitted. To this end, he made use of Emperor, cabinet, Diet, and mass media. They did what MacArthur told them to do. When one reform program failed, MacArthur—and the Japanese people, it is fair to add—assumed that changes in cabinet and Diet membership might do the trick. In this way those who were not retained in the cabinet or Diet could be blamed for their incompetence; that the reform program was impractical did not matter. MacArthur was right, always: his motives, pure and sincere, aimed at nothing but democracy and peace. His purity, however, made his democracy dogmatic, and his sincerity chilled any opposition.

MacArthur's stern warning against "mass violence," which was in reality a loud cry of hunger, expressed his abhorrence of the Communists who incessantly criticized his reform programs. His warning also reflected his determination to keep everything in his Japanese garden lovely. Fortunately for him, "disorder" and "communism" were already synonymous in the Japanese public mind, and his use of these terms was effective public relations. But his appeals to public order when the people of Japan were starving made democracy seem irrelevant to any but the rich.

The desperate economic situation, with or without communist agitation, did not improve. Growing frustration among the people, coupled with the visible impotence of the Yoshida cabinet, led the labor unions to declare a general strike for February 1, 1947. "I will not permit," Mac-

Arthur responded on January 31, "the use of so deadly a social weapon in the present impoverished and emaciated condition of Japan." He told the Japanese laborers that he had reluctantly intervened "only to forestall the fatal impact upon an already gravely threatened public welfare." Without naming the Japanese Communists as the potential users of this "deadly social weapon," MacArthur made clear that they were nonetheless responsible: "The persons involved in the threatened general strikes are but a small minority of the Japanese people. Yet this minority might well plunge the great masses into disaster not unlike that produced in the immediate past by the minority which led Japan into the destruction of war." He was well aware, however, of the dilemma of "rationed democracy," since he took no other action against organized labor and disclaimed any intention of compromising or influencing the basic social issues.[94] MacArthur's last-minute intervention in the "legitimate right of laborers to strike" caused widespread disappointment among the Japanese people and confirmed their nagging suspicion that Japan's democratic objectives, whatever they might be, were judged strictly in accordance with the American interest. The laborers' frustration and resentment might well have contributed to the emergence of the short-lived Socialist cabinet in the national election of April 1947.

MacArthur's economic pacification, meanwhile, continued systematically. On February 20, 1947, he wrote to the US Congress that since the surrender, the economic blockade of the Japanese home islands had been not only continued but intensified, and that the results amounted to "economic strangulation."[95] A month later, at a press conference, he perhaps overstated its effectiveness: "No weapon, not even the atomic bomb, is as deadly in its final effect as economic warfare. The atomic bomb kills by thousands, starvation by the millions."[96]

MacArthur did, however, try hard to secure enough money and food for occupied Japan and Korea. After he had sent his 1948 budget estimate to the War Department, the department requested from Congress $900 million for civil relief for Japan and Korea. On February 14, 1947, General Eisenhower informed MacArthur that congress was planning to reduce this figure by 50 percent, with ruinous consequences.[97] On February 20 MacArthur replied to Eisenhower and to Assistant Secretary for Occupied Areas Howard C. Petersen that unless the money was secured, the American victory in the Far East would be incomplete and would offer hope "for little more than an armistice between one campaign and the next."[98] His plea in favor of the full amount was seven pages long. The next day Eisenhower sent a cable to MacArthur: "Thank you very much for your very comprehensive statements which should help us materially in presenting our case to Congress."[99]

President Truman, having received numerous urgent reports on the Japanese food situation, was convinced that many Japanese were on the verge of death from starvation. One of his own emissaries, Edwin A. Locke, Jr., who had been sent to China as an economic adviser, met with MacArthur and Colonel Raymond C. Kramer, chief of the Economic and Scientific Section of GHQ in Tokyo. "Even if the required imports [4 million to 8 million tons] are obtainable," Locke told Truman, "there is almost certain to be widespread starvation and distress before food and textiles can be got into the hands of the needy." If the United States failed to provide the Japanese with foodstuffs, Locke feared, it would "create a desperate situation in Japan, with high mortality and perhaps social disturbances."[100] On June 19, 1947, Atcheson advised Truman: "Whether we like it or not, Japan is at present an economic responsibility of the United States and it is to our interest to assist in the process of getting the country on at least a minimum self-supporting basis."[101] Truman agreed. "President's office has requested," the Department of the Army told MacArthur on October 14, "pictures showing famine conditions, particularly emphasizing children, women and aged, breadlines, emaciated conditions, etc. These of course should be factual. No old pictures should be used."[102] Two days later the Public Health and Welfare Section of GHQ, SCAP, informed MacArthur that no such pictures were available, since famine conditions did not exist. Nor would they exist, so long as adequate food imports were continued.[103] The next day MacArthur replied to the War Department: "Famine conditions have been averted by the narrowest margin in Japan in calendar year 1947 by maximum use of indigenous food resources ... supplemented by the importation of minimum quantity of food from the United States." There was, accordingly, a regrettable lack of famine-stricken subjects to photograph. MacArthur suggested instead that publicity be given to the way in which imported US food had narrowly averted a famine in Japan. In this way he succeeded both in affirming his own administrative competence and in warning the Truman administration of disaster unless food imports were continued.[104] Photographic evidence of malnutrition could have been provided, but not without placing MacArthur in an unfavorable light. At the same time, he had to get more American food.

BUSTING THE ZAIBATSU

MacArthur wanted "to keep the Japanese economy going so that the Japs won't become an albatross around our necks."[105] But his economic policy, which was to destroy the existing Japanese economic structure and to keep importing food, made the Japanese just that. Japanese economic recovery was discussed, but proposals on how to achieve it differed widely. As early as October 1945 Colonel Raymond C. Kramer, chief of the Economic and Scientific Section, GHQ, said in MacArthur's presence that "he saw no danger in giving Japanese industry 'the green light,' since America [was] in a position to prevent or eliminate undesirable industrial developments in Japan." Kramer also spoke very highly of the Japanese people, "stressing their industry, discipline and honesty." They were, he said, "so far ahead of any other Far Eastern people as to be the 'natural leaders of Asia.' " He even predicted accurately that by 1960 Japan's position in world trade would have recovered to the point of making it a major competitor with the United States and Great Britain.[106] On the use of the atomic bomb Kramer commented that while the Japanese government seized on it as an excuse for getting out of the war, it "actually speeded surrender by only a few days."[107] Perhaps his frankness infuriated MacArthur; in any case, he left Tokyo two months later. Major General William F. Marquat, a MacArthur protégé who had shared the humiliation of Bataan, took over as chief of the Economic and Scientific Section, which made economic policy for Japan.

Another dissenting opinion was expressed by Max W. Bishop, who suggested to George Atcheson in January 1946 that GHQ's dissolution of zaibatsu was contributing to an imminent economic disaster. In April of the same year Robert A. Fearey, former secretary to Ambassador Joseph Grew in prewar Japan and now at the Office of the US Political Adviser, also cautioned the State Department and Atcheson that American economic policies, which appeared to be responsible for Japan's "persistently adverse economic conditions," were helping the rise of Japanese communism. If the zaibatsu busting did not stop, the Japanese people, realizing that the Americans were responsible for their chronic misery, might reverse their "current pro-American, prodemocratic and anti-Soviet, anticommunist tendencies."[108] His report arrived in Washington unclassified but was immediately classified "secret."

The Military Intelligence Division of the War Department concurrently shared a similar view; US prestige in Japan, it stated, undoubtedly depended in large part on solving Japanese economic problems.[109] Secretary of the Army Kenneth C. Royall was another who believed that the primary cause of the Japanese economy's wretched performance was the dissolution of the zaibatsu. As undersecretary of war he had visited MacArthur in Tokyo (from March 10 to 14, 1946) and seen his reign. He feared that MacArthur possessed too much discretionary power. Royall initiated changes in MacArthur's zaibatsu policy and asked the State

Department, which did not have a history of getting along with Mac-
Arthur, for cooperation. Royall's reasons, as cabled in his personal message to MacArthur, numbered four.

1. *Dissolution of* zaibatsu *was "un-American," because compensation for divested
    property was inadequate.* The State Department, however, took such in-
    adequacy as a matter of course. Its reason was that "if full compensation
    were paid, the former owners would retain the full power to resume their
    former positions of economic domination." MacArthur's reply to Royall
    was that breaking up the *zaibatsu* would "erect a solid bulwark against the
    spread of ideologies or systems destructive of both free enterprise and
    political freedom under democratic capitalism." The State Department said
    that was "soundly American."
2. *SCAP's* zaibatsu *program had been carried too far.* The State Department
    had more faith in MacArthur than Secretary Royall. "It is difficult to be-
    lieve," the department said, "that General MacArthur ... would permit
    this."
3. *Dissolution of* zaibatsu *would interfere with economic recovery.* MacArthur
    replied, "Japanese recovery would on the contrary be seriously jeopardized
    by delay in carrying out the program." Worse yet, the State Department
    feared that delay would make the Japanese business community wonder if
    the United States sincerely intended "to free them from the domination of
    the Zaibatsu," and whether "resurgent Zaibatsu interests" would now take
    reprisals against businessmen who tried to get ahead.
4. *A "committee of prominent private citizens" should be established to investi-
    gate MacArthur's* zaibatsu *program.* The success or failure of the program,
    MacArthur told Royall, hinged on the choice it presented between "free
    competitive enterprise which goes hand in hand with political freedom and
    a socialism of one kind or another under which political freedom is a myth."
    A review of the already controversial policy would make its success very
    doubtful, he said. The State Department agreed and said that such a
    committee "could not be kept secret, and the knowledge in Japan that the
    United States was uncertain about the program would greatly endanger its
    successful implementation."

Thus the State Department policymakers wholeheartedly agreed
with MacArthur's reasons why the program should continue and recommended that Secretary of State George C. Marshall try to talk Royall out
of his objections.[110] MacArthur vigorously continued to bust *zaibatsu.*
By paralyzing Japanese business initiative and failing to stabilize the
chaotic Japanese economy, he not only encouraged the growth of communism—a thought that was anathema to him—but also added to the US
financial burden. The Japanese people, though thankful, did not relish
this embarrassing dependency, a dependency that made MacArthur's
rule easier.

A surprise protest came from Socialist prime minister Katayama.
On the morning of September 4, 1947, Katayama requested an interview

with MacArthur to talk about a slowdown of *zaibatsu* decentralization. MacArthur replied that he would be busy for the rest of the week. The same day Katayama wrote to the "Dear General of the Army" that to further continue the decentralization would "deprive Japan of her capacity of self-support and international economic competition by further diminishing [her] already weak economic power," thus permanently reducing Japan to an object of US charity. "I believe that there is no reason why the General Headquarters should not give assurance to the Japanese industrial circles," he dared to opine, "[that] it is not the intention of the General Headquarters to divide the Japanese enterprises into unnecessarily small units."[111] "My efforts in the interest of guiding Japan toward a peaceful and democratic reorientation," MacArthur wrote back on September 10, "are too well known to require reiteration." He then preached Katayama a sermon on the need for "meticulous adherence to Allied policy" in order to convince world opinion of Japanese sincerity. Any major change in current *zaibatsu* policy, MacArthur threatened Katayama, could lead only to "unwarranted suspicion which may actually result in a revision of controlling directives to include the imposition of additional and more rigid standards."[112]

THE ECONOMIC STABILIZATION PROGRAM

The US government knew it could not continue feeding the Japanese indefinitely; the Japanese themselves had to bear the burden of a drastic austerity program. Yet nothing reassuring was happening in Tokyo, because MacArthur habitually resisted any concrete policy advice from Washington. He thought he knew the Japanese situation best. He probably did. But he was not informing the people in Washington, except insofar as he urged them to keep sending Japan more food. This lack of communication between MacArthur and the highest US policymakers was not entirely of MacArthur's own making. Awe and deference among the people in Washington played a large part in perpetuating his aloof and often arrogant behavior. As George Kennan, chief of the State Department's Policy Planning Staff, told Secretary of State Dean Acheson, "the elevated nature of [MacArthur's] position there and the necessity of preserving his prestige in Japan meant that the government could not really exercise an effective control over his actions." Washington, he added, was so anxious to let MacArthur have his own way that it sanctioned his actions even when they were questionable.[113]

In deference to MacArthur's feelings—or what it believed to be his feelings—the State Department was willing to exercise "considerable forebearance over a period of some years," turning a blind eye to what was really going on in Japan.[114] MacArthur, however, showed no such confidence in the people in Washington, as he took their "considerable forebearance" for granted. Kennan later commented: "I do not recall any evidence that he took the initiative at any time to endeavor to get a better understanding with the people charged with the conduct of our foreign relations."[115]

Meanwhile the Defense Department was exercising something more than forebearance. "[W]henever an issue comes up with MacArthur," Secretary of State Acheson complained, "there is great difficulty in getting a firm attitude in dealing with MacArthur in the Pentagon."[116] William Averell Harriman, ambassador to the Soviet Union (1943–46), secretary of commerce (1946–48) and personal representative of President Truman (1950–51), spoke of "the kid gloves that the Defense Department had towards MacArthur."[117] The Chiefs of Staff, he said to Acheson, "were always treating MacArthur with gloves and never sent him the kind of orders or the kind of firm messages" that a "less temperamental officer" would have received.[118] "I agree with you," Acheson replied.[119]

Something had to be done quickly about the worsening Japanese economic situation in addition to getting more information swiftly and accurately from Tokyo. In early 1948 Kennan recommended that Secretary of State Marshall authorize "a full-fledged diplomatic representative in Tokyo who would not be a subordinate of the general in his military command" and "who would report independently to the Department of State." Marshall did not act on the recommendation. "I am sure," Kennan said, "it was out of consideration for General MacArthur's known feelings on this subject and out of a reluctance to propose any arrangements which would not be agreeable to him."[120] Kennan himself was sent to Tokyo to confer with MacArthur during the first three weeks of March 1948. Japan's future, he believed, depended on "what had really been done about the purges and about the decentralization of industry." Answers to these questions were also "necessary for proper study of the Japanese peace treaty."[121]

The concrete result of Kennan's visit to Tokyo was *Recommendations With Respect to US Policy Toward Japan*, which the State Department submitted to the National Security Council in June 1948. In this top-secret policy document the State Department urged that economic recovery should be made the prime objective of US policy in Japan for the coming period. In particular, "the revival of Japanese foreign trade," combined with "a long-term US aid program," should be encouraged. On the other hand, the department felt it should make clear to the Japanese government that economic recovery would "in large part depend on Japanese efforts to raise production and to maintain high export levels through hard work, a minimum of work stoppages, internal austerity measures and the stern combatting of inflationary trends."[122] On June 8, 1948, MacArthur received a full text of this recommendation from the Department of the Army. Finally, on December 10, 1948, the US government issued to MacArthur an interim directive, *Economic Stabilization in Japan*, which the Department of the Army had drafted. "You," MacArthur was ordered, "will direct the Japanese Government immediately to carry out a program of economic stabilization by adopting whatever measures may be required rapidly to achieve fiscal, monetary, price and wage stability in Japan to maximize production for export."[123]

On December 19 MacArthur wrote to Prime Minister Yoshida that "the American people so long as called upon to underwrite existing deficits in the indigenous resources required to sustain the Japanese life [were] entitled to the maximized industry of the Japanese people . . . and that by positive Allied intervention many obstructions incident to improvidential political conflicts, unobjective labor strife and destructive ideological pressures [might] best be avoided." When this notion was "reduced to language which all may understand," MacArthur bluntly explained, it amounted to "prompt achievement of that degree of economic self-sufficiency which alone can justify and insure political freedom." But he did not say how the Japanese could promptly achieve economic self-sufficiency. Instead, he told Yoshida that no political freedom exists "as long as people's livelihood is dependent on the largess of others," and that Japan's economic stability would become "an impregnable barrier against evil and destructive ideological pressures." The task of achieving such economic stability, he further explained, would call for "a reorientation of Japanese thought and action. . . . for increased austerity in every phase of Japanese life and for the temporary surrender of some of the privileges and immunities inherent in a free society." Among the things to be surrendered were "interference by management or labor with the acceleration of production"; "political conflict over the objectives"; "ideological oppositions"; and "any attempt to delay or frustrate its accomplishment." Therefore, the Japanese people were expected to "rally with vigor and determination to the challenge of this objective." "If they don't," MacArthur assured Yoshida, "Japan may perish."[124]

Despite all this, the State Department and the Department of the Army were not at all sure that MacArthur was actually going to implement the economic stabilization program. W. W. Butterworth, assistant secretary for Far Eastern affairs, lamented to Secretary Acheson, "General MacArthur has from the beginning resisted the efforts of the Washington agencies concerned to impose on Japan a stabilization program."[125] Secretary of the Army Royall decided to visit MacArthur in Tokyo. Before departure, however, he wanted to consult with Secretary Acheson. On January 25, 1949, Butterworth briefed Acheson. "One of the *chief reasons for Secretary Royall's visit to Japan* at this time," Butterworth said, "*is to make certain that the initiation of the economic stabilization program gets off to a good start.* As you know, he is taking with him Mr. [Joseph] Dodge of Detroit who will remain in Japan as financial adviser to SCAP." A visit from Royall was necessary because the Office of Far Eastern Affairs "[had] learned informally that General MacArthur [had] recently set up in Tokyo a high economic council." The members of this council were General Whitney as chairman, and Generals Marquat and Fox; their function, it appeared, was to serve "as a buffer between Mr. Dodge and SCAP with a view to watering down any recommendations which Mr. Dodge may make before they reach General MacArthur."[126]

Major General Marquat, chief of the Economic and Scientific Section of GHQ, SCAP, was already well known to the State Department as a man who had made numerous "most insulting" innuendos against and cast "a distinct slur on the War Department, the State Department, and their officials."[127] On January 26 Acheson and Royall met over lunch at the latter's office. General William H. Draper, undersecretary of the army, briefed both secretaries, especially on the urgent need for stabilizing the Japanese currency and for encouraging Japanese foreign trade. The same day, Acheson reported to President Truman, "Secretary Forrestal [James V., assistant secretary of the army] and I indicated that the first and primary problem was a clarification of Mr. Dodge's relationship with General MacArthur. If this could be a direct relationship we thought his work held much promise. If it had to be strained through the staff, and particularly through the economic committee recently established, we thought that it would be very difficult indeed."[128] Truman gave Dodge a personal rank of Minister (i.e., he became Ambassador Dodge), so that he could have "direct access to General MacArthur in order to achieve the best results."[129]

On February 1, 1949, Dodge with Royall arrived at Tokyo. On March 7 he announced his strict counterinflationary measures, commonly called the "Dodge Line." The Japanese government was not given an opportunity to refuse it. Dodge made this clear in his press statement.

> The hundreds of millions of dollars of aid received each year by Japan from the United States comes from the taxes imposed on the individual citizens and business enterprises of the United States. In turn these taxes have been paid from the wages of American workers and the production and profits of American business and industry. And the American citizen does not like to pay taxes any more than does the Japanese citizen.[130]

On April 4 Prime Minister Yoshida explained before both houses of the Diet the imminent severity of the Dodge austerity program. The State Department was pleased with his speech, calling it "a forthright effort to explain the unavoidably painful character of the corrective measures required to overcome the present economic crisis."[131] The "painful character" was apparent for Yoshida's conservative majority party; as the State Department put it, "Mr. Dodge and ESS [Economic and Scientific Section] forced the present government to eliminate or drastically reduce many of its campaign commitments."[132] Although a similarly hard line from GHQ had, as the department was well aware, been largely responsible for the downfall of the Katayama and Ashida regimes, the department was not worried about Yoshida's breaking of his campaign promises, because it thought that, with his stature and prestige, he was not likely to be displaced.[133]

Though initially reluctant to welcome Dodge to Japan, MacArthur appreciated his performance in stabilizing the Japanese economy. On May 2, 1949, he sent a telegram to the Department of the Army:

> Mister Dodge's departure today for the United States is a distinct loss to the occupation. . . . Please convey to the president my renewed appreciation for his having prevailed upon Mister Dodge to assume this responsibility of public service and my sincere hope that he will lend his hearty support to my own efforts to convince him that he should return to Japan just as soon as practicable to see the work he has so ably started through to its successful conclusion.[134]

Truman wrote to Secretary of Defense Louis A. Johnson, "I am very sure that he will go back to Japan."[135] Dodge did in fact return to Japan twice, from October 30 to December 4, 1949, and from October 7 to December 4, 1950.

The US government's and MacArthur's insistence on strict implementation of the Dodge Line meant the US government had concluded that the risk of a strong, capitalistic Japan becoming a future military threat to the United States was less than that of an economically feeble Japan becoming a prey to international communist encroachment. As early as September 1947 the CIA had clearly recognized the importance of Japanese economic strength. "The removal of U.S. control," it reported to the first National Security Council, "particularly if the economic problem remains unsolved, would open the way to vigorous Soviet penetration. The rehabilitation of Japan under Soviet influence or control (with provision of essential imports from continental Asia) would jeopardize the US strategic position in the Pacific, as well as any US position in China."[136] And in March 1948 the CIA had predicted that a collapse of

Chiang Kai-shek's Nationalist government might come at any time—certainly, within the next six months.[137] Once again Japan was destined to become the land of *Fukoku Kyohei* ("Enrich the Nation! Strengthen Its Arms!"), reminiscent of imperial Japan in the mid-nineteenth century. Conservative Japanese leaders did not miss the significance of the Dodge Line. They understood that the United States needed Japan as much as they themselves wanted American money and security. Before Dodge's arrival the CIA had reported (on April 22, 1948) to the National Security Council that certain "high Japanese officials" had recently shown "an increasing spirit of independence apparently attributed to their appreciation of a US need for Japan as a strong point in East Asia in view of the state of US-Soviet relations and of their deteriorating prospects in China and Korea." The CIA accurately forewarned that the Japanese would "exert their bargaining power to the utmost in relation to US aid in the rehabilitation of Japan."[138]

The US Congress, however, was expecting the Dodge Line to work a sort of miracle. Before the wish could become reality, Congress proposed to reduce aid money to Japan. On May 25, 1949, Tracy S. Voorhees, assistant secretary of occupied areas, US Army, alerted MacArthur about "the proposed drastic slashes in US budgetary appropriations below the levels recommended by Department of Army." He assured MacArthur that the department was doing everything to convince members of Congress that the slashes would have a "devastating effect upon U.S. objectives" in Japan.[139]

MacArthur, who was extremely offended by the US government's constant attempts to reduce aid to Japan, responded to the Congress: "The severe domestic financial stabilization program outlined by the Dodge mission was imposed as a prerequisite of United States economic recovery fund contribution." If this contribution were cut off, he warned, then the entire recovery program could be "materially undermined if not actually completely vitiated."[140] The House accepted MacArthur's argument and restored virtually the original request.[141]

In December 1949 MacArthur faced another, more drastic reduction in American foreign aid to Japan. This time the director of the Bureau of Budget (Frank Pace) proposed to reduce the GARIOA (Government Account for Relief in Occupied Area) budget from $350 million to $140 million and economic aid to Japan from $300 million to $97 million. On December 16 MacArthur sent a heated reaction in a personal telegram to Undersecretary of the Army Voorhees. He said that this US government action constituted

> a most devastating attack against the objectives of this Occupation and the United States program of world political, social and economic readjustment.

No more virulent onslaught against the progress of democratization of the Far East could be devised even if purposely planned as a deprecation of the significant accomplishments of the Occupation in blocking the further advance of subversive philosophies. It is inconceivable that there should be serious consideration of such an ominous withdrawal of United States financial support in this epochal period of international crisis. The proposed action amounts in substance to the complete undermining of the foundation of rehabilitation advancement in Japan and to relinquishment of United States leadership in Asia. The realistic basis for slashing 70 percent from carefully prepared budget estimates for Japan defies comprehension and can only be construed by the Oriental mind as an abandonment of policy.

MacArthur's fury boiled on for another five pages.[142]

On December 17 Voorhees reported good news to MacArthur: "With personal assistance of Secretary Gray [Gordon Gray, secretary of the army], the value of which I cannot overestimate, we have reached an agreement with Pace, director of Bureau of Budget, to restore GARIOA budget to 320-million-dollar figure as a line item in President's budget message but subject to further late review by BOB [Bureau of Budget]."[143] No wonder MacArthur viewed Washington bureaucrats as a gaggle of ignoramuses whose lack of knowledge of Japan undermined his great accomplishment. He never changed his view.

MAC ARTHUR'S LAND REFORM

From MacArthur's standpoint of making every Japanese laborer a good capitalist, his land reform was brilliant policy. On December 9, 1945, MacArthur issued the "Rural Land Reform" directive. "In order that the imperial Japanese government shall remove economic obstacles to the revival and strengthening of democratic tendencies, establish respect for the dignity of man, and destroy the economic bondage which has enslaved the Japanese farmer to centuries of feudal oppression," MacArthur ordered, "the imperial Japanese government is directed to take measures to insure that those who till the soil of Japan shall have a more equal opportunity to enjoy the fruits of their labor."[144] This "more equal opportunity" meant that absentee landlords had to practically give away their farm land to those farmers who actually cultivated it. As compensation for their generosity they could sadly watch the delirious disbelief on the faces of peasants, whom MacArthur praised as "perhaps the best agriculturists in the world."[145] In his *Reminiscences* MacArthur summarized the results of his land reform policy: "The redistribution formed a strong barrier against any introductions of communism in rural Japan. Every farmer in the country was now a capitalist in his own right."[146] In this he was quite correct.

Japan (Reluctantly) Purges Itself

"Purge" was a clean word. The US purge policy was intended to clean out any cancerous remains of the old imperial Japan. Among these remains were any and all Japanese whose past physical and intellectual activities were suspected of supporting Japan's war efforts. The definition of "supporting Japan's war efforts" remained broad and ambiguous. Complaints about its misapplication could be met with the argument that, in order to rid the body politic of cancer, some healthy tissue had to be sacrificed.

SCAP ordered the Japanese government to establish a comprehensive screening ladder composed of a national committee, prefectural committees, and city committees, to discover all potential purgees. SCAP reasoned that the Japanese people would benefit from the psychological catharsis of purging from their own ranks the very members who had led them down the road to Armageddon. But what was catharsis for some was agony for others. "Literally millions of people were required to fill out book-size questionnaires probing into minute details of their life history," Kawai Kazuo, an editor of *Nippon Times,* stated in his perceptive study *Japan's American Interlude*; "these questions, incidentally, had to be answered in English, creating a frantic run on the inadequate available supply of English translators and typists."[147]

Prime Minister Yoshida wrote several lengthy letters to MacArthur explaining the injustice that the purge could work upon those who did not deserve purging, and its negative consequences for Japan's "most important task," that of "rehabilitation of the ruined country." Yoshida placed the total responsibility and blame for militarism upon "a clique of professional soldiers, of high governmental officials, of right wing reactionary and some members of *zaibatsu.*" The ordinary Japanese people, he said, "were so completely unlike the agents of the Nazi Fascist Party and I know for fact that they had no real hand in the matter." Yoshida concluded his letter by saying to MacArthur that he wrote this for the sake of "the future of democratic and uncommunistic Japan."[148] MacArthur replied the next day by taking up none of Yoshida's recommendations: "There appears to be no justification for the exemption," he opined.[149] Yoshida later said, "Our efforts were fruitless."[150]

An extensive purge continued for two years. It has been defended in the following terms by Edwin O. Reischauer: "Lacking any clear label, such as membership in the Nazi Party had been in Germany, to aid the task of separating the sheep from the goats, the authorities were forced to couch the directive in rather vague but sweeping terms. . . . some 1,300 organizations were dissolved and almost 200,000 persons barred from public office. . . ."[151] In contrast Nishimoto Motoji, in a typical counter-argument, popular among Japanese conservatives, claimed that the ostensible purpose of the purge was

> to eliminate active exponents of militarism and ultranationalism, but the underlying purpose was to remove cultural, political and economic talent from Japanese affairs and thus render impotent the Japanese economic and social structure. Many Japanese cannot but regret that the purge policy has created a deeply rooted anti-American feeling which might hinder future cooperation between the two nations.[152]

His estimate of the number purged was about three hundred thousand in contrast with Reischauer's two hundred thousand.

There were also American policymakers in Tokyo who expressed apprehension. Robert Fearey wrote to Secretary of State Byrnes that the purgees were "most of the country's more capable leaders of conservative or rightist point of view." This, he thought, was unfortunate for two reasons. First, "their replacement by men of almost uniformly low caliber, frequently of very doubtful 'liberality' and as often as not more enthusiatic [sic] supporters, in lesser positions[,] of the war program than the men whose places they were taking, [had] and [would] continue to handicap the successful execution of plans of Japanese reorganization and reform." Second, "it would scarcely seem in American interest . . . regarding the desirability of closer American-Japanese than Soviet-Japanese ties in future, for the United States actually to assist leftist against rightist elements in the struggle for power, unless this should be an unavoidable consequence of some essential occupation purpose."[153] Fearey's view was prophetic of the forthcoming "depurge" of Japanese militarists and ultranationalists, ordered by MacArthur at the same time as the "Red Purge" (see chapter 11).

When the purge of "militarists" was completed in May 1948, the Government Section of GHQ assessed its effects optimistically.

> There was no chaos, no confusion and very little communism . . . and business had achieved a substantial degree of vitality in contrast to the conditions of paralysis prevailing when the Occupation began. A new leadership had arisen in the political, social and economic spheres, free of war guilt, higher in quality than that which was at the helm in August and September 1945, and with its eyes firmly fixed on the construction of a hopeful future.[154]

MacArthur's initial evaluation of the purge was clear from a secret and personal telegram that he sent to Undersecretary of Army William H. Draper on January 23, 1949: the purge, he said, had been completed in

Japan "without the slightest detrimental consequences upon its rehabilitation and with marked beneficial effect upon its political, spiritual and cultural renovation."[155] In his *Reminiscences,* however, he wrote that he "very much doubted the wisdom" of the purge because "it tended to lose the services of many able governmental individuals who would be difficult to replace in the organization of a new Japan."[156] Prime Minister Yoshida, one of "new leadership" created by the purge of his old colleagues, also shifted his opinion in his own memoirs, but in the opposite direction: "We have to admit," he wrote "that they [the purges] did exert a considerable influence in bringing about the democratization of all spheres of activity in Japan."[157]

The shift of power from the Emperor to MacArthur was analogous to the replacement, in 1868, of the Tokugawa Shogunate by the Meiji imperial oligarchy. A surface difference was that while the imperial government had centralized all government functions, MacArthur attempted to decentralize them. Yet MacArthur, with his autocratic idealism, hardly exemplified decentralization.

MacArthur tried hard to create an impression that, far from being a dictator, he was only assisting the Japanese people and their government along the road to democracy. It was, however, an impossible task. The Japanese people knew he was over and above even the Emperor, who served only as the expedient mechanism for facilitating American interests in Japan. To be sure, use of the existing Japanese authorities and their legitimacy by the US government and especially by MacArthur was a wise decision designed to maintain Japanese confusion at a minimum. But, because of the absence of fundamental social and political confusion, MacArthur perpetuated more than he erased the prevalent attitude of obedience among the Japanese people toward authority.

I should point out that the Japanese people's loyalty to the Emperor entailed their devotion to the person of the Emperor and to the institution of imperial supremacy. Thus, even the traumatic transition from the Tokugawa Bakufu to the Meiji imperial government hardly required major modifications in the people's attitude toward the nation's supreme authority. The people's acceptance of change in the figure who personified authority was cogent testimony of their loyalty to the source of authority. In essence, the sovereign was seen as rightly deserving the loyalty and devotion of the subjects. In the light of this tradition, MacArthur seemed to evoke two different attitudes toward him among the Japanese people.

First, MacArthur, because he was alien, would never understand "things Japanese." He therefore was unfit even to provide acceptable policies for Japan and, needless to say, to occupy the highest authority in the nation. A mere military victory in no way made him the legitimate ruler. The defeat was a defeat in material things only. As *Nippon Sangyo Keizai Shimbun* (Japan's *Wall Street Journal*) editorialized:

> A racial culture never dies nor is it possible for any amount of external force to destroy it. Racial culture means the internal power of a race. It is possible that a strong prospering race is poor in its cultural realm and, conversely, it is equally possible for a race, while living in adversity and privation, to retain a superior culture of its own. . . .[158]

An official reflection of this attitude was the imperial government's desperate maneuvers, prior to its final acceptance of the Potsdam Declaration, to salvage "the prerogatives of His Majesty as a Sovereign Ruler." The conservative Japanese government, knowing very well that the Occupation by the foreign conquerors would eventually end, abandoned neither its hope that imperial sovereignty, despite the new Constitution, would be restored, nor its actual attempts to restore it.

Second, there were those to whom MacArthur appeared to symbolize a better political order. More importantly, he occupied the highest authority. This fact, at least, rendered him deserving of the people's due respect for and obedience to his reform directives. Most of all, MacArthur could not be worse than the militarists who had "lost the war." As Max Bishop perceptively observed, the Japanese people tended to "place more importance on the reasons and responsibility for *losing* the war than on those for *starting* the war."[159] Emmerson shared a similar view: "Japanese bitterness and resentment has been turned away from the nation's former enemies and focused upon military and political leaders."[160]

I often asked (in fact nagged) my uncles and neighbors to tell me about the war. Most of their comments were directed at the militarists who were "stupid enough to wage the hopeless war and lost everything that Japan had acquired since Meiji." They had no objection to the wars, no matter how many, that the Japanese Empire had won. Further, they were indignant that Tojo had failed his last and therefore most important test of honor by failing to commit suicide and—incredibly—had been arrested by American MPs at his residence. The code of the warrior, though anachronistic, lingered on.

With the old military and political leaders gone, the majority of the Japanese people accepted the new leader and his political doctrine without undergoing any significant psychological change. An alteration in the outward form of authority did not alter their loyalty and obedience. Form was substance. This Japanese attitude, though outwardly it meant that democracy was eagerly received, did not encourage a genuine "political reorientation of Japan." The uncritical enthusiasm with which the Japanese people shifted their allegiance from the old regime to the new one only exemplified their basic ideological promiscuity, if not their adaptability to the demands of the situation. The intensity of their reaction masked its superficiality, which went mostly unrecognized by the Occupation policymakers. Atcheson, for instance, assured President Truman that American government strategy in Japan had been "politically successful beyond expectation"; it looked, he said, as if their political policy would "continue to meet with far greater success than we would have hoped," and that any future obstacles would be "primarily economic in character." There could be no doubt that MacArthur had proceeded "with caution, restraint, wisdom and farsightedness."[161] Emmerson, however, added a few cautious remarks: "SCAP censorship and the natural Japanese inclination to please those in authority [did] not encourage criticism of occupation policies"; the average Japanese accepted MacArthur's supreme power as "inevitable" and was "quite prepared to do whatever he [thought] the Americans would want him to do." This attitude, said Emmerson, encouraged "a helpless dependence on the conqueror"; in such a mood, the Japanese were "ripe for education and guidance."[162]

Ozaki Yukio, Japan's leading Liberal statesman, epitomized the Japanese people's elation and bewilderment with their sudden freedom. At the opening session of the first postwar imperial Diet in December 1945 he stated: "We are grateful for our new freedom and our new liberty, even though they are rationed by MacArthur's headquarters."[163] Without intending to be sarcastic, he unintentionally put his finger on what was to become the unacknowledged program for American democracy in Japan: the censorship of forbidden thoughts.

5
Freedom
of Thought
in Public

The Potsdam Declaration had demanded guarantees for "freedom of speech, of religion, and of thought, as well as respect for the fundamental human rights." In addition, unless "a peacefully inclined and responsible government" were to be established by "the freely expressed will of the Japanese people," the Allied Powers would not withdraw from Japan.[1] Moreover, the *US Initial Policy* had declared:

> The Japanese people shall be encouraged to develop a desire for individual liberties and respect for fundamental human rights, particularly the freedoms of religion, assembly, speech, and the press. They shall also be encouraged to form democratic and representative organizations. ...[2] The Japanese people shall be afforded opportunity and encouraged to become familiar with the history, institutions, culture, and the accomplishments of the United States and the other democracies.[3]

These official positions taken by the US government did not differ from those of MacArthur, in whose judgment Japan was "more nearly a feudal society, of the type discarded by Western nations some four centuries ago."[4]

Immediately after the surrender, the imperial Japanese government offered confirmation that American assessments of how civil liberties fared in Japan were, alas, quite correct. Prime Minister Suzuki Kantaro, prior to his resignation in mid-August 1945, told the Japanese that regardless of the Potsdam Declaration "there would be no change in the prerogatives of his Imperial Majesty the Emperor."[5] The new prime minister, Higashikuni Naruhito, concurred in his first statement to the so-called surrender cabinet that the Meiji Imperial Constitution should stay in force, defending the supremacy of imperial sovereignty. And on August 21 an English-language broadcast by the Japanese government elaborated: "Since the Constitution provided for the exercise of imperial power through the cabinet, the Privy Council, the Diet, and hence provides for the collaboration and participation of the people in government, it is in reality a liberal and progressive document."[6] On August 25 the Higashikuni cabinet offered a classic imperial interpretation of the people's freedom of speech: "With reference to the supervision of speech and press, assembly, and organization, hereafter the policy will be to conform to the spirit of the Peace Preservation Police Law." Permission to organize, the statement continued, would be "granted immediately upon request," but the people's freedom of speech and of the press would be "interpreted from a standpoint of convenience and expediency."[7]

Censorship for Democracy

These realities of Japanese liberty and freedom accelerated American determination to reform the political structure and culture of the Japanese people. The Research and Analysis Branch of the Office of Strategic Services (OSS) shrewdly reported that the Japanese leaders appeared to be assuming that "reform in political practices rather than in political structure" would satisfy the Potsdam requirements.[8] On September 10, 1945, MacArthur issued his first civil liberties directive. He especially encouraged the mass media.

1. The Japanese imperial government will issue the necessary orders to prevent dissemination of news, through newspapers, radio broadcasting or other means of publication, which fails to adhere to the truth or which disturbs public tranquility.
2. The supreme commander for the Allied Powers has decreed that there shall be absolute minimum of restrictions upon freedom of speech. Freedom of discussion of matters affecting the future of Japan is encouraged by the Allied Powers, unless such discussion is harmful to the efforts of Japan to emerge from defeat as a new nation entitled to take a place among the peace-loving nations of the world.

3. Subjects which cannot be discussed include Allied troop movements which have not been officially released, false or destructive criticism of the Allied Powers, and rumors.
4. For the time being, radio broadcasts will be primarily of a news, musical and entertainment nature. News, commentation and informational broadcasts will be limited to those originating at Radio Tokyo studios.
5. The supreme commander will suspend any publication or radio station which publishes information that fails to adhere to the truth or disturbs public tranquility.[9]

This directive only confused the Japanese mass media. The Japanese press, which had been transformed into an extremely efficient propaganda organ under systematic government control, tended to interpret freedom of speech under MacArthur's regime as "anything goes." This tendency led to a vocal defense of the Japanese Empire by some. For instance, Domei, the nation's largest semigovernment news agency, declared that "the end of the war had come about because of the Emperor's 'benevolence,' rather than through Allied military superiority, and the occupying Americans were merely 'guests' of the Japanese Empire." Taking full benefit of its freedom of speech, Domei further informed the nation that: "(1) Japan might have won the war but for the atomic bomb, a weapon too terrible to face and one which only barbarians would use. (2) Japan could negotiate with the Allies as an equal. (3) Americans and Allied troops were committing atrocities. (4) Russian and other Allies were opposed to American interests and vice versa. (5) Crime was increasing since the arrival of the occupation forces."[10]

GHQ, however, found this confusion most convenient for its program of combining democracy with censorship. On September 15, 1945, Colonel Donald Hoover, chief of censorship of the Army Counter-Intelligence Service, called a meeting of top information officials of the Japanese government together with the leading editors and publishers of newspapers and magazines. The supreme commander, he told them, was not satisfied with the manner in which the Japanese government, press, and radio had observed the directive of September 10. To be sure, freedom of the press was "very dear" to the supreme commander—it was, indeed, one of the freedoms for which the Allies had fought. The Japanese, however, had shown that they were unworthy of the supreme commander's trust; they had not met the responsibility of a free press "cooperatively." Therefore, Hoover informed the Japanese, the supreme commander had ordered "a more severe censorship." Among the truths that the supreme commander wished held inviolate were "that the Allied Powers do not regard Japan as an equal in any way" and that Japan "has not yet demonstrated a right to a place among civilized nations." His scathing lecture continued: "One hundred percent censorship of the press and radio will continue to be enforced. No more false statements, no more misleading statements are to be permitted; no destructive criticism of the Allied Powers." Domei, he warned, had been suspended yesterday, for disseminating "news disturbing to the public tranquility"; the agency had also been prohibited from sending news overseas. To ensure Domei's compliance, the US Army stationed representatives in Domei to exercise "100 percent censorship."[11]

GHQ thus took upon itself the awesome task of deciding what was the news, what was the truth, what was public tranquility, and how the Japanese should handle all these elusive matters in print. The task was not only awesome but delicate, since GHQ, while practicing censorship, wanted to instruct the Japanese press and people in freedom of speech. Only two weeks prior to this American masquerade, the Japanese people had been tersely reminded by their own imperial government that their freedom of speech would be "interpreted from a standpoint of convenience and expediency."

When MacArthur wrote in his September 10 directive, "Freedom of discussion of matters affecting the future of Japan is encouraged," he expected the Japanese people to break out in iconoclastic criticism of prewar Japan, especially of imperial supremacy. He had badly misjudged the target at which criticism would be directed. On September 15 *Asahi Shimbun,* the nation's largest and most influential daily newspaper, criticized not the Emperor but "the use of the atomic bomb by the United States." *Asahi* called it "a breach of international law."[12] On September 17 *Asahi* argued that if the American official report was correct in asserting that Japanese atrocities in the Philippines cost the Japanese military occupation the support of the Filipinos, then the same logic would apply to the Allied forces now staying in Japan.[13] The next day MacArthur suspended *Asahi* for two days.[14] He also suspended the English-language *Nippon Times,* which began publication on September 15, for one day for failing to submit the prepublication galley proof of an undesirable editorial.[15]

Either because the Japanese press did not understand the September 10 directive and Hoover's warning or because MacArthur characteristically grew impatient with the newspapers' mistakes, he issued the so-called Press Code, on September 21. The ten-clause code deserves full quotation here, for it describes the journalistic ethics that MacArthur found most suitable for the Japanese:

1. News must adhere strictly to the truth.
2. Nothing shall be printed which might, directly or by inference, disturb the public tranquility.

3. There shall be no false or destructive criticism of the Allied Powers.
4. There shall be no destructive criticism of the Allied forces of occupation and nothing which might invite mistrust or resentment of those troops.
5. There shall be no mention or discussion of Allied troop movements unless such movements have been officially released.
6. News stories must be factually written and completely devoid of editorial opinion.
7. News stories shall not be colored to conform with any propaganda line.
8. Minor details of a news story must not be overemphasized to stress or develop any propaganda line.
9. No news story shall be distorted by the omission of pertinent facts or details.
10. In the makeup of the newspaper no news story shall be given undue prominence for the purpose of establishing or developing any propaganda line.[16]

A press release accompanying the Press Code informed the Japanese people that the code was "designed to educate the press of the Japanese in the responsibilities and meaning of a free press"; it would cover "news, editorials, and advertisements of all newspapers and . . . in addition, all publications printed in Japan."[17]

The Press Code tightened the meaning of freedom of speech. The imperial government had trampled on that freedom until August 1945. Now, for the sake of democracy, MacArthur threatened to follow suit. He wanted the Japanese mass media to become once more an effective propaganda organ—this time under American supervision. Censorship became a feature of Amerian-style democracy, not merely a legacy of past imperial oligarchy. It was a difficult beginning for the Japanese journalists just learning about freedom of speech.

On September 22 MacArthur issued the "Radio Code," which regulated the manner and matter of what went over the radio waves. It closely resembled the Press Code.[18] GHQ thoroughly controlled the Nippon Hoso Kyokai (Japan Broadcasting Corporation or NHK), a well-organized semigovernmental radio system. MacArthur understood the NHK's immense capacity for disseminating messages instantaneously throughout the nation. He ordered the Japanese government to submit, by December 1, 1945, a plan for the manufacture and distribution of home radio receivers of all types, plus repair parts and tubes.[19] MacArthur's tight control of the air waves was further demonstrated by his swift refusal of the Japanese government's request for resumption of overseas broadcast.[20]

On September 24 MacArthur issued yet another directive, *Disassociation of Press from Government.* Its ostensible purpose was "to further encourage liberal tendencies in Japan and to establish free access to the news sources of the world . . . and to remove [the Japanese Government] from direct or indirect control of newspapers and news agencies." Far from abolishing censorship, however, the directive foresaw no end to it. "The present system of distribution of news within the home islands will be permitted under strict censorship until such time as private enterprise creates acceptable substitutes for the present monopoly."[21] On the same day, MacArthur issued *Clarification of Censorship,* so that the Japanese mass media and government would understand what they should not say.[22]

The American policy of censoring the Japanese mass media did not result from a spontaneous decision by MacArthur. The *US Initial Policy* implicitly, and the *Basic Directive* explicitly, required him to exercise censorship for democracy. The *Basic Directive* stated: "You will establish such minimum control and censorship of civilian communications including the mails, wireless, radio, telephone, telegraph and cables, films and press as may be necessary in the interests of military security and the accomplishment of the purposes set forth in this directive." But, human frailty did not allow "minimum control and censorship." Censorship was (and will be again) exercised with a view to the censor's advantage— its historic function.

Free Discussion of the Emperor

On September 27, 1945, the Emperor paid an unprecedented visit to MacArthur. The Ministry of Imperial Household informed the nation that His Majesty's visit was "unofficial and informal." The Japanese people had never heard of such a curious imperial event; foreigners should visit the Emperor and not vice versa. This official announcement actually dramatized who now was the new head of state. The drama was further heightened by MacArthur's calculated absence from the reception committee. Two of MacArthur's staff welcomed the Emperor in formal attire, although MacArthur later stated, "I had, from the start of the Occupation, directed that there should be no derogation in his treatment. Every honor due a sovereign was to be his."[23]

The next day *Asahi Shimbun, Mainichi Shimbun,* and *Yomiuri Shimbun,* the nation's three largest daily newspapers, reported this meeting. On September 29 these newspapers published the official picture of both men standing side by side—"General MacArthur in shirt sleeves," as Emmerson described it, "towering over a pathetic little figure in a morning coat."[24] The Bureau of Information of the Japanese government attempted to suspend the three newspapers for their obvious desecration.

MacArthur immediately intervened and issued another directive, *Further Steps Toward Freedom of Press and Speech,* retroactively dated September 27—the day of his first meeting with the Emperor. With this new directive MacArthur became more explicit: "No punitive action shall be taken by the Japanese government against any newspaper or its publisher or employees for whatever policy or opinion it may express unless ordered by the supreme commander on the basis of publication of false news or reports disturbing public tranquility." MacArthur then proceeded to abolish twelve prewar laws and ordinances that subjugated the press to the government. Additionally, he ordered the Japanese government to submit a report to GHQ "on the first and sixteenth day of each month describing in detail the progressive steps taken by the Japanese government to comply with this order and the orders of 10 September and 24 September."[25]

The same day, September 29, Prime Minister Higashikuni welcomed new bureaucrats into the national government with the message: "You public servants should be aware of yourselves, first of all, as the Emperor's servants. Thus, abandon what is private and strive to serve him."[26] MacArthur did not find this kind of speech by the prime minister encouraging. On October 4, 1945, the *Stars and Stripes* published an interview with Minister of Home Affairs Yamazaki Iwao. Yamazaki said that anyone who advocated changes in the present political structure or abolition of the Emperor system was a Communist and thus should be arrested under the Peace Preservation Law.[27] He was removed by MacArthur, who was advocating just such structural changes.

The collective silence of the Higashikuni cabinet on civil and political liberties—except for its frequent public confirmation of the legitimacy of imperial supremacy—provided an excellent opportunity for MacArthur to issue, on October 4, the most comprehensive civil liberty directive that the Japanese people had ever even dreamed about. John Emmerson accurately characterized it as "the first political bombshell of the occupation."[28] MacArthur's satisfaction was Higashikuni's humiliation. The American authorities, Atcheson reported to Secretary Byrnes, had wanted the Japanese government to implement the Potsdam reforms on its own initiative. The Higashikuni cabinet, despite forty-five days in office, had achieved nothing in this respect. It had therefore "suffered the humiliation of having to act under orders—a humiliation apparently so heavy that it felt it necessary to resign."[29]

In the lengthy October 4 directive MacArthur ordered the imperial Japanese government to abrogate and immediately suspend "restrictions on freedom of thought, or religion, of assembly and of speech" and to encourage "the unrestricted discussion of the Emperor, the Imperial

Institution and the imperial Japanese government." The Peace Preservation Law, which provided the death penalty for those who had indulged in unrestricted discussion of the Emperor, was named first among sixteen undesirable laws and ordinances.

The immediate abolition was ordered of all governmental and municipal organs of thought control. The Ministry of Home Affairs, which had been the most skillful and tenacious of inquisitors, was itself condemned as dangerous, and thus virtually stripped of its authority. (This ministry ceased to exist on December 31, 1947.) The amazing directive continued: "Release immediately all persons now detained, imprisoned, under 'protection or surveillance,' or whose freedom is restricted in any other manner who have been placed in that state of detention." "Release immediately" meant within one week, by October 10, 1945. The seriousness of MacArthur's intentions was made clear in his last paragraph: "All officials and subordinates of the Japanese government affected by the terms of this directive will be held personally responsible and strictly accountable for compliance with and adherence to the spirit and letter of this directive."[30]

This directive of October 4, 1945, which some GHQ officers and Japanese liberals were fond of calling the "Magna Carta" of Japan, overwhelmed both extremes of the ideological spectrum. The leftist radicals, such as the long-oppressed Japanese Communists, welcomed it as a proclamation of their brave new world and even called the occupation forces "the Liberation Army." In fact, the Japanese Communists who had just been released from prison shouted a chorus of *banzai* in front of MacArthur's headquarters.[31] This *banzai* (literally, "Ten thousand years!") invoked eternal life for MacArthur. (According to Shiga Yoshio, a Communist leader released from prison, it was John K. Emmerson who arranged for a release of Communist prisoners.[32] Emmerson told me at the Hoover Institution in 1978 that Shiga's "recollection" was more like fiction.[33]) The Japanese conservatives and reactionaries, on the other hand, feared that the directive was a precursor of the final disintegration of the Emperor's prerogatives and a move towards anarchy.

On October 6, two days after the directive, Takagi Yasaka, professor of American constitutional law at Tokyo Imperial University, told Atcheson that Japanese leaders were "deeply anxious over the future of the Imperial Institution, especially since the issuance of the decree permitting free discussion of the Emperor and the Imperial Household." Professor Takagi, son of Baron Kanda Naibu and a confidant of Prince Konoye Fumimaro and Marquis Kido Koichi, emphasized to Atcheson that "a spontaneous development of Japanese democracy would be far more desirable than quick reforms imposed by the Americans."[34] But Mac-

Arthur and his staff, particularly in the early period of the Occupation, distrusted any Japanese opinions that implied even the slightest defense of the ancient regime. Accordingly, when the Japanese government, in the person of the conservative Shidehara cabinet, proposed to increase the domestic police force, MacArthur quickly denied the request.[35] On top of this, he wanted to eliminate Japan's notorious military police, the Kempei-tai. On November 4, 1945, MacArthur ordered the Japanese government to submit the name, rank, title, and present location of the chief of the Kempei-tai and his principal assistants including all headquarters officers. The Japanese government complied. MacArthur issued SCAPIN (SCAP Instruction) 606, *Abolition of Kempei-tai*, on January 16, 1946.

Emmerson summarized GHQ's mood well when he reported to Secretary Byrnes in February 1946 that "the specific provision authorizing free discussion of the Emperor aroused the most comment. Many among Japan's ruling classes were apprehensive that this would undermine the state, encourage lawless elements, and result in political chaos. None of these dire results has occurred, unless one defines 'undermine the state' to mean 'cast doubt on the Emperor system.' "[36]

Meanwhile, the Ministry of Imperial Household tried its best to publicize the new Emperor. "New photographs of His Majesty the Emperor will be granted to replace those in the schools, local government offices and diplomatic and consular offices abroad," it said. "The new imperial picture will show His Imperial Majesty," it promised, "in the imperial uniform recently instituted."[37] His new uniform happened to be civilian clothing instead of the traditional military uniform.

The Communists Speak Out

MacArthur himself had expected numerous dramatic changes in the Japanese mass media as a result of his October 4 directive. But the Japanese press did not know exactly what to do with this plethora of freedom, the proper use of which it had forgotten because of prolonged abstinence.

On October 24 Colonel Ken R. Dyke, chief of CI & E, summoned leading newspaper editors and the broadcasting executives of NHK and told them to fulfill their "obligations to establish a free and independent press or make way for papers that will." He accused the Japanese press of systematically ignoring MacArthur's October 4 directive on freedom of speech and thought with the exception of a meager "few perfunctory comments." He reprimanded them, because they had done "practically nothing to explain the historic significance of the document." Dyke reminded them that, contrary to their impression, the MacArthur directive was not aimed at suppressing "communism." A recent release of Japanese political prisoners, mostly Communists, he said, clearly spoke for itself. Colonel Dyke also charged that a lack of "full and frank discussion" on war criminals was regrettably apparent and his office had received complaints that newspapers consistently suppressed articles and letters calling for drastic changes in the imperial institution. Yet he assured them that GHQ had "no desire to lay down a blueprint for the press."[38] One month earlier, however, GHQ had begun enforcing the Press Code. "We have daily conferences with reporters from the Japanese press," said Don Brown, CI & E's PR man. In addition, newspaper and magazine editors were called in once a week for a meeting with the CI & E staff "to raise the standards of Japanese journalism."[39]

With all this pressure being brought upon them, the mass media started showing the effects of the October 4 directive. On October 21 all the policymaking officers of the *Asahi Shimbun,* including its bureau chiefs, resigned. On November 26 the management of the *Mainichi Shimbun* resigned at the demand of its staff. Shoriki Matsutaro of the *Yomiuri Shimbun* refused to step down. His refusal triggered a prolonged and bitter labor dispute, in which GHQ was deeply involved. When MacArthur named Shoriki in his list of war criminals, Shoriki and his associates resigned.[40] Atcheson wrote to Byrnes that in two months *Yomiuri* was transformed from "ultramilitaristic and aggressively pro-Axis" to "the most liberal of the great Japanese dailies."[41] He also reported to Byrnes that among the new magazines *Shinsei* seemed to be "the most promising." He strongly approved of such *Shinsei* articles as "The Responsibility of Marquis Kido Koichi" and "Public Men Who Danced to the Tune of the Militarists."[42]

The directive of October 4—soon known as the "Bill of Rights directive"—ordered the Japanese government to release immediately all political prisoners. "Political prisoners" since the Meiji Imperial Restoration of 1868 had meant people who opposed the expansionist policies of the Japanese Empire. There were not many. For the most part, they were Communists and Socialists. By fighting for their own ideological causes within the monolithic climate of prewar Japan they came to appear brave freedom fighters. One Japanese Communist leader, Tokuda Kyuichi, when interviewed by Domei just before release from prison, said that in 1929 about ten thousand Communists had been rounded up throughout Japan, two hundred had died as a result of police brutality, another two hundred had died from undernourishment and mistreatment in prison, and an estimated two thousand political prisoners were still detained as of October 1945.[43]

It was logical for MacArthur to assume that the immediate release of these political prisoners would dramatize to the Japanese people the nature and intention of the democratic Allied Occupation. The Military Intelligence Division of the Department of War, too, believed that the Japanese Communist Party provided "a healthy and active stimulant to Japanese political thought."[44] Having received MacArthur's blessing, the elated Communists turned their organizing skills to an aggressive and frequently reckless campaign. In less than a month the Americans were registering surprise. Atcheson wrote to Truman:

> Unfortunately, the most aggressive and vocal is the Communist group. The vigor of some of the Communist leaders is evidenced in the circumstance that, after eighteen years of imprisonment including solitary confinement which would have broken the bodies and spirits of ordinary men, upon their release they began making speeches before they were outside the prison gates. It is not unlikely that the Communist Party will become a problem and while it disclaims any connection with the Soviets, the presence here of Soviet occupation forces would undoubtedly give them indirect encouragement and would facilitate any liaison that may exist with Russian Communists.[45]

Bishop agreed with Atcheson that the Communists were both the most energetic and the noisiest group; within a few months of leaving prison, they had "increased their membership more than one hundredfold" and were attracting, according to his reports, as many as "5,000 enthusiastic members, supporters and spectators at one meeting." "The swing of the pendulum," he remarked, "is swift."[46] *Akahata* (Red Flag), the Communist Party's official daily newspaper, resumed publication on October 27, 1945, for the first time since its suspension in 1934.[47] Two months later "it had a circulation of 90,000 and by February 1946 this had risen to 250,000."[48] The actual membership of the Communist Party, however, was only 6,800.[49]

On December 19, 1945, MacArthur issued *Restoration of Electoral Rights to Released Political Prisoners.*[50] Mesmerized by GHQ's gesture, the Japanese Communist Party launched a concerted attack against the spiritual core of prewar Japan, the Emperor. To those Communists and their cohorts who, despite brutal government oppression and physical torture, had not recanted their political faith, the defeat of once-invincible Japanese militarism confirmed the historical inevitability of communist domination. The fact that they did not succumb, while the majority of their former associates did, encouraged them to feel morally superior to other political groups, which had supported Japan's war efforts. Thus, in the new climate of "equality for all," their denunciation of the Emperor appeared justifiable, if not tasteful. The Japanese Communists tactfully exploited the politics of martyrdom; since they had suffered most, they had to be right.

The Japanese people, still in shock and preoccupied with the scramble for food, clothing, and shelter, saw for the first time in their recent memory vigorous political rallies in the streets by the Communists. The Communists were supposed to be underground, in prison, or dead.

The Communist leaders kept up their intense verbal denunciation of the Emperor. In Emmerson's judgment, however, their attack "hurt the sensitivities of the Japanese and strengthened a defensive attitude."[51] The Military Intelligence Division of the Department of War concurred.[52] Most public opinion polls clearly indicated that even among the intellectuals, who did not enjoy freedom of speech in prewar Japan, only 10 percent were opposed to retention of the Emperor. MacArthur conceded that "well over 95 percent of the Japanese people are clearly disposed to retain the imperial institution."[53] The Emperor simply remained too sacred for the Japanese people to abuse him in public. They found enough other scapegoats around them: militarists who lost the war. The Japanese Communist leaders miscalculated the Japanese people's feelings in this respect. Their miscalculation was MacArthur's gain. The Communists became legal under MacArthur's discretion but they managed to remain unpopular.

MAC ARTHUR
AND THE COMMUNIST PRESS

Nosaka Sanzo returned from Yenan, China, in January 1946. An active Communist before 1920, he had fled to the Soviet Union to escape the anti-Communist raids in 1931. He was elected to the Executive Committee of the Communist International at Moscow. In 1935 he secretly returned to Japan and worked underground until 1943. He then went to Yenan to undermine the morale of the Japanese Army in China.[54] His return to Japan in January 1946 was a blessing to the Japanese Communist Party. As a brilliant political gimmick he advocated separate treatment of the Emperor, the Imperial Household, and the Emperor system. Public antagonism seemed to subside as people felt more secure that the Communists might not be after the Emperor's neck. Emmerson believed Nosaka's tactic would gain "increasing popular approval."[55] And the Military Intelligence Division of the War Department was impressed by Nosaka: "His tact, suavity, and moderation are in marked contrast to the attitudes of other Communist leaders, who are repugnant to most Japanese."[56]

To Japanese conservatives, however, the Communists' vocal attack on the Emperor was not only treason but *lèse majesté*. In fact, the editor of the Communist Party newspaper *Akahata* was so charged. But on October 9, 1946, the Tokyo Procurator's Office decided to drop the charge. "The decision," MacArthur said the same day, "is a noteworthy application of the fundamental concept, embodied in the new constitution . . . that all men are equal before the law, that no individual in Japan— not even the Emperor—shall be clothed in legal protection denied to the common man." And he went on to give the Japanese another of his lectures on democracy: "The free criticism of officials and institutions is essential to the continued life and growth of popular government. Democracy is vital and dynamic but cannot survive unless all citizens are free thus to speak their minds."[57]

With this sort of public encouragement by the supreme commander, the Japanese Communist Party understandably had a hard time believing that the MacArthur regime in Tokyo and the US government in Washington hated communism. However, MacArthur privately expressed his intense dislike of the Communists only a few days after he released them from prison. In mid-October 1945 he told Edwin A. Locke, Jr., Truman's emissary on the Chinese economy, that he was worried about "underground Communist agitation" in Japan. He also said such things as, "Many of the so-called liberal elements of Japan are Communistic," and, "Japanese Communism is dominated from Moscow."[58] As the activities of the Japanese Communist Party intensified, the traditional anxiety of Japanese conservatives about "dangerous thoughts" came face to face with American public endorsement of the people's political liberties. Hatoyama Ichiro, leader of the Liberal Party, the largest and most powerful of all the political parties, who was considered next in line for the premiership, expressed the fear prevalent among his associates. On November 25, 1945, Hatoyama, accompanied by his aides, visited the Government Section of GHQ to explain his political ideas for the future of Japan. He said that basic individual freedoms must be guaranteed. The Government Section asked him, "in the form of interrogation," to explain why he then publicly denied the same freedoms to the Communists. He replied that "the Japanese Communists were 'not like the American or British Communists' but were an un-Japanese party, acting as the agents of a foreign power and receiving funds from that power." The Government Section asked him to elaborate. "These fellows," he responded, "have been in jail for years and just got out. They are immediately running around actively campaigning. They have bought a printing press for 500,000 yen. Where did they get the money? It must have come from the Soviet Union." He went on to warn his interrogators that "the Japanese were excitable, unstable and erratic by nature." "If they go in one direction," he said, "they are apt to go too far. There is now danger that they will swing too suddenly and too radically to the Left. It is also part of Japanese nature that those in power tend to oppress and deny the rights of those not in power. It is therefore essential that there be a safeguard against [the] 'dictatorship of the majority.' "[59] Hatoyama was more than familiar with the "part of Japanese nature" that made "those in power tend to oppress and deny the rights of those not in power": as education minister in 1932–33 he had summarily dismissed liberal professors from Kyoto Imperial University. By "dictatorship of the majority" he meant democracy. After this meeting the Americans concluded that Hatoyama was "not impressive as a person of great conviction, forcefulness or leadership" and that he was "more of a 'politician' than a 'statesman.' " He was also "inclined to be verbose and indefinite."[60] MacArthur purged him a day before he was to become a prime minister. Yoshida Shigeru took over the premiership.

The Japanese conservatives' fear of communism culminated in a letter of December 27, 1946, from Prime Minister Yoshida to MacArthur, whom he addressed as "My dear General." The letter requested the inclusion of lèse majesté in the Japanese criminal code, then being revised. Because the Emperor's position was "truly a high and lofty" one and it was "undeniable that the Emperor is ethically the center of national veneration," Yoshida reasoned that "an act of violence against the person of the Emperor . . . should be considered as of a character subversive of the State, and deserving of severe moral censure and a severer punishment than any act of violence against the person of an ordinary individual." Yoshida, an impeccable guardian of the ancient regime, considered such specially severe punishment "natural from the standpoint of Japanese national ethics." He argued that the same applied to the members of the Imperial Family because they occupied "an important place in respect to succession to the throne." He then cited an example from abroad: "The fact all the countries under monarchial [sic] system such as England have special provisions relating to acts of violence against the person of the sovereign demonstrates beyond dispute the truth of the above statement."[61] This request of Yoshida's came after MacArthur had praised the decision of the Tokyo Procurator Office to drop the charge of lèse majesté against five Japanese, including an editor of Akahata.

MacArthur, taking an uncharacteristically long time, replied to Yoshida on February 25, 1947. The Emperor, he said, was "entitled to no more and no less legal protection that that accorded to all other citizens of Japan who, in the aggregate, constitute the State itself." "To hold otherwise," he informed Yoshida, "would violate the fundamental concept that all men are equal before the law." It followed that there was "even less basis for rationalizing a special position for other members of the Imperial Family." Regarding the physical protection of the Emperor, MacArthur clearly outsmarted Yoshida by arguing that the Japanese people's respect and affection for the Emperor formed "a sufficient bulwark" that did not need to be "bolstered by special provisions in the criminal law implying suzerainty." Concerning Yoshida's view that severer punishment for offenders was "natural from the standpoint of Japanese national ethics," MacArthur tersely reminded him of the Emperor's self-repudiation, in the rescript of January 1, 1946, of "a peculiar Japanese national ethic distinctly differing from universally recognized ethical principles." Furthermore, there was "no statutory provision in British law" comparable to Yoshida's reference, nor was there "the slightest analogy to the situation now existing in Japan." He concluded his letter by emphasizing that the American experience demonstrated "the adequacy of general legislation to punish crimes against even the head of the State." "All articles of the penal code relating to crimes against the Imperial House," MacArthur accordingly commanded Yoshida, "should be eliminated by appropriate ordinance."[62]

Yoshida waited awhile to present another request, as he knew the aggressive propaganda of the Japanese Communist Party would eventually aggravate MacArthur enough to make him reconsider. On August 6, 1949, when MacArthur was seriously contemplating banning the Japanese Communists from the world of legitimate politics, Yoshida asked his permission "to bring the police into closer liaison with government" so that it could take "swift, vigorous and effective action."[63] On August 8, MacArthur rejected his plea by informing him that, "with SCAP's moral support," the Japanese police were "capable of handling any anticipated internal disturbance without intervention of occupation forces."[64] Nevertheless, MacArthur firmly believed that communism was just another version of oppressive totalitarianism. The persistently aggressive Communist activities posed a trying political test of democratization. MacArthur was caught in an ironic dilemma: the Japanese Communist Party, which had officially hailed the American Army as "the Liberation Army," was in fact the most vocal and articulate iconoclast. MacArthur naturally welcomed such healthy indications of emerging democracy. Yet the US government in Washington and the MacArthur government in Tokyo came to be intensely embarrassed by their apparent support for the growth of Japanese communism.

This dilemma persisted until MacArthur, with the eager assistance of the Japanese conservatives, solved it by instituting an official "Red Purge" (described in chapter 11). Another irony was that, due to vigorous American efforts, the Japanese people by the time of the Red Purge understood, at least ideally, what civil and political libertarians ought not to do. The Red Purge reminded them of the prewar imperial persecution of "dangerous thoughts." Communism again became an ideology of political martyrdom. Particularly among the intellectuals and university students, the pendulum of sympathy swung to the Communists' defense.

How the Censorship Was
Administered

GHQ did not, however, single out Communist or leftist organizations as targets of censorship. On October 4, 1945, GHQ had summoned the editors of the nation's five largest daily newspapers, *Asahi Shimbun, Mainichi Shimbun, Yomiuri Shimbun, Tokyo Shimbun,* and *Nippon Keizai Shimbun,* and announced its mandatory prepublication censorship effective from the next day. Since prepublication censorship had so far been operated under the US Eighth Army's Counter-Intelligence Section, this announcement was intended only to inform the Japanese that prepublication censorship would now be handled by the Civil Censorship Division of the Civil Intelligence Section, GHQ.

The procedure under GHQ was as follows. The editors of newspapers or magazines first submitted galley proofs, in duplicate, of all items intended for publication, to the Civil Censorship Division. American officers translated them, and an inspection officer marked parts to be deleted in red pen. One proof was returned to the paper and the other copy was retained in the censorship office for comparison with the published version. The editors had to rewrite or paraphrase so that the entire article, after censorship, appeared natural to Japanese readers. Under no condition could the editors resort to painting in black ink the parts to be be deleted, leaving them blank, or using such conspicuous signs as XXXXX.[65] After appropriate rewriting, final page proofs were required for submission. Foreign news dispatches in English or French could be submitted for the censor's scrutiny in the original, but the publisher was held responsible for translating them accurately into Japanese.[66] GHQ's determined censorship efforts covered even marginal publications, which were required to bring in two copies of an issue immediately after printing, and to specify the names of the editors, the date of publication, and the publishers' telephone numbers and addresses.

GHQ's determination in controlling the mass media was reminiscent of two laws passed by the Meiji imperial government in 1875: the Law of Libel and Slander and the Newspaper Law. The latter had demanded that

> with the exception of the ordinary paragraphs of news, the writers of articles in newspapers or magazines (in which contributors are included) must sign their names and residences in every case where the discussion turns upon domestic or foreign politics, finance, the feelings (of the people), the aspect of the times, learning or religion, or matters affecting the rights of officials and people.[67]

The types of news articles that usually did not pass GHQ censorship were summarized by *Shakai Taimuzu* (Socialist Times) as follows: (1) news dealing with the misdeeds of American soldiers; (2) news that gave an unfavorable impression of the private life of American soldiers; (3) articles that threatened to give an impression of Japanese hostility toward or even dissatisfaction with the behavior of the occupation forces; (4) articles which reported harm or loss suffered by the Japanese people through the fault of the occupation forces; (5) articles that revealed the seriousness of the domestic food shortage; (6) articles that reported on policies of the Allied nations before they were announced officially; (7) articles that revealed disharmony among the Allied Powers (although any articles denouncing the Soviet Union were systematically suppressed at the beginning of the Occupation, this American practice began to disappear by late 1946); (8) articles that criticized the Allied policies; (9) articles that indicated GHQ's involvement in any domestic Japanese activities; (10) articles that gave an impression of defending the war criminals; (11) articles that suggested the new constitutional draft reflected Allied preferences. The *Asahi Shimbun* added to the list: (12) articles that reported American and Soviet involvement in the Chinese civil war; (13) articles that might influence the Tokyo Tribunal's decision on war guilt; (14) articles that reported arrests of war criminals before they were officially announced; (15) articles that attempted to justify any past wars of imperial Japan.[68] By January 1946 GHQ had rejected 670 newspaper articles.[69]

These prohibitions reflected not only the Press Code in action but MacArthur's extreme sensitivity to anything that might spoil the appearance of democratic tranquility in Japan. The phrase "American imperialism" was of course an absolute taboo, as the two words constituted an obvious contradiction. The atomic bomb was another favorite object of censorship. Matsuura asserts that GHQ only permitted as news the official American claim that the two bombs shortened the war and that they were for the sake of peace.[70] Robert Jay Lifton, however, interprets American atomic censorship differently in his excellent work *Death in Life: Survivors of Hiroshima:* "This censorship originated largely from fear that writings about the weapon could become a stimulus for some form of Japanese retaliation. But one cannot escape the impression that American embarrassment, guilt, and even horror at the effects of the bomb also played a part. . . ."[71] American sensitivity was acute enough, for instance, for a military observer to interfere in the middle of a radio speech by one candidate in the Hiroshima mayoral elections of April 1947, because he did not comment favorably about the bomb.[72]

FATE OF THE BOMB DOCUMENTARY

The Japanese attempt to make a film documentary about Hiroshima and Nagasaki became a legendary episode in the history of GHQ censorship. More than 30 cameramen together with nuclear physicists, medical doctors, biologists, and architects worked under the most trying conditions from August through December 1945. In early December, American MPs arrested a cameraman in Nagasaki and airlifted him back to Tokyo. GHQ immediately prohibited the work. The Japanese protested that the Americans should understand the Japanese desire to leave a record of the people who for the first time in the history of the world had been subjected to atomic attack: "The record will speak for the future of man." Considering the American sensitivity to any remaining signs of Japanese resistance, this defense took courage. GHQ replied that it was a task for the Strategic Bombing Mission of the US Army. Seeing the obvious documentary value, however, GHQ allowed the Japanese crew to complete filming. In February 1946 the 11,000-foot *Effects of the Atomic Bomb* (edited from 50,000 feet of film) was submitted to GHQ, which swiftly shipped it to Washington. Supposedly, not a scrap of the original 50,000 feet was left in Japanese hands. But the Japanese crew managed to conceal one print (more than half of the finished edition) in defiance of SCAP's order. This secret was kept well until the end of the Occupation.[73] *Effects of the Atomic Bomb* was returned in 1967 to Japan at Japanese public demand. The Ministry of Education, however, did not fully release the film to the public, reasoning that much of it would violate the privacy of those people who had been exposed to the bombs and that it contained too many cruel scenes.

The virtual press blockout on the atomic bomb persisted until September 1949 when the Soviet Union exploded its own. The end of American atomic monopoly seemed to ease GHQ's tight censorship of anything nuclear. American censorship in Japan relaxed, but American military defense precautions were sharpened. Indeed, the Central Intelligence Agency (CIA), successor to the Office of Strategic Services (OSS), had anticipated the Soviet nuclear bombs. On April 20, 1949, the director of the CIA urged the executive secretary of the National Security Council to better prepare the United States against possible nuclear attack from the Soviet Union.[74]

SOME BANNED BOOKS AND MOVIES

A few actual samples of "bad books" will indicate the scope of American censorship on behalf of Japanese democracy. Erskine Caldwell's *Tobacco Road* was not permitted to be translated. It described the dark side of American society, which either did not exist, or which MacArthur believed unnecessary for the Japanese to know. Translation of theoretical works on communism was discouraged. *Das Kapital* suffered a temporary suspension. GHQ demanded that the Japanese publisher first obtain permission from a surviving relative of Karl Marx. This unusual demand failed to deter the Japanese publisher but threatened to embarrass GHQ itself, which soon retreated to demanding that official permission be obtained from the Soviet representative in Japan (he was eager to grant it).[75]

MacArthur's desire to control the flow of foreign news into Japan was obvious from the beginning, when he issued the so-called Circular No. 12 entitled *Admission of Foreign Magazines, Books, Motion Pictures, News and Photograph Services, et cetera, and Their Dissemination in Japan.* These materials could be brought into Japan, provided they were "not detrimental to the purpose of the Occupation"—with GHQ deciding what was "detrimental."[76] The statistics on the foreign books passed for publication in Japan from September 1945 to December 1950 were yet another demonstration of American supremacy. By country of origin, they were: USA, 1,583; France, 657; Britain, 452; Germany, 466; USSR, 282; Italy, 64; China, 52; and miscellaneous, 282.[77]

Japanese Police Headquarters, wishing to participate in the campaign for democracy (and decency) through censorship, in January 1950 banned Norman Mailer's *The Naked and the Dead*, a best seller in Japan at the time. GHQ overruled the ban, saying that the action was "anti-democratic." On June 26, 1950, however, D. H. Lawrence's *Lady Chatterley's Lover* was successfully banned by the Japanese police authorities. The book also happened to be banned in the United States.[78] Although the choice of what to ban seems whimsical in some cases, it nonetheless reflected the seriousness of GHQ's attempts to reorient the psyche of the Japanese people. The Japanese, for their part, became increasingly disillusioned by the obvious inconsistency and pettiness of American censorship. GHQ's censorship, for example, was extended to specify desirable subjects in the design of Japanese postage stamps and currency.[79]

In the field of movie production, MacArthur issued a directive on October 16, 1945, entitled *Elimination of Japanese Government Control of the Motion Picture Industry.* Samurai movies, the Japanese all-time favorite, were included among the 236 films condemned as "nationalistic, militaristic, and feudalistic."[80]

THE SWITCH TO POSTPUBLICATION CENSORSHIP

Prepublication censorship ceased on July 5, 1948. This new policy came from Washington. On June 8, 1948, MacArthur received a top-secret cable from the Department of the Army informing him that the State Department's policy paper, *Recommendations With Respect to US Policy Towards Japan,* had been submitted to the National Security Council. In it the State Department urged that "censorship of literary materials and precensorship of the Japanese press should cease. This should not operate however to prevent SCAP from exercising a broad postcensorship supervision and from engaging in counterintelligence spot checking of the mails."[81] After that date SCAP switched to postpublication censorship of most publications except those of "leftist" intellectual magazines. From the end of 1949 until the end of the Occupation in April 1952, SCAP gradually relaxed postpublication censorship.[82]

A switch from prepublication to postpublication censorship would seem to imply a quantitative increase in freedom of thought. But the editors and reporters discovered to their surprise that prepublication censorship was much easier to cope with. Under prepublication censorship they could at least risk, without fear of suspension, writing what they thought GHQ would pass. If their news articles came back scored with GHQ's red ink, they simply did not print them. Under postpublication censorship, however, they could never know exactly what would pass. Yet any violation of the Press Code, as determined by GHQ's postpublication censorship, meant either an immediate suspension of publication or confiscation of the undesirable issues.[83] Such suspension naturally inflicted a severe financial loss on the publishers, and so was an effective means of thought control. Another efficient method was allocation, under the joint supervision of GHQ and the Japanese government, of scarce printing paper.[84] Postpublication censorship worked wonders for GHQ in silencing dissident Japanese opinions. The editors and publishers took great precautions and printed only the articles that they judged sufficiently safe.

One reporter recalled the most conspicuous difference between the censorship by GHQ and that by the wartime Japanese government: the latter, he said, "posed an omnipresent threat to my life, but GHQ's censorship never made me feel my life was at stake."[85]

MAC ARTHUR
AND THE FOREIGN CORRESPONDENTS

MacArthur's extraordinary sensitivity to the press was not limited to Japanese journalists; foreign correspondents, too, might be noted with disfavor and even deported. An episode involving Mark Gayn, the *Chicago Sun* foreign correspondent who wrote *Japan Diary*, will illustrate MacArthur's intolerance of bad publicity.

The *Washington Post* had published an article, supplied by the *Chicago Sun*, on Japanese land reform. The article was datelined Tokyo, June 4, 1946, and read in part: "Well-placed groups within headquarters have come to feel that wide transfer of land ... to landless 'smacks of communism.'"[86] On June 8 Secretary of State Byrnes asked George Atcheson, US political adviser, for clarification on behalf of the Far Eastern Commission.[87] "The news item," Atcheson replied to Byrnes the same day, "is entirely incorrect. There is no truth whatsoever in the quotations." He continued: "The author of these articles, Mark Gayn, has shown himself unreliable, malicious and subversive in his writing in regard to the Occupation and ... in addition, he is under suspicion here of lending himself to communist-controlled doctrines from Moscow."[88]

Mark Gayn was called into GHQ twice and asked to testify under oath before an investigation. He complained to the *Chicago Sun*, which immediately asked the War Department about GHQ's action against him. On October 19, 1946, the War Department asked MacArthur for an explanation.[89] On October 22 MacArthur told the War Department that Gayn had been interrogated to determine the source of "the apparent breach of security regulations." Gayn, he went on to say, was

> a constant menace to security regulations. He has a past record of suspect along this line. Our public relations officer suggested previously to the War Department his removal from the theater. His activities are unquestionably prejudicial to the Occupation. The matter does not involve in any way the question of the freedom of the press but has become a problem of subversive influence that defies propriety and administrative authority.[90]

On November 28 the War Department relayed some happy news to MacArthur: "Executive editor, *Chicago Sun*, reports ... 'Mark Gayn has been dropped from staff purely as economy measure.'" The *Chicago Sun*, however, said merely that Gayn would remain on the payroll until he either returned to the States or could make "a permanent connection in the Orient." The paper hoped that, in the meantime, his accreditation could be maintained.[91] But MacArthur did not want to see Gayn anywhere in the Orient. Twice before, he immediately told the War Department, "this theater" had recommended that Mark Gayn's accreditation be canceled. There were reasons: "He is believed to be the center of an intrigue which indulges in a type of communistic activity that daily becomes more serious and threatening." It followed that Gayn was "entirely unacceptable for any further assignment in this theater," and should be sent home without delay.[92] Soon after this, Gayn was off the *Chicago Sun*'s payroll and lost his accreditation. "In view Mark Gayn no longer a staff correspondent for *Chicago Sun* and as private citizen has no legal status in your theater," the War Department recommended to MacArthur on December 8, he should be "furnished orders to proceed stateside or to any other area he requests at earliest convenient date."[93]

Gayn, meanwhile, tried desperately to get *Colliers* to request that he be accredited as its correspondent. "No such request received here," the War Department cabled MacArthur.[94] If received, it would certainly be denied by the department. The same day, December 8, MacArthur informed the War Department that clearance had been given Mark Gayn and wife for Shanghai, effective December 15.[95] Gayn presently resides in Canada and continues to write on the US occupation of Japan.[96]

The case of Gayn may appear to have been an extreme measure on the part of MacArthur. It was not. MacArthur actually had a blacklist of newspapers. This became apparent in another exchange between the War Department and him.

On November 1, 1946, the War Department suggested MacArthur welcome a tour of the Pacific (Japan, Korea, and the Philippines) about to be made by some one dozen American newsmen, as a similar tour earlier had produced excellent public relations in the United States.[97] The next day MacArthur, who did not like any inquisitive journalists around him or even in Japan, replied that in view of the department's insistence, he would withdraw his objections. At the same time he requested that the list of invited people "should not include actual writers but should be limited to publishers and editors and should not include those connected with papers of known hostility to the Occupation." Among such papers, he continued, were "the *Christian Science Monitor*, [New York] *Herald-Tribune, Chicago Sun, San Francisco Chronicle, PM, Daily Worker,* and others of this stamp, whose articles and editorials have not only been slanted but have approached downright quackery and dishonesty."[98]

MacArthur's secret telegram leaked to the press. Drew Pearson, the syndicated columnist, reported it in full on December 3, 1946.[99] The next day Paul C. Smith, editor of the *San Francisco Chronicle,* sent a telegram to the War Department: "If the Pearson publication is accurate I feel strongly that I am due an apology from General MacArthur who may be supreme commander of Japan but nonetheless is just another American citizen charged with a heavy national responsibility."[100] On December 4 a personal telegram from the War Department was sent to MacArthur; it expressed surprise at his banning of the *Christian Science Monitor,* a nonpartisan paper, and the New York *Herald-Tribune,* a Republican one. The *San Francisco Chronicle,* it added, was not only Republican, but was edited by Paul C. Smith, whose war record in the Marine Corps and Navy was beyond reproach.[101] The War Department, which as it now informed him, was "always loath to make suggestions to MacArthur," had to make a definite suggestion.[102] On December 9, 1946, it told him that "the secretary of war had expressed the wish that the papers listed in [the] Pearson story be included among those invited."[103] "I will of course conform to the wishes of the secretary of war," MacArthur replied the same day.[104] The newsmen and executives of the blacklisted newspapers visited Japan in January 1947. As the War Department saw it, the visit was a great success.

Encouraged, the War Department asked MacArthur again on May 30, 1947, if he would accept another press tour of the Pacific. This time, however, the War Department put its request in the name of the secretary of war: "Your comments and views appreciated on proposal secretary of war invite group outstanding American news editors and executives visit Japan and Korea as his personal guests."[105] On May 31, MacArthur, who was in fact sick and tired of the newspaper men, answered that his staff was too busy to be "subject to the most intensive interrogation and to an examination which in effect transforms [the staff] into defensive witnesses against many preconceived fallacies." Mindful of past experience, he added an emphatic request that his message be protected from leakage.[106] Nevertheless, the War Department went on trying to persuade MacArthur that the press tour would be good for the cause of the Occupation and would greatly help the American public understand what was going on in Japan. For these reasons, the department urged MacArthur to accept the group.[107] MacArthur grudgingly accepted but requested the tour be postponed until July 1947.[108]

MacArthur's vigilant gatekeeping at the entrance of Japan was not his only method for isolating Japan from the rest of the world. He also tried to censor the flow of news in and out of Japan. For instance, on January 2, 1948, the *Daily Worker,* one of MacArthur's blacklist newspapers, carried a story headed "Tokyo Brass Censors News on Wallace and Eisenhower." They were presidential candidates. The *Daily Worker* also stated that the *Stars and Stripes* was under the censorship of Brigadier General Courtney Whitney, MacArthur's leading protégé. The War Department asked for MacArthur's comment.[109] "There is no repeat no slightest truth to the dispatch," he replied on January 8. "The Stars and Stripes is completely free from any dictation whatsoever and its news policies are left entirely to the discretion of its editors."[110] On June 24 Keyes Beach of the Chicago *Daily News* complained that a large part of GHQ, SCAP, did not want the American people to know what was going on in Japan. "Time and again in recent weeks officials of SCAP have flatly refused to answer legitimate inquiries," he said.[111]

What is going on? the War Department asked on July 9. The next day MacArthur replied: "The Beach articles have no repeat no foundation in fact. They seem to have resulted from correspondent's unreasonable irritation at being unable promptly to secure factual data."[112]

Correspondents kept on complaining, nonetheless. Secretary of the Army Kenneth C. Royall, who did not find MacArthur's omnipotence in Japan amusing, was concerned with the potentially serious consequences of bad publicity about the Department of the Army itself. On July 23, 1948, Royall sent a personal telegram to MacArthur: "Because we regard the issues involved so fundamental to the rights of the American people, we shall if necessary carry this to the Congress if that appears to be the only way we can get the information."[113] The best information MacArthur could give Royall was that the correspondents' allegations were completely untrue. "Every effort has been made by this headquarters," he assured Royall, "to give fullest publicity to the incidents of the Occupation and every assistance has been furnished to the press in gathering all information which is unclassified."[114] Of course, MacArthur was being less than candid. But Secretary Royall in Washington could not do much except threaten.

Sometimes foreign correspondents really did make dubious reports to the American public. On May 1, 1950, Japanese workers celebrated May Day throughout Japan. At the outer garden of the Imperial Palace in Tokyo there were some four to six hundred thousand people gathered.[115] Walter Winchell of ABC reported: "The Communist riots in Tokyo have sent fourteen American soldiers to the hospital with serious injuries. United States troops, ladies and gentlemen, are fighting back with only clubs and tear gas for weapons. They must not use guns. All leave for soldiers there have [*sic*] been canceled."[116] The Department of the Army asked MacArthur if that was true. On May 2 MacArthur replied indignantly that Winchell's statement was "complete fabrication." There had, he said, been absolutely no riots or disturbances whatsoever in Tokyo, where the May Day celebration had been "perhaps the quietest and most orderly since the surrender." Winchell's "willful prevarication," he thundered, "tends to destroy international relationships and aggravate the tension which plagues the world today."[117] The *Asahi Shimbun* extensively reported on the May Day rally but mentioned nothing about "communist riots," because none had occurred.[118]

Ironically, next day, May 3, MacArthur said that the Japanese Communist Party might be a constitutionally questionable entity. On May 17 Danton Walker of the *Philadelphia Inquirer* reported: "All leaves for United States troops stationed in Tokyo have been cancelled due to daily Communist riots there. Mobs sent fourteen US soldiers to the hospital last month. American soldiers are forbidden to use guns. Must use tear gas and clubs to quell rioters."[119] On May 18 MacArthur told the Department of the Army:

> The complete similarity of this attack to the one made by Walter Winchell ... tends to indicate a conspiratorial effort to damage the American position in Japan and in the Far East. It follows the usual norm of infiltrative Red influence in respectable publications whose underlying purpose is to undermine the confidence of the American public in its own national agencies. I believe that more positive steps should be taken by the Department of the Army to meet this situation.[120]

However, the first public fight between American GIs and Japanese Communists did not actually occur until May 30. Eight Communists were arrested and the Occupation military court severely punished them within a week.

American democracy, no matter how one interprets it, offered far more intellectual freedom and political liberties to the Japanese people than they had ever experienced before 1945. Precisely because of this achievement, it was unfortunate that MacArthur found it imperative to exercise such strict censorship of public expression, since the Japanese people had been led by American proclamation to believe that they were free to think and act. Such freedom was indeed what MacArthur promised in his *Statement to the Japanese Government Concerning Required Reform,* dated as early as October 11, 1945. He said: "The people must be free from all forms of government secret inquisition into their daily lives which holds their minds in virtual slavery and from all forms of control which seek to suppress freedom of thought, freedom of speech, or freedom of religion. Regimentation of the masses under the guise or claim of efficiency, under whatever name of government it may be, must cease. . . ."[121]

Following the model of the Canons of Journalism of the American Society of Newspaper Editors, the newly established Japan Newspaper Publishers' and Editors' Association adopted in 1946 their own "Canons of Journalism," when GHQ's prepublication censorship was at its height.[122] The gap between the real and the ideal, though narrow, was deep.

6
The New Constitution

With characteristic self-righteousness MacArthur dismissed the possibility of a spontaneous development of Japanese democracy. "We could not simply encourage the growth of democracy," he later wrote. "We had to make sure that it grew."[1]

"The problem was," as the Government Section saw it, "whether to permit and encourage the slow growth of local democratic institutions and political maturity and at some later time to advise the development of an organic law that would merge and reflect the new institutions, or to promote the early and drastic overhaul of the basic law and then build on that new foundation."[2] MacArthur and the Government Section decided on what they saw as "the wisest course," that of "immediate constitutional revision." The course of "slow natural growth," they believed, would take too long, and there could be no assurance that "a reactionary cabinet, privy council or Emperor would not, overnight, wipe out all the gains that might be achieved." Immediate constitutional revision "would give the Japanese people a goal at which to shoot, as well as a solid foundation on which to build."[3] Actually, the possibility of a "slow natural growth" for Japanese democracy was allowed to survive after the surrender for a couple of weeks at most.

"I instructed the Higashi-Kuni cabinet," MacArthur said, "to draft a plan for revision of the Constitution of Japan with the view of its democratization [*sic*] to permit development of the type of government and society required by the Potsdam Declaration."⁴ Prince Konoe (Konoye), minister without portfolio in the Higashikuni cabinet, met MacArthur and Atcheson on October 4, 1945, to receive their advice on governmental reform. Konoe, dealing with MacArthur through an interpreter, believed the supreme commander had said, "The Constitution should be revised. Revision must abundantly include liberalism." On October 8 Konoe secretly conferred with Atcheson, who emphasized "those points which SCAP considered to be basic."⁵ They were: (1) elimination of extra-constitutionality; (2) obliteration of the military influence in the government; and (3) constitutional guarantees for a bill of rights.⁶

Authors of the New Constitution

On October 9 the Higashikuni cabinet, due to the political bombshell of the October 4 "Bill of Rights," collapsed in humiliation.

THE RISE AND FALL OF PRINCE KONOE

The same day the Shidehara cabinet was formed. Prince Konoe became the lord keeper of the privy seal, a very powerful position. Although the function of the lord keeper did not include actually revising or amending the Constitution, Konoe proceeded with preliminary work. On October 11, 1945, MacArthur explicitly told Prime Minister Shidehara to revise the Meiji Constitution of 1889.⁷ On the same day Konoe received a formal order from the Emperor to work on a constitutional draft. In this way two separate formal committees on constitutional revision came into existence concurrently. The two committees fought for prestige and jurisdiction. Two days later the Shidehara cabinet, following MacArthur's order, appointed Dr. Matsumoto Joji to head the Constitution Problem Investigation Committee (Kempo Mondai Chosa Iinkai).

Konoe had served as prime minister when Japan invaded China in 1937, and in 1938 had advocated a "New Order" in Asia, thus engendering the Pacific war. His appointment as the principal draftsman for the new constitution accordingly brought swift disapproval in the United States as well as in Japan. "With regard to popular Japanese criticism of the undertaking of Prince KONOYE," Atcheson wrote to MacArthur and the Chief of Staff on October 23, 1945, "at present there would seem to be no reason to urge a change in the method of procedure."⁸ MacArthur and Atcheson could ignore criticism by the Japanese press but not by the American press. On November 2, 1945, the State Department telegraphed to Atcheson the New York *Herald-Tribune's* editorial of October 31. It read, in part:

> Of all the absurd blunders made by America in the Far East one of the worst is the selection of Prince Fumimaro Konoye to draft Japan's new Constitution. It is the equivalent of choosing a gunman to devise rules for a reform school. . . . His designation, with official American sanction, as the man to write democratic constitution of Japan is the ultimate in absurdity.[9]

Atcheson, writing to President Truman on November 5, attempted to extricate himself from this "ultimate in absurdity." "There is a curious story behind the activities of Prince Konoye," he began. "I was present on October 4 when he called on General MacArthur on his own initiative. The general mentioned that the 'administrative machinery' of the government should be reformed and Konoye's interpreter (who verified this to me later) could not think of the correct Japanese translation and passed the statement off with the only thing that came to his mind—'the constitution should be revised.'" The interpreter's translation was not inaccurate, however. "[When] Konoye came to me three days later to ask for 'advice and suggestions' in regard to constitutional revision," Atcheson continued to explain to Truman, "I told him and his companions, in a general way, what I thought was wrong with the constitution." Subsequently, he told Truman, Konoye "got himself designated by the Emperor to work on the matter." Atcheson then tacitly approved Konoe's move by providing a retroactive justification:

> This may cause some problems in the future but so long as we are using the Japanese Government to accomplish what we wish—or are permitting it to make its own efforts toward that end—it would not seem the part of wisdom to interfere at this juncture with an individual so engaged who is in the confidence of the Emperor and carries weight among the reactionaries because he himself is a feudal lord, especially as he was not arrested in the beginning. He is, of course, trying to save his own skin and the ethical question of using him for a very important purpose and then turning on him later is one which I myself would prefer not to solve.[10]

The New York *Herald-Tribune* editorial continued to disturb MacArthur as well as Atcheson. On November 7, 1945, Atcheson wrote a personal and confidential letter to Dean Acheson, undersecretary of state, who had appointed him as the US political adviser.[11] "We are very much worried over the question of the revision of the Constitution," Atcheson said. "Konoye has sent Professor Takagi to us to say that several draft articles have been prepared and to ask for consultation and advice, but we have been ordered by General MacArthur not to proceed with the discussions." (Professor Takagi taught American constitutional law at Tokyo Imperial University and was a confidant of Konoe.)

MacArthur's order made Atcheson apprehensive. We see here a beginning of conflict between MacArthur and the State Department—a conflict that MacArthur always won. "It is obvious to us now," Atcheson informed Undersecretary Acheson, "that General MacArthur, or his chief of staff and other members of the Bataan Club who act as his Privy Council or *genro*—wish if possible to keep the State Department out of this matter." (The Bataan Club was a half-admiring, half-derisive nickname for MacArthur and his devoted entourage who escaped from the Philippines to Australia after losing a bitter fight against the better-prepared Japanese forces. "I shall return" was MacArthur's famous promise to the Filipinos, which he kept.) Atcheson had some alarming news about Konoe's progress.

> Meanwhile, we learned from Japanese sources privately that Konoye's committee expects to have a complete draft prepared before the end of this month to submit to the government, and it seems to me that if we are to get our ideas abroad before a draft is published with all the trimmings of imperial sanction, etc., some action toward achieving our purpose should be taken at once. For, it goes without saying, any attempt to cause correction of a draft once prepared with imperial sanction will meet with difficulties and will cause unfortunate political repercussions which can not help but militate against our long-term objectives.[12]

On November 22, 1945, Konoe did in fact complete his draft and present it to the Emperor.[13] In his draft the first thirteen articles of the 1889 Imperial Constitution remained as before. This amounted to no change; supremacy of imperial sovereignty was perpetuated. Some drastic measure to discredit Konoe and his constitutional draft had to be taken, as Atcheson said, "at once."

On December 6 MacArthur named Konoe as one of 286 war criminal suspects and ordered him to report at Sugamo Prison by the noon of December 16.[14] Early in the morning of December 16 Konoe committed suicide.[15] Although the Japanese people felt shocked and sad, an *Asahi Shimbun* editorial was critical of Konoe's postwar activities, characterizing them as "dubious." It also branded him as "a weak personality."[16] The truth about who sanctioned Konoe as the draftsman of Japan's new constitution became quite clear from the available evidence, which revealed that MacArthur and Atcheson had initially encouraged him. Yoshida, then foreign minister, nevertheless remarked, "Nothing certain is known."[17] MacArthur's discussion of the new constitution in his *Reminiscences* mentions nothing about Konoe.

THE MATSUMOTO DRAFT

The Constitution Problem Investigation Committee of the Japanese Government worked solidly for three months, from mid-October to mid-January, frequently consulting with the cabinet ministers. All political parties submitted their constitutional draft proposals— impressive evidence of the degree to which Japanese politicians had grasped the essentials of representative democracy.

The Progressive Party proposal was denounced by the Government Section (GS) of GHQ as the "most conservative of all the proposals for revision." "Sovereignty remained with the Emperor," GS complained. Also lacking were "any clear guarantees either of individual liberty or the democratic process."[18] The Liberal Party proposed that although "the Emperor [be] divorced from all legal and political responsibility," he should still retain the infamous extraconstitutionality. "The Liberal platform," GS concluded, "differed little from that of the Progressives."[19] These two groups, the nation's most conservative, were not at all interested in changing the doctrine of the Emperor's supremacy.

The Social Democratic Party proposal fared better with American critics.

> An extensive bill of rights, including some economic guarantees, was provided for. Judicial independence was proposed. The Diet would amend the constitution by majority vote with a two-thirds quorum. Here we have emerging the shape and structure of a government of the people, with recognition of the place of the individual. The Diet becomes the supreme organ of state power. Civil liberties are to be guaranteed absolutely. The Emperor is removed from the exercise of political power.[20]

The Communist Party was more forthright: "Sovereignty would be reposed in the people, to be administered by the Diet. The Emperor system would be abolished. An extensive bill of rights was recommended, with particular attention to economic guarantees."[21] This actually looked best to GHQ. But GHQ could not say so publicly. Secretly, however, Atcheson admitted it to MacArthur: "Excluding the Communists," he said, "only the Social Democrats, who are still a minority party, are willing to consider the Emperor and sovereignty in something approximately our terms."[22]

Private citizen groups made still other proposals. "In general," commented the Government Section, "private groups favored reposing sovereignty in the people to be exercised by the 'cabinet' or the 'government.' The function of the Emperor would be to perform rituals and ceremonies."[23] GS singled out three "omissions" in the private proposals: (1) no provisions for guarantees against unreasonable searches and seizures and no protections for the individual in connection with accusations of and prosecution of crimes; (2) no suggestion that there be woman suffrage or equality of socioeconomic and political status for women; and (3) no recommendation for local autonomy.[24] GS observed sadly: "Only one private group proposed that the suffrage should be extended to all adult men and women, while in all of the proposals for extension of civil, social and economic freedoms, the removal of the constitutional and legal disabilities under which women suffered was not once mentioned."[25] Ideologically, these critical omissions revealed the Japanese people's blind spot.

In his *Reminiscences* MacArthur claimed that he "took no part in the deliberation of the Constitution Problem Investigating Committee, nor did any member of my staff."[26] His recollection bordered on a fiction if not deliberate deception. In mid-1946 MacArthur explained his deep involvement in the committee's work to Secretary of State Byrnes. "When the Shidehara cabinet assumed office [on October 9, 1945]," he said, "it acquired full responsibility in this matter." He ordered Prime Minister Shidehara, who was reluctant to touch the 1889 Imperial Constitution, to come up with a draft for a new one. "During that early period and subsequently until the government's draft constitution was formulated [on March 4, 1946]," he told Byrnes, "I held frequent personal conferences with state ministers with the view of their understanding of an acquiescence in the enlightened principles which of necessity would guide the revision to bring it within Allied general policy as interpreted in more specific form by the American government."[27] As for the involvement, also later disclaimed, of his staff, MacArthur informed Byrnes: "During that early period, the Political Adviser [Atcheson], upon instruction from the State Department, additionally held conferences with Japanese political leaders."[28] Because both MacArthur and Atcheson knew very well that the Matsumoto Committee consulted closely with the Shidehara cabinet ministers, they also "held frequent personal conferences with state ministers."

These conferences with the Shidehara cabinet members produced accurate knowledge of Japanese government thinking. "The Government plan," Atcheson informed MacArthur as early as January 7, 1946, "is to leave intact in principle the first four articles of the present [Meiji] Constitution." He said that these four articles were "the foundation stones and the pillars of the 'divine' Japanese State with which we have been at war." "Under the present government," Atcheson lamented, "it does not seem likely that there will be a purely voluntary revision which will provide a substantial and enduring framework of a democratic government."[29] Atcheson was already suggesting direct GHQ involvement in revising the Japanese Constitution.

On February 1, 1946, the Matsumoto Draft was submitted to Mac-

Arthur. It represented three months of hard work by the cream of Japanese legal authority. MacArthur immediately denounced it as "nothing more than a rewording of the old Meiji Constitution" and commented that "after three months of work, the Constitution was the same as always—worse, perhaps."[30] "The proposed revision," GS acidly remarked, "lags far behind even the most conservative of the unofficial drafts."[31] MacArthur proceeded to brand Matsumoto as "an extreme reactionary ... who ruled the deliberations with an iron hand."[32] GS, too, characterized him as "a thorough ongoing conservative who believed most fervently in the maintenance of the Emperor system and the doctrine of National Polity."[33]

What in the Matsumoto Draft was so infuriating to MacArthur? An example, which thoroughly destroyed American hope in Japanese ability or willingness to write a suitable draft constitution, shows that the imperial government was still adamant on one point. The Matsumoto Draft declared, in words strikingly similar to those in the 1889 Meiji Imperial Constitution, that "the Emperor is supreme and inviolable."[34] The Meiji Constitution had said that "the Emperor is sacred and inviolable." This semantic legerdemain even after the Emperor himself had denied his divinity on January 1, 1946, and after MacArthur himself had held frequent personal conferences with the Japanese cabinet members, was enough to trigger MacArthur's outrage. He ordered his own staff to prepare a thorough critique of the Matsumoto Draft as a prelude to drafting GHQ's version of a constitution.

A few excerpts from MacArthur's statement of rejection will explain the instant death of the Matsumoto Draft. The Japanese government, MacArthur said, hoped that "the liberalization of the language of the Meiji Constitution would be acceptable to SCAP, leaving the real Constitution in its loose and flexible form, open to such application and interpretation as the ruling groups might see fit to apply." He further accused the government of leaving imperial sovereignty untouched and of referring to the Japanese army and navy under the guise of "armed forces." In MacArthur's eyes

> the Matsumoto draft, if anything, reduces the rights and increases the duties of the people. No absolute guarantees whatsoever are provided. ... no provision making the Constitution the supreme law of the land. This omission is, of course, fatal, since it leaves the real Japanese state exactly as it was, and excludes from the operation of law the various extraconstitutional agencies which have been so characteristic a feature of the Japanese political structure.

He concluded sarcastically: "Their skill in fashioning facades involving no structural remodeling was notable."[35] According to Yoshida, however:

"Dr. Matsumoto explained that, since a great deal of alteration was bound to be demanded from all sides once the draft was made public, it was prudent to introduce as little change in the original draft as possible."[36] GS viewed Matsumoto's explanation differently: "Dr. Matsumoto claimed that his committee had made no real alteration in the terms of the Meiji Constitution quite deliberately," because a drastic revision "would only shock the moderates too severely, and cause them to assume an antagonistic attitude toward democracy." GS branded his explanation as "characteristic of the argument used time and again . . . by the ultraconservative against establishment of any form of popular representative government."[37]

There was some justice in GS's verdict. The real reason or "the aim of the government at that time," as Yoshida correctly remembered it, "continued to be to introduce no more change than thought absolutely necessary." In fact, Matsumoto himself on December 8, 1945, briefed the Budget Committee of the House of Representatives regarding "the Four Principles of Revision," one of which was that "no change was to be made to the principle of sovereignty residing in the Emperor." Yoshida said that "it was the desire of the government to satisfy the clause in the Potsdam Declaration dealing with the democratization of Japan without altering the fundamental principles of national government laid down in the Meiji Constitution."[38] This desire had in fact been identified by OSS's Research and Analysis Branch as early as September 1945, when it reported that the dominant Japanese leaders appeared to be assuming "that reform in political practices rather than in political structure will satisfy the requirements laid down at Potsdam. . . ."[39]

Yoshida, in fact, found nothing wrong with the 1889 Meiji Constitution; it had originated, he argued, in "the promises made to the Japanese people by the Emperor Meiji at the beginning of his reign." There was, accordingly, "little need to dwell on the fact that democracy, if we were to use the word, had always formed part of the traditions of our country, and was not—as some mistakenly imagined—something that was about to be introduced with the revision of the Constitution."[40] What had gone wrong with the Constitution, according to Yoshida, was that its spirit had become distorted over time, and this had led to national calamity. If "the promises made to the Japanese people by the Emperor Meiji"—promises made to a people whose thoughts and actions were effectively controlled by the imperial oligarchy—were what Yoshida called "democracy," then what the revised Constitution was about to offer to the people was, by these standards, no less than anarchy. It is noteworthy that Yoshida never even contemplated a structural revision of the Meiji Constitution that might have eliminated the distortions that he admitted it had undergone with the passage of time.

THE MAC ARTHUR DRAFT:
A "JAPANESE DOCUMENT"

MacArthur's disappointment with the Matsumoto Draft led him to conclude that "the most effective method of instructing the Japanese government on the nature and application of those principles he considered basic would be to prepare a draft constitution embodying those principles."[41]

Robert Ward in his well-researched article, "The Origins of the Present Japanese Constitution," has commented on this seemingly abrupt move by MacArthur as follows: "While General MacArthur is quoted as telling the Far Eastern Advisory Commission on January 30 that he had ceased to take any action in this field as a result of the Moscow Agreement, he apparently changed his mind within the space of the ensuing four days and initiated a number of moves which were to have sweeping consequences."[42] But in fact MacArthur did not change his mind at all. From the very beginning he had objected to the State Department's effort to make the occupation of Japan an Allied Occupation. So, when he said that the Moscow Agreement of December 26, 1945 (which created the Far Eastern Commission) took away his jurisdiction in the matter of the Constitution, he was making a public statement about an agreement that he privately (but not secretly) considered a disgusting diplomatic sellout of legitimate American prerogatives. His actions were consistent with his basic attitude: Who, after all, had defeated imperial Japan? When he also said he had ceased to take any part in the constitutional revision because of the Moscow Agreement, he was only being mendacious. MacArthur and his staff, as we have seen, frequently communicated their expectations for a new constitution to the Japanese leaders, who in turn frequently conferred with the Matsumoto Committee members. MacArthur even so informed Secretary of State Byrnes.

It is true, as Ward points out, that the constitutional revision did not become "an overriding priority" until February. This meant that MacArthur had expected the Matsumoto Committee to reflect his wishes. After reading the Matsumoto Draft, he totally lost his initial minimum faith in the Japanese government. Feeling betrayed, he abandoned his pretense of keeping hands off and instructed his protégé Brigadier General Whitney, chief of Government Section, to draft a model constitution that would incorporate the following MacArthur ideals:

I.

The Emperor is at the head of the State.

His succession is dynastic.

His duties and powers will be exercised in accordance with the Constitution and responsible to the basic will of the people as provided therein.

II.

War as a sovereign right of the nation is abolished. Japan renounces it as an instrumentality for settling its disputes and even for preserving its own security. It relies upon the higher ideals which are now stirring the world for its defense and its protection.

No Japanese army, navy, or air force will ever be authorized and no rights of belligerency will ever be conferred upon any Japanese force.

III.

The feudal system of Japan will cease.

No rights of peerage except those of the Imperial Family will extend beyond the limits of those now existent.

No patent of nobility will from this time forth embody within itself any national or civic power of government.

Pattern budget after British system.[43]

Just six days later, on February 10, 1946, the Government Section completed its draft and submitted it to MacArthur. With his approval Whitney and his associates on February 13 presented the so-called Mac-Arthur Draft to Matsumoto and to Yoshida, then foreign minister. "General Whitney informed me," Yoshida recollected of the meeting, "that GHQ was not satisfied with the Japanese draft . . . and that he had brought with him a model draft . . . and that he wanted us to turn out a version based upon this draft as soon as possible . . . and went on to say that it would meet with the approval of both the United States Government and the Far Eastern Commission . . . and that if this was not done, GHQ could not answer for whatever might happen to the Emperor."[44] "Failing action by the Cabinet," Whitney told Yoshida, "General MacArthur was prepared to lay the issue before the people himself."[45]

What the Americans told the Japanese was expedient political blackmail. The Americans knew very well that the Japanese conservatives would do almost anything to save the Emperor. Also, Whitney's statement to Yoshida that the MacArthur Draft would meet with the approval of the Far Eastern Commission (FEC) constituted a deliberate deception.[46] MacArthur had never consulted (and never intended to consult) the FEC—which operationally did not even exist—about the revision of the Constitution. He later disclosed, "I am certain that it [the new Constitution] would never have been accomplished had the Occupation been dependent on the deliberations of the Far Eastern Commission—with the Soviet power of veto!"[47] MacArthur's stance of nonconsultation consequently caused serious embarrassment to the State Department and perpetuated the bad relations between him and the FEC.

Yoshida and Matsumoto were, as Whitney observed, "visibly surprised and disturbed and said they would have to consider the matter and discuss it with the cabinet." The cabinet too received it "with a distinct sense of shock."[48] The profound dismay of the Japanese government was plain to behold when Yoshida complained that "the GHQ draft was of a revolutionary nature," and that the government "was not prepared to frame a new Constitution based upon such a model." The government accordingly "started negotiations with GHQ to see if there was not some means of coming to a compromise." When Matsumoto visited Whitney for this purpose, however, "he was told that the version formed a coherent body of laws and that . . . alteration in part of the text would affect the whole."[49]

The Japanese Government finally realized that MacArthur had no interest in compromising his version of what the United States wanted—or what Japan in future should want. A split ensued within the Japanese government: one supporting the new Constitution, while "Foreign Minister Yoshida spearheaded the standpatters supporting Matsumoto."[50] On February 21 Prime Minister Shidehara went out of desperation to seek MacArthur's advice. The next day Shidehara briefed his cabinet members about the meeting. MacArthur had told him that

> the welfare of Japan was foremost in his mind and that particularly since he had met the Emperor, it had been one of his primary concerns to safeguard the position of the throne; but that feeling within the Far Eastern Commission toward Japan was still of unwonted severity . . . especially [on the part of] the Soviet Union and Australia, being apprehensive that Japan might become powerful enough in time to make reprisals against the Allies.

It was in order to eliminate the possibility of more drastic reforms being proposed by the Far Eastern Commission, Shidehara explained, that the MacArthur Draft especially emphasized "the definition of the Emperor as the symbol of the State and the renunciation-of-war clause."[51] Of this episode the Government Section reported, with some distortion, that "the supreme commander declined to intervene" in the impasse within the Shidehara cabinet.[52] What is more intriguing is MacArthur's ruthless manipulation of the still nonexistent Far Eastern Commission, the commission he so despised.

The Shidehara cabinet remained divided. It managed, however, to come up with the First Japanese Government Draft on March 2, 1946, and deliver it to MacArthur on March 4. (This First Government Draft was not the Matsumoto Draft, which was never again brought up.) After intense discussions between the American and Japanese representatives, there emerged, on March 5, the Second Japanese Government Draft (the so-called Cabinet Draft); it closely resembled the original MacArthur Draft.[53] The same day MacArthur approved it. Robert Ward reports that "Premier Shidehara and other ministers burst into tears upon reading it."[54] Shidehara, however, told an AP reporter that the Japanese side proposed a new definition of the Emperor as the symbol of the State.[55]

The Shidehara cabinet still agonized, not over whether to accept or reject the Cabinet Draft, but over whether to accept it completely or conditionally. As a last resort Shidehara, accompanied by Yoshida, visited the Emperor late on the night of March 5.[56] "Hirohito did not hesitate," the Government Section reported. "He advised Shidehara that he fully supported the most thoroughgoing version."[57] Next morning, the Shidehara cabinet formally approved the draft. Its full text was published nationwide on March 7.[58] The *Asahi* welcomed it as an "epoch-making Peace Constitution" but also editorialized: "In all probability the Shidehara cabinet alone was not capable of drafting it single-handedly. It must have been made possible by a strong advice of SCAP, especially the American side."[59]

A remarkable piece of coordination between the Emperor and MacArthur was worked out in order to sanctify the draft constitution. Along with the text of the draft the Emperor's rescript was conspicuously displayed:

> I am fully aware of our nation's strong consciousness of justice, its aspirations to live a peaceful life and promote cultural enlightenment and its firm resolve to renounce war and to foster friendship with all countries of the world. It is, therefore, my desire that the Constitution of our empire be revised drastically upon the basis of the general will of the people and the principle of respect for the fundamental human rights.[60]

Beside the imperial rescript (of which this quote represents about one-quarter) MacArthur's unqualified approval prominently appeared: "It is with a sense of deep satisfaction that I am today able to announce a decision of the Emperor and the government of Japan to submit to the Japanese people a new and enlightened constitution which has my full approval."[61]

On June 26, 1946, the Government Draft was submitted to the Japanese Diet for deliberation. It was accompanied by a statement from MacArthur:

> The Government Draft now before the Diet is a Japanese document and it is for the people of Japan, acting through their duly elected representatives, to determine its form and content—whether it be adopted, modified or rejected. It therefore behooves members of the Diet to act upon this vital matter with the solemnity, with the wisdom and with the patriotism which they owe their country and the people they represent—scrupulously avoiding the influence of political creed, undue ambition, or self intrigue.[62]

The New Constitution: Whose Responsibility?

The House of Representatives debated extensively until August 24, when it approved the draft constitution by a vote of 421 to 8; 6 of the 8 opposing votes were from Communists who demanded the Emperor system be abolished.

In September and October 1946 the House of Peers as its final task studied the draft and approved it. On November 3 (Emperor Meiji's birthday) Emperor Hirohito proclaimed it law, and on May 3, 1947, it went into effect. After thirty-three years, no amendment to it has ever been introduced.

MacArthur proudly called the new Constitution of Japan "the single most important accomplishment of the Occupation."[63] Prime Minister Yoshida concurred, calling it "the most important single reform undertaken after the termination of the Pacific war."[64] MacArthur's exhilaration with the new Constitution was apparent in his letter of May 2, 1947, to Prime Minister Yoshida, informing him benevolently that he granted permission to fly the theretofore condemned Japanese flag. "Let this flag fly to signify the advent in Japanese life of a new and enduring era of peace based upon personal liberty, individual dignity, tolerance and justice."[65] Yoshida, a civilian, replied: "On the behalf of the Japanese nation I wish to express my profound gratitude and appreciation to you for restoring the national flag to the people of Japan for unrestricted display within and over the premises of the National Diet, the Supreme Court, and the prime minister's residence as well as the Imperial Palace." He assured MacArthur that the flying of the national flag would surely spur the Japanese people on to "new and higher efforts to become a truly democratic and peaceful nation."[66]

"I did not, however, try to force an American version of a Japanese constitution, and order them to adopt it," MacArthur recalled. True, he stopped short of issuing an actual written order to the Japanese government to adopt it. "The revision," he repeated, "had to be made by the Japanese themselves and it had to be done without coercion."[67] His excuse was closer to deception than to inaccuracy.

DEATH AND REBIRTH OF KOKUTAI

The new Constitution contained three significant features. The first was the fate of *kokutai:* MacArthur simply eliminated it from the Constitution because of its history. This monolithic ideological tradition, however, did not disappear, even from the surface, just because the new Constitution ignored it. In the official *Interpretation of the New Constitution,* published in November 1946 by the Yoshida cabinet, the dogma of *kokutai* was revived in a familiar but milder form:

> The national polity is the basis of the existence of the State and the national polity shares the destiny of the State. Therefore, if the national polity is changed or lost, the State loses its existence at once. . . . Considering the national polity of our country throughout her existence in the reliable part of her history is the unshakable, solemn fact, forming the basis of the existence of JAPAN, that the relation between the Emperor and the people is deeply rooted in the hearts of the people. The people have the Emperor as a focal point of adoration and are united through him.[68]

The majority of the Japanese people did not live up to the expectations of the conservative politicians, however. General disillusionment with anything that smacked of vainglory was still too fresh.

THE NEW LIBERTIES

The second feature was an unprecedented guarantee of political and civil liberties. The Government Section, GHQ, reported that "a bill of rights which gave absolute guarantees to the people proved another stumbling block. Many officials [of the Japanese government] were fearful lest the people abuse their liberties and apprehensive of a breakdown of governmental administration unless some legal method of checking or controlling excesses was provided. . . ." The Japanese people in their long national history had never had enough liberties to be able to abuse them. A "legal method of checking or controlling excesses" was a not-very-subtle euphemism for the familiar thought-control legislation, of which imperial Japan had enjoyed more than its share. "Throughout the discussion within the government and with SCAP," the Government Section continued, "there was a well-defined tendency to support the theory of state supremacy rather than individual freedom."[69] But SCAP's idealistic thrust for "the bill of rights" prevailed. In Ward's excellent summary: "The third chapter embodied what is perhaps the world's most extensive constitutional guarantees of civil rights. Besides all the normal protections, this extends to freedom of thought and conscience, academic freedom, the essential equality of the sexes, social security, and the right to work."[70] These extensive guarantees were a natural reaction to past persecution of those who had "dangerous thoughts" or inconveniently sensitive consciences. Theoretically, nothing the Japanese thought could any longer be considered dangerous. For this reason, the Constitution stipulated: "No censorship shall be maintained, nor shall the secrecy of any means of communication be violated." It did not, however, restrict the Americans who at that time were busy with prepublication censorship of all the major printed media, as well as radio content and the mails (which they opened).

Another unique feature of the Constitution was that the Supreme Court held the "power to determine the constitutionality of any law, order, regulation or official act." A conflict might arise, as Kawai Kazuo has pointed out, between the concepts of judicial supremacy and parliamentary supremacy, since the Constitution also declared that the Diet should be "the highest organ of state power, and . . . the sole law-making organ of the State."

Concerning the naming of the fifteen Supreme Court Judges, an interesting exchange took place between MacArthur and Prime Minister Yoshida. On January 31, 1947, MacArthur had stopped an imminent general strike, scheduled for February 1. But he knew that the Japanese people had lost their confidence in the Yoshida administration. On February 6 he wrote to Yoshida that he thought it was time for a general election. "It is necessary, in the near future," he said, "to obtain another democratic expression of the people's will."[71] On April 20 the nation's first election was held for the House of Councillors, which now replaced the House of Peers. Yoshida's conservative followers did not do well. Elections for the House of Representatives followed on April 25, and Yoshida's Liberal Party decisively lost its popularity. (It was this election that produced Japan's first Socialist cabinet and Socialist prime minister, Katayama Tetsu.)

Yoshida apparently knew he was going to lose. Before he left the office of prime minister, he wanted to make completely sure that the Japanese Supreme Court remained on his side. On April 23 he wrote to MacArthur: "I am taking this opportunity of advising you in advance that I expect to be able to announce the appointment of the president and fourteen judges of the Supreme Court on May 3rd."[72] That was the day when the Constitution went into effect. MacArthur immediately rejected Yoshida's maneuver: "I believe," he replied, "that the first panel of the supreme bench should be named by the first cabinet selected under the new Constitution. It may well be that there would be little difference in the personnel ultimately selected from those now named by your cabinet, but the impression upon public opinion, not only in Japan, but throughout the allied world, would be entirely different."[73] MacArthur perhaps did not anticipate that the elections of April 25 would make the Japanese Socialist Party the biggest winner.

THE NO-WAR CLAUSE:
DREAM AND REALITY

The third feature of the Constitution that will be discussed here is probably its most controversial one: the "no-war clause," article 9. Its origins are obscure. MacArthur went to some trouble to disclaim responsibility for it. Prime Minister Shidehara, he recounted, had come to his office at noon on January 24, 1946, and thanked him for a gift of penicillin. MacArthur noticed that "he then seemed somewhat embarrassed and hesitant." Upon being encouraged by MacArthur to "speak with the greatest frankness," Shidehara proposed "that when the new Constitution became final that it include the so-called no-war clause. He also wanted to prohibit any military establishment whatsoever."[74]

Note that this meeting took place on January 24 and that the Matsumoto Draft was submitted to MacArthur on February 1. This draft was what Shidehara had in mind as "the new Constitution" because he knew that no other government draft existed, and because he completely agreed with it. However, the phrase "when the new constitution became final" betrays MacArthur's intention not to tell all he knew, since there was in fact no reason why either Shidehara or MacArthur should have waited for the inclusion of the Constitution's most crucial and idealistic clause until such a late moment. A further exploration of the circumstances is called for here. The case against MacArthur rests on four main arguments. (1) MacArthur claimed that because of his "hands-off attitude," he was "not aware of everything that went on in the [Matsumoto] Committee." However, he told Secretary Byrnes that from October 1945 to March 1946 he "held frequent personal conferences with state ministers" to educate them about "the enlightened principles" of democracy. (2) As early as January 7, 1946, Atcheson told MacArthur that the Japanese government (i.e., the Matsumoto Committee) planned to leave intact the doctrine of imperial sovereignty exactly as codified in the 1889 Imperial Constitution. For MacArthur this alone was sufficient reason to reject the Matsumoto Draft. (3) If for the sake of argument the above evidence is discounted, and MacArthur "was not aware of everything" in the Matsumoto Draft, even so neither he nor Shidehara was at all sure on January 24 whether this draft, which was to appear on February 1, would be the final one for the Japanese Diet to deliberate. Shidehara, however, certainly hoped it would be. (4) Therefore, if Shidehara had voluntarily suggested the no-war clause to MacArthur, as MacArthur said he had, Shidehara must have been thinking of the Matsumoto Draft. It was the only draft then under study. Shidehara himself was deeply involved in consultation with the Matsumoto Committee, which his own cabinet had appointed.

The Matsumoto Draft, however, contained the clause on "the armed forces," instead of calling them "the army and navy." In the draft the Emperor retained the war and treaty-making power, which was made subject to Diet approval except in urgent circumstances (every nation, of course, wages war under "urgent circumstances"). An angry and disappointed MacArthur ordered Whitney to make future Japan constitutionally incapable of not only making war but also of defending itself. As MacArthur put it to Whitney, "War as a sovereign right of the nation is abolished . . . even for preserving its own security." Shidehara himself told an AP reporter on March 7, 1946 (the day the so-called Cabinet Draft was published nationwide) that during the GHQ-cabinet deliberation the Japanese side did not express any opposition to the no-war clause.[75] If, as MacArthur claimed, the Japanese side had proposed it, Shidehara would surely have said that the American side did not express any opposition to it. Yoshida speculated: "I have the impression that it was General MacArthur who suggested it . . . to which Baron Shidehara could very easily have replied with enthusiasm."[76]

MacArthur's belated attempt to deny his association with the clause had an embarrassing reason behind it. As the Cold War intensified, the American "loss of China" became complete, the Soviet Union exploded its own atomic bomb, and the Korean Peninsula seemed about to fall apart at any moment, MacArthur ordered the Japanese government to establish a National Police Reserve to maintain internal law and order in case of a Communist takeover of Japan. The National Police Reserve later became the present Self-Defense Forces, whose existence seems to violate the original intention of article 9 of the Constitution.

MacArthur steered an uneasy course between truth and fiction. "Should the course of world events require that all mankind stand to arms in defense of human liberty and Japan comes within the orbit of immediately threatened attack," he began his argument, "then the Japanese, too, should mount the maximum defensive power which their resources will permit." Article 9 was based upon the highest ideals, he went on, but there was no way in which it could be interpreted "as complete negation of the inalienable right of self-defense against unprovoked attack."[77] MacArthur claimed in his *Reminiscences:* "I stated this at the time of the adoption of the Constitution, and later recommended that in case of necessity."[78] The fact of the matter is that he did not officially state this "at the time of the adoption of the Constitution," on November 3, 1946. He said it officially for the first time in his January 1, 1950, message to the Japanese people, when the United States and the Soviet Union in Asia and Europe seemed ready to decide militarily who should rule the world.

The Japanese Communist Party did not think Japan should renounce its right to wars of self-defense. Nosaka Sanzo was considered by US Military Intelligence to be "the only Communist leader who has won any popularity among the Japanese people."[79] On June 28, 1946, in the course of the House of Representatives debate on the draft constitution, he and Prime Minister Yoshida exchanged views on Japan's absolute renunciation of any and all wars. Nosaka said: "There are two kinds of war. One is unjust war, war of invasion, such as Japanese imperialists waged against other nations. The other is just war—self-defense against invaders. Japan should retain the right to just wars of self-defense."[80] Yoshida replied: "To admit the possibility of war in self-defense would, in itself, provide an incentive to embark on other types of conflict, it being a well-known fact that practically every war in recent years had been undertaken on that plea." Members of the House of Representatives applauded. Encouraged, he said to Nosaka, "I think your opinion does more harm than good." More hearty applause followed.[81] Yoshida's interpretation was precisely what MacArthur had intended at the time of the original conception of the Constitution, when he denied Japan's "inalienable right of self-defense," as he put it, "even for preserving its own security."

On June 25, 1950, the Korean War broke out. On July 8 MacArthur "authorized" (i.e., ordered) the Yoshida government "to take the necessary measures to establish a national police reserve of 75,000 men." Also, he ordered that the Maritime Safety Agency should be expanded by an additional 8,000 men. These measures, MacArthur assured Yoshida, were for "the maintenance of internal security and order and the safeguard of Japan's coastline against unlawful immigration and smuggling."[82] And on July 14 Yoshida in the Diet urged the need for national security. "To us," he pleaded, "the battle of Korea is not a 'fire across the river.' It demonstrates how real and imminent is the menace of communism. We see before own eyes the sinister arm of Red aggression reaching out for its hapless victim."[83] The Japanese people, who had no idea what transpired beyond the Pacific Ocean, regarded MacArthur's volte-face as evidence that he was human after all. MacArthur's moments of true glory had all been on the battlefield, but he dreamed of a perfect society in which peace would reign forever. He wrote the most idealistic constitution he could imagine, a monument to the spirit of pacifism, which though influential throughout Eastern and Western history had never before been codified. Article 9 of the Constitution embodies MacArthur's dream as much as the Japanese people's:

Aspiring sincerely to an international peace based on justice and order, the Japanese people forever renounce war as a sovereign right of the nation and the threat or use of force as a means of settling international disputes. In order to accomplish the aim of the preceding paragraph, land, sea, and air forces, as well as other war potential, will never be maintained. The right of belligerency of the state will not be recognized.

Three years and two months after its birth, the dream was dead. Article 9 became its epitaph.

The FEC Takes on MacArthur

Throughout the process of writing the new Constitution, the Japanese government refrained from raising substantive questions about the manner in which the constitutional revision was being implemented. Perhaps that was the price of Japan's unconditional surrender. The Japanese government essentially reacted to the American suggestions, recommendations, threats, and impositions. The Far Eastern Commission (FEC), however, found MacArthur's monopoly of power repulsive. The following examination of the infighting between the FEC and MacArthur will illustrate MacArthur's style of governing as well as the US government's determination to keep Japan American.

MacArthur's unqualified approval of the draft constitution, issued on March 6, 1946, without prior consultation with the FEC, triggered a major flare-up over who was the official policymaker in the Allied Occupation of Japan. On March 10 the FEC protested formally that it was "somewhat apprehensive that this approval may be misunderstood by the Japanese public and taken to mean that this particular draft has the approval of the powers represented on this commission." To avoid this misunderstanding, the FEC requested MacArthur to tell the Japanese people that his personal approval did not "preclude favorable consideration of other proposals or drafts which may be submitted to the Diet for study and comparison." But MacArthur had no desire whatsoever to see any other proposal in the Japanese Diet; this draft was the one that the Japanese Diet had to deliberate.

The FEC also wanted MacArthur to "make clear to the Japanese government that the Far Eastern Commission must be given an opportunity to pass upon the final draft of the Constitution to determine whether it is consistent with the Potsdam Declaration."[84] Two days later, on March 12, Secretary of State Byrnes reassured the FEC that "before the Constitution becomes constitutionally effective, it [would] in some way or other come before the Far Eastern Commission."[85] He meant that the FEC had the prerogative to examine all constitutional drafts before MacArthur and the Japanese government took any final action on them.

Byrnes's reassurance did not comfort the FEC at all, especially because the first postwar election of the House of Representatives was scheduled on April 10, 1946. The FEC was well aware that this election would exert the most decisive influence in adopting the draft constitution. MacArthur, too, believed that it "would, in fact, be a plebiscite."[86] Because of "the very short period" that was available to "the parties of a more liberal tendency to circulate their views and organize their support," the FEC believed that holding the election so early might well "give a decisive advantage to the reactionary parties," and thus embarrass the Japanese government; it might also "give an undue political advantage to the political party preferring this Constitution."[87] On March 20 the FEC demanded that the election be postponed. The FEC's reason for the postponement was identical with the April 10 *Izvestiya* editorial, which the US Embassy in Moscow cabled to MacArthur and the State Department.[88]

MacArthur replied to the FEC that postponing the election "would inevitably result in greater advantage to the more experienced and better-organized reactionary group." "Should the result of the election prove disadvantageous to the purposes of the Occupation," he bluntly said, "the remedy is always in my power to require the dissolution of the Diet and the holding of a new election."[89] To make sure the election result pleased him, MacArthur purged the undesirables and thoroughly screened all the candidates prior to the election. The election was held as scheduled on April 10, 1946. MacArthur was delighted with its result: "Democracy has thus demonstrated a healthy forward advance."[90] But *Pravda* said the result confirmed the dominance of the reactionary parties that had been responsible for the crimes of Japanese imperialism; MacArthur, it added, supported these parties.

The FEC, realizing that it could hardly change the substance of the draft constitution, resorted to questioning MacArthur about the "method and machinery" by which it was to be adopted, in order to ensure that it would embody the "freely expressed will of the Japanese people."[92] Two days after the election, the FEC presented to MacArthur the following questions:

"(a) To what extent and in what manner have other drafts of constitutions been brought to the knowledge of the Japanese people and how have they been discussed?
"(b) What evidence have the Japanese people shown of applying democratic principles in considering a new constitution?
"(c) In what manner have the Japanese people been encouraged to abolish the Imperial Institution or to reform it along more democratic lines?"[93]

The FEC requested MacArthur, if he himself could not come to Washington, DC, to send a member of his staff to answer the above questions.

MacArthur could not believe that he was subject to this kind of "insult." He immediately sent a furious response to the FEC chairman, Major General Frank R. McCoy, an American, in the form of a personal and confidential telegram to McCoy himself. Personal, because MacArthur knew McCoy was deeply in awe of him. Indeed, when McCoy was appointed as US representative to the FEC, he asked the War Department to inform MacArthur of his regret at being unable to consult with him before accepting the post.[94] "It had been my purpose," MacArthur told McCoy, "to take no formal action on any constitutional reform finally adopted by the Japanese people"; this was "American policy." The Far Eastern Commission, however, was "reversing American policy in this respect by insisting that the formality of its approval be a prerequisite to final adoption of any such reform by the Japanese people." The FEC's attitude, MacArthur continued, was "capable of doing immeasurable harm to the Occupation as it [would] undoubtedly prejudice many Japanese people against the instrument itself who [would] therefore look upon it as a thing forced upon Japan at the point of Allied bayonets."

The Japanese people could not exercise their will freely, he emphasized, if "the threat of disapproval by the Allied Powers" overshadowed all constitutional debate. "My own personal approval of the Government Draft," he said, "was designed to give moral support and encouragement to the liberal forces struggling for reform against tradition, prejudice and reaction. . . . It did not commit the Allied Powers in any way or even the supreme commander himself except on general principles."

The FEC had "no executive power," MacArthur continued; such power was "reserved exclusively to the Supreme Commander." The FEC was "not empowered, in my opinion, to require prior approval of any action taken by either the supreme commander or the Japanese government." The requirement was therefore an "encroachment upon the authority of the supreme commander." Following, as it did, upon "the effort of the Far Eastern Commission to interfere with the elections just concluded," it tended to "undermine the authority of supreme commander" and "confuse the Japanese Government and people."

MacArthur had not finished yet. "What is at stake," he specified, "is the retention of American influence and American control which has been established in Japan by the American government in a skillful combination of checks and balances designed to preserve American interests here. There is a planned and concerted attack to break this down. It exists in the Far Eastern Commission in a most definite and decisive form under the veneer of diplomacy and comradeship therein." His peroration was truly apocalyptic. "I beg of you to protect in every possible way including the veto power, the position and policy of the United States Government," MacArthur pleaded with McCoy. "Appeasements, small as they may seem, rapidly become accumulative to the point of danger. If we lose control of this sphere of influence under this policy of aggressive action, we will not only jeopardize the occupation but hazard the future safety of the United States."[95]

McCoy immediately consulted with John C. Vincent of the State Department's Office of Far Eastern Affairs. Vincent briefed Secretary Byrnes on April 19. "There is general agreement among concerned American officials," he informed Byrnes, "that (a) General MacArthur should not have approved the draft constitution (b) that his defense is not to the point." Concerning the retention of American control of Japan, he said, "General McCoy, I am sure, is as fully aware of his responsibility in this connection as is General MacArthur. So am I. But we must at the same time bear in mind that the control of Japan is, by agreement, an Allied responsibility."[96] He recommended MacArthur be assured "that we are fully aware here of the need for protecting his position as executive authority and that we are also conscious of the importance of preserving American influence in the control of Japan." At the same time he believed in telling MacArthur "simply, without legalistic argument, that the Far Eastern Commissions (*sic*) policy decision of March 20 is in accordance with the Terms of References adopted at Moscow."[97]

The next day McCoy drafted his personal reply to MacArthur. Vincent edited it, and Byrnes approved it by signing "OK as changed."[98] "I realize," McCoy began, "as do the State and War Departments, the problems which face you and the difficulties under which you are laboring. I can assure you that all of us here concur in the general principles you have set forth, are fully alive to the necessity of safeguarding your position and share your desire to protect United States vital interest in the Far East." But, McCoy reminded MacArthur as diplomatically as possible, the FEC did have some right to review: "Our view is in accord with yours that the commission should take no formal action on a new Constitution unless the Constitution fails to fulfill the policy provisions of the Potsdam Declaration and the Instrument of Surrender.... Again let me assure you that I have constantly in mind the interests of the United States and that I will always protect your flank and rear."[99]

Such, then, was the FEC chairman's supposedly admonitory reply to MacArthur. McCoy belatedly told the FEC members on May 29: "He [MacArthur] is in full agreement with the need for a closer working arrangement and understanding between SCAP and the commission and stands ready to do everything in his power to further this end. [But] it is impossible for him to send an officer to act as his deputy in the broad matters involving constitutional reform, as he has given his personal attention to this question and there is no officer in a position to express in detail his views."[100]

George Atcheson, who had also been deeply involved in the constitutional revision (especially the Konoe fiasco), supported MacArthur by attacking the FEC. The FEC's "startling and incomprehensible attitude based on misconception and lack of knowledge of situation," Atcheson wrote on June 21 to John H. Hilldring, assistant secretary for Occupied Areas in the State Department, "has disturbed us here very much." He vehemently defended the Constitution: "Neither General MacArthur nor anyone in headquarters has had [the] slightest intention or inclination to 'jam' Constitution through this or any Diet. . . . The draft is a Japanese document. . . . I hope that the American delegates can do some missionary work among FEC members."[101]

While jealously defending his monopoly of executive powers, MacArthur was well aware that he had gone beyond a reasonable exercise of his power in relation to the FEC. He therefore tried to explain to Secretary of State Byrnes that the FEC's function in matters of constitutional reform was apparently "limited to the formulation of guiding policy." Knowing very well that the FEC had no "guiding policy," he dared to tell Byrnes that "in the absence of any such policy statement from the Far Eastern Commission, the Supreme Commander is clearly unrestricted in his authority to proceed in the implementation of the Potsdam Declaration and surrender terms as he interprets them." Nevertheless, he did not consider himself autocratic. "I have acted meticulously," he declared, "in accord with the instructions received from the United States government."[102] MacArthur's uncompromising haste to complete "the single most important accomplishment of the Occupation" was more the result of his personal race against the FEC than of the "foremost concern" for the welfare of Japan that he expressed to Prime Minister Shidehara. Before the FEC as the legitimate policymaking body for the Occupation of Japan began its business, he wanted to finish this most prestigious task by himself.

The FEC met for the first time on February 26, 1946, in Washington, DC. By then, MacArthur had already rejected the Matsumoto Draft, ordered Whitney and his staff to prepare the MacArthur Draft, and presented it to the Shidehara cabinet, which agonized not over whether to accept or reject it (rejection was never available as a choice) but over how to interpret the Emperor's position as "the symbol of the State." By February 26 MacArthur, in a calculated show of generosity, had persuaded the Japanese government that some members of the still nonfunctioning

FEC would abolish the Emperor system and worse yet eliminate the person of the Emperor himself, and that he could not answer for such an outcome if the Japanese government turned down the MacArthur Draft. By February 26, the "single most important accomplishment" was practially accomplished. Thus MacArthur was able to inform Byrnes proudly:

> In this matter speed is of the essence due to the fact, too readily lost sight of, that the Japanese people are now subject to their present wholly undemocratic constitution and will remain subject thereto so long as reform is delayed. Such delay, furthermore, but serves the interests of those who would much prefer that such reforms be not instituted at all.[103]

MacArthur won this race with a combination of shrewdness and bulldozing. Yoshida, while claiming ignorance as to why MacArthur moved in such haste, nonetheless volunteered to guess that "one can only put it down to that impulsiveness common to military people of all countries."[104]

The completion of the new Constitution left the FEC with hardly any significant policymaking responsibility. No wonder, then, that MacArthur later called the FEC "little more than a debating society."[105] This debating society persisted, however, and contemplated holding a referendum on the new Japanese Constitution as late as November 1948. This FEC move caused serious worry, especially within the State Department. Alice Dunning wrote a top-secret office memorandum to Max W. Bishop, chief of the Division of Northeast Asian Affairs, that the Constitution was "an American-inspired document and any number of votes cast by the Japanese against the document, however small, would merely supply ammunition to those who oppose[d] the American position in the occupation of Japan."[106] The referendum was never held.

The Constitution and Its Critics

The drastic nature of the new Constitution inevitably engendered criticism. Most conspicuous were the complaints that it was "made in America"; that it was imposed upon the unwilling Japanese government by the alien conqueror; and that it killed the spirit of what was once authentic Japan.

"Made in America," no doubt. "Imposed upon the unwilling Japanese government," no doubt. These criticisms were not significant, however, because the conservative Japanese government was clearly incapable of drafting a new, more democratic constitution; all it was capable of was obstinately holding on to the imperial Constitution. Robert Ward's case against the Constitution is harder to answer. "Most serious of all,"

he has asserted, "is the damage this constitution may have done to the
very cause it was intended to serve—the democratization of Japan." This
is indeed the most serious criticism. "By imposing upon the Japanese a
constitution hopelessly unsuited to the political ideals and experience of
the vast majority of the population," Ward charges, "the long-term interests of democracy may have been ill served." He elaborates on the
damage: "Instead of a system of government based upon and geared to
the social, economic and political realities of Japanese society, a hollow
but elaborate facade modeled after an idealized version of Anglo-American
political institutions was hastily patched together. The result was an
enormous gap between political fact and constitutional fiction, the true
extent of which has been carefully concealed by a variety of devices."[107]

Ward's reasoning appears sound. But he presumes that the Japanese are so rooted in tradition that they could hardly change their political
orientation or preferences. When he argues that the new constitution is
hopelessly unsuited to Japanese political ideals, he seems to be referring
nostalgically to a "Golden Age" that happened somewhere between 1868
and 1945. True, Japan was an extremely structured society. The vast
majority of the population was well conditioned to perpetuate its own
subjugation in the name of loyalty and patriotism. Soon after the surrender, however, the disillusioned people abruptly rejected hierarchy and
the bureaucracy that supported it. *Nippon Sangyo Keizai Shimbun* heat-
edly but accurately expressed the people's resentment:

> There is no country where people are so slighted by the governing class as
> in Japan. All government officials, from top to bottom, should now radically
> rectify their haughty attitude toward the people. If they don't, it will be
> necessary to regard them as opponents of liberalism and treat them as crim-
> inals who are restraining the development of Japan's new peaceful nation.[108]

One should also reflect on why American idealism was so passionately involved in the Occupation of Japan. Partly responsible was the
American war propaganda that had depicted imperial Japan as the land
of human enslavement. The reality of postwar Japan confirmed the American policymakers' perceptions; they saw selectively what they wanted to
see. But what they saw was not out of focus, even if they did not look very
hard at it. One should remember, too, that the young Meiji semirevolu-
tionaries in the nineteenth century eagerly sought after idealized foreign
political theories and practices as long as these served their own cause.
The celebrated Meiji Constitution of 1889 itself was an idealized version
of Prussian constitutional absolutism.

The history of Japanese political theories was and still is a story of
continuous pragmatic grafting of major foreign ideologies onto indigenous

ones. The scars left by grafting often faded into comfortable assimilation, as things formerly foreign became Japanese political ideals and experiences. They were "the social, economic and political realities of Japanese society." It is reasonable to expect, then, that the Japanese should try democracy based upon popular sovereignty for the first time in their history. Such audacity on the part of a people who, thanks to love of unanimity, give a surface appearance of conservatism, was one of the most powerful ingredients in both their spectacular prewar industrialization and their postwar recovery.

The Japanese people may not have fully understood "democracy" in terms of their own freedom and liberty. However, their temporary lack of understanding does not necessarily constitute a justification for condemning popular sovereignty in the new constitution. After all, the Japanese people had had enough experience with monolithic ideologies that could not survive without "thought control." Japanese reality during the 1940s was a nightmare, the end of which encouraged a mood of idealism and risk taking in conqueror and conquered alike.

Another criticism of the Constitution comes from a different perspective. Kawai Kazuo in his perceptive essay *Japan's American Interlude* writes "from the point of view of the Japanese, which Westerners may find hard to understand." The Constitution, he argues, "arbitrarily changes the fundamental nature of the Japanese state—the unique characteristic of Japan which makes it Japan."[109] By "the fundamental nature of the Japanese state," Kawai means *kokutai*, the traditional mystic notion of the Japanese state as an organic whole. He therefore denounces the new Constitution in which the Emperor became "the symbol of the State" and the nation's sovereignty rested in the people, because it "arbitrarily violated the *kokutai* ... which was the essence of the Japanese state."[110]

Kawai elsewhere points out correctly that "there does not seem to be any such entity as the 'Japanese soul' or the 'Japanese temperament' which innately predestines the Japanese to any particular pattern of behavior."[111] Nevertheless, he argues that *kokutai* "has almost mystic significance" to most Japanese; that it legitimizes "the naturally ordained supremacy of the Emperor." *Kokutai* is "inextricably imbedded in the social organization of Japan whose orderly hierarchical structure logically calls for a capstone at the top."[112] This is why he claims that the doctrine of popular sovereignty "did violence to Japanese social reality as well as to Japanese political theory." He even goes so far as to assert that "the doctrinal basis of the new constitution, so out of keeping with the facts of Japanese life, could hardly appeal to the Japanese."[113]

One may reasonably ask, however, if Kawai has been successful in elevating *kokutai* to the same mystic but often incomprehensible level as the "Japanese soul." To claim that the doctrine of popular sovereignty is alien to Japanese political theory (or the Japanese way of life), and hence should be abandoned, is tantamount to saying that beef, the main ingredient in *sukiyaki,* is not part of the Japanese people's traditional diet and therefore should not be eaten by them. It was only in the last quarter of the nineteenth century that ordinary Japanese began to eat beef—a practice of which they had not even heard until the sixteenth century, and then only as a repulsive peculiarity of "Southern Barbarians."

Kawai advocates constitutional revision retroactively based upon "a sounder historical foundation."[114] He asserts that "the basic problem of 'national polity,' the essential nature of the Japanese state" is far more important than any other constitutional questions such as "the exact circumstances under which the prime minister may dissolve the lower house of the Diet, the spelling out in practice of the relations between the national authority and autonomous local authorities, the specific implementation of the bill of rights, and all the rest. . . ."[115] But I doubt if Japan's "national polity," or the essence of what makes it Japan, could be materialized into workable concepts without discussing first those "subsidiary" constitutional questions such as the bill of rights. In fact, the Ministry of Education spent years articulating the essential nature of the Japanese state. Its masterpiece was an ideological monolith whose existence demanded strict regimentation of thought. *The Cardinal Principle of Kokutai* and *The Way of the Subject* were the logical climax of Japanese intellectual fascism. To assume the existence of *kokutai* as the guiding principle of democracy without taking the people's rights into account is analogous to guaranteeing a cure without knowing what the disease is. If an argument such as Kawai's holds, no political revolution would ever be justifiable, because it would change "arbitrarily" the essence of the ancient regime.

A PERSONAL COMMENT

I should like to add my brief personal comment as one who grew up during Japan's most passionate era of pacifism. I empathize with the members of the Japanese generation that "lost the war"; they were bound to be humiliated when a foreign victor with his unquestionable supremacy and overbearing though generous paternalism wrote the constitution for Japan. Yet, as Kawai too concedes, the constitution "did conform to the best standards of a true parliamentary democracy."[116]

I learned in the primary and secondary school curricula nothing about the imperial mythology, nothing about *kokutai,* nothing substantive about the past imperial wars, but everything about democratic principles if not practices, and everything about the original sin of the atomic bomb. As an extracurricular activity, I enjoyed reading the imperial mythology; it stirred my imagination in the same way as Greek mythology or *Robinson Crusoe*. The Meiji Constitution is to me a monumental document which excites my sense of history; *kokutai* to me is not only devoid of any mystic significance but also frightening with its exclusivism.

Because *kokutai*, as Kawai explains, "is inextricably imbedded in the social organization of Japan, whose orderly hierarchical structure logically calls for a capstone at the top," I am naturally suspicious of any attempt to bring back any such "logical" regimentation. Even a cursory review of intellectual and political freedom in prewar Japan shows how this regimentation was utilized to suppress dissident voices that challenged the "natural validity" of the hereditary social hierarchy. The imperial oligarchs and bureaucrats characterized the dissidents as "undesirable." The "undesirable" became the "dangerous," hence persecuted.

I have already described how Yoshida called this abnormal ideological homogeneity "democracy," based on "the promises made to the Japanese people by the Emperor Meiji." His account of how the spirit of the Meiji Constitution "became distorted with the passage of time" borders on semantic gimmickry, if not outright historical and political fiction.

The Emperor is, as our constitution stipulates, "the symbol of the State." The Emperor should be relieved from the awesome burden of being a logical capstone to the social edifice. Popular sovereignty, if not exercised, leads to a corruption of wisdom. Here I do not imply that the defeat in the war proves the evil of imperial sovereignty. The defeat or victory has nothing to do with my advocacy of popular sovereignty.

The postwar generations, I am sure, will not suffer any identity crisis, because they have not been indoctrinated in *kokutai*. They also will not perceive an inconsistency between their belief in popular sovereignty and their personal goodwill toward the person of the Emperor. After all, there is no logical reason why they should.

"The imperial Japanese government," in the scathing words of GHQ-SCAP, "arrogated unto itself the positions of guides of the people's morals, keepers of the people's conscience and arbiters of the people's destinies. The people are not consulted."[118] That criticism constituted a fair warning in the eyes of the American occupation authority: "It would, indeed, have been strange if the principal proponents of democracy—inherent in which is the right to free choice of one's own form of government—had undertaken to impose their own system of government upon the conquered country."[119]

Such simple but decent thinking did not change their actual behavior at all. MacArthur and his staff willingly became the new guides of the Japanese people's morals, keepers of their conscience, and arbiters of their destinies. To be sure, MacArthur's reform policies were animated by a spirit of freedom of thought and action. In his 1946 New Year's message to the Japanese people, MacArthur forcefully declared:

> The shackles of militarism, of feudalism, of regimentation of body and soul, have been removed. Thought control and the abuses of education are no more. All now enjoy religious freedom and the right of speech without undue restraint. Free assembly is guaranteed. The removal of this national enslavement means freedom for the people, but at the same time it imposes upon them the individual duty to think and act each on his own initiative. It is necessary for the masses of Japan to awaken to the fact that they now have the power to govern and what is done must be done by themselves.[120]

But he did not trust the political conscience and intelligence of the Japanese. Hence, he practiced censorship. In other words, the Japanese did not have to torment themselves pondering what they as responsible individuals should or should not utter in public.

The Japanese conservatives attempted to preserve the structure of imperial sovereignty; their strategy was to inject some democratic practices into it to placate domestic and foreign suspicions. MacArthur, ironically, did the reverse: he abolished imperial sovereignty and injected undemocratic practices for the sake of achieving democratic ends. Curiously, there was hardly any major public disorder throughout the drastic transition from the once-mighty hegemony to the more powerful foreign military government. In other words, MacArthur prohibited a public "trial-and-error" learning of democracy, because the "errors" would constitute "public disturbances" and that would make his occupation of Japan imperfect. His last-minute intervention in the proposed general strike was a dramatic example of his sensitivity in this regard. Probably, the Japanese people's acquiescence in the face of authority nicely matched the American propaganda for democratic law and order. This law and order, guided by censorship, prevailed throughout the American administration of defeated Japan.

MacArthur's idealistic rhetoric appeared to fortify his autocratic style of governance—a style that, in the eyes of the Japanese people, did not symbolize the essential meaning of democracy. But, to the dismay of the Japanese conservatives, the vast majority of the people welcomed the substance of the new Constitution. A painful irony for those involved in the governance of Japan was that, when the democratic reforms started working, the "rationed democracy" became obvious. The gap between principle and practice continued to irritate the Japanese and to embarrass the American policymakers. Perhaps, this embarrassment was the most precious lesson of democracy that the Americans left for the Japanese.

PART TWO
FROM INDOCTRINATION TO EDUCATION

Education in occupied Japan was fiercely political; to the US government, it was the best instrument for achieving basic ideological change. The American authorities demanded that there be no nationalism, no militarism, and no communism in Japanese education. They indoctrinated the Japanese incessantly. From the beginning, the officially sanctioned mode of political and ethical thought was never neutral.

For the Japanese people, there was nothing new about having their educational system politicized. Since its inception the Japanese imperial government had constantly endeavored to control the thoughts and actions of teachers and students. True, the government reacted to the voices and moods of this touchy educational elite. But the deliberate attempt to domesticate the minds of the intelligentsia ironically perpetuated their traditional prestige. Since the Meiji Restoration in 1868 the intelligentsia had hardly failed to think "politically." Indeed, the word "intellectual" in Japanese society automatically connoted "political."

I do not mean to imply that the students and professors were "liberals," while the government was "reactionary." Rather, the academics did not hesitate to express their views on government policy. Japanese universities tended to band together in protection against government invasion. But protection of the academicians, who had a more-or-less unified point of view, had virtually nothing to do with those who spoke out boldly on the crucial issues of the day and who were silenced as dangerous to public peace and tranquility.

The American occupation authorities found it encouraging that some Japanese professors and students had voiced their opinions at the risk of their physical safety. As Secretary of War Henry L. Stimson told President Truman before the Japanese surrender, Japan's liberals "yielded only at the point of the pistol"; their liberal attitude, he added, had not been "subverted in the way which was so general in Germany."[1] MacArthur urged all professors and students to engage more in political discourse. The Japanese intelligentsia, whose longing for political thought and action had been frustrated especially since the 1920s, was not sparing in its praise for the American forces: the Americans epitomized the democratic virtues. The intelligentsia plunged into freedom of speech and freedom of individual conscience and thought. Their fascination with these freedoms, though apparently a sudden infatuation, had deep roots; it was a romantic longing that had survived severe thought regimentation.

Two factors contributed to the swiftness, if not the thoroughness, with which the American policies were implemented in Japanese schools. First, the psychological and physical deprivation of the people nurtured their inferiority complex regarding the invincible Americans. This superior-inferior relationship, which MacArthur did not strive to eliminate, lent impetus to the American propaganda with its guarantees of a brave new world. Second, the traditional Japanese appetite for learning, long suppressed by the imperial government, craved new substance, which American ideals in part supplied. America became undoubtedly the most popular and urgent subject for the Japanese people to study. The Japanese attitude toward America during the Occupation resembled the climate of the early Meiji era (from the 1860s through the 1880s), when an avalanche of Western intellectual and technological knowledge overwhelmed the nation. Yet Meiji Japan had reacted as its self-confidence increased; its nationalistic frustrations and ambitions had found concrete embodiment in the 1889 Meiji Imperial Constitution and the 1890 Imperial Rescript on Education. It was reasonable, then, to anticipate a similar reaction in favor of Japanizing the American "excesses" after the end of the Occupation.

It was, however, only a matter of time before GHQ-SCAP, the extraconstitutional government, became the target of the intellectuals' political outspokenness. GHQ neither expected such critical attention nor found it entertaining. MacArthur and the Japanese government accordingly demanded that education be politically neutral. A familiar cycle began anew.

In charge of Japanese education at GHQ-SCAP was, as we have seen, the Civil Information and Education Section (CI & E). It was established on September 22, 1945, to become what might be termed the "American Ministry of Japanese Education." The Education Division in CI & E dealt daily with the Japanese Ministry of Education. There were regular meetings between the CI & E chief and the Japanese minister of education and between the Education Division chief and the Japanese vice-minister of education. CI & E advised MacArthur on education policies for democratizing future Japanese generations and ensuring, through the mass media, that the Japanese people understood "the true facts of their defeat."[2] CI & E was also to eliminate "militarism and ultranationalism, in doctrine and practice, including military training from all elements of the Japanese educational system."[3] Further, it was instructed to "keep the supreme commander factually informed of public opinion."[4] MacArthur's concern for his own popularity is legendary. A Public Opinion and Sociological Research Unit was established within CI & E.[5]

"The Japanese themselves quickly developed an almost compulsive fascination with their own changing public opinion," says Kawai. But his assessment of the CI & E personnel is not at all flattering:

> The chief of CI & E was a Marine Corps reserve lieutenant colonel who in civilian life had been a small-town high school principal. The members of his staff . . . were mostly people of about the same level of background and experience. The education officers of the district military government teams . . . were generally young men of even less background and experience. Their incomparable idealism and intense dedication to their work should have served as an inspiring example, but many Japanese educators and particularly the university professors were conscious only of their own wider experience or greater erudition and tended to be supercilious toward these American educational officers and their ideas.[6]

Maeda Tamon, the first postwar education minister, was blunter in 1956: "Many of those who carried out the occupation administration of education were persons of extremely limited knowledge and experience in the field."[7]

The CI & E staffs were, however, far more knowledgeable than these assessments indicate. It should be noted that both Kawai and Maeda made their statements in the postoccupation period, when the Japanese government was trying hard to rectify what Japanese conservatives called the "American excesses" during the Occupation. It is true that the CI & E staffs initially showed that they had only limited knowledge of the Japanese people and of education in general. But as they became more involved with Japanese education and personnel, their behavior and attitude began to reflect their experience. Their growing knowledge was not necessarily received kindly by Japanese conservatives, who wanted the CI & E to change the Japanese educational system as little as possible.

The Japanese Ministry of Education, now under CI & E's direct supervision, was not amenable to change. One confidential report, written by two retired senior Ministry of Education officials and submitted to GHQ in late 1946, confirmed American suspicions that the ministry was a stronghold of clannish bureaucrats who were desperately resisting any American attempts at reform. The authors were Kaneko Kenji, a Tokyo Imperial University graduate who had been a professor at Hiroshima Higher Normal School and later senior superintendent in the Ministry of Education; and Iwamatsu Goro, also a Tokyo Imperial University graduate who had been a professor at the Naval Academy and chief secretary to the education minister. The Ministry of Education officials, they said, were "very conservative," always trying "*to keep the present conditions,*" but they were also "mostly opportunists." These opportunists who had been "extremely pro-German," now with the defeat were pretending "to have been pro-American, *simply from fear* against the omnipotent GHQ." What these officials said was different from what they believed, so the Americans should handle them "with great care." Almost all the high officials in the ministry, they continued acrimoniously, were from the clique of Tokyo Imperial University. This academic clique was "controlled by [the] 'Tuesday clique,'" which had originally been a chess club. The Tuesday Club was "a breeding bed of evil plots and schemes, a kind of educational underworld." The authors were worried: "Americans are very frank and honest, so, our great concern is that *you may be deceived* by those courteous and smiling Japanese officials with dangerous hidden tricks, schemes and very tactful to handle men."[8] "This is something to bear in mind although it is from a Japanese source," said CI & E chief Donald R. Nugent.[9]

SCAP's education reforms covered literally every aspect of the Japanese educational system. I shall concentrate on the dominant themes of the reforms and interpret the manner and matter of the curriculum tailored for occupied Japan. The following chapters will deal more with substantive themes than chronological narrative. To help the reader make comparisons among related events and themes, I have from time to time gone over the same ground as in the preceding chapters.

One last introductory remark for a rough comparison between the American and the Japanese educational ladders in 1945. According to Nugent, "universities in Japan approximate the upper division of American universities, Japanese 'higher schools' are comparable to American junior colleges, 'middle schools' to high schools, and 'primary schools' to primary schools."[10]

7
The 1890
Rescript
on Education

The two most important documents of imperial Japan were the 1889 Meiji Constitution and the 1890 Imperial Rescript on Education. The 1889 Constitution codified the sanctity and inviolability of the Emperor. The 1890 Rescript on Education made the Japanese educational system the means by which the people's loyalty to the throne was nurtured. Conversely, MacArthur's intense determination to destroy the Meiji Constitution reflected the thoroughness of the people's devotion to the divine Emperor. Amid the lethargy that followed surrender, the imperial Japanese government struggled to prevent its imminent disintegration. The government was preoccupied with morality, imperial benevolence, respect for law and order, collective altruism, and all slogans for social cohesion.

The 1890 Rescript in 1945

In his surrender rescript of August 14, 1945, the Emperor asked his subjects to "bear the unbearable," "protect the national polity [*kokutai*]," and "strive for world peace and progress." The next day,

August 15, 1945, the Suzuki cabinet resigned at 3:20 P.M. But four hours later Suzuki assured the nation in his radio broadcast that imperial Japan had accepted the Potsdam Declaration with one condition, namely, that there would be no change in the prerogatives of His Imperial Majesty.[1] In other words, the Emperor still ruled the nation. Suzuki deliberately ignored the full meaning of unconditional surrender. Education Minister Ota Kozo, also resigning, quickly confirmed Suzuki's contention: on August 16 he ordered all prefectural governors and school principals to make sure that the people continue devoting themselves to defending the divine national polity, and to enhancing the national strength as best they could. He said that such was a proper response of loyal subjects to the Emperor's wish.

On August 18, at a press conference on his inauguration day, Education Minister Maeda Tamon (who was to hold office until January 13, 1946) declared that "the foundation of Japanese education could not exist" without the 1890 Rescript on Education and the 1945 rescript on the surrender. "I would like to solve Japan's future educational problems," he confidently said to the reporters, "by translating the imperial rescripts into concrete policies."[2] Maeda had graduated from Tokyo Imperial University in 1909 with a degree in German law; he had served the Ministry of Home Affairs, had been deputy mayor of Tokyo, a member of the *Asahi Shimbun's* editorial staff, and—before the war—director of the Japanese Cultural Library in New York. He knew everybody liked peace, and this was a sentiment that MacArthur himself liked to hear, especially from the mouths of Japanese leaders. "With dauntless bearing," Minister Maeda said, "we should defend the national polity [*kokutai*] and international peace."[3] Maeda was supposed to be a liberal, and the US State Department was counting on his liberalism.

New prime minister Higashikuni lost no time in answering the demand of Japanese leaders that the imperial sovereignty and *kokutai* would be left untouched even under the Allied Occupation. The Higashikuni cabinet unhesitatingly told the nation that the people's new freedom of speech must, like the old freedom, "conform to the spirit of the Peace Preservation Law." This law included the death sentence for *lèse majesté*, the definition of which was frighteningly broad. Higashikuni said that the people's rights of expression would be interpreted from the standpoint of "expediency." The imperial government, not at all sure of itself, was hence intensely distrustful of the people, and had to rely on its time-honored tactic of muzzling public opinion.

The Japanese leaders kept reassuring themselves that imperial sovereignty had to remain sacred and inviolable or else the nation would decay. But Japanese reality right after the surrender rewarded perfidy, not loyalty. The people were about to lose faith in virtually everything. They were exhausted after their long history of servitude for the glory of the empire—a servitude that had rewarded them with an unprecedented unconditional surrender. "Surrender" should not have existed in the Japanese military vocabulary. The people were tired of the official prohibition of anything spontaneous or self-gratifying that the imperial government said would weaken the spirit needed to fight a victorious war. They were starving and did not care if the imperial rescript was dead or alive.

Realizing this, Education Minister Maeda bewailed popular indifference as "the root of our recent moral decay."[4] Hoping to rehabilitate the Japanese people, he proposed an old remedy for a new disease: they should faithfully obey the 1890 Imperial Rescript on Education, because its most precious virtue was the harmonious relationship it prescribed among the people and their loyalty to His Majesty. He told this to the nation's educational leaders on October 15, 1945, at the Central Seminar for New Educational Policies. There was nothing new.

While the Japanese leaders were busy defending the Imperial Rescript on Education as if it were a battle flag, SCAP appeared totally unconcerned. American silence on what the Japanese believed crucial to the Emperor's sovereignty encouraged them to publicize vocally—though with not as much confidence as they professed—the rescript's validity. The seriousness of the issue was in fact recognized in a personal letter of December 9, 1945, from Commander J. J. Schieffelin, Military Government in Kyoto, to his friend Brigadier General Ken R. Dyke, chief of CI & E. "The Imperial Rescript on Education," Commander Schieffelin wrote, "is their 'Gettysburg Address.' " The rescript, however, was also "narrowly nationalistic," and a new one was needed. He insisted upon "a rather brilliant Japanese educator" to draft one. This Japanese educator, wary of possible *lèse majesté*, had asked Schieffelin "not to mention his name for the time being." The Japanese educator did produce a mock imperial rescript on education in archaic Japanese and modern English. Schieffelin liked it very much. "SCAP may be missing a best bet," he told Dyke, "if the idea of a new rescript is rejected." Indeed, "if SCAP wished to use the immense existing tradition of obedience and respect which pervades the schools," the Emperor should be encouraged to "produce a new rescript." Schieffelin recommended that the enclosed draft rescript could be used by the Emperor and reminded Dyke that "speed" was crucial. Schieffelin concluded that if SCAP wanted "a streamlined way of improving the thinking of these people, this could be it."[5] Dyke referred Schieffelin's letter to the Education Division, which debated the possible merit of the rescript for the US Occupation but took no action until July 1946.

What MacArthur wanted was not only to improve but actually to revolutionize the Japanese way of thinking about self-government. He planned to constitutionally prevent the Japanese from fighting another war in the future. To disarm the Japanese mind, which he believed filled with a suicidal devotion to a religious mythology of the Emperor, Mac-Arthur condemned "the doctrine that the Emperor of Japan is superior to the heads of other states because of ancestry, descent, or special origin."[6] He told this to the Japanese people in his directive of December 15, 1945, entitled "Abolition of Governmental Sponsorship, Support, Perpetuation, Control, and Dissemination of State Shinto (Kokka Shinto, Jinja Shinto)." With it he intended to destroy the psychological foundation of imperial sovereignty. As proof of compliance, he ordered the Japanese government to submit "a comprehensive report" to GHQ by March 15, 1946. He then reminded every Japanese of his personal accountability for noncompliance.

The Emperor Renews
the Charter Oath

The most important example of compliance came immediately. The Emperor denied his divinity in his 1946 New Year's message to the Japanese people: "The ties between us and our people have always stood upon mutual trust and affection. They do not depend upon mere legends and myths. They are not predicated on the false conception that the Emperor is divine and that the Japanese people are superior to other races and fated to rule the world." He asked his people to unite firmly "in its resolve to face the present ordeal." "Love of family and love of country are especially strong in this country," he reminded them. "With more of this devotion should we now work towards love of mankind." His particular emphasis was on filial love and loyalty, because the Japanese were "liable to grow restless and fall into the Slough of Despond." Excessive radical tendencies, he added, were becoming more prevalent and undermining public morality, with the result that there were "signs of confusion of thought."[7]

"Confusion of thought" was an understatement considering the massive introduction of American-rationed democracy, the public outspokenness of Communist orators for the first time in the nation's history, and the sheer apathy if not disgust of the people toward the imperial government. The Emperor, for consolation and solution, turned to his grandfather Emperor Meiji's Charter Oath of 1868. "We wish to make this oath anew," he said, "and restore the country to stand on its feet again."

The oath, however, was a firm but self-serving proclamation for the young oligarchs envisaging their own imperial glory. True, it declared that "deliberative assemblies shall be widely established and all matters decided by public discussion." But such visionary promises had been forgotten overnight. The real intention of Meiji oligarchs was well revealed when the oath also proclaimed that "knowledge shall be sought throughout the world so as to strengthen the foundations of imperial rule."

The Emperor's advocacy of the Charter Oath as a manifesto of Japanese freedom and liberty merely underlined the superficial way in which the Japanese leaders had approached the meaning of democracy. Similarly, that "rather brilliant Japanese educator" of Commander Schieffelin's letter said in his mock imperial rescript that "Our subjects" must grasp "the true meaning of the Charter Oath." A crushing defeat had not diminished the conservatives' belief in imperial supremacy. Indeed, they saw no inconsistency between democracy and imperial sanctity.

"The Emperor's New Year's statement pleases me very much," MacArthur said publicly. He was generous with his compliments: "By it he undertakes a leading part in the democratization of his people. He squarely takes his stand for the future along liberal lines. His action reflects the irresistible influence of a sound idea. A sound idea cannot be stopped." Nonetheless, on January 4, 1946, Education Minister Maeda capitalized on the Emperor's message and issued a highly emotional directive to all prefectural governors and heads of all schools:

> I cannot help being filled with trepidation when I think that the Emperor graciously teaches us that by cleansing ourselves from this mistaken idea we may realize the close relationship between the Sovereign and his subjects; that is, the Sovereign and his subjects belong to one family. I am deeply impressed by the magnanimity of His Majesty's will and our desire to serve him devotedly cannot but be augmented ever more.[8]

The press responded by branding his statement "pitiful" and "a foolish directive" that would exert "a very strong retarding effect on school education."[9]

Tanaka Revives the Rescript

The reaction of the press did not disturb Minister Maeda. Again in January 1946, at the Imperial Diet session, he said that the spirit and letter of the Imperial Rescript on Education had been "unfortunately misinterpreted" by self-righteous reactionaries and militarists. If the Japanese people once again read the rescript with reflective humility and purity of mind, Maeda reassured the Diet, "we shall regain the true understanding of the Emperor's wisdom and affection in the rescript."[10] He actually believed that the 1890 Imperial Rescript on Education encouraged individuality to blossom and freedom and liberty to flourish. Under Maeda's leadership the Ministry of Education established the Civic Education Section for disseminating a democratic way of civilian life. The section concluded that a new civic life should be based upon the spirit of the Imperial Rescript on Education, regardless of past unfortunate misinterpretation.[11]

The Japanese government's struggle to secure "the correct interpretation" amounted to twentieth-century political alchemy, because regardless of correct or incorrect interpretations by the government, the Japanese people had experienced the reality of minimal civil liberties, and realized that nothing was about to change. From now on, the Japanese government took different stances toward GHQ and the Japanese people. To the Americans it insisted that the real responsibility for the war rested with the militarists and ultranationalists who had misconstrued everything for their own selfish motives. The real imperial rule, which suited the Japanese, was a parliamentary democracy. But to the Japanese people, who had amply experienced the multiple layers of official lies, the government emphasized the urgent need for the people to vigilantly safeguard the Imperial Household. The favorite full-time exercise of leading Japanese politicians was to try to convince MacArthur and his subordinates that the Meiji Imperial Constitution was in fact a brilliant document on parliamentary democracy. The MacArthur regime did not believe their plea at all; and lack of American faith in the guilelessness of Japanese "misinterpretation" of the Meiji Constitution brought not only a shattering rejection of the Matsumoto draft constitution but the conservatives' lasting nightmare, the present new Constitution.

The Japanese leaders' chorus on the ageless virtues of the Imperial Rescript on Education made the American authorities suspicious of that document as well. CI & E began talking about what it should do. On July 10, 1946, Second Lieutenant Scott George, language officer, Education Division, discussed with W. K. Bunce, Religions Division, the question of the imperial rescript and portraits in the schools. George reported to Lieutenant Colonel Mark T. Orr, chief of the Education Division, that there was "no objection to the possession and display of an Imperial Portrait by a school," if it were treated "not as an object of religious veneration." Concurrently, the Japanese government announced that a new portrait was being prepared, a portrait that would show the Emperor in civilian clothes instead of the familiar military regalia. "New portraits," George said, "will be placed on walls of schools." He also informed Orr that the rescript was not "a suitable document to serve as the basis of the new Japanese education." But, George recommended, "a new imperial rescript on education" should be considered, because the Japanese would desire it.[12]

Bunce made harsher remarks than George: "The 1890 Imperial Rescript on Education is a Shinto-Confucianist document written for the purpose of keeping down 'radical' (i.e., democratic) tendencies." He denounced it as "the 'bible' of modern state Shinto." "From it," Bunce told Orr, "militarists and ultranationalists drew much of their ammunition." As MacArthur's Constitution had been debated in the Diet, Bunce inevitably compared the rescript with it: "By the most liberal interpretation, it is out of spirit with the new draft constitution. . . . It should not be read in the public schools or included in textbooks, except perhaps at the college level where it might be included as an historical document." Concerning the Imperial Portraits, Bunce suggested that the Ministry of of Education should prohibit "school-conducted bowing toward the portraits."[13]

Mark Orr, chief of the Education Division, asked some of his staff to review both George's and Bunce's memoranda. Arundel Del Re, an Italian civilian adviser, wrote to Orr that he agreed with both of them and strongly endorsed "the desirability of a new imperial rescript on education."[14] Ken Dyke, chief of CI & E, had hired Del Re in Tokyo on October 15, 1945, at the extraordinary monthly salary of 3200 yen (extraordinary when a university professor's monthly salary was 300 yen or so).[15] In contrast Edwin F. Wiggleworth, an education officer in Higher Education, wrote Orr that he believed a rescript of any kind to be "unnecessary." Worse, he could foresee "some harm" if a new one were issued.[16]

But while the American authorities were contemplating how to bury the 1890 Rescript on Education, Education Minister Tanaka Kotaro (in office from May 22, 1946 to January 31, 1947) tried to revive it. (Tanaka, after graduating from Tokyo University in 1915, studied in England, France, Germany, and Italy. While in Europe he converted to Roman Catholicism and remained a devoted Christian thereafter.[17]) On June 14, 1946, Tanaka spoke to the nation's prefectural governors: "Recently the people's morals have greatly deteriorated; they even question the content of the Imperial Rescript on Education. Indeed, there are hardly any Japanese who now pay as much respect to His Majesty the Emperor as foreigners do to their own heads of state."[18]

Minister Tanaka had been defending the ancient regime and the Emperor even before MacArthur landed in Japan. The US State Department initially thought of him, like his predecessor Maeda, as a liberal. But a few excerpts from his public statements show that he belonged to a unified ideological front of Japanese conservatives. In his article entitled "Nippon kunshusei no goriteki kiso" (Rational foundations of Japanese monarchy), written in March 1945 but revised after the surrender, Tanaka said: "The Emperor rules our Japanese Empire. This is the historical fact, since the very origin of the nation. It also remains the unchangeable principle of the future. The Japanese people believe in this with their flesh and blood." "But," he lamented, "we cannot expect foreigners to understand this. They need theoretical explanation." The "foreigners" were the occupying Americans. If the Japanese failed to sell them on the mythical significance of Japanese *kokutai,* Tanaka feared that "they would suspect it as the ideological foundation of ethnocentric and militaristic nationalism. That would invite a grave consequence."[19] Accordingly, he ventured on the difficult task of making the dogma of *kokutai* simple.

The Ministry of Education had already spent decades on writing up a definitive study, *Kokutai no hongi* (The cardinal principles of *kokutai*); it had been completed in 1937, about forty days prior to the Japanese invasion of China. Even that book was not a satisfactory explanation, but the broadest conceptual gaps were usually bridged by leaps of faith. Tanaka proved no exception, maintaining that Japanese history offered sufficient reason for the existence of *kokutai.* Neither the Meiji Restoration of 1868, he argued, nor the "termination" of the recent war could have been accomplished "without the Emperors' thundering proclamations." Only these proclamations could have freed the Japanese people from "an eternal shifting between anarchism at one extreme and dictatorship at the other." Therefore, he confidently concluded, "as long as Japanese nationality exists, our special *kokutai* remains as the absolutely necessary pillar for the nation's political stability and healthy development."[20]

Realizing that GHQ had not formally abolished the 1890 Rescript on Education, Tanaka said in the Diet on July 15, 1946, that the nation should abide by it. The spirit of the rescript, he said, had to be put into practice, and other materials such as Japanese classics and the Bible should be utilized extensively to form the basis of a new educational system for Japan.[21] His choice of time and place for this statement was dramatic: an address to the Draft Constitution Committee of the House of Representatives, which was ready to accept MacArthur's Constitution. The Constitution advanced popular sovereignty, while the rescript defended imperial sovereignty. Tanaka, fully understanding the basic contradiction between the two sovereignties, still insisted on the imperial rescript.

Tanaka's speech appeared to challenge the indecisiveness of American authority. In fact, it generated quite a commotion in the Education

Division, CI & E, GHQ. Bunce, after reading Tanaka's remarks in the *Nippon Times,* wrote to Mark T. Orr. "It is my opinion," he said, "that the Rescript on Education positively ought not to be permitted in the schools." Bunce could not see "any connection" between Tanaka's advocacy of the Japanese classics and "the degradation of morals now being witnessed in Japan." Positively angry, Bunce asserted that Tanaka's reference "is to the old hocus-pocus about the 'Imperial Way'."[22]

Tanaka on the Defensive

On August 6, 1946, Eileen Donovan, women's education officer, wrote Chief Orr a lengthy and articulate memorandum on the question of the rescript. Her memorandum, which Orr circulated among all staff of the Education Division, decided the rescript's fate. It crystalized the American attitude toward all remnants of the Japanese Empire and indicated a tougher American approach to the Japanese Ministry of Education. "All over Japan today there is confusion," Donovan wrote, "both in the minds of the Japanese and in the minds of Military Government officers," concerning the proper handling of the rescript. She acknowledged that the issue was "one of paramount importance, demanding immediate priority, inasmuch as a delay of nine months in promulgating our policy in the matter [had] already resulted in an awkward situation [Mr. Tanaka's remarks]."[23] "The origin of this rescript," she assessed correctly, was the "reaction against the fear of overwesternization."

> The rescript has been, more than any other element, the catalytic agent accelerating those reactions which together have produced the anachronism, the survival of archaic paternalism based on primitive superstition, which was the prewar Japanese state.
> These one hundred thirty Chinese characters were the Magna Charta of Japanese national ideology which inspired the acts and theories of militarists and ultranationalists.[24]

Concerning loyalty and filial piety, two primary virtues stressed in the rescript, Donovan objected that they were "not loyalty and filial piety as Western minds understand them, but a feudal concept, the blind unreasoning loyalty of the 47 ronin, the loyalty which condones every other sin," while the filial piety was "the cult of the Emperor worship which has made a religion of patriotism." To the rescript's proclamation that these virtues were "the source of Our education," she retorted: "What kind of philosophy of education is this? What room is there for an inquiring mind here?"[25] The more obvious danger, however, lay in the direct statement, "guard and maintain the prosperity of Our Imperial Throne *coeval with heaven and earth*," since it indicated that "the chief end of moral conduct should lie in desire for prosperity of the Throne."[26] There can be no doubt," she bluntly concluded, "it [the rescript] is completely and utterly in opposition to the 'rights of man' spirit of the new Constitution."[27]

Twice she consulted Thomas L. Blakemore, a legal expert for POLAD, who told her that the rescript was not a law in the strict sense; rather it was the Emperor's personal proclamation and "therefore [would] not automatically go out with the new Constitution."[28] This implied that the rescript had to be formally banned by SCAP.

Donovan suggested to Orr that the Emperor issue a new rescript on education. Education Division already had the draft, which it called the "Kyoto Rescript," sent by Commander Schieffelin to Ken Dyke in December 1945. Donovan believed it to be "an excellent document" that merited "our thoughtful consideration."[29] The best course, however, would have been no rescript at all. "If we had abolished the Rescript nine months ago," she lamented, no need for a new one would exist, "*but* now Mr. Tanaka's face could be saved by the issuance of a new one."[30] His endorsement of the old rescript, she urged, should above all be prevented from being considered SCAP policy because "this [would] cause trouble for CIE both sooner and later, sooner in the minds of the Japanese and the Allied personnel here, and later in the writings of the news commentators and historians who critically analyze the occupation policies."[31] Officers of Education Division read her memorandum and made brief comments: "Old rescript should be abolished at once and nothing substituted. What do we care of [sic] Tanaka's 'face' particularly in the light of his recent remarks to Diet, press and over radio"; and, "I agree 100%. If we don't settle this important matter, and fast, it will certainly be embarrassing, and maybe worse."[32] Meanwhile Joseph Trainor conceded separately in a memorandum to Orr that Minister Tanaka's strong defense of the rescript had a point, "since we have done nothing to put it out of force." It was, he added, "an emotional document—beyond the meaning of the words." Perhaps because of this Trainor recommended that "the rescript *should* be out of the schools."[33] Del Re, who had taught English at Taihoku High School in Japanese-occupied Formosa (Taiwan) from 1936 to 1943, urged Orr immediately to order the vice-minister of education to draft a death sentence for the Imperial Rescript on Education and Imperial Portraits in the schools.[34]

In September 1946 the vice-minister of education did indeed submit to Orr a draft in Japanese and clumsy English.[35] Del Re believed it "somewhat weak and ambiguous in the English translation." He and his colleagues rewrote it completely, not only for the sake of clarity but also to prevent the "not infrequent possibility of this instruction being watered down at prefectural and local levels."[36] On October 8, 1946, the vice-minister, through the press, issued a directive to prefectural governors and heads of all schools: "You should refrain from considering the Imperial Rescript on Education as the sole source for educational philosophy in our country." He encouraged them to synthesize "ancient and modern, oriental and occidental ethics, philosophy, religion, etc." Most importantly, "respectful reading of the Imperial Rescript on Education should be discontinued hereafter." "Copies of Imperial rescripts and instructions are to be kept at schools," he said, but those concerned were "not to deify them in reading them and in [their] custody of them."[37] The announcement must have pained Tanaka severely, for two months later he resigned from the Ministry of Education to become a member of the Diet.

The switch from education to politics was easy for him. Tanaka believed that "education is politics." It was, he said "common sense" that "only a thin paper" should separate education and politics, and that educational philosophy should be "identical" with political philosophy, so that a theorist "should find no contradiction or inconsistency between the two." But he insisted that educators must remain "neutral and vigilant," because "a national government always tries to impose its political ideology upon education." As the worst examples he cited Communist Russia, Nazi Germany, Fascist Italy, and ultranationalist Japan.[38] Tanaka had said this when he was director of school education, controlling the nation's primary and secondary schools. Prime Minister Yoshida, a most political man during the US Occupation, recognized that Tanaka consistently used education to advance his belief in the Emperor's sovereignty, and rewarded him with the highest public post in the field of education. As education minister Tanaka vigorously defended the Imperial Rescript, a policy that had roots in his personal life. He had married a daughter of wealthy Matsumoto Joji, who was the cabinet-appointed chairman of the Constitution Problem Investigation Committee. In early 1946 this committee came up with a draft constitution that still codified imperial sovereignty and retained Japanese armed forces. Yoshida, then foreign minister, admired the Matsumoto draft. MacArthur was furious. It was the hope of Japanese conservatives that imperial sovereignty could perhaps be salvaged in the area of education. Education Minister Tanaka carried the burden of this gamble.

Tanaka's plight attracted some sympathy. The report, already referred to, by the two retired Education Ministry officials called him "a scholar and a good professor," but added that he "miserably lacks ability as a politician, just as it was entirely against our expectation when he was pushed upon a lime-light stage [*sic*] by his powerful millionaire father-in-law, a former minister without portfolio Joji Matsumoto."[39] Thus it was truly ironic that Education Minister Tanaka, by defending the rescript with a touch of desperation, aroused such acute suspicion in GHQ that the rescript was doomed. To ensure its demise, Government Section stepped in and forced both the House of Representatives and the House of Councillors to issue separate resolutions on June 19, 1948.[40]

THE NEW EDUCATION COUNCIL

But Prime Minister Yoshida did not give up so easily. This true conservative wanted to revive the spirit of the rescript in a different form, because he believed that the nation's morals were rapidly deteriorating. On May 7, 1949, he established an Education Council (Bunkyo Shingikai) within his cabinet. Nugent was shocked by Yoshida's move, for nobody had told him about this council in advance. He called in Education Minister Takase on June 8. The top-secret conversation that followed clearly conveys Nugent's anger and Takase's humiliation.

NUGENT: I was dumbfounded to hear about the new Education Council not from you but from the newspaper reports. If the council has been doing the Ministry of Education's work, it means that the close relationship between the CI & E and the ministry has broken down. If the prime minister is doing your work, then he took education in his own hands.

TAKASE: The prime minister believes that the only remedy for the moral degradation of the Japanese people is through education. That is why he established the council.

NUGENT: But why did he ignore the Japan Education Reform Council? [This council, a think tank for the cabinet, was an outgrowth of the Committee of Japanese Educators that had worked with the US Education Mission to Japan in March 1946.]

TAKASE: This new council is different, because it is not a public body. The prime minister formed it as his personal advisory board exclusively on the morality question.

NUGENT: If the prime minister wanted advice it is you who should have advised him, not an outsider. Within GHQ I advise General MacArthur on education. If the general were to appoint a group of people in addition to me, I would be very embarrassed.

TAKASE: I understand very well what you mean. But I am one of the council's members.

NUGENT: The press reported that the council is contemplating a draft of a new proclamation on education as a replacement for the Imperial Rescript on Education.

TAKASE: I do not know about it. I think the chief cabinet secretary, when interviewed, said that only as his personal opinion.

NUGENT: If the council is planning to issue a new proclamation on education without consulting you, I consider it a grave matter.

TAKASE: Since the Imperial Rescript has been abolished, I should think the prime minister urgently wants to have a new document on the nation's morality.

NUGENT: What I am deeply concerned about is the relationship among the CI & E, the Ministry of Education, and this council. If the Prime Minister had consulted you, you would have informed me. But I received no information from you.

TAKASE: The council has never met yet. I do not think that any decision has been made on drafting the new proclamation on education.

NUGENT: If so, shouldn't the prime minister correct the newspaper report, which is to the contrary?

TAKASE: If a correction were necessary, the chief cabinet secretary should do so.

NUGENT: According to the press, however, the first task of the council is to issue a Yoshida Rescript on Education. GHQ is gravely concerned as well as very annoyed. First of all, the council was reported to us as a fait accompli. Second, there are already the Ministry of Education, the Japan Education Reform Council, and education committees in the Diet. What else could the new council be doing? Third, Japan's important newspapers are all against the new proclamation and consider it a political move. Ever since the beginning of the Occupation, GHQ has been making every effort to avoid confusing politics and education.

TAKASE: The prime minister did establish the council at the May 7 cabinet meeting. I apologize for not consulting you earlier because of the time factor.

NUGENT: To tell you the truth, already on May 3 I acquired a list of the council members. [He did not say how he acquired it.] We spent an entire week on screening them. I personally believe that the nation's education is handled well by the Ministry of Education and the Japan Education Reform Council. Frankly speaking, I do not have any interest in the council's reason for existence or its worth.[41]

THE END OF THE RESCRIPT

A new rescript on education was never issued. It was a wise decision on GHQ's part. The new one would have caused an uproar among Japanese liberals and radicals, and unless the Americans had dared to write it themselves, as they had the Constitution, the Japanese government could not have agreed on its wording. The Fundamental Law of Education, promulgated on May 31, 1947, was the people's declaration on what, ideally, democratic education should be, and it eliminated the need for an imperial rescript on education.

Tanaka Kotaro became chief justice of the Japanese Supreme Court in 1950. Though starting as an inexperienced politician, Tanaka grew sophisticated and better at making politically expedient remarks. Soon after his appointment as chief justice he wrote to his friend in Philadelphia, Michael Francis Doyle, who was a member of the Permanent Court of International Arbitration at The Hague.

> Now I feel my grave responsibility to guard the sanctity of justice and law against any political influence. I hope I may contribute something constructive to the cause of world peace as well as to stability and harmony within my own country. I am convinced that the Christian conception of natural law, which is universal for human beings and which has remained unchangeable throughout all human history, is the surest way of protecting society from anarchy and moral corruption.[42]

Tanaka should have said this when he was an education minister. MacArthur might have considered him for prime minister.

8
Democracy
Now
or
Never

By the time the Occupation began in mid-August 1945 the food situation, already strained by a long war, was approaching disaster. For the Japanese, a bowl of sweet-potato mush was now a delicious feast. Scarce rice was too precious to eat. In the midst of devastated cities, where the only sign of recovery was an extortionist black market, students and teachers together struggled to make their hunger endurable. But the occupation authorities remained unsympathetic. The plight of Japan, MacArthur bluntly told the Japanese, was their own fault.

The frightened imperial Japanese government, eager to please MacArthur, declared publicly its willingness for democratic reforms. In future, it told the people, Japan must honor human rights and cherish democracy as the only way of life. The government's frequent and feverish publicity for liberty and equality astonished the hungry Japanese people, who had never heard such words before. They had been conditioned by the government's habitual equation of democracy and anarchy.

The Japanese government's publicity helped GHQ assess how much Japan's leaders knew about democracy. MacArthur's idealism, the Japanese quickly discovered, was not easily satisfied. Every statement issued by the government was subject to his revision. The government, swallowing his demands, then added more democratic terminology, while each side strove to outdo the other in democratic fervor. But such escalation of democracy—seen as reckless American reforms by Japanese leaders—was not what the government secretly wanted. The fate of imperial sovereignty appeared too precarious for the government to enjoy this festival of democracy. Its worst fears were realized in the new Constitution, which replaced imperial supremacy with popular sovereignty.

Although food, shelter, and clothing preoccupied the nation, the defeat of the undefeatable Japanese Empire had engendered among the people a deep distrust of the government and of any authority professing absolutism. Also, the chaos in the nation's once-efficient educational hierarchy encouraged the students to demand what they thought were their legitimate rights. Prewar slogans in favor of military heroism and nationalistic sacrifice vanished from Japanese daily life faster than American peace slogans replaced them. The Japanese government, though paying lip service to democracy, stood bewildered. But it tried to comply with MacArthur's orders. The government, through the Ministry of Education, released an avalanche of memoranda to Japanese teachers and students. So did MacArthur. Such paper democracy in the midst of a paper shortage had a bewildering effect on those for whom it was intended.

Education for Democracy

In his inaugural address of August 18, 1945, the first postwar education minister, Maeda Tamon, announced the creation of five new committees in the Ministry of Education. They would upgrade and expand scientific education, he said, because future educational policy would be based "on the advancement of scientific education."[1] One reason for such emphasis on scientific education was the two nuclear attacks, which had shattered Japanese morale, once considered invincible, and exposed the scientific gap between Japan and the United States. Japan's realization of its technological poverty in 1945 was reminiscent of the mid-nineteenth century, when Western gun boats threatened Tokugawa Japan. *Mainichi Shimbun* editorialized on September 7, 1945, that a nation with the atomic bomb would not need extensive conventional armament in the future.[2]

The preoccupation with science was prevalent throughout the Ministry of Education. According to the chief of the Bureau of Lower Elementary Education, in the girls' schools, while feminine virtues were to be encouraged, guidance was especially to be given in "how to conduct

daily life more scientifically."[3] The Ministry of Education swiftly implemented a nationwide promotion of scientific education for "the establishment of the civilized Japan."[4] As an incentive the Ministry gave special
scholarships to those students who studied science.[5] "The Education
Ministry is endeavoring," Minister Maeda emphasized in a press release
of September 11, 1945, "to wipe out militarism, foster culture and scientific thinking, promote moral sincerity and love of peace, and thereby
build up a new nation of culture and high moral standards and contribute
to the peace and progress of the world." He also informed the nation that
all textbooks would soon be "radically revised," and that physical training and sports would be reformed "to foster a spirit of fair play," although
students would be asked to continue their agricultural and war relief work.[6]
These remarks were designed to impress MacArthur and his staff.

On September 15, 1945, the Ministry of Education announced the
first comprehensive government policy on the future of Japanese education, *Shin Nippon kensetsu no kyoiku hoshin* (Educational plan for building a new Japan).[7] Maeda proudly declared it "my own."[8] It preceded not
only all SCAP directives on Japanese educational reform but also the
birth of CI & E. "The Ministry of Education," Maeda stated, "considers
it imperative that future education strive more than ever to secure and
perpetuate *kokutai* [national policy], to disregard militaristic thoughts
and practices, and to establish a peaceful nation." For the sake of these
distinctively Japanese ideals, he explained, textbooks had to be "fundamentally revised." Due to the circumstances, however, the ones currently
in use were to be continued with deletions. By the "circumstances" he
meant that no appropriate replacements were available. For scientific
education he wanted a policy that would be not merely pragmatic; science,
he urged, "should root its foundation in an eternal search for truth, in
purely scientific thoughts"—or in other words, be scientific. In more concrete terms this meant that "academic and scientific institutions should
administer and promote their research solely for the sake of a peaceful
Japan and world community." Given the nation's subsistence economy,
his idealistic notion of science amounted in the event to sheer impracticality.

Minister Maeda also expected much from "religion." He reasoned
that a new, morally sound Japan could be built by cultivating the people's
religious sense. More beneficially, "the vigorous religious activities of all
sects would reveal to the world Japan's religious sincerity." He failed
entirely to ask if the new ideology of democracy might contradict the old
ideology of the Japanese Empire. The Ministry of Education, which had
published *The Cardinal Principles of Kokutai* in May 1937 and *The Way
of the Subject* in July 1941, could not destroy its favorite mythology.

Although infused with such appealing words as "science," "non-

military," "peace," and "harmonious world community," Maeda's proclamation was the conservative Japanese government's shrewd attempt to
protect the doctrine of imperial supremacy. For this the government
deliberately glossed over the imperial regime's blatant abuse of civil liberties, memory of which was still fresh. Because of such past abuse, the
conservative Maeda feared that the Japanese people, disgusted with
authority, might abandon even the sacred imperial sovereignty. The Japanese conservatives expected their antimilitary and pro-democratic statements to blunt the American zeal for reform and minimize any imminent
national overhaul.

The Research and Analysis (R&A) Branch of the State Department
scrutinized Maeda's statement and concluded that Japanese policymakers
would probably "continue to consider that defense of the national polity
includes perpetuation of the philosophy of militant nationalism"—to the
general detriment of American policy. Although Maeda had explicitly
stated that militaristic terminology should be deleted from textbooks,
R&A dismissed his gesture as necessitating "only the use of other expressions to describe the same situation."[9] The difference between what
the Japanese government wished to keep and what the US government
demanded the Japanese abandon became all too apparent. This gap
stemmed from the Japanese reading of the Potsdam Declaration. In it
the United States encouraged "the revival and strengthening of democratic tendencies among the Japanese people." The Japanese government managed to read into this an acknowledgment that the United States,
the self-proclaimed champion of democratic ideals, recognized the existence of "democratic tendencies" under past imperial governance. The
Japanese government failed to grasp that democracy and imperial sovereignty, as the US government saw them, were total opposites.

The R & A Branch, therefore, wondered why the Ministry of Education had not yet come up with any proposal to "revise the courses in
Japanese ethics and history," the two subjects most responsible for inculcating militarism. To liberate Japanese education, R & A recommended
use of "external pressures" or the "force of combined student-faculty
demands." Otherwise, it foresaw no real change except an improvement
in scientific training.[10] R & A's was the first American critique; its tone
and thrust indicated the kind of educational policies being formulated
within GHQ.

CI & E REFORMS THE MINISTRY
OF EDUCATION
Unaware of the American policymakers' disappointment,
the Ministry of Education continued to instruct Japanese teachers and

students. On October 3, 1945, the Ministry of Education abolished military training, dismissed all military officers on the staff, disposed of arms and equipment for military training, and made plans to reeducate teachers. It also decided to abolish the traditional practice of having the education minister appoint the chief officers of various public bodies connected with the ministry (his approval, however, could still be asked).[11] The next day MacArthur dropped upon the Japanese government the Occupation's first political bombshell, the "Bill of Rights" directive, which toppled the Higashikuni cabinet. Suspecting that the Ministry of Education neither understood democracy nor was willing to digest it, CI & E called in Minister Maeda and his top aides on October 13 and told them what they were expected to do. The American expectations were typed on the official paper of the Japanese imperial government and headed "Concerning Change in Constitution of Ministry of Education." This CI & E memorandum should be introduced here briefly, as it was the precursor to MacArthur's first sweeping education directive.

CI & E uncompromisingly told Maeda that it was "of urgent necessity to take speedy and forceful measures in realizing every educational plan." The urgent necessity was reconstruction of Japan "into a new peaceful civilized country." "For that purpose," CI & E told him, "it has been decided to change completely the constitution of the Ministry of Education." The American changes numbered seven:

1. A new Bureau of School Education, to carry out reforms in elementary and secondary education.
2. A new Bureau of Textbooks, to rewrite textbooks.
3. A new Bureau of Social Education, to cultivate the moral sense of the Japanese people and to improve national culture.
4. Abolition of the old Bureau of Moral and School Education, which preached blind loyalty.
5. Abolition of the old Institute of Research in Racial Characteristics and the Seminary of Moral Training, because they perpetuated racism.
6. A new Institute of Educational Investigation, for reeducating teachers with "a strong conviction in democracy."
7. Division of the Ministry of Education into six bureaus, to further decentralization and democratization.[12]

The American proposals bitterly displeased Minister Maeda. He had just one month earlier announced his own voluntary changes, which he believed satisfied GHQ.[13] CI & E ignored his announcement because the Americans understood Maeda's covert intention: to keep imperial sovereignty alive. Maeda did not know exactly what to do with CI & E's informal suggestions, which demanded major changes in the center of power. The Ministry of Education, under his command, did make numerous minor changes, however—mostly to remove from the schools what little remained of militarism.

Apparently dissatisfied with the piecemeal Japanese attempts, MacArthur issued his first educational directive, "Administration of the Educational System of Japan," on October 22, 1945.[14] In it he ordered the Japanese government to revise the content of all educational instruction "in harmony with representative government, international peace, the dignity of the individual, and such fundamental human rights as the freedom of assembly, speech and religion." He did not forget the important psychological task of reminding the Japanese people of the total devastation brought on by the Pacific War. Students, teachers, and the public would be fully informed about "the part played by militaristic leaders, their active collaborators, and those who by passive acquiescence committed the nation to war with the inevitable result of defeat, distress and the present deplorable state of the Japanese people." He was of course eager to justify an imminent and extensive political and military purge. MacArthur pitted the Japanese people against the Japanese militarists, hoping the opposing sides in the conflict would line up as "democracy versus fascism." The Japanese people showed unbounded enthusiasm for democracy, as if the more fanatic they became in its behalf the less they would suffer the misery of defeat and the humiliation of the Occupation. They were well advised to do so, for MacArthur's denunciation of "passive acquiescence" included all remaining Japanese except the prewar political prisoners, who happened to be hard-core Communists.

INDIVIDUALITY AND GUILT

MacArthur's judgment was a harsh one, given the social realities of imperial Japan. Public and private political morality had long been practically identical and were encouraged to be so. Rhetorical, all-embracing slogans such as "The Emperor's Wish," "Loyalty," "Patriotism," "kokutai," and "the Japanese Soul" reinforced the symbiosis of sovereign and subjects. The more intangible a political shibboleth, the more symbolic and untarnished it could grow, and so the more unifying force it could exert. Ideally, each individual Japanese had his own assigned lot, and his performance had an intrinsic relation with others' performance. The stability and security of the empire depended upon the perpetuation of such an interdependent system, not upon selfish assertions supported by individual conscience. There was no individual conscience as such, unless it implied dangerous egoism at the expense of the collective welfare. But orderly competition—in scholarship or athletics, for example—was of course strongly encouraged for the sake of the empire's mental and physical welfare. Individual effort, no matter how trivial it might be, was regarded ultimately as a state concern. The identification of the individual with the state was one of the primary themes in education. This identity served as a powerful reinforcement for the doctrine of state supremacy. The state was the condition for individual excellence; its prosperity was its subjects' pride and its perpetual glory was the dream they were encouraged to share. What was good for the state was good for the individual. Crucially lacking was any serious debate on what the "glory" or "prosperity" of the state might mean. The imperial oligarchs, supported by zealous patriots, suppressed all dissidents with insidious thoroughness. Suppression culminated in an abnormal homogeneity that enabled Edwin O. Reischauer to justify MacArthur's sweeping purge because of the impossibility of separating, as he put it, "the sheep from the goats."

This condition of Japanese thought contrasted with the American belief in individuality—an individuality that was expected to metamorphose totalitarian Japan into a democratic Asian wonder boy. It was reasonable to assume, as the US government and MacArthur did, that as belief in individuality spread, imperial sovereignty would wither and popular democracy would eventually prosper. The American assumption was correct, and the Japanese government clearly knew this. That is why the Japanese government persistently resisted popular sovereignty in the new Constitution, while trying to salvage the Meiji Constitution and the Imperial Rescript on Education.

The Japanese leaders were more comfortable with the familiar tyranny of the oligarchic cliques than with the tyranny of the ignorant masses, which was what they imagined popular sovereignty to be. For those Japanese leaders whose faith lay in the inviolable supremacy of the Emperor, popular sovereignty based on individual conscience was rank anarchy, not merely one cost of losing the war.

MacArthur, however, kept returning to the theme of "war guilt," as if it were something that only the defeated could expiate. Was the "democratization" of Japan a penalty for losing the war? Japanese conservatives appeared to believe so. That was not a brilliant way to encourage peace, enlightenment, and democracy in a people who felt they had been already punished enough by their wartime sacrifices and postwar hunger. Hiroshima and Nagasaki prevented them from believing the victor was unquestionably right. MacArthur had no such doubts. To ensure that the Japanese understood the causes of the war and their defeat, GHQ-SCAP compiled a *History of the Pacific War* and distributed fifty thousand copies to elementary and middle schools.[15] He also encouraged students and teachers to "evaluate critically and intelligently the content of instruction" and to "engage in free and unrestricted discussion of issues involving political, civil, and religious liberties."

THE STUDENT MOVEMENT

The students quickly and energetically responded to MacArthur's call. In September 1945 students at Mito High School led the nation's first postwar strike, demanding the dismissal of their authoritarian principal. They appealed directly to the Ministry of Education, whose reputation depended upon its skill in maintaining law and order. The ministry swallowed their demand, thus ending the strike after thirty-seven days.[16] Even at the Peers' School, training camp for the hereditary class hierarchy, ten professors with support from progressive parents asked the president to resign. They said they would present the matter to the Ministry of Imperial Household for deliberation.[17] After these incidents the Ministry of Education urged the resignation of school principals and teachers who had supported militaristic doctrines. The latter understood the ministry's gesture to portend a mass educational purge. Their understanding was accurate.

While numerous strikes were in progress, university and high school students vocally demanded: (1) reinstatement of liberal teachers and resignation of promilitary and nationalistic ones; (2) resumption of instruction in the social sciences, which the imperial government had persecuted as harboring dangerous thoughts; (3) the establishment of autonomous student self-government; (4) equal educational opportunity for women.[18] These student demands reflected American propaganda for democracy. The Ministry of Education had no choice but to join the American campaign and unprecedentedly yield to various student requests. The ministry did so, however, with great reluctance. It was particularly upset by the students' vocal demand for a part in school administration.

The ministry's top officials tried to convince the students to behave more reverently toward authority. Tanaka, chief of the Bureau of School Education, in 1945 cautioned the students "not to misunderstand the true meaning of Freedom." "Schools are domestic societies tied by Love and Teaching," he explained. "The importance of the Code between Teachers and Pupils will always be the same regardless of time." His real message was one of obedience to the 1890 Imperial Rescript on Education, which he believed was a natural law containing in it the universal virtues of loyalty and filial piety. School troubles should be dealt with in "a domestic and self-governing manner"; schools that exposed their private problems to public gaze would always discredit themselves.[19] "Students should not participate in the administration of their schools," the ministry's officials candidly told reporters of *Tokyo Shimbun.* They even offered the classic imperial choice of "love it or leave it": "If they don't agree with the school's policy they should leave the school, which would be the honorable thing to do. They had the right to select the schools they wanted to enter and they should have studied the school's policy before enrolling."[20]

Such remarks revealed a highly selective memory. The ministry during the past seventy years had vigilantly exercised its talent for standardizing the administration of the nation's educational system. All schools ruled the students alike—efficiently at that. Thus when officials said that the students "had the right to select the schools they wanted to enter," the right they referred to amounted to supporting the status quo. The student strikes intensified.

Education Minister Maeda gave some ground while replying to a House of Peers member. School authorities, he said, could not be considered invariably right in all disputes with their students, and were "expected to reform where they are found in the wrong." Nevertheless, students were minors who had yet to learn to govern themselves, and for this reason the authorities were determined to deal firmly with them if they strayed from their proper functions.[21] "Their proper functions," as far as Minister Maeda was concerned, were to honor the Imperial Rescript on Education. The Ministry of Education underestimated the students' intelligence, which it had habitually inhibited by a series of oppressive measures. The following letter from a group of middle school students to *Asahi Shimbun* reflected the gap between the ministry's mentality and the students' attitude:

> We middle school boys have been educated thoroughly in militarism. . . . However, we are rapidly changing our views and becoming greatly interested in political affairs. We grew up through the periods of the Manchurian Incident, China Incident and World War II. Accordingly, we took it for granted that a state should make war. Now for the first time we see a nonwarring Japan . . . a miserably defeated Japan. The reality is quite contrary to all that we have formerly been taught. . . . Please give us enough time. Please do not throw us out of school with fine diplomas, but without the fundamental knowledge we should have acquired.[22]

The students' letter appeared in December 1945. The same month President Nambara Shigeru of Tokyo Imperial University warned against the interest that students were taking in politics. "It is not desirable," he said, "that the student participate in university administration because of its difference in character from other enterprises in general." Reform of the educational system, he nonetheless argued, should be carried out "in accord with public opinion."[23] Nambara was, however, to oppose the establishment of a board of trustees, which the CI & E suggested as a transmitter of public opinion. Another letter to the editor of *Tokyo Shimbun*, however, supported the students' role in school reforms. "Those who cannot criticize the school's operation," the letter read, "will not be able to criticize government policies or social problems after they graduate from school."[24]

Anticipating what was soon to become the general intellectual orientation of student groups, the newly established Social Science Student Association of Kyoto Imperial University announced that capitalism in Japan was being analyzed.[25] The Japanese Communist Party, now basking in the prestige of its long martyrdom, found the emerging student movement a congenial one. Takeda Takeshi, a prominent Communist leader, became actively involved in student affairs.[26] The Communist Party, however, created embarrassment for itself when it kept denying any connection with the Soviet Union. The denial was understandable, because the Japanese people held an acute enmity toward the Soviets. Also, the Japanese Communists wanted to avoid provoking MacArthur, who had given them unprecedented legal freedom. Students observing the Communists' dilemma tended to lose respect for them; the Communists, they thought, should have openly avowed their support for the Soviets instead of denying it in order to curry favor with the Americans.[27]

The possibility of Communist Party affiliation with the increasingly leftist students' organizations did not alarm an American observer in December 1945.[28] On the contrary, the Research and Analysis Branch of the State Department made an unusually optimistic, if not accurate, assessment of the student strikes then in vogue: "Given the genuine encouragement of liberalism in the universities which appears probable under Maeda and Tanaka, university students may again make a positive contribution in the struggle to restore academic freedom in Japan."[29] Both Maeda and Tanaka were, of course, prominent conservatives.

RETURN OF THE LIBERALS

MacArthur in his first education directive ordered Maeda to carry out a thorough screening of all personnel of all educational institutions to remove career military staff, active exponents of nationalism, and "those actively antagonistic to the policies of the Occupation." He also ordered the immediate reinstatement of teachers who had been dismissed for their liberal or antimilitary opinions. Solemn language was used to impress upon the Japanese people the seriousness of his directive: without exception, "all officials and subordinates of the Japanese Government affected by the terms of this directive, and all teachers and school officials, both public and private," would be punished if they failed to comply.

Minister Maeda invited back the university professors who had been forced to resign for their "dangerous thoughts." He told them, as if to give official sanction to the new order, that "free discussion of the theory of the Emperor as an organ of the state would no longer be considered a violation of national polity."[30] He instructed presidents of universities, colleges, and high schools to reinstate "liberal teachers."[31] On November 24, 1945, the Ministry of Education published the names of 140 new heads of higher and professional schools.[32] They were supposed to represent the new liberalism in education. "University professors are delighted with their new academic freedom. Most of them are bursting to talk of many things long prohibited," John K. Emmerson reported.[33] The resignation of Waseda University's president triggered a vigorous power struggle between senior and junior faculty members over the right selection procedure for a new president. At Kyoto Imperial University the entire Department of Economics tendered its resignation. The department, which was strongly nationalistic, had been involved in one of the most notorious academic freedom cases in modern Japanese history. Hatoyama Ichiro, minister of education in 1933, had eagerly persecuted the liberal professors as dangerous. In 1946, when he was about to become prime minister, MacArthur accordingly declared him a dangerous war criminal suspect.[34] (Especially in the early period of the Occupation, MacArthur and his staff categorized those few Japanese who had opposed the Japanese military regime and the Pacific War as "the liberals." Their true political persuasion did not matter. For instance, the Research and Analysis Branch of the State Department called Education Ministers Maeda and Tanaka "liberal forces." Leftists and Communists, the most ferocious attackers of Japanese militarism, also were "liberals.")

Education Minister Maeda tried hard to propagate democracy. On November 2, 1945, at a conference of prefectural governors, he unveiled proposals for reforming Japanese education. He did not say that GHQ had imposed them. But, more important to him than the reforms per se, was what he called "the present deplorable state of moral degeneration," which he believed stemmed from the people's disregard of the Imperial Rescript on Education. "I should like to promote morality," he told the governors, "by attaching great importance to moral education and encouraging the cultivation of religious sentiment."[35]

EDUCATION PURGE

The cultivation of religious sentiment also appealed to MacArthur. Before cultivation, however, weeds had to be uprooted. He ordered the Japanese government to punish any official of a Christian university who had committed "inexcusable subversion of such institutions to militaristic and ultranationalistic ends." The president and his cohorts at Rikkyo Gakuin (presently Rikkyo University) in Tokyo were named for immediate dismissal. MacArthur listed eighty-two institutions for investigation and called his order dated October 24, 1945, "Violation of Religious Freedom."³⁶ While Christianity was being salvaged, MacArthur purged Japan's most ancient indigenous religion from the schools. On December 15, 1945, he ordered: "The dissemination of Shinto doctrines in any form and by any means in any educational institution supported wholly or in part by public funds is prohibited and will cease immediately." He also prohibited all public schools from conducting any visit to Shinto shrines and any rites, practices, or ceremonies associated with Shinto.

MacArthur also banned the Ministry of Education's two ideological mainstays, *The Cardinal Principles of Kokutai* and *The Way of the Subject,* together with "all similar official volumes." Prior to this ban, Education Minister Maeda had ordered destruction of the remaining stock of *The Way of the Subject.* He called its existence "inconvenient." He was promptly assailed by *Asahi Shimbun* in an editorial of December 4, 1945: "*The Way of the Subject* is not a piece of paper. More importantly the minister should say what he has against this book's ideological basis. Thought cannot be dismissed by the destruction of books. One thought should be conquered only by another."³⁷ But Maeda did not have another thought. And he did not order destruction of *The Cardinal Principles of Kokutai,* because he believed in the supremacy of imperial sovereignty and the ethnocentric purity of the Japanese nation.

Tanaka, director of the Bureau of School Education, accurately expressed the ministry's limited interpretation of MacArthur's abolition of Shinto when he said that Japanese school children and students would no longer be told to regard the Emperor as divine, but that it would be "all right to regard the Emperor as the object of reverence as a Sovereign Ruler."³⁸ Later the Ministry of Education instructed the prefectural governors that the prohibition on shrine worship did not include the Imperial Palace.³⁹ Pupils and teachers could still line up neatly and bow deeply in the palace's direction. This deliberate flouting of basic democratic principles, however, only accelerated the severity of American reform. To Japanese leaders the future appeared increasingly bleak.

Sensing American impatience with the Japanese government, the Ministry of Education, in an announcement of January 17, 1946, ventured to encourage students and teachers to actively participate in the body politic. Practically no restrictions on their activities were imposed. The ministry only requested them not to let politics interfere with their normal duties and not to canvass for political parties during school hours.⁴⁰ While the Ministry of Education was parroting MacArthur's democratic terminology, MacArthur himself was planning a mass dismissal of every militaristic and nationalistic teacher he could find. On October 23, 1945, one day after MacArthur's first education directive, Lieutenant Robert King Hall of the Education Division, CI & E, was assigned to draft an appropriate directive on screening teachers. On October 29 Hall submitted his sixth and final draft to Brigadier General Ken Dyke, who then secured MacArthur's approval.⁴¹ And on October 30 MacArthur issued an order to the Japanese government entitled "Investigation, Screening, and Certification of Teachers and Education Officials."⁴² With this order MacArthur intended to eliminate "militaristic and ultranationalistic influences" from the Japanese educational system and to debar from teaching those teachers and officials "having military experience or affiliation." To this end he ordered a precise statement on acceptable teachers. The Ministry of Education responded immediately and two days later delivered the first draft of a plan of implementation. It was rejected on November 6 as insufficiently representative of Japanese society, lacking precise standards, and failing to establish enough committees for thorough screening.⁴³

To make sure the Ministry of Education did understand MacArthur's directive, Education Minister Maeda was called in on November 17 for a meeting with Dyke, Hall, and Lieutenant Colonel H. G. Henderson. They presented him with the following points.

1. "When the plan is complete a trial run will be made on a small prefecture near Tokyo."
2. "The plan must have many more committees"—in villages, counties, and prefectures.
3. "The local village committees should report on every teacher not merely the ones they consider ineligible."
4. "The local committee should only recommend, not actually dismiss the teacher. The county should take action, and the prefecture should review the cases. The national committee should act as a court of appeals."
5. "Each of the universities and *semmon gakko* [professional schools] should have its own committee and its findings should be reported to and reviewed by the national committee."
6. "Publicity should be given to all phases of this screening [so that the parents will realize that] their children will get the best of education." Publicity

should also be given dismissed teachers, to encourage other undesirables to resign voluntarily.

7. "The plan should include a definite set of precise standards, not a mere rewording of the general policies laid down by the Allied Powers."[44]

Two weeks after this meeting, on November 30, the Ministry of Education submitted a revised draft to Hall. He still did not like it. During December 1945 the Ministry of Education officials and Hall frequently conferred to write a precise statement to CI & E's satisfaction. It was not easy. At last, on May 7, 1946, the Ministry of Education came up with a statement. It resembled very closely MacArthur's directive of January 3, 1946, against Japanese war criminals. The Ministry of Education first condemned the visible evils of the past such as any persons who advocated "militarism, ultranationalism, despotism and totalitarianism." Second, the ministry purged those who "opposed the policies of the Allied occupation forces." The prohibition of criticism of the occupation policies was consistent with the ongoing prepublication censorship of the mass media. The ministry also decided to purge the personnel who, since the Manchurian Incident of 1931, had participated in "intelligence propaganda service, or thought guidance" through their works, essays, or lectures.[45] The Manchurian Incident was specified because the US government believed the Japanese invasion of China, not Pearl Harbor, was the beginning of the Pacific War.

The Ministry of Education, as CI & E suggested, set up the hierarchy of committees to discover the potential undesirables.[46] Before actual screening began, however, a total of 115,778 teachers and educational officials resigned.[47] The initial screening was completed by the beginning of the new school year on April 1, 1947. The screening continued, however. After passage of the Board of Education Law in 1948, all candidates for board membership were screened. By the end of April 1949 the Ministry of Education reported to GHQ that a total of 942,459 persons had been screened and 3,151 had been declared unacceptable.[48] One should perhaps admire the ministry's tenacity or rather the American insistence on separating the 3,151 goats from nearly a million sheep.

CHRISTIANITY TRANSPLANTED
Since Christianity had been declared officially superior to Shinto, was it perhaps advisable to mass-produce Christian teachers? President Nambara of Tokyo Imperial University apparently thought so. On February 11, 1946, anniversary of the nation's traditional foundation day, he delivered to the students a lengthy address entitled (by the official translators) "Creation of New Japanese Civilization." "One must

realize," he said, "how impossible it is to reach the real wakening of the individual as a human being simply by cultivating human nature." This real awakening was possible, he continued, through "discovery of God" and "the subjection of self through its discovery." Japan urgently needed "a religious Reformation," because emancipation from the nationalistic Japanese theology could be accomplished "only by another religion."[49] To confirm the weakness of the Japanese indigenous religion, Nambara pointed to the defeat in the war. His new civilization demanded a "revolution of the Japanese spirit itself." This revolution should not stop at being merely a change in the political and social systems; it should be, in addition, "a subjective spiritual revolution, intellectual and religious in nature."[50] To the student audience he declared that they were "the chosen champions for that campaign." There was, he assured them, "no more significant and appropriate mission than this for those pure and sincere souls who are impassioned lovers of truth."[51]

The president of the nation's most influential university was advocating Christianity. "Dr. Nambara has recently proposed the establishment at Tokyo Imperial University of a chair in Christianity," confirmed Max W. Bishop to Secretary of State Byrnes. Bishop informed him that Nambara's speech had been "praised privately by leaders of the American Education Mission now in Japan as a courageous, enlightened, and forward-looking statement."[52] Nambara became chairman of the Committee of Japanese Educators who worked with the US Education Mission during March 1946. Despite a critical national paper shortage his speech was published as a booklet for wider circulation.

MacArthur, now a saintly figure in the eyes of the Japanese Christians, continued to spread the gospel. Christianity was what he called "the advanced spirituality of the world." It is within such a political context that Nambara's proposal should be understood. Bishop worked hard to make the proposal a reality. "Establishment of such a chair," he told Secretary Byrnes, "the first of its kind in a Japanese government university (where chairs of Shintoism and Buddhism have already existed), will be important in establishing freedom of religion in Japanese public institutions."[53] The project, he added, had been "the earnest prayer and hope of all Japanese Christians"; it would result in the education of "many fine Christian students" at Tokyo Imperial University and would thereby "contribute much to the promotion of international peace."[54] However, when the chairs of Shintoism and Buddhism had been summarily eliminated from all public universities, it was reasonable to expect that, in order to avoid the appearance of conferring an official sanction, neither GHQ nor the Ministry of Education would advocate chairs of any religion. Nambara must have been aware of this complication, as he told the Office of the US Political Adviser that "the projected chair is not intended to replace a former one in Shintoism"; indeed, "the proposal was made quite independently."[55] This statement, while it may not throw his sincerity into question, surely reveals his political naiveté.

The sticky question of how to finance the chair in Christianity rose immediately within the Japanese government. Nambara was in favor of private endowment, Bishop told Byrnes, "not only because of the favorable time element, but also because the chair would thereby be free from governmental entanglement."[56] Although Tokyo Imperial University and the Ministry of Education insisted that "the chair or professorship of Shintoism should be abolished" and "its fund should be given to [the] university," the Ministry of Finance refused. Angry, Bishop complained that the ministry was indirectly "sabotaging . . . 'freedom of religion' in the key university of Japan."[57] But, as informants inside the Ministry of Finance told Bishop, what the ministry actually said was that since the chair in Shintoism "was created by the support of right-wing influence . . . it should be abolished and the fund should be returned to the government"—without being used by the university for any other purpose. Bishop nonetheless concluded that the Finance Ministry had ruined a fine opportunity to encourage religious freedom.[58]

Concomitantly, the idea of establishing a university of Christianity began circulating among foreign missionaries and the Japanese faithful. Ralph E. Diffendorf, a prominent Methodist missionary, became president of a Japan International Christian University Foundation, headquartered in New York.[59] Even the Ministry of Education appeared unusually enthusiastic about Christianity. After an International Christian University Research Institute was formed in late 1947, the Ministry of Education sent Hidaka Daishiro, chief of the Bureau of School Education, to deliver a greeting. "There is nothing comparable to Christian culture," he declared, "that can better grow true roots and enable them to develop into never-fading blossoms of civilization in our future peaceful Japan." In order for Japan to avoid past errors and set a good future example, he continued, the Japanese would have to cultivate "Christian love," which he defined as "a universal love of mankind consecrated by the love of God."[60] He became the vice-minister of education in 1951, and retired from the ministry in 1952 to teach as a professor at the International Christian University.

Joseph C. Grew, former ambassador to Japan (1932–1941), assumed the position of American national chairman to raise funds for the International Christian University.[61] When Grew was requested by *Contemporary Japan* to write an open letter to the Japanese people for its 1949 Christmas issue, he chose to write on the university and asked his friend

W. Walton Butterworth, assistant secretary of state, to review a draft.[62] In it Grew quoted a remark of Fleet Admiral C. W. Nimitz: "I know of no better way in which to bring to the Japanese people the enlightenment on spiritual and moral values and education as we know it than through the offices of International Christian University. These are requisites in leading the Japanese toward the desired goal of a free and democratic form of government."[63] Butterworth liked Grew's message to the Japanese people.[64]

Fund raising went well: the Japan International Christian University Foundation informed Dean Acheson, secretary of state, that more than $1.5 million had been pledged as of June 1949.[65] MacArthur became honorary chairman of the fund-raising committee.[66] He gave the project his enthusiastic support.[67] And Grew came to Japan in October 1950 to further promote International Christian University. This university now exists in Mitaka, near Tokyo.

Textbook Revision

Both the Japanese imperial government and MacArthur were well aware of the urgent need to revise national textbooks. The Japanese government wanted to carry out this important task unilaterally. The wish was understandable, because Japanese pupils literally memorize textbooks. The government wanted this familiar relic of the imperial past to remain unchanged.

On September 22, 1945, when the Occupation had barely begun, the Ministry of Education announced that Japanese textbooks had to defend and promote the mythic imperial polity (*kokutai*), "high moral education," "culture and agricultural production," "the scientific spirit and its concrete application," and "physical education and hygiene."[68] On October 3 the ministry ordered teachers and school officials to delete undesirable militaristic words and references from the textbooks. On October 13 CI & E explicitly told Education Minister Maeda to establish a new Bureau of Textbooks to expedite textbook revision. Two days later, Maeda announced that the bureau existed. Minister Maeda hoped with a touch of confidence that GHQ would be delighted with the voluntary Japanese deletion of militarism from all teaching and learning materials. But GHQ was already planning a major overhaul of Japanese education. On September 30, 1945, only one week after CI & E had been formed, Lieutenant Robert King Hall of the Education Division was assigned to survey the textbooks in morals (*shushin*). Japanese history and geography were quickly added for scrutiny. Intensely alarmed by an initial cursory look, CI & E speeded up its critical investigation.[69]

The Office of the US Political Adviser, too, began collecting opinions from Japanese scholars. George Atcheson reported to Secretary of State Byrnes the results of conversations with prominent Japanese historians whom GHQ considered "progressive." They were very eager, Atcheson wrote, "to correct the nationalistic interpretation of history" and "to publish material which will accurately explain Japan's social and political development." They were also hoping to make contact with their US counterparts and "to get access to books and research material."[70] These historians pointedly named "reactionary professors" in the universities and said that very few law professors were truly liberal in their political views.[71] The Matsumoto committee, which had just then been established with the generous assistance of Japan's leading legal scholars, eventually confirmed the historians' assertion.

RECALL AND REVIEW
In his first directive on education MacArthur promised that "new curricula, textbooks, teaching manuals, and instructional materials designed to produce an educated, peaceful, and responsible citizenry [would] be prepared and [would] be substituted for existing materials as rapidly as possible." On November 10 Hall orally instructed the chief of the new Bureau of Textbooks, Arimitsu Jiro, to stop the printing presses.[72] Hall wanted to examine line by line every textbook of morals, Japanese history, and georgraphy. On November 23 he ordered the Ministry of Education to translate all textbooks on these three subjects. Japanese Nisei translators would recheck the ministry's translation.[73] To gather more information Hall conferred extensively with Arimitsu, eminent professors in education such as Kaigo Tokiomi, and teaching faculty of large private universities in Tokyo. He even acquired the lecture notes of some professors whom GHQ suspected of being undesirable.

During early December 1945 various staff reports were completed and more CI & E meetings followed. A consensus in the CI & E policy recommendations emerged. On December 13, 1945, Ken Dyke reported the six recommendations to MacArthur.

1. All the textbooks in morals, Japanese history and geography—textbooks, it was emphasized, that had been compiled by the Ministry of Education— had proved, after the page-by-page survey, "to be most pernicious." They totaled 50 out of 173 nationally prescribed textbooks. They also occupied a substantial percentage of a student's time at each educational level. The approximate figures were, respectively: elementary school, 20 percent; secondary school, 14 percent; continuation school, 10 percent; higher school (college prep), 17 percent; and normal school, 15 percent. It was therefore

recommended that these three subjects "should be suspended immediately." Subjects such as "Principles of a Democratic Society," "New World Peace Structure," "Economic Reform," and "Position of Women in a Democratic Society"—all prepared by CI & E—were to take their place.[74] Dyke informed MacArthur that the Ministry of Education and CI & E were also preparing "stopgap textbooks" for the beginning of the new Japanese school year on April 1, 1946.

2. CI & E had translated the Ministry of Education's ordinances regarding these three dangerous subjects. They too had proved totally undesirable and should be suspended immediately.

3. The Ministry of Education should be ordered to collect all textbooks of those subjects throughout the nation for pulping, and to submit a full report on its handling of the matter. This nationwide textbook retrieval should not be limited to schools; it would also have to include "private homes and institutions," even though it might assume "the nature of 'witch-hunting.'"

4. The Ministry of Education should be ordered to submit to GHQ a detailed plan for revising the textbooks to be used from April 1, 1946, on. The plan must include, for instance, names of writers and selection of suitable subject matters.

5. While appropriate textbooks were being prepared, the Ministry of Education would have to submit to GHQ a substitute program for those suspended courses. The program was to "have for its objective the presentation of the fundamental truths about the world in which the Japanese students are living."[75]

6. Since there was no nationally prescribed, standard curriculum for Japanese universities, Dyke suggested, banning specific textbooks was "not a solution to the problem." Pernicious teachings, he added, might be continued under any other course title. Rather than merely banning books, screening of teachers in accordance with the directive of October 30, 1945, "should be applied with full force to universities."[76]

Because of Hall's order to stop printing textbooks, an acute textbook shortage had ensued. Representatives from the Japan Middle School Principals' League pleaded with CI & E for a quick remedy. The vice-minister of education also wrote to CI & E that the situation was desperate.[77] But CI & E took the situation to be inevitable and continued to review every textbook. The Ministry of Education, busy translating into English not only every existing textbook but also all manuscripts for revised textbooks, tried to maneuver itself out of such a formidable workload. CI & E was intensely annoyed by the ministry's subtle but unmistakable delaying tactics. On December 19, 1945, CI & E called in two Ministry of Education officials, Sekiguchi Isao, chief of the Bureau of Social Education, and Teranaka Sakuo of the Civic Education Section. This meeting was held because the Ministry of Education had without CI & E's approval compiled and printed various pamphlets on how to vote democratically for the coming election on April 10, 1946. This was the important election that would decide the fate of MacArthur's new

Japanese Constitution. The following excerpts from their exchange show that CI & E was determined to see every piece of paper coming out of the Ministry of Education.

NUGENT [chief of the Education Division]:   Who chose the writers for the pamphlets?

SEKIGUCHI: Mr. Teranaka and I chose them. . . .

NUGENT: Did Minister Maeda tell you the pamphlets could be printed and distributed without submitting English translations to us for approval?

SEKIGUCHI: No, he did not. These copies are galley proofs. The pamphlets have not been printed in final form.

NUGENT: Do you intend to submit English translations before going any further with this project?

SEKIGUCHI: Is complete translation necessary? Would a synopsis be sufficient?

NUGENT: Aren't you aware that all documents published by the Ministry and distributed to the schools must be approved first?

SEKIGUCHI: It is my error. We did submit our general plan.

NUGENT: To whom?

SEKIGUCHI: To the Education Division through the General Affairs Bureau of the Ministry of Education.

NUGENT: When?

SEKIGUCHI: A week to ten days ago.

NUGENT: In English?

SEKIGUCHI: Both in English and in Japanese. . . .

NUGENT: Why do all writers favor retention of the Emperor System?

SEKIGUCHI: . . . It is only coincidental that they all supported the Emperor System. . . .

NUGENT: Who chose the final articles for publication? On what basis?

SEKIGUCHI: The pamphlets do not contain articles representing the leftist viewpoint. The articles were chosen to cultivate political judgment. . . .

NUGENT: Did you study all of the articles carefully?

SEKIGUCHI: No.

NUGENT: We must have complete English translations of all the pamphlets. No copies whatsoever must be printed or distributed until they have been approved by us.

SEKIGUCHI: We will do as requested. We will submit English translations as far as they can be made, one by one.[78]

Immediately after this meeting, Teranaka pleaded with Nugent that the Ministry of Education be permitted to distribute the pamphlets as originally planned with the objectionable pages removed. Nugent denied his request. In the afternoon of the same day Teranaka came back to see Nugent and apologized that the Ministry of Education had not submitted the plan to the Education Division, although earlier he and Sekiguchi said they had.[79] This conference, however, did not stop the ministry's procrastination. MacArthur took it as Japanese insubordination, and on January 17, 1946, he formally ordered the Japanese government to submit to GHQ all textbooks and teaching manuals in English.[80]

THE TEXTBOOK SHORTAGE

On December 31, 1945, one day prior to the Emperor's abrogation of his divinity, MacArthur issued a directive entitled "Suspension of Courses in Morals (*Shushin*), Japanese History, and Geography." He ordered the Japanese government (1) to immediately suspend all these courses until GHQ permitted their reinstatement, (2) to issue no instructions of any kind on the subjects, (3) to collect all textbooks and teachers' manuals for paper recycling, and (4) to submit to GHQ in English the substitute programs for the courses, as well as a comprehensive plan for thorough revision of the textbooks.[81] These were exactly Dyke's recommendations.

On January 19, 1946, the Ministry of Education orally instructed textbook publishing companies to ship all textbooks remaining in stock to the paper mills. On January 23 the ministry again instructed them, this time by letter, and again on January 30, by telegram. The publishing companies were told that they had to bear the entire financial loss.[82] As the Ministry of Education had originally given the paper mills all the collected textbooks free, the mills stood to make an enormous profit in the middle of a desperate national paper shortage, CI & E objected, insisting that some rebate should be returned, not to the publishers, but to the schools that had collected the texts. The amount of the rebate was substantial, 15 million yen. The alert and anxious CI & E also questioned one item of 500,000 yen for bookkeeping cost. The Ministry of Education agreed to add some of it to the rebate fund.[83]

The public schools, from the elementary level through the teachers' colleges, made use of 425 textbooks. By early 1946, according to an internal CI & E memorandum, 155 national textbooks had "been surveyed, page by page, with deletions marked and recorded."[84] School officials and teachers, too, began to delete passages describing the glories of the past Empire. "Such deletions," CI & E said, "were made by inking out, cutting, pasting pages together and similar devices."[85] Scissors and soft-brush pens had to be used so extensively that reprinting, as CI & E quickly conceded, became "impractical."[86] The American leniency in the way the textbook deletions were handled marked a clear contrast with American policy toward the mass media. Newspapers, magazines, and radio broadcasts bore no trace of how deletions had been made. Textbook censorship was less stringent because otherwise, the American censors said, "it would have left the schools entirely without textbooks."[87]

Actually, it did leave the schools entirely without textbooks. Production of what were commonly called "stopgap textbooks" was close to a disaster. Allocation of printing paper during the 1946–47 school year was only one-quarter of actual needs, and only 40 percent of the allocation was delivered.[88] This pitiful situation forced Education Minister Maeda to declare in the House of Representatives in December 1946 that the students would learn Japanese history without textbooks.[89] The Japanese government reallocated to textbook production some of the precious printing paper earmarked for newspapers. "Without this help from the newspapers," CI & E acknowledged, "virtually no textbooks could have been ready for the pupils by the beginning of the 1947–48 school year."[90] The paper shortage was so serious that CI & E itself had to write its numerous intra- and interoffice memoranda on scrap paper.

To cope with the textbook shortage the Ministry of Education, which had jealously monopolized textbook publishing since the nineteenth century, even permitted privately published books to be used in the middle schools. Also, the ministry promoted extensive use of circulating movie pictures, slides, and radio broadcasts for disseminating the new ideology of democracy. The use of the mass media was CI & E's pet idea. For instance, "The Education Hour," a daily program on Radio Tokyo, began on October 22, 1945, the same day MacArthur issued his first education reform directive. The program was halted four days later because a Japanese commentator's speech on textbooks was "inappropriate."[91] CI & E allowed it to resume on November 12, 1945, "with precensored lectures."[92]

The Japanese Cabinet, eager to convince MacArthur of Japanese compliance, decided on November 28, 1945, to punish Arimitsu Jiro for neglect of his duties. The "neglect" was as follows. In November 1945 Lieutenant Hall told the Textbooks Bureau chief that all Japanese textbooks had to be translated into English and be censored by the Education Division. But he was careless and let six textbooks be published uncensored.[93] His punishment was a reduction of 10 percent in his salary for one month. The humiliation alone was punishment enough, but CI & E considered 10 percent too small a reduction and on April 17, 1946, requested the cabinet to reconsider. The cabinet obliged and on May 25 reduced his salary still further—by 10 percent for six months.[94] Ironically, Hall had appeared to be more tolerant of Japanese mistakes than this punishment would imply. In an internal memorandum of November 7, 1945, he stated: "The long period of isolation from democratic procedures and Western knowledge has made it inevitable that all officials, however willing, will fail through ignorance unless given technical assistance. This method of guidance maintains their effectiveness by avoiding their public humiliation."[95]

CI & E was very serious about censoring every textbook in the land

and not eager to be taken lightly by the Japanese. American sensitivity about Japanese violations was apparent when early in 1946 GHQ's routine opening of Japanese mail caught "an anonymous letter from a girl in Nagano City ... to another girl in Tokyo, informing her of the use of banned textbooks in her school."[96] GHQ immediately dispatched a Japanese staff to investigate this offense. According to the staff report, the case turned out to be "nothing."[97] In general, the Japanese people were encouraged to believe that even a minor violation of American orders, if it was caught, would invite an unpleasant consequence. The Ministry of Education sent out some top bureaucrats to various corners of the archipelago to make sure that school teachers and officials obeyed American directives.[98] The CI & E officials, too, made numerous and extensive inspection tours throughout Japan.[99]

NEW TEXTBOOKS FOR OLD

While the old textbooks were censored, MacArthur ordered the Japanese government to begin drafting new ones. By July 1946, according to CI & E, "some 446 textbooks in revised manuscript" had been cleared for publication.[100] Geography textbooks were not difficult to compile. The Japanese government requested and MacArthur granted permission to reopen courses in geography on June 29, 1946.[101] But writing Japanese history was troublesome, even though CI & E told the Ministry of Education that "the histories should be an honest story of the Japanese people." Nobody particularly wanted to lie, but CI & E volunteered to define "historical honesty."[102] The Ministry of Education submitted to GHQ the names of historians for drafting new history textbooks. GHQ thoroughly investigated them prior to formal assignment in May 1946.[103] Three history textbooks were to be prepared, for the elementary and secondary schools and the teachers' colleges, respectively.

At least two CI & E employees combed the manuscripts in English translation, one with a black pencil and the other with a red pen. A few samples of this American editing will suffice. In the manuscript for the teachers' colleges the Japanese author (Takeuchi Rizo) described Japan's natural elements: "The rain brought about by summer monsoon invigorates the growth of plants, the mountains and hills are covered with woods, the plains are fit for paddy fields and are also for hunting and farming." So far, so good. From the sentence immediately following, however, a censor deleted these words: "and the scenic beauty of nature, everchanging agreeably according to the season; these are favourably combined to make life exceedingly comfortable." The phrase "patriotic spirit" was deleted by the red pen and changed by the black pencil to "thinking about the country," while "the chronicle of Emperors" was changed to "the legends of Emperors." One famous crown prince (Shotoku, A.D. 573–621) sent an ambassador to China with a special message that originated the designation of Japan as "the land of the rising sun." The message read: "The ruler of the land where the sun rises begs to write to the ruler of the land where the sun sets to inquire after his health." The American censor deleted this historical fact without a comment. Dictator Toyotomi Hideyoshi united war-torn Japan in 1591—another historical event that every Japanese recognized as part of his heritage. The American censor deleted it completely.[104] Clearly, the Americans did not like comments or assertions about the Emperors or Japan in general that sounded too positive. After this kind of editing, CI & E could confidently conclude that "emotional treatment did not appear in any form."[105]

In September 1946 the Ministry of Education was permitted to publish the first new Japanese history textbook, *Kuni no ayumi* (The footsteps of the nation). On October 12, 1946, MacArthur permitted the Japanese government to resume Japanese history courses, provided that Japanese schools used "only those textbooks prepared by the Ministry of Education and approved by General Headquarters, Supreme Commander for the Allied Powers."[106]

Although in March 1946 the US Education Mission had strongly recommended against using the Ministry of Education for textbook compilation, GHQ continued to use it for that purpose. No doubt the Americans sincerely wanted Japan to have local autonomy at some time in the future, but the exigencies of the present seemed to encourage centralized autocracy. Unfortunately for the growth of local autonomy, these exigencies never disappeared. CI & E was well aware of this danger when it reported that the present system of textbook publishing and printing was in fact "a private monopoly system subsidized and sanctioned by the Ministry of Education." However, "the urgency of other projects" required that any remedy for the monopoly be postponed.[107] At the same time the CI & E wondered how Japanese teachers liked their new history and geography. Six hundred questionnaires were sent out to them by the Ministry of Education. The replies, a remarkable 520 of them, were mailed back to the CI & E.[108] The teachers said they liked the new textbooks.

Concurrently with the textbook revision, on November 10, 1945, Hall also ordered Arimitsu to begin preparing a teacher's manual.[109] The manual must be prepared, Hall said, in terms of "Japan's responsibility for war" and "the unique position of teachers in reeducating Japan."[110]

The completed manual did in fact provide a representative sample of American expectations for Japanese teachers. Issued by the Ministry of Education on November 9, 1946, it bore the peremptory title *Guiding*

Principles for Instruction in Japanese History. "In teaching history," ran the GHQ-approved text, "materials which propagate militarism, ultranationalism, and State Shinto shall be excluded, as well as antiforeign ideas." Without mention of these ideals that had meant so much to Japan, the teaching of Japanese history required a unique definition of history. And in fact a definition was provided. "Stress should be put on concrete aspects of the development of national life from social, economic and cultural viewpoints rather than on the history of peace and war and the vicissitudes of powers and struggles for political power." This almost meant that Japan ought to forget virtually its entire modern period, between 1868 and 1945, during which the Japanese Empire was either at war or in preparation for it. A nationalist perspective was also taboo. "Looking at history with dogmas and prejudices should be avoided, and historical facts showing international friendship, interdependence, and exchange of civilization for mutual benefit should be cited from the viewpoint of world history. Thus, a contribution shall be made to the peace of the world and the development of world civilization."[111] Japan was encouraged to think of joining the United Nations in New York. Indeed, on January 20, 1947, before the new education was launched nationwide, Mark T. Orr, chief of the Education Division, said to the press: "Emphasis is placed on an objective study of international relations and the machinery of the United Nations."[112]

The memorandum war between the Ministry of Education and CI & E–SCAP astonished Japanese teachers and students. When Karl C. Leebrick, assigned to the Office of the US Political Adviser, informed George Atcheson of the school officials' request for "more instructions and assistance from their own or from occupation authorities," he accurately depicted the psychology of a group caught unprepared by sudden change. Education Minister Abe (in office from January 13, 1946, through May 22, 1946), succeeding Maeda, diagnosed the type of confusion from which the nation was suffering. On January 15, 1946, when interviewed by *Mainichi Shimbun,* he said that the word "democracy" was on everybody's lips but its meaning seemed to be misunderstood. "The Government," he concluded, "must lead the nation towards democracy by establishing a relationship between the protection of the state system [*kokutai*, that is] and democracy, the Emperor System."[114]

Under these circumstances it is easy to see why school administrators and teachers were, as Leebrick wrote, "hesitant to act on their own initiative for fear of later rebuke or punishment."[115] Their fear bore witness to the success of the deliberate imperial policy of the previous seventy years. Local autonomy was unheard of; reverence for central policy direction was made as unshakable and unquestionable as reverence for imperial supremacy. Indeed, "local leadership" in the context of traditional Japanese government sounded like a contradiction in terms. Local autonomy was, GHQ said, "another notable omission" among the various constitutional drafts that Japanese interest groups submitted. But the Ministry of Education sincerely believed that its publicity for democracy and eagerness for compliance would please the Americans. "The cooperation of the Japanese Ministry of Education and of school authorities is on the surface complete," Leebrick reported to Atcheson.[116]

What was the intention of SCAP's numerous uncompromising directives? It was, as SCAP acknowledged, "political education." Ideological reeducation was "inevitably bound up" with "governmental and political reforms."[117] That is why MacArthur's first and most important business during the Occupation was to write a new constitution for Japan. After pushing this new constitution at maximum speed past the Japanese ultraconservatives, MacArthur had to teach the Japanese people how to use it in their daily lives—"to insure," in the words of the official directive, "the permanence of the democratic structure . . . on the solid foundation of an informed citizenry."[118] In support of this principle he became a passionate teacher. "An awakened people," the directive continued, "conscious of their sovereignty and fully aware of their privileges and responsibilities as members of a democratic state represent the only real insurance against the possibility of eventual perversion by aggressive and unscrupulous extremists of the objectives achieved during the Occupation."[119] MacArthur truly worried about "the possibility of eventual perversion." Recall that the new Constitution contained several concepts shocking to the Japanese tradition of governance—most radically, popular sovereignty over and above imperial sovereignty.

MacArthur's intense campaign for generating popular support for the new Constitution revealed the urgency he felt in the face of Japanese political apathy—an apathy reinforced by the people's maddening preoccupation with rice. His campaign themes clearly illustrated this:

a) To help change the present cynical, and therefore, passive attitude toward government to one of more positive participation. . . .
b) To help develop in the Japanese people an acute awareness of their rights as well as their responsibilities under the new Constitution.
c) To assist in eliminating age-old concepts of law and order as engendered by a totalitarian type of government.
d) To assist the Japanese people in recognizing the fallacies behind opportunistic promises and nondemocratic ideologies and the benefits of living in a free, democratic state.[120]

Numerous pamphlets such as *How to Hold a Civic Gathering* were published.[121] MacArthur gladly encouraged many civic organizations to participate in his "Democracy Now or Never" propaganda. All mass media were mobilized by CI & E to promote democracy to the Japanese people.[122] CI & E sponsored conferences on democracy throughout Japan.

The Ministry of Education with American urging joined in the Occupation's biggest campaign. In August 1947 the ministry published *The Story of the New Constitution.* Initially for use in seventh-grade social studies, it proved so popular that it was soon distributed to all the grades of the junior high schools. CI & E proudly declared that about seven million copies of it had been printed—a Japanese publishing record.[123] But CI & E discovered, to its dismay, that "most school people refuse to regard the teaching of politics as a legitimate school responsibility." "A combination of lethargy and fear" still prevailed among them even as late as November 1947. CI & E was also discouraged by "the belief of many Japanese that their democratic responsibilities, if any, ended with voting."[124] "The only solution to the mess," Howard Bell urged Orr, "is to develop *habits* of 'political' participation through the formative years"; the Americans had to "accept the responsibility of cultivating political literacy."[125] CI & E told the Ministry of Education that "political education will receive major attention."[126]

"Political education" in the schools was called "civic education" and was taught in social science courses. The new social science inculcated the virtues of peace and pacifism; it spoke of aggression as evil and displayed unbounded faith in rational discourse. Such an attitude would contribute, as both Japanese and Americans agreed, to the solution of any future international disputes. Also, a scientific attitude was seen as a peaceful attitude. A renewed fascination with science pervaded Japanese school curricula. This "new science" (new because completely objective) made Japanese mythology, folklore, and even a sense of historical continuity into something shameful and tainted with defeat.

While Japan was groping for new guiding principles of education, MacArthur, too, wanted someone to tell him that he was right. In March 1946 the United States Education Mission arrived in Tokyo.

9
The United States Education Mission to Japan

On March 8, 1978, in New York, I asked George Stoddard, chairman of the 1946 US Education Mission to Japan, "Who wrote the mission's report?" "Mostly I did," he replied.[1] On November 21, 1977, I had asked the same question of Ernest R. Hilgard, another member of the mission and then a professor of educational psychology at Stanford University. "George Stoddard, I, and one other person whose name I cannot recall right now, wrote it," he answered. "What did the other twenty-four mission members do, then?" I asked. "Well, some did extensive sightseeing, and some others went out a lot at night. Mr. Stoddard was kind of an authoritarian chairman. I don't mean it pejoratively. But he tended to decide things first and then ask the mission members for consent."[2]

MacArthur praised the *Report of the United States Education Mission to Japan* as "a document of ideals high in the democratic tradition." "In origin," he added, "these ideals are universal. Likewise universal are the ends envisaged by the mission."[3] But one American critic was not impressed. Veteran educator and publicist Carroll Atkinson, then a columnist for the *Honolulu Star-Bulletin,* wondered about the members' qualifications. "With beautiful thoughts for the most part and here and there a down-to-earth observation," he wrote, "it is just about what one would expect to come from a group of traditional educators making a brief tour of the country." He continued: "Few, if any, of these committee members knew a thing about the Japanese and their previous educational backgrounds and practices, except what possibly they may have read—and as yet there is not very much literature on the subject."[4]

Isaac L. Kandel, a mission member from Teachers College, Columbia University, countered in the same journal by citing MacArthur's praise in full. "The Mission," he retorted, "was not invited by General MacArthur to impose American or any other educational theories on the Japanese, but to help the Japanese to reconstruct their own educational system."[5] He had a point. "We do not come in the spirit of conquerors," the mission had declared, "but as experienced educators who believe that there is an unmeasured potential for freedom and for individual and social growth for every human being."[6] Nevertheless, the mission's faith in the capacity of American education to mold Japan remained impressively unshaken throughout their three-week stay in March 1946.

Origins of the Education Mission

The State Department's press release on February 18, 1946, stated that the US Education Mission had been created because MacArthur requested it.[7] The idea of a mission, however, had been well expressed in a private letter that A. B. Chapman, a soldier, wrote from Japan to his friend Senator John L. McClellan (D., Arkansas), who was on the Committee on Naval Affairs. It was dated October 16, 1945.

Chapman wrote that many Japanese educators were "anxious to reform the educational system and the way of living in Japan." They admitted, he said, that the Japanese educational system was "totally void of freedom of thought, progress, initiative and individual volition." Because of their paralyzing fear of the imperial government, however, they did not want "to commit themselves to changes and have us move out and leave them to the mercies and unmercifulness of the same Japanese government." Chapman himself believed that the Japanese educational system was "the very heart of the evils which caused the suffering and bloodshed during the past four years in the Pacific Area"; it would, he added, "undoubtedly be an arsenal for the thriving of those evils in the future." He therefore suggested that "a committee of educators from amongst the colleges and high schools in the United States be appointed along with a congressman and a senator to come over to Japan and talk with the Japanese educators and Japanese people." He urged that this committee "make a study of the needs and possible remedies of Japanese education and return to the United States and make recommendations to Congress and the president for action." The committee should be formed immediately, he said, "because soon the people will become complacent with a situation embodying an army of occupation and the old Japanese regime, in part, and a change will be more difficult and less effective."[8]

On October 31, 1945, Senator McClellan sent a copy of Chapman's letter to Secretary of State Byrnes, saying that "I sincerely believe something should be done about it."[9] Both Chapman's and McClellan's letters were circulated among the State Department's Division of Economic Security Controls, Division of Cultural Cooperation, and Division of Japanese Affairs. Concurrently, in Tokyo, MacArthur was getting ready to request the US government to send an education mission. Robert King Hall said on November 7, 1945, "A request for an Educational Mission of American leaders in education is being initiated through channels."[10]

Perhaps it was mere coincidence that Chapman's plea for an education mission occurred practically at the same time as MacArthur's. In any case, on January 4, 1946, MacArthur sent a telegram to the War Department in Washington: "Rehabilitation of Japanese educational system given high priority in occupation operations. Estimated 18 million students, 400,000 teachers, 40,000 schools represent major medium for influencing Japanese life throughout, and action in accomplishing occupation mission." The Ministry of Education was trying hard to please MacArthur, but the Japanese educators were "technically unqualified to plan and initiate complete reforms." Hence, he requested an education mission from the States to study four major areas: (1) "education for democracy in Japan," (2) "psychology in the reeducation of Japan," (3) "administrative reorganization of the educational system of Japan," and (4) "higher education in the rehabilitation of Japan." MacArthur also listed the names of twenty-six potential mission members.[11]

After receiving MacArthur's formal request Acting Secretary of War Kenneth C. Royall wrote to Secretary of State Byrnes that the reform of Japanese education did indeed seem to be State's job and that the mission should be undertaken immediately. In deference to MacArthur's devotion to Christianity, Royall suggested to Byrnes that "Catholic and other sectarian advisors who are not considered in the cable be given weight in the formation of the mission."[12] Dean Acheson, acting secretary of state, replied to Royall that he would be glad to undertake such responsibilities.[13] Acheson, however, was worried about the diplomatic wisdom of the US State Department assuming the exclusive responsibility of sending an American education mission. What would the USSR and Britain, the two nations that most resented the American monopoly of the occupation of Japan, say about another all-American mission? Acheson consulted John C. Vincent of the Division of Far Eastern Affairs. Vincent replied to William Benton, assistant secretary of state, that he saw no objection to the department assuming the responsibility. "As a matter of fact," he told Benton, "I feel, that in the Japan theater, it would be advisable that we do so." The possible reaction of the Far Eastern Commission did not perturb him, since the commission was "free at any time to draw up policy papers with regard to reorientation and education in Japan and General MacArthur would be guided thereby."[14] Vincent then expressed the prevailing attitude of the US government toward the Far Eastern Commission: "MacArthur wants expert advice as to how he should proceed now. It might take the Far Eastern Commission many months to agree on policy and in the meantime MacArthur cannot be inactive."[15]

Assistant Secretary Benton assumed the task of forming the US Education Mission. After consulting with MacArthur and the War Department, the State Department named as chairman of the mission George D. Stoddard, who was then state commissioner of education for New York and president-elect of the University of Illinois.[16] Benton knew Stoddard well: he was one of the five members of the US delegation to the London conference for establishing the United Nations Educational, Scientific, and Cultural Organization (UNESCO), and Benton headed the delegation. They liked each other.[17]

For historical interest I list the names of all the members of the mission and their occupations at the time of appointment:

Wilson M. Compton, president, Washington State College
George W. Diemer, president, Central Missouri State Teacher's College
Frank N. Freeman, dean, School of Education, University of California
Virginia Gildersleeve, dean, Barnard College
Willard E. Givens, executive secretary, National Education Association
Mildred MacAfee Horton, president, Wellesley College
Lieutenant Colonel T. V. Smith, professor of philosophy, University of Chicago
David H. Stevens, Division of Humanities, Rockefeller Foundation
Alexander J. Stoddard, superintendent of schools, Philadelphia
William C. Trow, professor of educational psychology, University of Michigan

These members are the ones who were on MacArthur's list and who accepted the invitation. The State Department invited the following members "in order to complete the group":

Harold Benjamin, director, Division of International Education, Office of Education

Leon Carnovsky, associate dean, Graduate Library School, University of Chicago

George S. Counts, professor of education, Columbia University and a vice-president, American Federation of Teachers

Roy J. Deferrari, secretary-general, Catholic University

Kermit Eby, director of research and education, Congress of Industrial Organizations

Ernest R. Hilgard, head of Department of Psychology, Stanford University

Monsignor Frederick G. Hochwalt, National Catholic Education Association and chairman, Education Section, National Catholic Welfare Conference

Charles Iglehart, formerly professor, Union Theological Seminary and Methodist Episcopal missionary to Japan, adviser to CI & E, SCAP

Charles S. Johnson, professor of sociology, Fisk University

Isaac L. Kandel, professor of comparative education, Columbia University

Charles H. McCloy, professor of physical education, University of Iowa

E. B. Norton, state superintendent of education, Alabama

Pearl Wannamaker, state superintendent of public instruction, Washington

Emily Woodward, State Department of Education, Georgia[18]

The churchmen were included at Royall's suggestion, and also in deference to MacArthur's evangelistic zeal.

Concurrently with the selection of members, MacArthur on January 9, 1946, ordered the Japanese government to set up a Japanese counterpart, the so-called Committee of Japanese Educators, to work with the US Mission. He also suggested that this Japanese committee should continue after the US Mission left and that it study Japanese education and submit periodic recommendations to the cabinet, the Ministry of Education, and CI & E.[19] The Japanese government took his suggestion and the committee evolved into the Japan Education Reform Council, a government think tank.

The Mission at Work

In February 1946 the members of the US Mission met in Washington, DC, for preliminary conferences. The State Department handed out a large amount of background information about past and present Japan. Sir George Sansom, a leading Western authority on Japanese history, briefed the members. On the way to Japan the mission stopped at Honolulu and Guam for more briefings. The members arrived in Tokyo in two separate groups on March 5 and 6, 1946. On the morning of March 7 they received a briefing on public relations. Don Brown, CI & E's PR man, informed them that the Japanese were "extremely interested in this mission": "They want to know, he said, "what you think about Japan, what you think about the Japanese educational system, what you recommend be done with it." "Because of your unique position," Brown cautioned, "whatever you say is really to be taken as coming from the Commander." This careful attitude was necessary, said Brown, a newspaperman, because Japanese journalism had "all the worst aspects of American journalism plus bad aspects of its own." There was very little respect by newspapers for veracity or integrity, and Japanese reporters were "capable of doing very strange things with statements you make." One mission member, Compton, asked Brown, "The less we talk the better off we are?" "Yes," replied he. Another member, Horton, worried about even talking with the Committee of Japanese Educators assigned to cooperate with the mission: "Is it safe for us to speak freely in that group?" Brown responded, "Unless Colonel Nugent or the Education Division suggests otherwise, I would say that you have complete freedom there." He assured the mission that the Japanese committee members would "not be speaking freely to the Japanese press."[20]

CI & E had compiled a booklet, *Education in Japan*, to give the mission "the essential facts about the Japanese educational system" and about reforms in progress.[21] During the first two weeks the mission studied the booklet and listened to numerous lectures by the CI & E staff.[22] This routine was broken by occasional field trips to the picturesque ancient capitals of Kyoto and Nara, and by talks with the Committee of Japanese Educators which prepared its own statement for the US Education Mission.[23] The mission spent the third week writing its report.

The mission's style of operation was well conveyed in a CI & E memorandum to the Ministry of Education entitled "Tentative Schedule of US Education Mission." The accent was on leisure: "Formal meetings in morning only. PM reserved for field trips or committee meetings. Use Saturday and Sunday for travel. Japanese plan 3 evenings' entertainment per week, such as operas, symphonies, plays, exhibits, etc. (Monday through Friday only)."[24] Chairman Stoddard read the CI & E–prepared schedule for the mission. "I think I am speaking for the whole group in expressing our deep sense of appreciation," he thanked Colonel Nugent, "for all these physical, intellectual, and recreational preparations which have been made."[25] The Japanese government spared no expense; altogether, it spent 165,000 yen for the mission's stay in March 1946. Fifty thousand yen was for entertainment, and 50,300 yen for their domestic traveling expenses. The rest, 64,700 yen, went for the expense of

Japanese personnel and other necessities such as writing paper and pencils.[26] The total of 165,000 yen did not include the mission members' lodging.

On March 8, Education Minister Abe Yoshishige (in office from January 13 through May 22, 1946), succeeding Maeda, welcomed the US Mission. His speech of welcome sounded like a plea. "I would like to ask America," he begged, "not to deal with us simply from an American point of view." His apprehensions were realistic. "You must know that it was a great failure for Japan to have treated Korea and China in such a manner. America, as a victorious country, is in a position to do anything it pleases with Japan." A victorious people, he continued, always tended "either consciously or unconsciously" to impose its own culture, and there were "some young idealists among the Americans coming to our country who tend to use Japan as a kind of laboratory in a rash attempt to experiment in it on some abstract ideals of their own, ideals which have not been realized yet even in their own country."[27] MacArthur did in fact think of Japan as "the world's great laboratory for an experiment in the liberation of government from within."[28] It was brave of the Japanese education minister to caution the mission but futile for him to expect "some young idealists among the Americans" to behave differently from the supreme commander.

"Mr. Abe has given us a warm welcome," Stoddard diplomatically responded. "We have not come here to criticize; we have come to study and to learn." He went on to emphasize the basic tenets of the mission: "(1) We believe in the individual and civil rights of the Japanese people. (2) We believe that there is a tremendous potential for freedom and for individual and social growth in every child, youth and adult. (3) We shall look for what is good in the Japanese educational system." "In short," he said, "we are here to help in a process of social evolution."[29] Isaac L. Kandel was more blunt: "The mission did not need to be reminded but they welcomed the plea of the then minister of education."[30]

It should be remembered here that the new Constitution, just then being extensively publicized, and numerous other SCAP directives had already established the dominant political atmosphere and direction. The US Education Mission did not deviate from MacArthur's expectation. "I am glad," Wilson Compton wrote to MacArthur, "to have witnessed at first hand the evidence of the masterful way in which you, in behalf of the Allied Powers, are administering the difficult affairs of a difficult people in an extremely difficult time."[31] Emily Woodward, too, believed that "General MacArthur is doing a magnificent job in Japan and the Japanese seem devoted to him."[32]

In the remainder of this chapter I shall discuss the mission's report, *Education for Democracy in Japan*; with some related issues and developments.

The Virtues of Peace

"We believe," the mission said,

in the power of every race and every nation to create from its own cultural resources something good for itself and for the whole world. That is the liberal creed. We are not devoted to uniformity; as educators we are constantly alert to deviation, originality, and spontaneity. That is the spirit of democracy. We are not flattered by any superficial imitation of our own institutions. Believing in progress and social evolution, we welcome cultural variety all over the world as a source of hope and refreshment.[33]

The mission wished to clarify the two crucial terms, *"liberalism* and *democracy."*[34] "We should preach to Japan only in terms of our painfully hammered-out practice: it is the responsibility of all in authority to find out how much can be allowed rather than how much can be forbidden." "That," declared the mission, "is the meaning of liberalism." "Democracy is not a cult," it warned, "but a convenient means through which the emancipated energies of men may be allowed to display themselves in utmost variety."

The mission preached that democracy was best conceived "as the pervasive spirit of ever-present freedom."[35] Otherwise, "liberty carried to abnormal lengths [would] yield irresponsibility, anarchy and chaos."[36] "Duties," it emphasized, "keep rights from cancelling each other out. The test of equal treatment is the taproot of democracy, whether it be of rights to be shared or duties to be shouldered."[37] The mission continued to wax eloquent: "Education cannot proceed in a vacuum, nor is a complete break with a people's cultural past conceivable." Some continuity must exist, the mission believed, "even in a crisis such as the present."[38] To find continuity, or "to discover what is worth preserving as humane ideas and ideals," the mission thought it necessary that all educational officials in Japan analyze "their cultural traditions."[39] From such analysis, the mission promised, the new Japan would acquire "a legitimate and inspiring basis for loyalty and patriotism."[40] However, the mission warned that the Japanese search for a new identity should be carried out within "the consciousness of a worthy national culture, so as to avoid the dualism that comes from the constant addition of new elements."[41]

The mission nonetheless went on to follow MacArthur's lead and constantly add new elements. In trying to find "the consciousness of a worthy national culture," the Ministry of Education was pressed to the limit. Here a comment is in order on Japanese adaptability to foreign influences. Grafting of foreign ideas onto native stock has been the rule not the exception in Japanese history. Frequently the grafting has worked well: a successful synthesis of old and new has long formed part of the Japanese ideological climate. The ambiguity inherent in continually adopting one half of an idea and rejecting the other half is a Japanese norm that contrasts with the general American preference for an either/or choice. When the mission worried about "the dualism that comes from the constant addition of new elements," it was expressing its lack of faith in Japanese pluralism, if not its ignorance of Japanese patterns of cultural synthesis. The Japanese people's ability to adopt foreign elements pragmatically has freed them from the mental discomfort of what an American might perceive as inconsistency among these elements. Only when the imperial Japanese government tried to create a monolithic national culture did Japan succumb to intellectual bankruptcy. It was, of course, this monolithic culture that the mission meant to denounce when it declared: "The course in morals as taught in the Japanese schools of late years was aimed at an obedient citizenry."[42]

Japan needed new morals—democratic ones. The question was, how should Japanese teachers and students be expected to acquire them? The mission volunteered the answer: "Where teachers are well prepared, are independent minded, are loyal from love, and have few enough students per teacher to individualize instruction, ethical training tends to take care of itself, informing each pedagogical part with the spirit of the moral whole."[43] To the Japanese teachers who had to teach hopelessly crowded classes, this must have sounded either incomprehensible or depressing. The legal limits in elementary and secondary schools were respectively eighty and sixty students per class, but the limits were exceeded.[44]

Further light on democratic ethics was shed by the mission when it wrote: "Women must see that to be 'good' wives, they must be *good*; and to be 'wise' mothers, they must be *wise*."[45] Both virtues were essentially civic: "Goodness does not spring from narrowness, and wisdom is not a hothouse plant. It grows from wide social experience and from political practice."[46] What the mission wished to stress above all was that students "should be introduced to the heroes of civil life, so that the virtues of peace may become as personalized as the vices of war."[47] The mission could not close its eyes to "the pitiable economic status" of Japanese teachers, but failed to come up with any recommendations: "Economic factors are important but they are not supreme." In fact, they could probably be ignored entirely: "Nowhere can happiness be taken for granted; wealth does not assure it, lack of wealth does not prevent it."[48] For ordinary Japanese teachers and pupils, happiness at this stage was a full stomach.

On April 11, 1946, ten days after the mission departed, Education Minister Abe admitted in a directive to presidents of higher educational institutions and prefectural governors that the government could do little to alleviate current hardships. "It is, therefore, necessary," he reasoned, "that attempts be made by teachers to help themselves"—even to the point of starting self-help organizations. He did, however, caution them "not to be too radical, or to allow themselves to be taken advantage of by any political parties." Protecting the teachers, Abe even warned the presidents and governors "not to impose too many restrictions on such [self-help] groups."[49]

Concerning Japanese history and geography, the mission confirmed the on-going SCAP reforms, saying of Japan that "its recorded history has been consciously confused with mythology, and its geography protectively and even religiously self-centered."[50] To avoid recurrence of these faults, the mission recommended that responsibility for compiling textbooks in history and geography should be taken away from the Ministry of Education and given to specially established "councils of competent Japanese scholars" who would "develop authentic and objective sources for the rewriting of Japanese history."[51] The mission then passed to the usual remarks about world peace and the contribution that democratically educated Japanese could make to it.[52]

The Fundamental Law of Education

CI & E censored every Japanese manuscript to make sure not a trace of aggressiveness or nationalism reached Japanese pupils. But it could not resist the power, prestige, and organization of the Ministry of Education, which it expediently used for compiling all textbooks. To codify democracy and pacifism as part of Japanese education, CI & E suggested that the Ministry of Education draft a fundamental education law to replace the Imperial Rescript on Education, which CI & E had just abolished. Joseph Trainor from CI & E and Sekiguchi Isao from the Ministry of Education conferred frequently on this subject. Their first meeting took place on November 12, 1946. They discussed the future role of democratic principles in Japanese education and agreed that Sekiguchi would present the first draft of a new education law at the next meeting on November 18, which he did.[53] It was evident from the draft that Sekiguchi and the ministry had had a hard time understanding what the Americans meant by "coeducation." When Trainor questioned him, Sekiguchi tried to explain his idea of coeducation "over a period of an hour and a half," by "jumping from one to the other without much continuity."[54] He was told to come back on November 21.

He returned punctually with the ministry's second draft. "Mr. Sekiguchi again managed to produce a statement that avoided the use of the word democratic," Trainor complained to Orr and Nugent. Sekiguchi replied that "it was apparently an oversight," which Trainor thought was "a little horrifying." On equal opportunity of education Sekiguchi had written: "All people shall have equal opportunity to receive education correspondent to their ability and their aptitude as provided by law without discrimination because of race, creed, sex, social status or family origin." The phrase "as provided by law" was his shrewd way of altering the principle of coeducation and equality of educational opportunity later by enacting another law. Trainor denounced it as "a startling addition." Trainor told Sekiguchi this was worse than the first draft. Sekiguchi then replied that "he could not write a statement about coeducation in principle until he discussed it with the Minister of Education [Tanaka] and all the Bureau Chiefs." Trainor rejoined that it was he, Sekiguchi, who had been assigned the responsibility of drafting this document, so he should "sit down and write." The new deadline was November 29.[55]

On the appointment day Sekiguchi came back with the third draft. This time he brought with him two versions. The other version, not his, "would be understood," Sekiguchi said, "without any vagueness by all Japanese whereas his version would not be understandable to most Japanese people." But, he said, his version was written in "good Japanese." Trainor told him that the education law should be written clearly "so that people could understand what is meant." "Mr. Sekiguchi seemed completely startled by this concept but nonetheless somewhat intrigued," he reported to Orr and Nugent.[56] On December 2 another meeting took place between them. Sekiguchi and the Ministry of Education, realizing that they could no longer procrastinate or vacillate, presented a far more satisfactory draft. Both Trainor and Sekiguchi agreed that each would write a final draft in English and compare them at the next meeting on December 9, which they did. The final draft was submitted to the Education Division for comment.[57]

On March 31, 1947, the Fundamental Law of Education came into existence to reinforce the ideals embodied in the new Constitution, especially the ideal of representative democracy. "The realization of this ideal," declared the education law, "shall depend fundamentally upon the power of education." Primacy of individual dignity and conscience and the nation's permanent pacifism also became foci of the new educational philosophy. The law's most controversial article was not on coeducation, but on political education; it stated that "the political knowledge necessary for intelligent citizenship shall be valued in education" (article 8). Every word in this short sentence is pregnant with possibilities for ideological interpretation and counterinterpretation. Well aware of this, GHQ vigilantly supervised Japanese use of political knowledge and liberties in schools.

EMERGENCE OF TEACHERS' UNIONS

The Japan Teachers' Union was to make extensive use of article 8 in its drive to politicize the teaching profession. Politicization led to unionization. Both GHQ and the Ministry of Education, in fact, encouraged teachers to unionize.

Two major teachers' unions were emerging. The Nippon Kyoikusha Kumiai (Japan Educators' Union) had been established on December 2, 1945, by a well-known Christian, Kagawa Toyohiko. He was interested not only in the economic betterment of educational administrators but in the strong defense of the Emperor System. One day earlier, Hani Goro, "the social historian, writer, and leftist," as CI & E described him, had founded the Nippon Kyoin Kumiai (Japan Teachers' Union). This union wished to promote democracy and to demand a fivefold increase in pay. The two unions openly derided each other, the one as "reactionary" and the other as "Communist." But Hani's leftist Japan Teachers' Union began winning the favor of the nation's teachers.[58]

The teachers' economic crisis was so serious that Vice-Minister of Education Yamazaki Kyosuke told Nugent and Orr on June 25, 1946, that "this might become a mass movement creating great trouble and mass resignations by the teachers." The Ministry of Education wished to issue immediately a press release regarding a proposed increase in teachers' salaries. Nugent and Orr approved.[59] Both CI & E and the Ministry of Education wanted the teachers to be intellectually and politically alert. The Ministry of Education told them in its 1947 *A Tentative Suggested Course of Study:* "Standardization indeed baffles the purposes of education. Regimentation reduces teachers to mere dull machines. Hence, the importance and necessity of lively activities on the part of teachers."[60] Both CI & E and the Ministry of Education, however, remained on their guard as to the direction in which the teachers' unions were moving.[61]

Psychology in the Reeducation
of Japan

"From a deep sense of duty, and from it alone, we recommend a drastic reform of the Japanese written language."[62] Such was the US Mission's recommendation in the second area to which MacArthur had directed them. The recommendation was indeed a radical one. Even MacArthur was moved to remark that some of its ramifications could serve only "as guide for long-range study and future planning."[63]

THE MISSION'S PROPOSALS FOR
LANGUAGE REFORM

Although Chairman Stoddard told me that the mission's report was mostly his work, he was quick to add, "I did not write the language section. George Counts did."[64] Counts did not, however, initiate the mission's controversial ideas on language reform. To discover the origin of these ideas, it is necessary to review certain foreign policy documents.

During my research at the US National Archives in March 1978 I found a confidential memorandum entitled "The Exclusive Use of Katakana as Official Written Language." It was written before the Japanese surrender and dated June 23, 1945. The author was Lieutenant Robert King Hall, then chief of the Education Section of the Planning Staff for the Occupation of Japan at the Civil Affairs Staging Area (CASA), Monterey, California. As soon as the Occupation began, Hall came to Tokyo and served as CI & E's educational reorganization and language simplification officer. In that capacity he briefed the US Education Mission on Japanese language reform. His confidential memorandum, then, has some bearing on the mission's report.

In the memorandum, Hall recommended that "all written communication be restricted to *katakana,* and that the use of materials in *kanji* be prohibited."[65] *Katakana* is the simplest written form of the Japanese language. *Hiragana* is a written form that is curvy and slightly more complex than *katakana. Kanji* is a Chinese ideograph or character, and visibly far more complicated. The Japanese people used and still use a combination of these three forms.

Hall, then, was recommending the simplest medium. Although lengthy, his reasoning will be quoted here, for from it stemmed the initial American attitude toward Japanese education reform and in fact toward Japan itself. First, he emphasized the benefits his idea would bring.

1. *Prohibition of* kanji *would greatly assist in barring access to pre-war propaganda.* Nearly all serious writing in Japan has been done in the past in the medium of *kanji.* If all books and written materials in *kanji* were prohibited, possession of such materials becomes illegal. It is not recommended that materials already existing in *kanji* should be destroyed. It is sufficient that libraries be impounded. The knowledge represented in the impounded books would thus be preserved and the occupying forces would avoid the stigma of "bookburning."
2. *The exclusive use of* katakana *would ease the problem of censorship.* Censorship demands the highest level of discriminating linguistic ability. There does not now exist anything remotely approaching an adequate supply of linguists competent to censor *kanji.* . . . An adequate command of spoken Japanese is far simpler to acquire. Acquisition of the *katakana* then requires two or three weeks. Every member of the occupying forces, whether he reads Japanese or not, would become in effect a rough censor. Mere recognition of the type of writing would become sufficient. No translation to determine the content of that writing would be necessary.
3. *The use of* katakana *will shorten the time required for children to reach the same proficiency level in schools.* In prewar Japan a very major portion of the time devoted to elementary education was spent in acquiring facility in *kanji.* This time would be saved and could be utilized in other branches of instruction. Children would thus reach a productive level at an earlier age and would increase the labor supply without reducing the educational standard of the country.
4. Katakana *would increase national business efficiency.* It is widely used now in telegrams, in military dispatches, and in certain newspapers directed to the lower classes. It can be efficiently written on a standard occidental typewriter with a simple substitution of keys. . . .

On the practicality of his proposal he had this to say:

1. *The use of* katakana *does not impose illiteracy upon Japan.* All literate people in Japan read *katakana.* In fact, many who cannot read *kanji* read the simpler *katakana.* The use of romanized transcription, *romaji,* is not practical despite its obvious linguistic advantages, because it is not generally read in Japan, and accordingly its immediate adoption would virtually make Japan an illiterate nation. Illiteracy would be more dangerous to the military government than access to antagonistic propaganda. A modern nation without written communication would be reduced to chaos.
2. *Translation into* katakana *of necessary documents now in* kanji *is simple.* The difficulty is no greater than that of transcribing shorthand notes into typewritten copy. It can be done by any secretary who knows both systems.

3. Katakana *has a propaganda value*. It is one of the few, and
   certainly one of the most remarkable, native Japanese inven-
   tions. Its use should be a matter of national pride. Proper education of the Japanese people should convince them that its
   use is preferable to the continued use of a foreign and adopted
   kanji.
4. *There is a precedence [sic] for a major change of this sort.* Japan
   within the past two decades has shifted to the metric system of
   measures in an attempt to modernize their industry.... The
   centralization of authority in the Japanese government makes
   possible radical changes which would be nearly impossible in a
   decentralized government.
5. *The change will become permanent.* The closing of schools early
   in 1945, combined with the chaos that will attend any occupation, whether under combat conditions or under an armistice,
   will produce a two-to-five-year gap in the education of the
   present generation in *kanji.* This lapse, following a period under
   military government during which the *kanji* is officially forbidden, will effectively end the widespread use of *kanji* as a national
   language. *Kanji* is too difficult and requires too long a period of
   study ever to survive being driven underground for any period
   of time. It is not something that can be kept alive by word of
   mouth. If education in *kanji* is prohibited for even a period of
   ten years it is highly likely that *kanji* writing will become a "dead
   language," studied in the future by scholars as a medium to the
   "Japanese Classics."[66]

Hall sent this memorandum to Major General John H. Hilldring,
director of the War Department's Civil Affairs Division. Hilldring found
the suggestion "not practicable." But he did consult Eugene H. Dooman
of the Department of State.[67] Dooman, born in Japan, spoke Japanese
fluently, and before the Pacific War had worked at the US Embassy under
Ambassador Joseph Grew, another Japan expert. Dooman replied to
Hilldring:

It is our view that the prohibition of Chinese characters could not be enforced. Even if it could be, the elimination of Chinese characters under
conditions of military occupation would probably have consequences of a
most serious and far-reaching character, not only in drastically limiting intellectual and cultural pursuits, but in impeding in most drastic form the
operation of the normal economy of the country.[68]

Although Dooman's apprehension was sensible, the idea of radical
language reform persisted. On November 12, 1945, Colonel Ken Dyke,
the CI & E chief, assigned the task of Japanese language reform to Hall.
Dyke's reasons for proceeding with the reform were identical with those
in Hall's memorandum.[69] On March 13, 1946, Hall briefed the US Education Mission on Japanese language revision. "This," he admitted, "is a

very controversial subject." It would, he added, be "quite inappropriate of an officer of this headquarters to attempt to speak for the Japanese people."[70] Inappropriate or not, he had already decided to drastically change the Japanese written language for the Japanese people. The Japanese scarcely anticipated that CI & E was actually contemplating this, but what they wanted was irrelevant.

At this particular briefing Hall described only technical aspects of the three basic Japanese written forms. Dr. Ando Masatsugu, who was a distinguished philologist, a member of the Imperial Academy, and former president of Taihoku Imperial University in Japanese-occupied Taiwan, then spoke to the mission through a Japanese interpreter. Ando, echoing Hall's contention, said that the present Japanese language posed "obstacles to the raising of the people's intelligence level." But he cautioned, they should not be overhasty in their attempts or there would be undesirable future effects.[71] He therefore recommended, as "the most timely and fastest solution," reducing the number of Chinese characters in Japanese.[72] Ando's commonsense recommendation was not radical enough for Hall at this juncture. It was never raised again.

Two weeks later, in its report, the mission called the written Japanese language "a formidable obstacle to learning."[73] Its assumption was identical with that of Hall, who had said in his memorandum that "written Japanese is perhaps the most difficult language in common use today."[74] Regardless of how "mentally alert and remarkably diligent" the Japanese pupils were, the mission found disappointing "the results achieved by the inordinate amount of time allotted to recognizing and writing Kanji."[75]

> On leaving the elementary school the pupils may lack the linguistic abilities essential to democratic citizenship. They have trouble reading common materials such as daily newspapers and popular magazines. As a general rule, they cannot grasp books dealing with contemporary problems and ideas. Above all, they usually fail to acquire a degree of mastery sufficient to make reading an easy tool of development after leaving school.[76]

Since the mission could not say bluntly that the Japanese language stunted the Japanese people's intellectual growth, an ample amount of euphemism was employed. The mission readily acknowledged that "certain esthetic and other values residing in the Kanji can never be fully conveyed by a phonetic system." Eventually, however, *kanji* should be replaced in popular usage by a phonetic system, preferable *romaji*, since it offered more advantages than *kana* in terms of "the growth of democratic citizenship and international understanding."[77] Both domestically and internationally, the Japanese were moving in directions that would require a simplified and therefore more efficient written language, for foreigners' use no less than their own.[78] "A language," the mission concluded, "should be a vast highway, not a barrier."[79] Again, the mission's reasons were practically word for word those of Hall.

The mission's proposal constituted, at the least, an astonishing break with the Japanese cultural heritage. And yet it seemed anxious to deny that any such break was called for. Its report included such remarks as: "Education cannot proceed in a vacuum, nor is a complete break with a people's cultural past conceivable"; The Japanese people should "analyze their cultural traditions in order to discover what is worth preserving as humane ideas and ideals"; and "Language is so intimate an organism in a people's life that it is hazardous to approach it from without."[80] The mission was confident that mass dissemination of information at the cost of the Japanese written language would push the nation closer to democracy. The role of the "difficult" Japanese language was held to be more important than the role of the imperial government in persecuting "dangerous thoughts"; indeed, the mission failed to consider the latter at all. Perhaps it did not want to remind people of how SCAP's "democratic" censorship had already been practiced. In any case the mission revealed an astonishing naiveté. After all, was there any historical evidence for a relationship between phonetic written language and democracy? Both Germany and Italy had had such languages for some time.

The Education Mission's language reform pleased the man in charge of the mission at the State Department. "The most striking single element, in my judgment," wrote Assistant Secretary of State Benton to Secretary Byrnes, "is the revelation that the literacy of the Japanese people had been greatly overrated and the recommendation that Japan foster the widespread use of an alphabet." Benton, without raising any doubt, happily claimed that "this proposal, if adopted, can contribute enormously to the democratization of the Japanese way of life." The mission's chairman, after all, had told him that "the much vaunted literacy rate in Japan is another Japanese myth."[81] Three days later, in his press statement of April 22, Benton emphasized the importance of the proposed language reform. And a few days later Wilson Compton wrote to Benton: "I think that fundamentally that recommendation [language reform] is more important than all the rest because without the language reform the other reforms in my judgment cannot be fully effective. I personally would have preferred a much stronger statement on language reform in our report and a stronger challenge to the Japanese to do something about it."[82]

Sir George Sansom, who had briefed the mission's members before their departure for Tokyo, was surprised by its report. "I doubt whether the mission's view is justified," he wrote in *Pacific Affairs*.

> With a knowledge of 1,000 characters, a child leaving primary school can read a good deal more than newspaper headlines, especially if side-*kana* are used. . . . It must be remembered also, that knowledge of 1,000 characters is the basis for a very large vocabulary, since combinations of two characters represent compound words, and the possible combinations of 1,000 things taken two at a time are very numerous. Moreover, there is no reason to assume that an intelligent child on leaving school will not add to the number of characters it can read, just as an occidental child adds to its vocabulary.[83]

Sansom's observation should have prevailed, to say the least, among the American educators who believed in (to quote the report's introduction) "an unmeasured potential for freedom and for individual and social growth in every human being." But the mission was so far from being interested in exploring the "unmeasured potential" of the Japanese students that it doubted even their ability to learn their own language.

In April 1946 Hilldring, to whom Hall had sent his language memorandum, was appointed assistant secretary of state for occupied areas. He read the mission's report. Impressed, he changed his mind about Japanese language reform, which he had originally believed "not practicable." Under his and Benton's urging the State Department drafted the policy paper, "Reform of the Japanese Writing System and Language Problems," and in November 1946 submitted it to the State-War-Navy Coordinating Committee (SWNCC) for deliberation. The SWNCC was the official policymaking body of the US government for occupied Japan. While it was debating, Hilldring wrote George Atcheson in Tokyo, urging him to solicit MacArthur's support. Hilldring wrote Atcheson, because the War Department (i.e., the Department of the Army) at the SWNCC meetings insisted that the State Department's idea would place MacArthur in an awkward and definitely unpopular position.

Hilldring presented his rationale to Atcheson: "The Department [of State] believes that the present Japanese writing system is an important factor in preventing the development of an adequately informed electorate required for the proper functioning of a democratic system. At present, the Japanese written language stifles independent and original thinking on the part of the average Japanese, processes so necessary to the healthy development of a democracy."[84] After consulting with MacArthur, Atcheson replied to Hilldring: "It has been General MacArthur's feeling and that of the Civil Information and Education Section that this is a matter which should be left to the Japanese themselves." "General MacArthur is of the opinion," Atcheson continued, "that nothing more can be done than is being done at present and therefore believes it unwise to agitate the question further." Atcheson added his personal observation:

> I do not speak Japanese, but I am told by some qualified experts that romanization would merely touch the fringe of the problem; that Japanese students in the primary and secondary schools actually devote no more time solely to studying Japanese than do students in such schools in the United States in studying English; and that the real waste in language study lies in the study of Chinese and Japanese classics rather than of modern ideas.[85]

The State Department withdrew its policy paper on the Japanese language from the SWNCC.

While Atcheson and Hilldring were exchanging opinions on language reform, the originator of this infamous proposal, Robert King Hall, went home to the United States to receive a prestigious Guggenheim Fellowship. Under this fellowship, in 1946/47 he wrote *Education for a New Japan*, which Yale University Press published in 1949. In his memorandum of June 23, 1945, Hall had cautioned against a sudden change to *romaji*. However, he changed his mind after his involvement with the US Education Mission. In *Education for a New Japan* he expounded at some length (pp. 293–410) the virtues of *romaji* and the corresponding vices of *kanji*. A few quotations will suffice to convey his new infatuation with *romaji* as well as his condescending attitude toward Japanese intelligence. "A rapid and complete change to *romaji* in elementary and secondary schools appears highly desirable to ensure the rapid production of a population mass which is literate but which is unable to read in the traditional *kana-majiri* [common Japanese writing style], as an insurance against defection and backsliding in the program." He was generous enough to concede that "the Japanese themselves must make this final election [i.e., final choice of alternatives]." "But if they be thoughtful," he pontificated, "they can only arrive at one solution. Japan has available against the attrition of ignorance and the encroachment of nationalistic conservatism one of the most subtle and yet powerful allies of democracy—a phonetic writing system."[86] After the Guggenheim, Hall became an assistant professor of comparative education at Teachers College, Columbia University, where George Counts and Isaac Kandel, the mission's members on language revision, also taught.

A ROMANCE WITH ROMAJI
The Ministry of Education, in deference to the mission's pleas for *romaji*, created in June 1946 a Romaji Education Committee

(Romaji Kyoiku Kyogikai). This committee was composed of thirty-five leading educators, journalists, and ministry officials. At its first meeting the vice-minister of education expressed caution on *romaji*, especially "in the light of our nation's present condition and our cultural heritage."[87] The committee dissolved in October 1946, when it submitted a report to the Ministry of Education recommending the introduction of *romaji* in schools.

The vice-minister of education, probably to appease Hall at CI & E, declared that *romaji* "enhances the efficiency of social life and elevates the people's cultural standard."[88] Of course, neither MacArthur nor CI & E told the Japanese government that the adoption of *romaji* education was up to the Japanese people and that if they wanted none of it, so be it. Unaware of MacArthur's rare hands-off attitude, the Ministry of Education began experimental *romaji* education in April 1947, for the third grade and above. CI & E was anxious enough to launch monthly analyses of children's magazines concerning the use of romaji.[89] Reflecting American enthusiasm, the Kenkyusha Publishing Company published Japan's first all-*romaji* magazine, *Robin*, for children on April 1, 1946. More followed. There were fourteen magazines printed in *romaji* in December 1946 and twenty-seven in September 1947. By October 1950 the number had dropped to only two.[90] The Japanese romance with *romaji* was superficial.

"Is Romaji Enlgish?" I once asked my teacher. "No," he replied, "it is Japanese written in English alphabet." Pupils were confused; and the Ministry of Education itself was indecisive.[91] The mission's proposal fizzled. Sadly, one mission member (Compton) continued to believe it the most important one in the report. Conservative Japanese fear of "Americanization" or "cultural colonization of Japan" may well stem from this proposal, which in effect invited the Japanese people to commit cultural suicide.

CALLIGRAPHY AND CULTURE

The American passion for cleaning up the Japanese language did not exclude calligraphy. As Japanese as the kimono, calligraphy was a compulsory subject in the schools. The members of the US Education Mission did not believe in what appeared to them a waste of time. Soon after the mission left, the combined Japanese and American Committee on Curriculum Revision declared that "writing should be emphasized as a tool, rather than an art."[92] It promptly relegated calligraphy to a noncompulsory course. "At that day," CI & E chief Nugent recalled in 1949, "the Japanese were willing to continue or discontinue a subject if we said 'boo.' So the combined committee means nothing. It can be considered an American decision."[93]

In 1949, when the US occupation authority began slowing down radical reforms and reviving things indigenously Japanese, the Calligraphy Promotion Council energetically pressured the Ministry of Education to make the subject compulsory. The Ministry of Education appointed a committee composed of Japanese language and calligraphy people to make recommendations, if desirable, for change. According to a CI & E internal memorandum, "CI & E had no part in naming the committee and attended none of its meetings. No pressure of any sort was exerted, either directly or indirectly."[94] The committee recommended no changes and CI & E thought the matter was settled.

But the Calligraphy Promotion Council, assuming correctly that the Ministry of Education did not make a final decision on anything important, pleaded directly with CI & E. "The use of fork and knife is as indispensable for Europeans and Americans as chopsticks for the Japanese. Likewise penmanship is as indispensable for children in Europe and America as calligraphy in [the] Orient," reasoned the council's chairman Bundo Keichi. As for concrete benefits, he unhesitatingly declared that "the usual practice of calligraphy with a soft brush-pen spontaneously fosters a tender and graceful temper and also amend (sic) evil conduct." For this reason, "there were only [a] few who committed crime among those [who] pursued calligraphy."[95] Calligraphy also helped pupils "cultivate the presence of mind, noble spirit and assume a proper posture from childhood."[96] Because of the American ban, he pointed out, the writing ability of Japanese students had deteriorated considerably over the last two years.[97] Bundo pleaded with Arthur K. Loomis, chief of CI & E's Education Division, to have calligraphy taught "even in the lower classes"; it was, he said, equally the wish of parents, pupils, and teachers.[98]

Loomis routed Bundo's petition to the Elementary and Secondary Education Branches. Pauline Jeidy, elementary school officer, replied to Loomis that when she asked the Japanese employees in her office they said calligraphy had nothing to do with the improvement of their penmanship or their artistic ability. They also told her that Bundo's claims for the virtues of calligraphy were groundless.[99] Monta L. Osborne, secondary education officer, met members of Bundo's group at least six times. He asked them to prove their claims. They presented "scientific" evidence. One sample Osborne relayed to Loomis was as follows.

Calligraphy contributes toward a complete personality and helps insure the success of the individual. Evidence: Once a man had three sons, A, B, and C. A was enthusiastic about Calligraphy; B was less enthusiastic, but studied the subject some; C almost completely ignored it. A became a Tokyo University professor, B a normal school instructor, and C a menial worker.

This example illustrated, Osborne said, "the hazy thinking of these groups."[100]

Loomis could not decide what to do with calligraphy. He asked his superior, Nugent, for action. Nugent told Loomis:

> The question of calligraphy in the Japanese curriculum will be one for the Japanese to decide for themselves. We will exert no pressure one way or the other. We will give no aid and encouragement to the Calligraphy Association—and will not answer their petition. We will give no opinions to the Min/E [Ministry of Education] on the subject. If the Japanese wish to make it compulsory 10 hrs a week in kindergarten, they can—altho I believe they will have better sense. In this matter, as well as in certain other areas which touch closely on the Japanese cultural background—with all the emotional concomitants—we will be well advised to keep our noses out and not make judgments on a straight utilitarian and materialistic basis.[101]

This perspicacious comment illustrates Nugent's growing understanding of the relationship between education and culture. In fact, two months later Nugent told Loomis that his policy was "turning over to the Japanese as rapidly as possible all responsibilities in the field of curriculum. We may offer progressively decreasing guidance."[102]

GOODBYE ROMAJI, WELCOME ENGLISH!

One last remark on *romaji*. After several years of earnest experiment in the schools the impracticality of the US Education Mission's idea for converting the Japanese written language to *romaji* became vividly clear to everybody. In December 1950 CI & E conceded that the use of *romaji* as the daily Japanese language "would require extensive revision of the vocabulary."[103] Since neither MacArthur nor the Japanese government was willing to change the Japanese vocabulary, CI & E abandoned faith in *romaji*, calling it "at best an auxiliary means of writing Japanese."[104] Even that was an excessively generous assessment of the Japanese use of *romaji*. CI & E's embarrassment showed, at least privately, when Nugent confided to Loomis: "I remember that some of the people we had working in 1946 in [CI & E] were hatchet men concerning anything Japanese in the Japanese curriculum. (Remember how one man was going to change the language overnight?)"[105] The "one man" was of course Robert King Hall, who by then was teaching comparative education at Teachers College, Columbia University, with emphasis on Japanese education.

In contrast to the unpopular *romaji,* English was explosively popular among the Japanese people, who had been prohibited by their government from studying the enemy's language. For instance, "Come Come *Eigo Kaiwa*" ("Come Come English Conversation"), a fifteen-minute program broadcast weekdays by the Japan Broadcasting Corporation, attracted a large audience.[106]

Administrative Reorganization of the Japanese Educational System

"The Ministry of Education has been the seat of power for those who controlled the minds of Japan," the US Education Mission correctly assessed. Since the mission presumed that "the minds of Japan" had been deprived of both liberty and literacy, it proposed that the ministry's powers be reduced.[107] In the new Japanese education, the mission urged, there should be a "new philosophy, new procedures, and a new structure" that would "recognize human personality as of paramount importance and the state as a means to that end." The interests of individual human beings were not to be subordinated to those of the state.[108] Decentralization of authority would, the mission affirmed, contribute to the democratization of education and thereby increase the Japanese people's freedom and wisdom. The concept of popular sovereignty, codified in the new Constitution, was extended to the nation's educational governance. In fact, a "national" educational policy no longer existed. All policy decisions were supposed to be "local."

The mission listed concrete measures for decentralization.

1. To remove pupils from the last remaining influence of imperial Japan, the mission recommended that "the ceremonial use of Imperial Rescripts and the practice of obeisance before the Imperial Portraits should be discontinued."[109]
2. In order to educate pupils about the inalienable and universal human rights and individuality, the mission urged that the number of years to be spent in compulsory schooling be expanded to nine, instead of the prewar six. The Japanese government liked this idea but was at a loss over where the necessary money for such a costly project would come from.
3. The mission felt that teachers, the crucial agents of instruction in democracy, "must have security in their positions, reasonable salaries and adequate retirement provisions."[110] These would give them financial independence. But since nobody had much faith in the Japanese economy, which was close to bankruptcy, the mission proposed that "teachers should organize into voluntary associations on local, prefectural, and national levels" so that they could "be effective in the best interests of youth and in the promotion of their own welfare."[111] Before the mission's arrival in Tokyo, the two

teachers' unions had already been promoting their own separate interests by attacking each other's reputations. Hence the mission's caution that economic factors were "important, but ... not supreme." What was supreme, in the mission's view, was "freedom to think, speak and act."[112]

4. With respect to primary and secondary schools, the mission recommended in each prefecture, each city, and each village that there be "an educational committee or agency, which shall be politically independent and composed of representative citizens elected by popular vote."[113]

DECENTRALIZATION
AND THE SCHOOL BOARD ELECTIONS

CI & E had been deliberating on efficient and permanent ways of reducing the awesome power of the Ministry of Education and at the same time enhancing local decision-making ability. Local boards of education looked especially appealing, and the mission recommended and the Committee of Japanese Educators endorsed them. After the mission left, CI & E in mid-1946 appointed the advisory education committees of local citizens "in every city, town and village." Nugent informed MacArthur that these committees "demonstrated the ability and the willingness of the Japanese people to assume additional responsibility for public school affairs."[114]

The Ministry of Education did not like decentralization at all. But since it could not attack the US Education Mission, it tried to discredit the Committee of Japanese Educators, the members of which the ministry itself had carefully chosen. Naito Takasaburo, secretary of the Archives and Document Section of the Ministry of Education, told Orr that the Japanese committee was "not really qualified to recommend in the field of administrative reorganization." Orr reminded him that the ministry itself had selected the members. Naito replied that what he really meant was that "they were really qualified but that they had no opportunity to hear the very enlightening and useful advice of the Ministry of Education."[115] The ministry, however, was encouraged to begin working hard on decentralization, and its attitude changed quickly.[116]

The Naimusho (Ministry of Home Affairs) strongly objected to the establishment of local school boards. This ministry, perhaps the most talented organ of thought control in Asia, understood well that American-initiated school boards would take away power and prestige from the central government in Tokyo. As the ministry was under the jurisdiction of the Government Section (GS) of GHQ, Trainor talked with two GS representatives named Tilton and Gradjanzev. The GS men assured him that the ministry could be persuaded.[117]

Encouraged, CI & E began drafting a bill for local boards of education. Arthur K. Loomis, at that time adviser on Administration and Finance in the Education Division, proposed that policy be made by a prefectural board of education.[118] But the members of Secondary Education Unit, Education Division, unanimously disagreed with Loomis, contending that a prefectural school board would still be too remote from the people. They suggested that the Japanese school board should more closely conform to the American pattern. They hoped the powerful Government Section would approve their idea, because its opposition, as they put it, "could not be overcome."[119] GS did not oppose. On the contrary, GS and CI & E, working closely together, told the Ministry of Education explicitly what they wanted from local boards of education. The ministry came up with a draft which GS and CI & E revised to their satisfaction.[120]

In June 1948 both houses of the Diet deliberated the bill on boards of education. The Diet was not sure it should pass the bill. On June 29, 1948, Education Minister Morito Tatsuo, who in 1920 had been forced to leave a position as assistant professor at Tokyo Imperial University for writing an essay on Prince Peter Kropotkin, the Russian anarchist, visited Mark Orr, chief of the Education Division, and said he had just learned from the Education Committee members of the House of Representatives that the Government Section was "not particularly anxious that the bill be passed." Surprised, Orr immediately telephoned GS, which replied to him that the bill "should be passed as soon as possible."[121] The next day Loomis of CI & E met the chairmen of the two Diet Education Committees and urged them to expedite the bill. They did, and five days later, on July 5, 1948, the Diet passed the Board of Education Law. On July 15, 1948, the Emperor promulgated it.

The law as originally drafted denied the right of teachers to run for local school boards. However, the Japan Teachers' Union (JTU) successfully lobbied for removal of this provision.[122] The law prescribed that the election for school boards be held on October 5, 1948. Everything looked good for what Nugent and MacArthur considered "the most important step taken thus far in limiting the power of the Ministry of Education and transferring authority over education from the national government to the local level."[123] They quite reasonably expected the transfer to proceed without major trouble. Reality, however, was not on the side of reason.

First, strong opposition to the election sprang up from an unexpected place: the Eighth Army Headquarters. The Eighth Army, commonly called the "Military Government" or "MG," stationed throughout Japan, was responsible for maintaining law and order and making sure that the Japanese obeyed the Americans. On August 23, 1948, Lieutenant Colonel S. B. Satterwhite, civil education officer, wrote a letter, informally but with the approval of his superiors, to CI & E expressing the

Eighth Army's misgivings. The Japanese, he said, still did not understand what this new law was all about. He urged that GHQ as well as MG launch a mass information campaign. Because the electorate was so poorly informed, October 5 was too soon for the elections; they should be postponed at least six months. Teachers, he added, should not be allowed to run for election, because if they did JTU would "dominate the administration of schools for the next four years." Further, he recommended that "the screening of candidates prior to the election be eliminated," for it would "scare off many of the best prospects for board members."[124]

There were some good reasons for the Eighth Army's acute anxiety. For instance, the Military Government in Osaka found out that there were only ten candidates for the school board. "One is a notorious black-market operator who is looking for 'gravy.' Three are Communists—two of whom are officials of the Communist Party. One is a disgruntled textbook publisher who feels he is not getting a sufficient slice of the textbook pie. All others are JTU [Japan Teachers' Union] members."[125] Disgusted, the American military men in Osaka tried to persuade other candidates whom they thought desirable to run. But these others told them that they did not wish "to run against such opposition"; that they had "no money and no backers"; and that they felt it was "inevitable that the bosses and JTU representatives [would] win out."[126]

Ironically, although the Eighth Army had requested no screening of candidates prior to the election, this report from the Military Government in Osaka was used to justify the ongoing screening of all candidates. On September 17, 1948, the Ministry of Education reported to CI & E that the 1,530 candidates were screened and that only 8 were found unacceptable.[127] Teachers were not screened; they had already been screened very carefully.

Both GS and CI & E took the Eighth Army's advice seriously, but only up to a certain point. For policy coordination Mark Orr, Loomis's successor as chief of the Education Division, met the GS representatives (Colonel Charles Kades and Justin Williams). GS was determined to carry out the October 5 election as scheduled. Kades told Orr that C. Whitney, chief of GS and MacArthur's favorite protégé, believed that the postponement "would be definitely harmful for SCAP," because it would indicate MacArthur's "distrust in the ability of the Japanese people." Although the Japanese people might elect members of the Teachers' Union and the Communist Party, such a "danger," GS said, was " 'inherent' in democracy." GS dismissed as negligible the danger that the Teachers' Union would dominate the nation's education. "The GS officials stated," Orr informed Nugent, "that they would be willing to share with CIE (STAND OR FALL TOGETHER) any repercussions."[128]

Realizing that GS and CI & E were taking no action regarding the Eighth Army's urgent request, its commanding Gen. Charles W. Ryder sent a letter of warning to his superior, MacArthur. His letter, dated September 11, 1948, was identical with that of Lieutenant Colonel Satter-white. MacArthur routed Ryder's letter to Nugent. On September 21 Nugent submitted to MacArthur a draft of the reply, which MacArthur approved the next day. The reply to Ryder was simple and short: "It is not considered advisable that the Board of Education Law be set aside, or modified, by this General Headquarters."[129]

But the Eighth Army's worry was confirmed by another discouraging report, this time from Herbert Passin of the Public Opinion and Sociological Research Unit, Analysis and Research Division, CI & E. Passin (presently an eminent professor of sociology at Columbia University and an authority on Japan) reported to Orr the results of a public opinion survey on the coming school board election. A Japanese organization, The Association for Public Opinion Science (Yoron Kagaku Kyokai), conducted the survey in Tokyo in early September 1948 with a sample of 744 scientifically selected persons. To the question, "Do you know that there will be school board elections soon?" 62 percent of the respondents said "Yes," 32 percent "No," and 6 percent "Have a vague idea." The majority (82 percent) of the respondents who knew about the election learned from newspapers and radio. To the question, "Do you know what the work of the school boards will be?" 53 percent replied "Don't understand," 29 percent "Understand a little," and only 12 percent "Understand well." When the respondents were asked (in a question allowing more than one choice) to name the "most desirable" election candidates, they named ordinary citizens oftenest (mentioned by 54 percent) not far ahead of JTU members (50 percent), and PTA members (50 percent). Communist Party members were oftenest mentioned under the head of "least desirable" candidates.[130]

Despite this evidence of the Communist candidates' striking unpopularity, Japanese conservatives were not satisfied. On September 9, 1948, former Education Minister Tanaka, chairman of the Education Committee of the House of Councillors, visited Orr to warn that "the CP [Communist Party] wants the JTU to dominate the elections at least to the extent of having fifty percent of the membership of each board" and that together they would attempt to control the nation's education.[131] It was certainly timely but unpleasant news for GHQ. Prime Minister Ashida Hitoshi, a conservative who was foreign minister in the Socialist Katayama cabinet, and Education Minister Morito, a Socialist turned conservative, after being pressured by Eighth Army representatives during a tour of the nation, also wanted to postpone the election. The prime minister called an emergency cabinet meeting. The cabinet decided that Education Minister Morito should formally request the postponement.[132]

On September 14, 1948, Morito visited the Education Division. "Mr. Morito expressed fears of Communists and Bosses," Orr told Nugent. Both Ashida and Morito, he added, feared that the candidates were not of "sufficiently high character." Orr sarcastically commented: "It was not quite clear why people of low character are well aware of the election and people of high character don't seem to be so well informed." "Mr. Ashida may wish to call upon General Whitney or even General MacArthur to discuss the problem with them," Morito suggested. But Orr told Morito that the supreme commander did not contemplate postponement.[133] MacArthur and GHQ, recognizing that the Japanese people hardly understood the idea of local school boards, made "strenuous efforts," as Richard B. Finn of the Office of the US Political Adviser put it, "to stimulate intelligent public interest."[134] The mass media were encouraged to publicize the school board issue.[135] The election was held on October 5, 1948.

The results of SCAP's "strenuous efforts" were depressing. The board members, Finn reported to William J. Sebald, US political adviser, were "either incompetent or thoroughly unfamiliar with educational problems," and "considerable public education and experience" would be needed before an effective system could be established.[136]

FAILURE OF DECENTRALIZATION

To encourage the needed public experience and involvement, Parent-Teacher Associations (PTAs) were established throughout the nation with American blessing. But the PTAs also disappointed the Americans. "These associations," Finn told Sebald, "have been victimized either by local bosses or by wealthy people eager to advance private interests."[137]

The Board of Education Law did eliminate the Ministry of Education's policymaking authority. As Osborne understood it, the prefectural and local boards of education had "almost absolute control over the curriculum." Once more, however, this American expectation was not fulfilled. Contrarily, the Ministry of Education's curriculum guide, *Courses of Study*, was swallowed whole by the local school boards, who took it literally as an instruction to them. Osborne asked Trainor to order the Ministry of Education to announce that these courses of study were neither mandatory nor about to become so when revised. "The schools," he added, "may use all of a course of study, a part of it, none of it, or toss the whole volume in the wastebasket as soon as it reaches the school."[138]

Such a policy, confirmed CI & E chief Nugent, was "especially important in Japan." Every effort, he told Loomis, must be made "to prevent the ministry from prescribing a curriculum for the country as a whole"; the ministry "should never be allowed even to entertain the idea that it is responsible for the curricula of Japan's schools."[139]

Unfortunately, the Board of Education Law was obsolete from the very beginning. One of the most obvious reasons was the lack of funds. When the nation, as a result of SCAP's effective economic strangulation, was scrambling for rice, money for education was budgeted last and ran out first in the national treasury as well as in local ones. Besides no money, no administrative talent existed in the numerous localities; and at the same time the nation's compulsory education, expanded to nine years, dramatically demanded more money and more managerial skill. The state of chaos was apparent. As Finn informed Sebald, "primary and secondary schools were in many cases without guidance or control to help them through the difficult transitional period." The solution, he concluded, appeared to be remote.[140] One solution, exceptionally "Japanese" no doubt, was the suicide of a man in charge. A mayor of a small town killed himself for having failed, despite his best efforts, to find money for education. Extreme, this action nevertheless conveyed the psychological state of many people who engaged in educational policymaking. Over a hundred mayors and village heads resigned and over twenty-five mayors and local assemblymen were recalled for their inability to secure money for education.[141]

What ensued was that the local boards of education turned for policy guidance to prefectural boards of education, who themselves were busy looking for guidance from the Ministry of Education (where guidance equalled directives) and for favorable allocation of precious money. The Ministry of Education did retain the crucial power of preparing the nation's educational budget.[142] With no money at each locality, it was an understandable arrangement. CI & E, because it scrutinized the ministry's budget allocation, felt comfortable with this arrangement. A rumor of money in Tokyo was sufficient to attract the local school boards; and their pilgrimage to Tokyo proved fatal for decentralization. Worse yet, the 1949 Dodge Line, a drastic austerity program for occupied Japan, eliminated the funds for urgently needed school building construction and further undermined the independence of local school boards.

While the nation's schools were crying out for money, local board members, including those in Tokyo, began voting themselves monthly salaries. The Japan Teachers' Union was responsible for this nationwide phenomenon, which happened right after the October 1948 election. It was an illegal move and local board members knew it. The Military Gov-

ernment was shocked. Its deep suspicion of the Teachers' Union appeared
to be confirmed. Realizing that whatever happened in Tokyo would influence the rest of the nation, on December 8, 1948, Tokyo Military Government Headquarters summoned Tokyo School Board members for a
serious talk on what the Americans thought was an outrageous gesture on
the part of elected public officials. Their talk went as follows:

COLONEL STERLING [commanding officer]: . . . Out in the provinces, every-
> body looks at Tokyo-To [City] for guidance. . . . In America,
> position as a member of a board of education is looked upon as
> an honorary one. In America, [it means] that you possess out-
> standing integrity, honesty and intelligence. . . . If you would
> forego salaries for yourselves, it will certainly carry great weight
> in the restoration of economic stability of Japan. . . . You have
> a splendid opportunity of making history in Japan now.

MR. YAMAZAKI [chairman of the School Board]:   . . . I understand your high
> ideal very well. . . . By law we are restricted from taking any
> other position. Unless we have a considerable wealth of our
> own, we cannot work as members of the Board of Education. If
> Tokyo-To were to set an example by voting not to accept sal-
> aries, this will mean only rich men will be in a position to be-
> come members.

COLONEL STERLING: On the other hand, if the members accept salaries, it
> will just be setting up of another bureau and practicing bureau-
> cracy.

MR. YAMAZAKI: I am not wishing for high salaries. . . . but unless we receive
> enough pay for living, only those with fortunes can become
> members. We have agreed to have the Tokyo-To Assembly
> decide the salaries for us. None of us wish to receive high sala-
> ries, but just enough to live on.

COLONEL STERLING: Aren't you thinking that Board of Education duties
> will take thirty days a month? . . . .

MR. HORIE: . . . The commanding officer must have some misunderstand-
> ing. We are determined to serve the board in a spirit of patri-
> otism and have no desire to make financial gains. . . . I am a
> Communist and represented the Communist Party when elected
> on this board, but today, I am not talking as a Communist. . . .
> The reason for need of salaries is not for financial gains, but
> because poor but qualified persons will not be able to run for
> the board in the future if salaries are not paid. . . .

COLONEL STERLING: . . . One should not look on the board position as his
> principal duty.

MR. MATSUZAWA: We do not wish to make the board our main source of
> income. . . . We desire just enough salaries to make our living
> stable.

CAPTAIN DUPELL: This board is already off on the wrong foot. . . . You are
> not following the examples nor advice given by the experts,
> with the excuse that "it's different in Japan." Why not hold

the board meetings in the evenings when most of the workers
are free to attend the meetings? In the United States meetings
are held in the evenings. . . .

MR. YAMAZAKI: . . . I am just expressing my frank opinion and presenting
my side.

COLONEL STERLING: I have not asked you here to scold you. . . . Do not be
disappointed if the Assembly votes not to pay any salaries to
the board members.

MR. HORIE: I fear qualified men will not be able to become members of
the board. Laborers will not be able to run for this position.
This is not democratic.

COLONEL STERLING: I am afraid you did not get my point. Everybody is
supposed to have another job by which he derives his living. . . .

MR. MATSUZAWA: I agree with you but under the present economic condition of Japan, an honest person working hard is not getting
enough and so in order to perform the board duties conscien-
tiously a little pay is needed to supplement his principal
salary. . . .

COLONEL STERLING: Tokyo-To will be setting an example if you vote yourselves salaries. . . . This will mean a tremendous burden on national finance. This will slow the economic recovery of Japan.[143]

This meeting was reported to Nugent who told Orr: "I am shocked.
. . . This pay situation, together with the influence of the JTU [Japan
Teachers' Union] on school boards, is going to make decentralization a
much greater danger than centralization ever was. Let's consider some
amendments to the Local Board Law to be introduced (with a club if
necessary) in the next regular session of the Diet." After reading the
transcript of the meeting, Nugent said, "Our MG [Military Government]
people are either being misquoted or they are more illiterate as regards
educational administration and procedure than the Japanese. . . . I consider this situation," he said, "very serious, indeed."[144]

Another reason for the failure of the local school boards was that
the popular vote elected many members of the Japan Teachers' Union
who were politically minded. These people, earlier encouraged by Mac-
Arthur and the Japanese government, were politically active. They leaned
to the Left. They displeased MacArthur and GHQ and made the Ministry
of Education unhappy. GHQ's displeasure with the JTU was especially
acute. CI & E met regularly, as Joseph Trainor said, with "the top brass
of JTU" to teach them the way of democracy. Their first meeting took
place on July 15, 1948. Trainor told them that the union was "not going
to be permitted to run the schools of Japan," and that it should stop
fighting all the time and "begin to show signs of 'growing up.' "[145] "Good!
Proceed on this basis," Nugent encouraged him.[146]

The JTU refused to grow up in the way GHQ wanted. On the contrary, to GHQ's and the Japanese government's sorrow, the union grew politically more combatant and ideologically more leftist. Accordingly, the Japanese government began to demand "political neutrality" from teachers, while steadily regaining the power and authority it had temporarily lost. Leftist board members and teachers retaliated by branding government members as evil reactionaries. The government thought the teachers were Communist subversives. Although the stage seemed to have been set for participation in democracy, the drama took a disappointing development when continental Asia, especially the Korean Peninsula, became an area of crisis for the United States—and perhaps for Japan.

From the very beginning of decentralization, the Ministry of Education did not at all enjoy losing power. To Japanese conservatives the rule of the masses, at its birth in Japan, resembled anarchy. They genuinely feared the Communists would exploit the situation. Knowing well that GHQ intensely disliked the Communists, they stressed the urgent need to fight back. To decentralize, they argued, was merely to dissipate the powers of government. It would therefore be very damaging and in fact would play into the hands of the Communists. They also urged that the Ministry of Education should remain unchanged and resume its prewar responsibility for "thought control." Former Education Minister Tanaka, who had gallantly defended the 1890 Imperial Rescript on Education, was "apparently an advocate of this position," Education Minister Morito told Orr.[147] At that time Tanaka was chairman of the Education Committee of the House of Councillors—the same committee that was deliberating the bill on local school boards.

Although the Japanese conservatives tried to fan GHQ's visible animosity against the Communists, GHQ was not so naive as to listen to them. As Orr told Nugent, "GS [Government Section] representatives distrust the Ministry of Education completely. This feeling of distrust has been expressed in every conference with GS officials." The Government Section, he continued, believed that the ministry was "struggling to retain every possible thread of power," and that its bureaucrats were hoping for the Americans either to delay decentralization "or, better still, to permit the retention of certain critical powers at the national level— and in the hands of the Ministry of Education."[148]

In other words, the Ministry of Education did not believe the Japanese people could understand democracy without a tutor. The ministry wished to practice "guided democracy." But MacArthur, a past master of guided democracy, did not believe the Ministry of Education capable of following in his footsteps. When, on March 27, 1948, the ministry had proposed expanding into "the Ministry of Education, Science, and Culture," he believed Science and Culture would be too much for it to manage adequately.[149] The Government Section thought even education was more than the ministry could handle; in fact, the GS staff told Orr it was "feasible that the Ministry of Education be abolished" and that "a Bureau of Statistics [to collect educational data] would be sufficient at the national government level."[150] The ministry's proposal for expansion was ignored. After the Occupation ended, however, the Board of Education Law was amended (in 1956) to abolish the popular vote and, instead, to empower the Ministry of Education to appoint all board members.

Higher Education in the Rehabilitation of Japan

The US Education Mission, for what it called "the crown of every modern educational system," namely, the university, reaffirmed three popular ideals:

> [1] it guards as a treasure beyond price the tradition of intellectual liberty, stimulates freedom of thought, perfects methods of inquiry, promotes the advancement of knowledge, cultivates science and scholarship, nurtures love of truth, and serves as a source of perpetual enlightenment of society; [2] it prepares young men and women of talent, through acquaintance with the best thought and finest aspirations of all ages and peoples, for positions of leadership in the improvement of family and community life, in the more efficient and humane conduct of industry and government, and in the fostering of understanding and goodwill among the nations; [3] it trains selected young men and women for technical proficiency in both old and new professions, being ever sensitive to the changing and emerging needs of society.[151]

The mission's message, however eloquent, had no more effect on the academic clique-forming instinct of the Japanese university than the distant echo of a priestly incantation. This instinct, carefully nurtured, ruled supreme in the nation's academic hierarchy. Even outside the academic community, elites prevailed; thus "85 percent of the executive officials" in the Japanese government bureaucracy in 1948 were "graduates of the law department of Tokyo Imperial University."[152] Of course, each imperial university did its best to create similarly incestuous elites out of its own graduates.

Japanese academic cliques were a product of the Japanese ideological tradition. The Japanese academic community (especially in the imperial universities) had created a system that perfectly mirrored the authoritarianism of the community at large. A senior professor with permanent chairship protection, which was more than tenure, literally controlled the lives of students and junior professors who wished to continue following an academic career. Subservience of the student to the professor remained unquestioned. There was a concrete demarcation in authority and privileges between the senior professor and the junior professor that stayed inviolable. The professor's favor, personal or professional, not only required the eternal obligation of his subordinates but also formed an ethos of inextricable bondage that none dared challenge. Any differences of opinion with the senior professor were best left unmentioned. Exchange of faculty members among the universities (a practice so common in the United States that nobody ever bothers to talk about it) was unheard of. The senior professor did send his students to the universities of his choice with his eyes firmly fixed upon territorial expansion. In this way cliques of like-minded persons, promiscuously called "colleagues' by the professors who had originated them, were established without conscious expenditure of effort. Such cliques, thanks to the tenacity of dogma, excluded those of different minds. "Difference," when judged by scholarly orthodoxy, was always equated with "inferiority," if not with "threat."

Dr. Ueda (T.) of the Tokyo University of Commerce, the son of the famous scholar Ueda Bin, was interviewed by CI & E in late 1945. The Ministry of Education, Ueda bluntly said, "still continues to function in the old leisurely bureaucratic and inefficient manner and remains a preserve of the Tokyo Teidai [Tokyo Imperial University] which occupies the key positions and is thoroughly imbued with the worst Japanese bureaucratic traditions."[153] Other professors, at Waseda and Keio Universities, concurred with him.

Fighting University Elitism

When the US Education Mission asserted that "the conservatism of Japan in higher education can be broken" and went on to urge that "in the interest of world welfare and the welfare of Japan, we think that it should be," it was referring to such autocratic academic cliques. In fact, the mission pointedly declared that "the preferential treatment given today to the graduates of imperial universities" should be eliminated.[154] To remedy the situation the mission recommended increasing the number of universities and colleges, so that elitist higher education might be eliminated. Accordingly, in October 1946, the Ministry of Education formed the University Accreditation Association.[155] Walter Crosby Eells, adviser on higher education, lectured in various influential quarters on the urgent need for establishing accreditation standards.[156] The University Chartering Committee was established by cabinet order in January 1948 to "determine whether any prospective higher institution has sufficient potentialities to be given the right of establishment."[157] Further, the School Education Law of March 31, 1948, established the four-year university. To keep the government out of the campus, this law made clear that "the president shall govern all the affairs of the university and supervise all the staff of the university," and "the university shall have a faculty meeting to discuss and deliberate on important matters."[158]

On May 31, 1949, the National School Establishment Law became effective; it consolidated the then-existing 249 institutions of higher education into 68 new national universities. The new university followed in theory the American land-grant university system: each prefecture was to have at least one senior university.[159] Richard Finn of the Office of the US Political Adviser anticipated in July 1949 that "the exclusive character of Japan's prewar university system, in which six imperial universities clearly dominated the field, [would] be radically altered by eventual establishment of over 200 colleges and universities."[160]

The target was reached, but the effects were not as anticipated. In 1945 there were 48 universities with a teaching staff of 6,888 and 98,825 students. By 1952, when the Occupation ended, there were 220 universities, 36,978 teachers and 399,513 students.[161] Junior colleges, which came into existence in 1950, by 1952 numbered 205 with 8,328 teachers and 53,230 students.[162] This dramatic proliferation of higher educational institutions neither pleased everybody nor interfered with the imperial universities' power and prestige. On the contrary, it served, under the straitened financial and intellectual conditions that prevailed everywhere, only to strengthen the supremacy of the imperial universities. After all, the Japanese government was not eager to change the imperial universities, because most high government officials were alumni of those universities and believed that any reform constituted a lowering of academic standards. Also, both the American and the Japanese authorities considered it democratic to keep their hands off the universities, as the prewar imperial government had manipulated them far too much. While every institution of the conquered empire underwent drastic reform, the imperial universities kept their prewar prerogatives and aura of prestige. Ironically, it was they who fiercely preached democracy and academic freedom.

The proliferation of new universities particularly offended the first postwar education minister, Maeda. Writing in 1956, he derided it as "seemingly insoluble." "The abuses and evils inherent in this jerry-built and completely overexpanded system seem to be," he complained, "all but without remedy." This deplorable situation stemmed from "a mistaken sense of the principle of equality of educational opportunity" and "the tendency of the Japanese people, who have little individuality, to follow any system which, on the surface at least, offers the appearance of equality and uniformity."[163] The principle of equal educational opportunity, according to Maeda's "correct" interpretation of it, would only have confirmed the academic status quo, that is, the autocratic and deeply entrenched monopoly of the imperial universities. Women would have continued to be virtually denied higher education. Maeda's contention that the Japanese people had little individuality and did not understand equality mirrored his own arrogant indifference to their welfare and intelligence. It was the same Maeda, it will be recalled, who was infatuated with the 1890 Imperial Rescript on Education, which had encouraged, he believed, true individuality and liberty, although the imperial regime had done its best to suppress both.

DEFINING ACADEMIC FREEDOM

The new Constitution, extensively publicized by the Japanese government and SCAP, contained an article guaranteeing academic freedom. The US Mission, before proceeding to an explanation of academic freedom, criticized past Japanese scholars as both "insular and insulated," as conformists, and as elitists who created a gap between them and "the unidentified millions of the Japanese people."[164] "Academic freedom exists," the mission said, "when the faculties of any university or college, public or private, are allowed to experiment with ideas, as well as with apparatus, in the search for new knowledge. . . . One sure way to preserve academic freedom is to give authority to the faculties themselves in academic affairs." As a further protection, the mission encouraged establishment of "national associations of teachers, professors, and of universities" that should be governed by "the spirit of social responsibility to use the rights of the scholar and scientist for the good of all."[165]

The mission also recognized the intimate connection between academic and economic freedom: "If an institution of higher learning is worthy of freedom to serve society, it is worthy of freedom from intellectual surveillance. Caution is therefore necessary whenever an issue arises that puts financial pressure upon academic freedom."[166] As a safeguard the mission recommended that university faculties be freed from the tyrannical system of civil service ratings, under which a superior rated his subordinates according to the government's scale.[167] It was, in fact, the rating system, with its mechanisms to ensure intellectual accountability, that under the prewar Ministry of Education had been partly responsible for the successful conversion of Japan's best minds into efficient sycophants.

The Japanese Association of University Professors was established on December 1, 1946. It followed the pattern of the American Association of University Professors (AAUP). The AAUP's charter, however, contained a definition of academic freedom while the Japanese Association's did not.[168] However, it was this Japanese Association, in October 1949 when the Red Purge was raging throughout the nation, that bravely came up with a clear statement defending intellectual freedom. The association grew to over 5,200 members in ninety-two universities, public and private, by 1951.[169]

SCIENCE AND POVERTY

The US Education Mission also deemed it necessary to comment on Japanese science. "In the world of science," it generalized, "Japan's participation has been to a great extent imitative and absorptive rather than creative and original."[170] But the mission did not recommend original research. Rather, given Japan's physical deprivation, research and development were needed "to expand the sources of employment and livelihood."[171] The mission went on to warn Japanese scientists that "the scientific character" would contribute more to national well-being than "scientific results."[172] The scientific character, the mission wrote, "demands humility in the presence of evidence, patience before the hard task of accumulating facts, and a cooperative spirit in sharing discoveries and putting to universal use the technological fruits of this inner spirit of science."[173] This rhetoric was altogether typical of the mission's tendency to become enmeshed in the tangled web of its own eloquence. Indeed, the mission's numerous recommendations, not unreasonable in theory, failed to consider the troublesome economic factors. The mission knew that American fire bombing had severely damaged or totally destroyed the buildings of almost two-thirds of the universities and almost half of the other higher institutions.[174] It nonetheless urged the universities to expand their libraries and other research facilities. The poverty of Japanese library facilities inspired a donation from the Rockefeller Foundation and the American Library Association of 150 sets of scientific journals published during the war period in the United States. It went to Tokyo Imperial University in March 1947. President Nambara hailed the gift as "spiritual food."[175]

In December 1947 a US Library Mission came to advise on the establishment of the National Diet Library of Japan. The Library Mission submitted its report to MacArthur on February 8, 1948, which he called in a press release "of inestimable value to the Japanese people."[176] The National Diet Library Law was passed by unanimous vote of both Houses of the Diet and put into effect on February 9, 1948.

10

The Facade of Japanese Autonomy

During the Occupation Japanese universities faced two major administrative reorganization plans. Both of them were initiated, in the name of decentralization, by Walter Crosby Eells, adviser on Higher Education in the Education Division, CI & E. Bewilderingly, his idea of decentralization was to reassemble the already decentralized policymaking authority of individual universities under a larger organization such as prefectural government or the Ministry of Education. Eells's passion for recentralization was contagious, especially to the Ministry of Education with its nostalgia for absolute control. Japanese universities united in fear and vehemently fought back.

The Universities Defeat Eells's Plans

On January 12, 1948, Eells came up with a draft plan whereby a prefectural government, in which the faculty played no part, would govern the university. The Japan Education Reform Council (JERC), the Ministry of Education's think tank, had previously opposed any such plan, but Eells had dismissed its opposition as "not very convincing or compelling."[1] He next submitted a detailed version of his draft to Mark T. Orr. In it he proposed to set aside, in university governance, the jealously guarded prerogatives of autonomous faculty. One of his recommendations empowered the Ministry of Education to approve or disapprove the appointment of university presidents after they had been elected by the faculty.[2] It was a betrayal of the faculty's high expectation for postwar democracy.

The Education Division was caught entirely by surprise. "This is fantastic in view of our attempts to decentralize, in view of everything that we have said in our check note to the chief of staff," Trainor warned Orr.[3] Eells wanted to present his plan to the Japan Education Reform Council for discussion. But Trainor advised Orr to treat "the Eells plan as classified at the moment"; if presented, it would cause embarrassment.[4] Another problem was that, since it came from CI & E, it would "be construed as the viewpoint of the Headquarters."[5] CI & E could hardly present this plan of Eells's "that he has cooked up himself."[6] Trainor's anxiety was intense, since he saw the decentralization issue as critical. He suggested internal study of the Eells draft. After that, CI & E could ask Nambara if the JERC, of which he was vice-chairman, would ask it for ideas. "Unless he agrees," Trainor insisted, "I am against giving any plan for them to discuss."[7]

Eells, however, started talking extensively with many Japanese who, he said to Orr, "have sent delegations to CIE to discuss their plans."[8] As Finn told Sebald, Eells's idea "provoked a storm of opposition from all groups in Japan"—especially the former imperial universities.[9] The Japanese universities argued that a prefectural government lacked sufficient administrative and financial capabilities to maintain a university, and that such critical deficiencies threatened the university's autonomy as well as its survival. They reminded CI & E that Japanese universities (unlike their American counterparts) had not come into existence because of local needs but were "national" in the sense that they attracted students from throughout the nation and educated them in ways that went far beyond local needs.[10] Nambara of Tokyo University presented exactly the same argument to the staff of the US political adviser.[11] CI & E readily accepted this argument, and Eells's plan died in early 1948. Eells interpreted the successful opposition of the universities as politically disturbing and ideologically suspicious. His revenge was the Red Purge, which he would soon spearhead with pleasure.

Secondly, in March 1948, Eells came up with a slightly different idea of control, a Board of Trustees, an American-inspired prototype, for Japanese national universities. His draft, "Outline of Proposed Law Governing Universities," triggered other heated debates between the universities and the Ministry of Education.[12] This time CI & E was not going to give up easily. The long summer vacation did not pacify the universities, which made concerted efforts to persuade the ministry to abandon the proposal. Tokyo University, the JERC, the Zengakuren (All-Japan University Student Federation), the JTU, and the Japanese Academy of Sciences all drafted alternative plans and submitted them to the ministry. It liked none of them. Nambara himself energetically denounced Eells's new proposal. The Ministry of Education and CI & E were very unhappy with Nambara.

Privately Nambara met with Orr to discuss it further. Orr invited him to a dinner at his own residence in early July 1948. They evidently had a pleasant evening, but came to no closer agreement.[13] In his letter of thanks Nambara enclosed a copy of a joint opinion by the presidents of seven national universities (all former imperial universities). He was of course one of them. The message to Orr was blunt: A Board of Trustees "would create possibilities of numerous evils and dangers for the future."[14] As Finn observed correctly, Nambara's Japan Education Reform Council had lost much of its influence.[15]

Each month the opposition to the draft grew. Nonetheless, Education Minister Shimojo Yasumaro (in office from October 19, 1948 to February 16, 1949) announced that he was ready to send the draft bill to the Diet for consideration. Nearly a hundred universities responded by closing their campuses. In February 1949 the president of Osaka University (one of the nation's most influential institutions) headed a massive street demonstration by students and faculty. The opposition to the draft bill appeared to paralyze the Ministry of Education. A new education minister, Takase Shotaro (in office from February 16, 1949 to May 6, 1950), was appointed. On May 24, 1949, he announced the bill's withdrawal from the Diet. He said that only a minority of students was responsible for the agitation and strikes on the campuses. He did not say that the Ministry of Education had given up. Agitation and strikes mushroomed. "The ministry has, however, been almost powerless to do anything about student agitation," Finn informed Sebald.[16]

On August 5, 1949, the ministry announced it had completely abandoned the idea of a Board of Trustees. Finn did not believe the faculty could govern, however. He told Sebald that there was at present "no effective system of control for most colleges and universities."[17]

A Lesson in Planning

These two major reorganization plans were made within the political context of the growing American alarm over worldwide communism. Appropriately the Zengakuren, a radical leftist organization, initiated the fierce attacks on the proposed Board of Trustees. The rest of the academic camp willingly joined in the offensive. It was no accident that the Ministry of Education in October 1949 warned that government-supported educational institutions must remain politically and ideologically neutral. Neither students nor faculty understood exactly what that meant. They did, however, understand the ministry's warning as an interference with their political liberties. The press also denounced the ministry in scathing terms.[18]

One year and a half after the US Education Mission left Japan, the physical condition of the nation's educational resources had not improved at all. US Political Adviser William J. Sebald admitted at the November 1947 meeting of the Allied Council for Japan that many classes were being held in disused factories or even in the open air, that elementary and secondary schools were being forced to share the same crowded premises, that numerous school buildings were in disrepair, and that new construction, where authorized, was being held up by lack of funds and materials. The shortage of teachers, he continued, was estimated at forty thousand. It was the paper shortage, however, that had hit Japanese students hardest; only a small proportion of the required textbooks were available at any level, and very often the only textbook was the one in the teacher's hand. Sebald, however, praised the Japanese government because, despite "tremendous odds," it had dared to introduce the new expanded educational system in April 1947.[19] MacArthur, too, praised the Japanese initiative: "The reform of Japanese education," he characteristically remarked, "is a Japanese problem which must be solved by the Japanese themselves and integrated by them into the social fabric of the democratic society now emerging."[20]

Actually, the Japanese government had no other choice but to begin the expanded program in April 1947, long before the autumn rice harvest with its contribution to pupils' physical strength. The Japanese were of course very eager for their children to resume their schooling. Nevertheless, the Yoshida cabinet agonized over Japan's uncertain economic prospects in undertaking the program. From agonized doubt it passed to active opposition, which was "very strong."[21] Education Minister Takahashi and chief of the Bureau of School Education Hidaka frequently visited Orr to report on the cabinet's internal discussions. The cabinet requested the Ministry of Education to present the Education Division with "cold facts descriptive of the present economic status of Japan."[22]

The Education Division did not have to be reminded of the miserable economic status of Japan. Well aware of it, the Education Division even so insisted that Japan launch the new mass education. Its dictate, of course, prevailed. Meanwhile the schoolroom shortage and many other physical deprivations that Sebald described did not improve at all. The Dodge Line—the American-imposed austerity program—eliminated money that had been budgeted for school building construction. The Ministry of Education was in a state of shock.

On April 7, 1949, Education Minister Takase made an urgent plea to Major General William F. Marquat, chief of the Economic and Scientific Section (ESS). The following verbatim account has been translated from Japanese records.

TAKASE: If the budget for construction were completely eliminated, our program of compulsory education that the Americans advised us to implement could not be carried out. This would be a grave shock to the people, not only educationally, but also socially, ideologically, and politically. We are deeply worried about the consequences. So, the cabinet has decided to reallocate some money from the budget for public works. I beg your reconsideration.

MARQUAT: The Japanese Government told us that the budget for public works was the absolute minimum. Now you say there is room in that budget. What are we at GHQ to believe?

TAKASE: We are even using horse stables as classrooms. The situation is desperate and miserable.

MARQUAT: Teaching beyond your ability is like spending beyond your means. The Japanese are especially prone to go on planning sprees without calculating the cost, and then to beg GHQ for more money. We at GHQ assume no responsibility for such planning.

TAKASE: The compulsory nine-year schooling is a product of American recommendations. Our people strongly support this. If you do not approve the money for construction, I fear it may diminish their trust in the [US] occupation authority.

MARQUAT: You don't have to worry about their trust in the occupation authority. If no money existed, neither GHQ nor the Japanese government could spend it. After all, the Japanese themselves must pay for the construction.

TAKASE: As this is an earnest desire of the Japanese government and people, I beg your special consideration.

MARQUAT: I shall give as much support as I can after I study the Japanese proposal.[23]

The school construction budget remained completely eliminated. Finn put the situation in a nutshell when he observed that until more money could be devoted to education, there would be little prospect for great improvements.[24] The Ministry of Education's *Bricks Without Straw*, a two-volume study submitted to CI & E on September 15, 1950, conveyed vividly with photographs the "tremendous odds" against which the Japanese people were battling.[25] This American attitude of praising "Japanese initiatives" in public was symptomatic of the dilemma of imposed democracy. The more drastic was the American reform, the more extravagant the American publicity for Japanese initiative.

More Policy Recommendations

In conjunction with the report of the US Education Mission, four other pertinent documents should be briefly mentioned here.

REPORT OF THE UNITED STATES
EDUCATION MISSION TO GERMANY

While the Mission to Japan was studying Japanese affairs, the National Education Association of the United States proposed an identical mission to Germany. On March 19, 1946, William G. Carr, the association's acting secretary, formally requested Robert P. Patterson, secretary of war, to "send a committee of educators, with purposes similar to that which is now in Japan, to Germany for a similar study and report."[26] The association's executive secretary, Willard E. Givens, was on the US Mission to Japan. The secretary of war referred the matter to Assistant Secretary of State Benton, who was then administering the Mission to Japan. Benton, especially after reading the mission's report and talking with Stoddard, became convinced of the benefits of a similar mission to Germany. On August 23, 1946, the US Mission to Germany went to the American Zone, where it stayed one month. The *Report of the United States Education Mission* was submitted to Lieutenant General Lucius D. Clay, deputy military governor, in Berlin on September 21. Later Patterson and Benton received copies.

In striking contrast to the Mission to Japan, the Mission to Germany approached its subject with humility—a humility bordering on admiration. "No country—unless it be ancient Greece or Rome—has contributed more generously to the common treasures of our civilization," the Mission to Germany stated. "No approach to the German educational problem dare be blind to this achievement or lacking in gratitude for it."[27] Naturally, the mission never dreamed of abolishing the German language in order to denazify the psyche of the German people. On the other hand, the Mission to Japan thought the Japanese people's outstanding trait was "good manners." "Japanese civilians, at least, are noted the world over for their formal gentility," the mission noted approvingly.[28] The Mission to Germany declared, "Nowhere in the world has it been possible to erect the structure of successful democratic self-government upon starvation or economic disorder.²⁹ To the Mission to Japan, however, economic factors were "important, but . . . not supreme."

THE FEC ON JAPANESE EDUCATION
On March 27, 1947, the Far Eastern Commission (FEC) in Washington, DC, formally adopted a policy directive entitled "Policy for the Revision of the Japanese Educational System." "Education should be looked upon," began the directive, "as the pursuit of truth, as a preparation for life in a democratic nation, and as a training for the social and political responsibilities which freedom entails. Emphasis should be placed on the dignity and worth of the individual, on independent thought and initiative, and on developing a spirit of inquiry."³⁰

MacArthur received this FEC policy statement as a directive on April 5. He was supposed to obey the FEC. On April 11, a day after the statement had been made public in Japan, MacArthur said he welcomed the FEC's "definite policy." At the same time he dismissed it by saying that it "introduced no new policy" and required "no shift in present emphasis."³¹ The directive was a belated one. Not only did it contribute to MacArthur's contention that the FEC was no more than a debating society, but it also epitomized the bureaucratic inefficiency of its multinational administration. Fortunately for the United States, MacArthur gladly and majestically took care of the inefficiency.

THE US CULTURAL SCIENCE MISSION
In contrast to the twenty-seven-member Education Mission, the US Cultural Science Mission, which arrived in late September 1948 and left in early January 1949, consisted of only five professors: George K. Brady, professor of English, University of Kentucky; Charles E. Martin, professor of international law and political science, University of Washington; Edwin O. Reischauer, associate professor of Far Eastern languages, Harvard University; Luther W. Stalnaker, professor of philosophy, Drake University; and Glenn T. Trewartha, professor of geography, University of Wisconsin.³² They conferred extensively with Japanese colleagues and wrote their own report.

The report pleased Nugent, who informed MacArthur that the mission had made "a definite contribution to higher education in Japan and to occupation objectives."³³ The recommendations for Japanese scholars were:

1. Research, which in the past has tended to be too theoretical, should in the future be made more "positivistic" and practical in direction.

2. An effort should be made to overcome the excessive emphasis
on the historical approach and antiquarian studies which in the
past has resulted in the neglect of the study of modern and contemporary problems.
3. The ivory-tower isolation of Japanese scholars should give way
to a new attitude of cooperative research in which some significant projects and more definite problems are envisaged than
has frequently been the case in the past.
4. The present economic and social crisis in Japan calls for all the
leadership the country is capable of producing and the call is
for Japanese scholars to cast off the cloak of isolation assumed
in the past and to step forward to meet the challenges squarely.
5. The Japanese cultural scientists, individually and collectively,
should develop a greater sense of social responsibility and
should strive to contribute more consciously and more directly
to the society in which they live.[34]

By "cultural science" the American professors meant "social science,"
which by its very nature should embrace a wide variety of scholarly
opinions. Accordingly, the report criticized the "many serious evils" of
the Japanese chair system, particularly "the feudal relationship between
senior and junior members of a faculty and the serious inbreeding of teaching and research staffs." What was needed, according to the report, was
"a general lowering of interfaculty and interdisciplinary barriers."[35] Unfortunately, the Japanese academic community believed that each department should remain autonomous. As this autonomy symbolized academic freedom, the walls of departmental sovereignty were never lowered.

Both the Cultural Science Mission and the Education Mission had
defined academic freedom not merely as a professor's intellectual freedom
within the classroom, but also as his freedom to exercise a full range of
political and civil liberties—a freedom that made his participation in the
body politic a moral obligation. This definition of academic freedom differed from the one put forward in 1940 by the American Association of
University Professors, which is still in force. The AAUP recommends
that "a teacher should be careful not to introduce into his teaching controversial matter which has no relation to his subject," and that when he
speaks or writes as a citizen, "he should remember that the public may
judge his profession and his instruction by his utterance." Thus the
AAUP's concept of academic freedom constricts a professor's words and
deeds, whereas the academic freedom that the American missions wished
to confer on Japanese professors encouraged them to act freely in accordance with their own consciences. One reason for the difference was
that the Americans perceived only too accurately how little academic
freedom or political liberty Japanese scholars had enjoyed in their daily
lives of late. That is why GHQ and the Ministry of Education insisted

especially during the initial period of the Occupation that all Japanese educational personnel should become involved in leading public issues to fulfill democratic responsibility as citizens.

THE GUIDE TO NEW EDUCATION
IN JAPAN

The US Education Mission had suggested that Japan find "the consciousness of a worthy national culture." The Ministry of Education discovered that the Japanese people themselves were primarily responsible for losing this consciousness of worth. "The Japanese people are scientifically backward and have a poor sense of logic," the ministry declared—words that should have reassured MacArthur, who believed that Japan was about four centuries behind Western nations.

The ministry's confession of national inferiority was published on May 15, 1946, as a *Guide to New Education in Japan.* Intended for elementary and secondary school teachers, it chiefly illustrated how far the Americans were prepared to press their demand that the conquered cheer for the victor's justice. "This manual," affirmed Brigadier General Ken R. Dyke, CI & E's first chief, in its foreword, "represents the first concrete evidence of a studied effort to reeducate the teachers of Japan."[36] Dyke could say this because his office had closely supervised the Ministry of Education's drafting of the "manual," plus several rewritings.[37]

The guide pleased CI & E. A satisfied boss was easy to work with and ready for more flattery. The Ministry of Education, with CI & E's approval, made the guide also available to teachers of middle, youth, and girls' schools. In the midst of the acute paper shortage during 1946 and 1947, the Ministry of Education printed 436,020 copies of the guide.[38] "The Ministry of Education does not intend to force the contents of this book on educators," the ministry magnanimously stated. "Therefore," it continued, "educators neither need to memorize this as a textbook themselves nor teach it as a textbook to pupils."[39] This attitude, suddenly arising less than a year after the paralyzing surrender, bewildered the nation's teachers, who had no experience of making their own educational policy decisions. The *Guide to New Education* was an official publication of the ministry. More imposingly, the CI & E chief heartily endorsed it. Japanese teachers strongly suspected that they had better memorize the guide and teach it as a textbook to pupils. Indeed, Chief Dyke confirmed their suspicion when he said that the guide gave "the teachers in a clear and summary form an outline of the basic facts accounting for the present situation in Japan," and would "point out the lessons which should have been learned."[40]

These "facts" and "lessons" were painful to teach. In the guide the Ministry of Education asked the Japanese people, as the first requirement of national rebirth, to "apologize most humbly to the world for the sins they have committed." "Apologizing for misbehavior," the ministry cautioned, "does not end by merely saying that they are sorry, or passively carrying out the demands of the Allied Powers because there is no alternative."[41] Instead, the Japanese people had to "show by their conduct that the establishment of a new Japan can only be accomplished by fulfilling voluntarily, of their own accord, the obligations stated in the Potsdam Declaration or any other directives issued by the Allied Powers." After the people had complied, "hardship and shame" might be "transfigured to joy and honour."[42] Even MacArthur could not have asked more.

The ministry itself naturally wondered how Japan had come to be in its present condition. Its answer was that there must have been "general defects" in the body politic, especially "in the wrong way of thinking of the people themselves." "Let us now examine," the ministry coaxed, "these defects and shortcomings."[43] The defects the ministry discovered in the Japanese outlook and character numbered five.

1. *"Japan is not yet sufficiently modernized."* To substantiate this the ministry reminded the teachers that "on street corners where motor vehicles rush by there are people who are having their palms read and their fortunes told."[44] As for an explanation, Japan since the Meiji Restoration had "learned how to use steam engines and electrical apparatus," but had "not adequately learned the scientific spirit which had built these things." Worse, some Japanese believed the Japanese way of doing things was better. That had been "a big mistake," because this minority became the nation's leaders and "gave little thought to Western culture, underestimated their power, and plunged the nation into war . . . deceived, fought and were defeated."[45] The ministry that had done its best to suppress the spirit of inquiry now equated it with victory. The United States represented both. As further confirmation of America's virtues, the ministry encouraged the teachers to "make better use of our abilities to embrace and assimilate and take in the fundamental principles of Western Civilization, digest these principles and be able to use them as our own."[46] Education Minister Abe's plea to the US Education Mission not to Americanize Japanese education was ignored even within the Ministry of Education. After all, the first task of the civilian Japanese government was to please the military conqueror. The Japanese were good at it.[47]

2. *"The Japanese Nation does not sufficiently respect Humanity, Character, nor Individuality."* Human beings were endowed with a "free will," the ministry stated, and could "aspire to make their lives logical, righteous and good, beautiful and comfortable, religious and modest, and strive for these attainments."[48] By working toward these enlightenments they would develop "humanity." That ought to be "the aim of life."[49] The ministry defined "character" as exemplifying rationality. It followed that someone whose

various activities were "disrupted, contradictory, or ununified [sic]" possessed little character. The blunt implication was that the Japanese people had been personally disorganized and therefore lacking in humanity. As for individuality, it was "a nature peculiar only to that particular person."[50] Individuality was a difficult concept for the ministry to define, because it had had no practical experience with it. Customarily the ministry defined individuality as egoism, if not as that most feared quality of all—anarchism. When one did not respect Humanity, Character, or Individuality, the ministry warned, the consequence was a society in which human relationships tended to be patterned after master-servant relationships. This pattern of hierarchy, as Japanese as the cherry blossom, stunted the growth of valuable individual attributes. The ministry, paralyzed by the shame of unconditional surrender to the former "devils and beasts (American and British)," told the teachers that "Japan may find the cause of the war and the cause of her defeat in this weakness."[51]

3. *"The Japanese lack critical spirit and are prone to obey authority blindly."* This, of course, was what the ministry exemplified to the teachers by faithfully obeying American dictates. The ministry seemed aware of this uncomfortable fact, as it also stated: "One of the attributes of the Japanese people is that those higher in rank have always loved and guided those below them, from which the virtues of loyalty and filial duty generated [sic]." Ironically, the ministry was intimately familiar with the past horror of "the virtues of loyalty and filial duty," since it went on to attack "the idea that officials are better than civilians." Also admonished was the government's routine indifference to the people's freedom of speech and other fundamental human rights and the "employing [of] torture and secret service agents." Such abuse deprived the people of "the ability to exercise political discretion and judgment," and forced them to submit "blindly to the orders of the government."[52]

4. *"The Japanese people are scientifically backward and have a poor sense of logic."* These primitive people had manufactured the Zero, one of the best fighter planes of World War II, as well as two of the world's largest battleships. Yet the Ministry of Education neither intended to be humorous nor could afford to be sarcastic. The ministry said that the people who "are inclined to obey authority blindly" were the same ones who "did not have the ability to think logically."[53] A logical and scientific mind was equated with a democratic mind, one that would obey authority only selectively. The ministry saw overwhelming evidence of Stone Age Japanese logic and science in the indigenous myths and legends. The myths and legends had been taught "in history textbooks as historical facts," said the ministry scornfully. The ministry omitted to say, however, that it had not only written and published those "historical facts" but coerced teachers and pupils to memorize them as universal truths. As further evidence of Japanese backwardness, the ministry calmly pointed out that "students accepted them and did not try to find out whether they were true or not."[54] When some of them did try to find out, they were swiftly condemned as "dangerous to public peace and tranquility." After all, the Japanese myths and legends were those of the Imperial Household, and who had dared to question them? As further proof that daily life in Japan was devoid of science the ministry offered the Japanese written language, which, it declared, was an "extra irrational burden" and hampered "our scientific spirit."[55]

5. *"The Japanese are self-satisfied and narrow-minded."* "Those who are unable to discard feudalistic feelings," the ministry delicately informed the teachers, "take an arrogant and egoistic attitude toward those below them who are blindly obedient to their superiors." The ministry continued on this very familiar subject and said that arrogance gave rise to self-satisfaction. Two examples of Japanese narrowmindedness were Japan's condemnation of Christianity and the Japanese race superiority complex. The ministry, however, reassured the teachers that it was "natural for anyone to have pride and confidence in one's own race, to love his fatherland" and that there was "nothing to criticize in that." What, then, had gone wrong? Japan had self-righteously attempted to subjugate other nations; that, too, was "the cause of the war and also the cause of the defeat."[56] In the subsequent chapters of the guide the Ministry of Education frequently praised the democratic virtues of the West and denounced the feudalistic vices of Japan.

For all its dogmatism, the guide was full of unresolved issues. One such issue was language reform, which was still causing the ministry keen annoyance. The ministry was yet to hear from MacArthur, who said in December 1946 that the language issue should be left wholly to the Japanese themselves, and that the Americans should refrain from interfering. However, the ministry well knew the impossibility of actually changing the Japanese language to the Roman alphabet; indeed, it advised the teachers that such a change would be "not desirable," since at the present time it would cause "inconvenience to the people."[57] If a majority of the people were to favor adopting the Roman alphabet "at some time in the future," the ministry was prepared to approve.[58] Such a future, the ministry was sure, would never come.

Another conspicuous feature of the guide was that the ministry openly endorsed "a healthy development of the Teachers' Union ... for the democratic life and discipline of teachers."[59] The ministry notably deemphasized the teachers' need for a full stomach; officially, the major issue was spiritual fulfillment.[60] Such a statement sounded unfeeling in 1946, when the people were desperate for food and when MacArthur reviled them for creating "disorders and violence by mass mobs."

The Ministry of Education advocated democracy, pure and uncompromising, as the only form the new social arrangements could take. That the new democracy was uncompromising was merely a reflection of the Japanese government's habitual authoritarianism, which had enabled it to create a totalitarian regime with such ease. The ministry condemned imperial Japan but exonerated itself by declaring early that militarists and ultranationalists had abused the magnanimous imperial wishes for the sake of their ambitions. The ministry, the master of thought regimentation, told teachers and students that they were narrow-minded and tended to obey authority blindly. While packing the guide with official denunciations of the Japanese people, the ministry tried to preserve the principle of imperial sovereignty at all cost. Thus the ministry informed teachers that the prewar official effort to clarify the national characteristics was good; that the National Spiritual Culture Research Institute and other similar government organizations (which existed solely for the purpose of thought control) were good; and that even *The Way of the Subject* and *The Cardinal Principle of Kokutai* were good. "These movements were in the right," the ministry boldly declared, "insofar as the ideal of the Japanese people was to cease to imitate Europe and America, to be conscious of the national characteristics in an independent attitude, to respect the history of the country, and, by letting grow the strong points in the national traits, and by developing a culture of their own, to contribute to the welfare of the world."[61]

In the late nineteenth century such an ideal could have been a healthy reaction for an imperial Japan that had become infatuated with the West. But Japan's reactionary leaders went beyond nostalgia for the historical past and entered the realm of myth and legend. They even discovered an "Original Family" to which all living Japanese owed their filial duty forever. This family happened to be the Imperial Household. The reactionary leaders also believed in a one-dimensional picture of society, that of the sovereign and his subjects. Despite their own imitation of Germany, they called on the Japanese people "to cease to imitate Europe and America" and "to respect the history of the country." The Imperial Household presided over their military victories with detached benevolence. In December 1941, when the Emperor and his civilian advisers were not watching, the "militarists and ultranationalists" attacked the United States and—incredibly—lost the most important war. The loss, of course, was not just theirs but Japan's. Pacifism, in occupied Japan, became the supreme virtue, although the reactionaries equated it with cowardice and defeatism.

After the surrender the Emperor's loyal advisers reported many times that he had not wanted the war with America, and desperately wished for its termination in August 1945. They said it was not the Japanese system of imperial governance that had caused such unprecedented human misery; the real fault lay with the militarists and ultranationalists, who had been nurtured by the Japanese people. Thus blame for the war fell not upon the imperial government but upon the people's "defects." The Japanese people had to apologize to the world by voluntarily showing how peace-loving and scientific they could become in the near future. Thus the Ministry of Education was denouncing defects once praised as unique Japanese virtues—defects that the ministry itself had been responsible for inculcating. By denouncing them, the ministry had perhaps been indirectly analyzing its past involvement in Japanese empire building.

If so, its self-analysis did not include questioning imperial sovereignty, which was unquestionable.

The ministry recanted in public, hoping that the Americans would then forgive its past mismanagement of Japanese education. It also hoped that the recantation would somehow transform it, in the eyes of Japanese teachers, from an object of fear to a source of friendly advice. It was no accident, then, that in March 1946 Tanaka Kotaro, soon to become education minister, made the following statement:

> The cause of our defeat can be traced neither to the low quality of natural science that failed to invent an atomic bomb nor to inadequate political science that failed to administer the controlled national economy. The true cause is our starting a war that could not be permitted from the standpoint of morality. The cause of the defeat resides in the defects of the people's morality.[62]

In other words, the *Guide to New Education* effectively combined the victor's propaganda with the loser's self-abasement before it—a rare phenomenon in world history.

The ministry's public confession, however, was completely useless as a cure for the problems it diagnosed. Its only real contribution was to reaffirm the Japanese experience at its most basic level. Once again the Ministry of Education was to indoctrinate the nation's teachers and students. This time, however, Western qualities were extolled and Japanese ones downgraded. Somewhere in the process, the Ministry of Education managed to come out cleaner than the Japanese pupils.

An Imperial Offering to Democracy

The Emperor and Empress were deeply concerned about the future of twelve-year-old Crown Prince Akihito. His upbringing, they believed, should be consistent with the novel concept of popular sovereignty. The Prince must understand what American democracy would look and feel like and anticipate a new Japan without a hereditary nobility.

In March 1946, the Emperor asked George D. Stoddard, chairman of the US Education Mission, to find a suitable American female tutor for the Crown Prince. Conceivably he intended to demonstrate his willingness to offer up the Crown Prince as a kind of human sacrifice for the greater cause of future Japanese welfare; in any case, it was clever imperial diplomacy. The Emperor even entertained members of the US Mission at the Imperial Palace. The members, however, were not very impressed with him. Emily Woodward was downright insulting: "He is a timid little man obviously nervous over all that is going on about him."[63]

After returning to the United States, Stoddard worked hard to find a special woman tutor. Kate Smith, whose voice had sold so many war bonds, announced on the radio to the American people that the Emperor of Japan was looking for a tutor for the Crown Prince. One woman actually applied directly to the Emperor.[64] Stoddard recommended two final candidates to the Imperial House. One was Miss Mildred A. Chaplin of the University of Hawaii and the other Mrs. Elizabeth Gray Vining of New Hampshire. The choice was announced on August 6, 1946. "Imperial Household has decided on Vining repeat Vining," MacArthur communicated to Stoddard in a telegram.[65] Stoddard immediately asked Vining if she would accept the invitation. She would.[66] Vining (b. 1906), a widow who had become a prolific author (her *Adam of the Road* won the 1943 Newbery Medal), remained as tutor until 1950. She published an account of her experience in Japan in *Windows for the Crown Prince* (1952). Pleased with Stoddard's work, William Benton wrote him: "I am keenly interested in this particular matter because undoubtedly the future Emperor will reflect the influence of his American tutor in the years to come."[67]

Both the Emperor and the Empress, delighted with their son's new learning, wished to accelerate "the influence of his American tutor" in a manner befitting to his station. In January 1949 the Empress informally suggested to William J. Sebald, then acting political adviser to MacArthur, that the fifteen-year-old Crown Prince receive preparatory school education in the United States and higher education in England. MacArthur agreed with the idea but felt that "the boy should first learn to speak English and that the aim should be a four-year standard course in the United States without a period at a foreign preparatory school." Sebald, too, found the suggestion a good one, "both in the interests of the United States–Japanese relations and in the interests of weaning the young Prince away from the enervating atmosphere of a royal court in which feudal customs may gradually reappear."[68] Sebald, however, asked W. Walter Butterworth, assistant secretary of state for Far Eastern Affairs, for his frank comments.

"I am inclined to believe," Butterworth replied to Sebald, "that it would be an almost impossible adjustment for one who has been brought up in the atmoshpere of Japanese court life to be suddenly placed, at an early age and with only a rudimentary knowledge of English, in an alien country and among boarding school boys most of whom would have already been in the same class for several years." Butterworth reminded Sebald of the wartime animosities "still too fresh in the public mind"; the Japanese, he added, were "hypersensitive about such matters." He continued: "A further two years of schooling in Japan under the very competent instruction of Mrs. Vining with emphasis on English language and Western culture seems to be indicated. This would bring the Prince to college age." If the Empress still desired that the Prince receive a university education abroad, Butterworth said, then the Americans should encourage it. He, however, wished the Prince would stay away from the United States, because of the possibility of embarrassing racial incidents there. Besides, educating the Prince in England would "lend itself less readily to charges of American 'colonization' of Japan." He told Sebald that Secretary of State Dean Acheson concurred with the above view.[69]

Crown Prince Akihito received his university education not at Oxford but at Gakushuin in Tokyo, a private university famous for attracting the prewar Japanese peerage. By then, however, the Occupation was ending. Perhaps the Empress considered the future Emperor's Americanization no longer necessary diplomatically and unpopular on the domestic front.

In 1872, when Meiji Japan, bold yet insecure, had suffered an identity crisis, Japan's first education minister, Mori Arinori, proposed the abolition of the Japanese language and its replacement by English. He found good reason for this drastic change in "the commercial power of the English-speaking race [that] now rules the world" and in "the power of steam and electricity." He believed that the "meager" Japanese language had never enabled the Japanese people to "grasp the principal truths from the precious treasury of Western science and art and religion." "The law of state [i.e., all the laws and regulations needed for governing a modern society] can never be preserved in the language of Japan," he argued. "All reasons suggest its disuse." It was David Murray, Mori's own American appointee in the Ministry of Education, who persuaded him to abandon his romantic infatuation with the West.[70]

In March 1946, when Japan was about to assume a thoroughly different national direction, epitomizing another identity crisis, the US Education Mission, for similar reasons, recommended the abolition of the Japanese written language and adoption of the English alphabet. The mission's members showed a quasi-colonial sense of superiority that did little credit to their credentials as scholars and still less to their common sense. At the time, however, they do not seem to have had any doubts about their accomplishment. For instance, on May 9, 1946, George S. Counts of Columbia University Teachers College wrote William Benton: "If any important part of our recommendations should be adopted, the sending of the mission will go down in history as one of the most extraordinary events in the educational development of our time.... I regard my membership on the mission," Counts stated, "as a great honor."[71]

Another member, Emily Woodward, said: "The Japs [sic] are daily be-coming more like Americans, but they still have a long road to travel before redemption to new political and economic concepts."[72] In general, the US Education Mission's recommendations for transforming Japanese education looked like an eloquent—and rather idealistic—summary of the American system.

"I felt that the mission failed in one very important respect," Counts more recently reminisced to me. "They seemed to assume that they should introduce the American educational system in Japan, not realizing that education is always an expression of a particular society and cul-ture."[73] This defense, however, cannot be applied to the US Mission in March 1946, since it was deeply hostile to Japanese culture anyway, and would not have acted differently even if it had appreciated the relation-ship between that culture and the Japanese educational system. Counts also told me that he was the only member of the mission "who had ever visited Japan before," meaning that the other members had no knowledge of Japan. But it was Counts who, for all his knowledge, had written with the passionate assistance of Robert King Hall the highly controversial language recommendation—a recommendation that served to gravely discredit the entire report.

The mission's most conspicuous achievement, however, was to pro-vide intellectual confirmation of SCAP's on-going political reforms, which were to pacify Japan forever and democratize the hearts and minds of the Japanese people.

PART THREE
THE
PRICE
OF
PEACE

11
The Red Purge

PART THREE

PRICE
OF
PEACE

Who first attacked whom on the Korean Peninsula did not matter in Japan; what did matter were the drastic political and intellectual changes caused in Japan by this first American war against communism. Under MacArthur's auspices American cold war attitudes were immediately translated into a repressive official policy of the Japanese government, commonly called the "Red Purge."

From the very beginning of his reign in Tokyo, MacArthur had looked on communism as the ultimate threat to his most cherished political and religious beliefs. As early as September 1945 he began sending numerous top-secret telegrams to the War Department, warning of ominous Soviet activities in North Korea.[1] Because MacArthur's propaganda on behalf of political liberties had been so insistent, the Japanese people by the time of the Korean War had a good general understanding of what the new political slogan, democracy, meant. When American policymakers, "for the sake of democracy," purged the very Japanese Reds whom MacArthur had earlier released from jail, American declarations on human rights began to sound hollow to Japanese ears. Those Japanese intellectuals who had always liked to study Marxism, but were never allowed to put it to open test, now faced the same old fight for their intellectual freedom. This time their persecutor was not the familiar imperial government that had thrived on intellectual intolerance, but a supposedly democratic popular government that was believed to flourish on ideological diversity. These leftists vigorously attacked the Red Purge. By so doing they became the purge's prime targets.

Due to their long isolation from the international communist movement, these intellectuals tended to develop, as Kawai has aptly put it, "their own idealistic, bookish Marxism."[2] Besides being idealistic, and frequently fanatic, the Japanese Communists were neither experts in understatement nor gentle persuaders. Their public rhetoric succeeded in frightening the Japanese conservatives, embarrassing the moderates, and mesmerizing themselves as well as their cohorts. At the same time, of course, they infuriated the American policymakers who had given them political freedom. The Americans felt that the Japanese Communists had betrayed them, but were nonetheless jealous of the Communists' organizational ability and dedication. This American envy was well expressed by Walter Crosby Eells, who became a prominent hunter of Japanese Communists. He said, "Many times in Japan we wished that the non-Communist students would exhibit one-half the zeal and passionate devotion of the Communists."[3]

Prelude to the Purge

The Japanese general public showed remarkable tolerance toward the Communists' aggressive rallies and propaganda. The new tolerance stemmed from a popular assumption that it was democratic not only to be political but also downright sympathetic, especially to the Communists. It was the Japanese Communists after all who had dared to oppose the imperial regime, went to jail, and even died under brutal torture. In postwar Japan the Communists enjoyed the prestige of martyrdom. Communism, however, implied the Soviet Union, a nation the Japanese people heartily disliked. Consequently, the Japanese Communist Party publicized its independence from the Soviet Union—a stance that only made the party itself appear hypocritical. The steadily declining number of Communist seats in the House of Representatives indicated the changing public attitude. Of the 466 House members, 4 were Communists in 1947 and 1948, 36 in 1949, 29 in 1950, 22 in 1951, and none in 1952. These statistics also show the impressive success of the Red Purge.

From the beginning of the Occupation, the Japanese government had two strong preferences: that the Communists should stay in jail forever; and that the doctrine of inviolable imperial sovereignty should forever prosper. MacArthur, however, released the Communists, and they immediately attacked the Emperor System. The Japanese conservatives' nightmare was confirmed. MacArthur, as delighted as the conservatives were discomfited, encouraged Japanese workers to organize their own labor unions and even to overcome the *zaibatsu* (family-centered financial conglomerates). They eagerly obeyed his wish; labor unions mushroomed. MacArthur did not anticipate that they would be friendly to Communists.

But the plight of Japan's economy encouraged Japanese workers to become radicalized. It also greatly encouraged the Communists in the political agitation that they aimed at the frustrated workers. MacArthur soon found this effective dissemination of Communist propaganda very annoying. The Cold War, vigorously waged not only in occupied Japan but everywhere, did not ease his anxiety. It was only a matter of time before MacArthur and the Japanese conservatives came to agree that communism was in fact a most dangerous dogma. A tacit, and eventually explicit, agreement materialized when the Japanese labor unions declared a general strike for February 1, 1947. On January 31 MacArthur prohibited it. Yet the threat of it frightened both GHQ and the Japanese government. "There can be no doubt," confirmed Prime Minister Yoshida, "that the projected general strike of February 1947 was instrumental in inducing GHQ to review and change its policy towards the Communists and adopt a sterner attitude."[4]

Soon after his intervention in the general strike MacArthur introduced various economic stablization programs. He even halted economic decentralization, which he had earlier preached was essential for Japanese democracy and economic recovery. Recentralization of the scattered *zaibatsu*, he anticipated, would revive the steadily disintegrating Japanese economy. Also, in March 1947 MacArthur publicly suggested that peace treaty negotiations should begin, so that the Occupation could end. Future Japanese security, he recommended, could be taken care of by the United Nations. Prime Minister Yoshida, when interviewed by the Associated Press on March 19, said he preferred American protection to that of the United Nations. "We are having our battles with the Communists, too," he said. More explicitly, he added that Japan had "a very dangerous enemy to the north."[5] The *New York Times* published his interview on March 20, 1947. S. Tsarapkin, the Soviet chargé d'affaires in Washington, DC, protested to Dean Acheson, acting secretary of state, that "Yoshida, in the capacity of the head of the Japanese government, which capitulated to the Allied Powers, made a hostile attack against the Soviet Union, one of the Allied States."[6] Acheson replied to Tsarapkin that he would begin an inquiry. He sent Tsarapkin's letter to George Atcheson in

Tokyo and asked what was going on. Atcheson replied to Acheson that nothing was going on. Acheson then wrote to Tsarapkin that there was no evidence Premier Yoshida had made the remark attributed to him. "Only one American correspondent present at the interview reported such a remark and it appears that his inaccurate reporting was due to language difficulties."[7] He did not tell Tsarapkin that Yoshida, a former ambassador to England, spoke excellent English.

Japan's economy, already reduced to subsistence level, grew weaker. Ordinary Japanese people blamed the government. The Japan Communist Party through its daily newspaper *Akahata* (Red Flag) kept up its biting criticism of the government for failing to remedy the people's plight. Communist street agitation met with surprisingly widespread sympathy. But the conservative government discounted Communist zeal as neither filling the stomach of the people nor contributing to the future of the American-Japanese alliance. Meanwhile even government employees, whom MacArthur and the Japanese government thought should never go on strike, did so willingly and frequently. Both MacArthur and Japanese conservatives decided that government workers, at least, should be stripped of their right to strike. On July 22, 1948, MacArthur wrote Ashida, the new prime minister, a lengthy letter urging an immediate and comprehensive revision of the National Public Service Law, which allowed them that right. Quoting the late President Franklin D. Roosevelt, MacArthur said that a strike by government employees, "looking toward the paralysis of government by those who have sworn to support it, is unthinkable and intolerable."[8] On July 31, the Ashida cabinet issued Cabinet Order 201 to ban a strike by government employees. On December 3, 1948, the National Public Service Law was revised on the initiative of Yoshida, who had formed his second cabinet on October 19. The idea was, as Yoshida put it, to "prevent them [the Communists] from obtaining control of the unions and so menacing the economy."[9]

In early January 1949 Truman's special envoy, Joseph Dodge, came to institute a drastic austerity program. The national budget appeared to balance on paper. But the daily life of the people continued to be wretched. The Japanese Communists drew new strength from the situation and campaigned energetically on the people's behalf. The Japanese government grew desperate. In January 1949, in the midst of the election campaign, the government told newspaper editors that press support for any particular party candidate was illegal, and that "they had to give equal space to competing parties and could not attack anyone." This was a new interpretation of the new election law, and *Akahata*, fully understanding what the government was up to, questioned it. Caught by surprise, General Whitney of Government Section, who was well aware of what the

Russians might think, told the Japanese attorney general and the members of the election supervisory committee that their interpretation violated the law of the land, the Constitution.[10]

The Japanese government responded with another scheme for controlling Communist propaganda: it instituted an innovative system of newsprint allotments. Paper was to be distributed to the official organs of all political parties on the basis not of their circulation but of how many votes each party had received at the last general election. Since *Akahata* was considered a party organ, the monthly allotment to the Communist Party was reduced from 86,000 pounds to 20,000. "The Democratic Party, which had no official publication, received 34,000 pounds of scarce newspaper each month. The Democratic-Liberals, who published an almost unknown review, were allotted 94,000 pounds monthly and the Socialists, who printed a small weekly, received 34,000."[11]

Mao took power in China in January 1949, and the Soviets split the atom in September of the same year. The United States grew extremely nervous. MacArthur and Yoshida seriously considered outlawing the Japanese Communist Party. John Gunther wrote: "Yoshida wants to suppress and outlaw them bag and baggage; SCAP is reluctant to do so, for fear of driving them underground and because it does not want them to infiltrate into the Socialists and other left parties." Yoshida, however, claimed that GHQ had often made such a suggestion informally. "The first formal suggestion coming from GHQ," Yoshida said, "was contained in General MacArthur's Fourth of July message in 1949."[12] On that date MacArthur raised a question, in which an answer was provided. He asked "whether any organization that persistently and publicly advocated a program at variance with the aims of democracy and opposed established order should be permitted to function as a legal party."[13] The Japanese press understood that MacArthur wished the government to declare the Communist Party illegal.[14] The party was dismayed.

MacArthur's statement of July 4 may have been, as Yoshida asserted, "the first formal suggestion coming from GHQ." Before that, however, Yoshida himself had openly attacked the Communists. On May 11, 1949, at the first annual Prime Minister's Dinner at the Tokyo Correspondents' Club, Yoshida said: "True, we do not see eye to eye with the Socialists. We abhor Communism. In that sense, we are definitely of the Right. But we hope and believe that we are also in the right."[15] The truth was that Yoshida, encouraged by MacArthur's statement, wished to accelerate his attack on communism. On September 2, 1949, he submitted to MacArthur for review a draft of a speech scheduled on September 4. In his draft Yoshida said: "General MacArthur, drawing a sanguine picture of our achievement in the past four years, exhorts us to great efforts.

By spiritual regeneration as well as physical rehabilitation we should yet achieve true greatness and be, as he says, a bulwark of human freedom." To achieve it, he continued, "we must combat communism, which under alien instigation seeks to create confusion and destroy social order by deceit and intimidation. We should boldly confront and overcome this sinister force. . . . Most of our Communists, I believe, are victims of ignorance and delusion, who can be won back to good citizenship, if we give them a chance for reflection and self-awakening."[16] MacArthur made a notation on the margin of Yoshida's draft, "Entirely unobjectionable."[17] After making these statements Yoshida noticed that "the Japanese Communists became openly antagonistic in their attitude towards the United States the following year."[18]

Although MacArthur stated as late as November 1949 that Japan did not need any armed forces for its internal and external security, on January 1, 1950, he advocated reinterpretation of the Constitution's article 9 (the so-called no-war clause) so that Japan would be prepared for the unpleasant ramifications of Communist encroachment in Asia. Concurrently, in January 1950, the Cominform reprimanded Nosaka Sanzo, perhaps the most popular Japanese Communist, for "his heterodox view that the Communist could aspire to control the government through ordinary parliamentary processes and that socialist reforms were possible even under the Occupation."[19] Nosaka recanted. Yoshida wrote that "from that time onwards" the Japanese Communist Party advocated a revolution by force.

Yoshida Clamps Down

GHQ had been keeping the Japanese Communists under close surveillance. On October 25, 1947, Major General Charles A. Willoughby, chief of Military Intelligence Section, GHQ, reported to MacArthur that "a usually reliable source," who had "contacts with three important officials in the Communist Central Headquarters," as well as with Tass, the official Soviet news agency, which had "acted as a 'cover' for the Soviet Embassy in dealing with Japanese informants," had told him that the Soviets had become "dissatisfied with the overaggressive, revolutionary type of leadership TOKUDA has provided."[20] Tokuda Kyuichi was one of the Japanese Communists whom MacArthur released from prison in October 1945. On July 6, 1948, Willoughby reported to MacArthur that "a complex liaison network, depending primarily upon illegal and covert movements of Koreans to and from Japan and Korea," was being used to infiltrate Cominform agents into Japan, and that Cominform "directives, policy guides and funds" were being "conveyed to the Japan Communist Party."[21]

SCAP-GHQ responded vigorously. In February 1949, according to Yoshida, "GHQ for the first time initiated steps aimed at legislative action openly directed against the Communist threat." GHQ's suggestion resulted in the Organization Control Law of April 1949. This law "prohibited all ultranationalistic and antidemocratic political associations ... and reserved to the government the right to call in responsible officials of such organizations for questioning and to demand the presentation of data whenever such action was considered necessary." Prime Minister Yoshida was very satisfied with this law, which, he said, "served its purpose until the Occupation ended." After the Occupation he wanted to establish "a committee within the Diet along the lines of the US House Committee [on] Un-American Activities." He had to give up this project because of "too many difficulties."[22]

On May 3, 1950, the anniversary of the proclamation of the Constitution, MacArthur became more aggressive. The Communist Party, he said,

> has cast off the mantle of pretended legitimacy and assumed instead the role of an avowed satellite of an international predatory force and a Japanese pawn of alien power policy, imperialistic purpose and subversive propaganda. That it has done so at once brings into question its right to the further benefits and protection of the country and laws it would subvert and raises doubt as to whether it should longer be regarded as a constitutionally recognized political movement.[23]

"I myself was almost disposed to agree [with MacArthur's desire]," Yoshida conceded, "to see the Japanese Communist Party declared illegal."[24]

On May 30, 1950, the Communist Party held a rally on the outer grounds of the Imperial Palace in Tokyo. Mingling with the Japanese police were several American soldiers who were taking pictures of the rally. Someone started a scuffle that lasted five minutes. Five of the Americans received minor injuries. This was, as John Gunther reported, "the first time in the history of the Occupation that any Japanese had attacked and injured GIs."[25] Eight Communists "were quickly arrested and promptly brought to trial before an Occupation court." One defendant received ten years at hard labor, one seven, and the rest five years.[26] It was, Gunther thought, "a rush job."[27]

Yoshida did not think it was a rush job. On June 4, he said publicly that the trial had "clearly shown [that] the principal force that brought about the shameful affairs was ... members of the Communist Party and a few students who, instigated by them, acted as their catspaw." He added that his government "might even have to consider outlawing the Communist Party."²⁸ Accordingly, the police authorities proceeded to ban all outdoor meetings and permit only indoor meetings. Since there were practically no large auditoriums left in Japan because of successful American air raids and no money to rebuild them, the official ban on outdoor meetings was effective in controlling the size of Communist gatherings.

On June 3, 1950, the Communist Party sent an open letter to MacArthur condemning the arrests and trials and demanding the immediate release of those sentenced. MacArthur, who was not used to being challenged, swiftly responded by ordering the Japanese police "to confiscate all available copies of the letter and to search for additional stocks." The police found many copies "in quarters related to the Communist Party."²⁹ As if he had been waiting for this kind of public incident with the Japanese Communists, on June 6 MacArthur ordered Prime Minister Yoshida to purge—that is, to "remove and exclude ... from public service"—the twenty-four members of the Central Committee of the Japanese Communist Party. MacArthur's rationale for the purge was a scathing one: the Japanese Communist Party had "sought through perversion of truth and incitation to mass violence to transform this peaceful and tranquil land into an arena of disorder and strife as the means of stemming Japan's notable progress along the road of representative democracy and to subvert the rapidly growing democratic tendencies among the Japanese people." The Communist Party's "coercive methods," he charged, bore "a striking parallel to those by which the militaristic leaders of the past deceived and misled the Japanese people, and their aims, if achieved, would surely lead Japan to an even worse disaster." Yoshida, to whom MacArthur's order was hand-delivered at 9:30 A.M., could not have agreed more.³⁰

The same day, at 7:30 P.M., the Japanese Communist Party issued an appeal headed "To All Patriots Throughout Japan!" "If you succumb to the Yoshida cabinet's outrageous policy," it declared, "the freedom of every Japanese will be violated and the whole race will be enslaved. Hitler and Tojo proved that."³¹ (MacArthur and Yoshida found the comparison with Hitler and Tojo "downright libel."³²) Continuing its appeal, the party boldly asserted that "reactionaries at home and abroad, who could not stand against the Communists as they fought bravely for Japanese peace and independence and opposed creation of military bases in Japan, began to suffer death agonies."³³ But it was the party's death agony that was about to begin. The next day, June 7, MacArthur ordered Yoshida to purge (i.e., fire) seventeen editors of *Akahata*. His reasoning was simple: *Akahata* had

> for some time assumed the role of mouthpiece for the most violent of lawless elements within the Communist Party and as such defiled its news

columns and editorial pages with licentious, false, inflammatory and seditious appeals to irresponsible sentiment in the efforts to provoke defiance of constituted authority, disrupt the progress of economic revival and create social unrest and mass violence. All this calls for prompt corrective action to safeguard the public peace.

He would not, however, actually suspend *Akahata* because it would violate freedom of the press, and was therefore "repugnant" to him. This order, too, was hand-delivered to Yoshida, at 5:10 P.M.[34]

What was going on, proclaimed *Akahata* the same day, was "an open suppression of the Japanese Communist Party and the people who hope for peace and independence"; the same thing, it made clear, had happened under Hitler. As for the Yoshida cabinet, it was violating the Potsdam Declaration and the Japanese Constitution and betraying the Japanese race. *Akahata* did not stop there. "The reactionaries' dream," it predicted, was "to drive the Communists underground." All of this the Yoshida cabinet was doing "for the sake of foreign plutocrats."[35]

The Yoshida cabinet issued orders for the arrest of "lawless elements," who predictably went underground, some escaping to China. On June 25, 1950, the Korean War broke out.[36] On June 26, MacArthur ordered Yoshida to suspend *Akahata* for thirty days.[37] The same day police raided all known Communist cells throughout Japan.

MacArthur's zeal in fighting domestic and foreign communism pleased the Emperor, who was supposed to stay out of politics. "Two sources close to Emperor have informed me on confidential basis," Sebald reported to the State Department, "of Emperor's sincere gratitude to US for prompt action taken and his suggestion that Japanese government might wish to consider issuing public statement to this effect." But the Japanese government, Sebald said, "reportedly feels Japan cannot, as occupied country, too brashly interject itself into Korean operations notwithstanding genuine desire to assist US wherever possible."[38]

From July 18 all Communist or pro-Communist publications were suspended indefinitely. (*Akahata* did not resume publication until May 1, 1952, three days after the US Occupation formally ended.) Encouraged and protected by SCAP, the Japanese government hunted down Communists and their sympathizers, real or imagined. Yoshida summarized the result of the nationwide hunt: the total number fired from their jobs was, he claimed, "some twenty-two thousand." The Red Purge, he rationalized, "was the alternative chosen by us to making the Communist Party itself illegal." He attributed the purge's success to "the support of public opinion."[39] "Public silence" would have been more accurate, since if anyone had defended the Communists, he would have been considered a sympathizer and therefore purged as a matter of course. That the purge did succeed there can be no doubt, as William Sebald saw when he reported to the State Department on July 19, 1950: "Government's anti-Communist moves keeping JCP on run and hampering effectiveness of its efforts."[40]

The Red Purge in Education

Fear of the Red Purge spread swiftly. It was particularly acute in the nation's educational circles. Communist teachers, a minority, and their non-Communist colleagues alike braced themselves for yet another official crusade against holding the wrong ideas. Their memories of a similar crusade before 1945 were still painfully vivid. GHQ wanted the Communists and their sympathizers to fear and tremble, to the point of resigning voluntarily from teaching. GHQ and the Japanese government saw the Japan Teachers' Union, which included practically all elementary and secondary teachers, as the bastion of the Communists. The thought of Japanese youth receiving its first impressions from Communist teachers was anathema to them.

Not only communism but the nation's pervasive pacifism—a successful product of American indoctrination—alarmed GHQ. The Americans decided that pacifism had had its day, and that Japan should prepare for combat against communism. But, to their dismay, communism fascinated the "nation's future brightest." In 1948, when applicants to the law department of Tokyo University were asked to write an essay on the future of Japan, "70 percent favored communism, 20 percent nihilism, and only 3 percent Christianity," reported one Japanese Christian pastor to GHQ.[41] It was indicative of the nature of the US Occupation that the pastor, like MacArthur, viewed the reform of Japan in terms of communism versus Christianity. To GHQ these percentages proved that elementary and secondary school teachers had been preaching communism to their innocent pupils. Such action justified the purging of all suspects. "In 1948," Walter Crosby Eells reported, "about twelve hundred Communist or allegedly Communist teachers were advised to resign and most of them did so."[42] These were 1,200 out of the total of 499,860 elementary and secondary school teachers in 1948—a mere 0.24 percent of the total. For GHQ, however, that was too many.

THE PRIMER OF DEMOCRACY

GHQ's Red Purge actually started early in the Occupation, in 1946. MacArthur, desiring Japanese youth to grow up in an atmosphere where democracy was unquestioned, wanted a handy manual. Dr. Howard M. Bell, a specialist in social studies and in curriculum and textbooks, suggested one called a *Primer of Democracy*.[43] He was assigned to collaborate with the Ministry of Education on drafting this primer. Bell was an excellent choice for this task. His views were firm: "Unless Americans start demonstrating and teaching the virtues of democracy with something like the aggressiveness and zeal with which the Russians are preaching what they consider the virtues of communism, we are in for some real trouble."[44]

Bell closely supervised the Japanese authors of the primer, especially Professor Otaka Asao of Tokyo University, who was the principal author and editor. Their collaboration worked well. "We are going to have an unusually good book," Bell reported to Orr on April 13, 1948.[45] Two months later Bell made another progress report to Orr. The primer had been "revised, often rewritten, four times by the original author and later by Profesor Otaka." In the course of the revision, every sentence had been "checked and doublechecked against the Japanese manuscripts."[46] The eleventh chapter, "Democracy and Dictatorship," was, he emphasized, the most important one, for it contained "the direct and deliberately caustic references to the Communist Party of Soviet Russia and its boss." He said the rest was "essentially preparatory."[47] But this blatant attack on the big neighbor whose representatives participated in the Occupation seemed to "worry the policy gentlemen of the ministry [of Education]." Ministry officials told Bell that chapter 11 violated "the spirit, if not the letter, of the Fundamental Law of Education." "I don't think so," replied Bell. "To pull the punches in chapter eleven," he reasoned to Orr, [would] "largely destroy the book's potential effectiveness." Furthermore, "in view of the ideological intensity of this so-called cold war and our comparatively meek performance to date, it would seem both illogical and timid not to speak of things as they are." "I am personally very pleased with them," he said of the Japanese authors under his direction.[48]

A completed draft of the *Primer of Democracy* was circulated within GHQ-SCAP in September 1948.[49] Response was in general favorable. Brigadier General Whitney, chief of the influential Government Section, who with his master MacArthur was least friendly to the Communists, said that he had "no objection, except for certain references to the Soviet government in chapter 11, 'Democracy and Dictatorship,' which would seem to violate paragraph 3 of SCAPIN 33."[50] SCAPIN (SCAP Instruction) 33 was the Press Code, which ordered the Japanese press to make "no false or destructive criticism of the Allied Powers." But the Cold

War was getting hotter already in Japan as well as in Europe. Chapter 11 remained as written.

With American blessing the Ministry of Education published the *Primer of Democracy* on October 30, 1948, for use in high schools and adult education classes.[51] It had taken more than two years to write. *Stars and Stripes* hailed the *Primer of Democracy* with superlatives: "This is certainly the most complete, most accurate and most objective book on a subject which has probably been more written about than any other. . . . the Japanese reader will know everything about democracy and be able to apply it."[52]

The Japanese Communist Party did not agree; it denounced the primer as violating article 8 of the Fundamental Law of Education, which stipulated that all schools remain ideologically neutral. On February 4 and 5, 1949 the party announced in *Akahata* that this serious matter had to be reported to the Allied Council for Japan. All that this meant, how-ever, was that at the council meeting the Soviet representative could formally attack the United States, as was customary. The American rep-resentative at the council was not likely to be disturbed; in fact, Nugent told Whitney that "the United States would welcome the opportunity."[53] MacArthur himself regarded the Allied Council as merely "a debating society." The *Akahata* editors also advocated that the Japanese personnel responsible for the primer should be prosecuted (Nugent thought there was "little likelihood of prosecution"[54]). On March 15, 1949, the Japa-nese Communist Party filed formal charges of malversation against the two former ministers of education, the present minister of education, Takase Shotaro, and the principal author-editor Otaka Asao.[55] Nothing substantive came of it. The angrier the Communists, the happier grew CI & E. Walter Crosby Eells contently said that the primer had been described as "an outstanding indictment of communism and as a very effective countermeasure to the spread of Communist propaganda." Why? "It was vigorously attacked in Communist propaganda—an excellent recommendation for it."[56]

On June 27, 1949, the first group of repatriated Japanese soldiers from Siberia arrived in Japan. Upon landing some of them shouted the praises of Soviet communism. The Military Intelligence Division of the War Department had anticipated such a reaction as early as August 1946. Of the approximately 785,000 Japanese prisoners of war under Soviet control, "selected Japanese military and civilian personnel . . . ," it pre-dicted, "presumably are receiving political-indoctrination from the Soviets and, when returned to Japan, may become an important factor in influ-encing Japanese thought." Not only ideologically pro-Soviet, these repatriates, the War Department suspected, could "form a possible nucleus for a military organization which might be used to 'liberate' Japan."[57] CI & E accordingly published a portion of the primer as the *Story of Democracy* for the Japanese repatriates, "to offset the indoctrination in communist ideology."[58]

The other vigorous attack came from the opposite end of the ideological spectrum. Catholics hated the *Primer of Democracy*. Both the indigenous Catholics and the foreign missionaries who were their mentors tried to stop its distribution. The *Missionary Bulletin* asked John O'Donovan, Catholic adviser to CI & E, to review the book. He made his views explicit in his memorandum to Nugent. In chapter 1, which was "the most important chapter of this book," he complained, "there is no reference to the Supreme Being as the source of all human dignity and human rights." Although authority in democracy appeared to come from the people, they were not "the ultimate source of the authority." "God," he pronounced, "is the source of all authority." In the United States, he reminded Nugent, "the President solemnly swears on the Holy Bible to defend the Constitution, so help me God." This omission was serious enough for O'Donovan to declare that "while Christianity can get along without democracy it is not at all certain that democracy can survive without Christianity." Besides this critical deficiency, he added, "the discussion of communism is rather disappointing." The primer mentioned nothing about "its denial of God" and "its rejection of the worth and dignity of the human person." This was "not going to help greatly in the battle to save Japan from communism."[59]

Nugent reported to MacArthur that the Catholics in Japan condemned the primer for being "too secular." Also, they objected to "not only the interpretation of democracy set forth in the textbook under review but also to all those concepts of democracy introduced since the beginning of the Occupation by SCAP."[60] Exasperated, Bell lamented, "The Communists don't like us because we had unkind things to say about communism, and the Catholics don't like us because the things we said about communism were not unkind enough. It's hard to please everybody!"[61]

POLITICIZATION AND CONTROL

Howard Bell could ignore the Catholics but not the Communists. Soon after the *Primer on Democracy* was completed, he urged that CI & E immediately launch anti-Communist education in all Japanese schools. "Originally," Bell said, "my idea of a political education program for Japan was a positive one—to present the promise of democracy." While GHQ was doing this, however, the Communists had "made considerable progress in selling their bogus bill of goods to many politically innocent Japanese." "Ideologically," he declared, "we have an enemy that needs to be dealt with, and now." Speed was paramount, for political education in the Soviet Union formally began at the age of three. "We might at least begin with the age of six or seven." He proposed that CI & E issue "a clear-cut order to bring the Communist-democracy (really Russian and American) conflict out in the open, through classroom discussion and school and college assemblies." He was, however, worried about the lack of trained personnel to carry out a controversial new political education: "We will have to send a boy out to do a man's job."[62]

Mark Orr, impressed by Bell's argument, wrote an identical memorandum to his superior, Nugent.[63] CI & E's anxiety, which bordered on fear, was understandable. The Japan Teachers' Union (JTU), organized in late 1945 with generous American endorsement and the Ministry of Education's blessing, was becoming increasingly aggressive in its political and economic demands. It appeared to be making actual educational policies for the nation's elementary and secondary schools. The most vocal on local school boards were union members.

On college campuses the Zengakuren (All-Japan University Student Federation) ruled supreme. Organized formally on September 18, 1948, it grew rapidly and leaned heavily to the radical left, behaving as if it owned the universities. In December 1948 the Ministry of Education reported to CI & E that the number of institutions of higher education affiliated with the Zengakuren had reached 266, which was practically all of the nation's higher educational institutions, and that Zengakuren students numbered 222,581, which was 60 percent of the nation's university student population. These statistics were definitely inflated, but skeptical CI & E believed that even more students were involved.[64] Orr recommended to Nugent that CI & E immediately begin "combating communism on college campuses."[65] However, the spectacular popularity of these two organizations did not mean that their respective members adhered to the organizations' leftist ideology. Instead, the organizations served as the most convenient and effective rallying centers for the members' physical and psychological needs in a nation in crisis.

In May 1947 Japan's first Socialist cabinet came into being under Prime Minister Katayama. He was also a Christian. MacArthur hailed the event as a reflection of "complete religious freedom" that offered "hope for the ultimate erection of an invincible spiritual barrier against the infiltration of ideologies which seek by suppression the way to power and advancement. This is human progress."[66] Christian Socialist Katayama, cheered by MacArthur's effusive rhetoric, appointed Morito Tatsuo as the new education minister (he was in office from June 1, 1947 to October 15, 1948). Morito himself, when he was a young Socialist assistant professor of economics at Tokyo Imperial University, had suffered merciless persecution by the imperial government in 1920 for publishing an article on the Russian anarchist Kropotkin; he was dismissed from teaching, and the Japanese Supreme Court upheld the dismissal. The appointment of Morito as education minister was very good news to the Japan Teachers' Union and Zengakuren, but GHQ was becoming impatient with their political activities. Indeed, GHQ found both organizations repulsive and tried hard to reduce their influence.

The Katayama cabinet, knowing GHQ's displeasure, agonized over an appropriate approach to the politicization of the nation's education. Education Minister Morito's dilemma was especially painful, because he did not wish the students and teachers to experience the same kind of persecution he had suffered. On June 29, 1948, he visited Orr. The basic problem, he said, was that of "determining how to fight communism in the school and maintain civil liberties at the same time"; only some 20 percent of the students of higher institutions, he added, were involved in campus strikes. Although ex-Education Minister Tanaka, a member of the House of Councillors, advocated as a solution that the Ministry of Education resume thought control of the students and teachers, Morito told Orr that personally he was against it.[67] Orr suggested nothing to Morito. The next day, June 30, Morito courageously affirmed in the Diet that student political activity was "a constitutional right and to ban it might increase the likelihood of underground activities and alienate more students."[68]

Morito had misread Orr's silence. This liberal stance by the Ministry of Education was not exactly what GHQ wanted. GHQ intensified its efforts at making the Communists and leftists feel undesirable. Before the first election for local school board members, on October 5, 1948, representatives of the Military Government (Eighth Army) visited numerous campaign sites and derided leftist candidates.[69] On October 6, 1948, a day after the election, the Ministry of Education issued a statement on political activities of students and teachers. Freedom of research and political comment should be respected in the schools, the ministry blandly observed. It requested school staff, however, to "observe political neutrality and maintain the order of the institution."[70] GHQ wanted the Ministry of Education to denounce communism in blunter terms, but the ministry under Morito was reluctant to do so. Fortunately for GHQ, the Katayama cabinet crumbled a week later. Ashida, foreign minister in that cabinet, became prime minister and kept Morito as education minister.

Captain Paul T. Dupell, civil education officer of the Tokyo Military

Government, delivered a bristling speech at Nippon University on February 3, 1949. (It was the same Dupell who had angrily told Tokyo School Board members to do exactly what school board members did in America.) Communism, Dupell said, "thrives like a disease festering in filth." He had neither much respect for nor trust in students and teachers. "Being readily susceptible to bombastic, emotional propaganda," he told the academic audience, "students are easily instigated to strike." Communist teachers, he said, "become so obnoxious that they have to be discharged for incompetence and undesirability." Far more dangerous, he warned, was the teacher "who quietly and unobtrusively spreads the doctrines of communism in his classroom." He saw the danger of communism everywhere. "We see no difference," he declared, between the Communists and "the former Nazi and Japanese militarists." "With Communists, the end always justifies the means. Liberty and human dignity mean exactly nothing." Obviously, then, "Communist cells which exist in your universities should be wiped out as being contrary to the Japanese Constitution and the Fundamental Law of Education." Dupell reminded the students: "Remember that no one forces a student to remain in a higher education institution against his will. If a student doesn't like the policies or tradition of the school, he has the right to withdraw voluntarily."[71] That was exactly what Ministry of Education officials had earlier told the students who were demanding that school administration be made less inflexible and militaristic.

Dupell's speech did not impress everyone, even at GHQ. "We must not become the 'anticommunist' branch of SCAP," cautioned D. M. Typer of the Education Division. Since they were engaged "in an historically significant experiment," he said, their "every word and deed" would have to stand the already urgent test of history. The future would be even more demanding. "Useless name-calling," then, was a waste of time and effort.[72]

The future might be demanding, but there would not be a future at all if the present menace—the alleged threat of communism—were left to devour the politically innocent Japanese. The picture of Japan's future that CI & E painted, with Loomis warning Orr of "the danger of violent revolution" and of "feudalistic reaction," was precisely the justification needed for the Red Purge.[73] "The danger of violent revolution" came, of course, from the Japanese Communists. CI & E decided to suppress this danger, while closing its eyes—hesitantly perhaps, but deliberately—to the danger of feudalistic reaction. Typer's sensible warning was quickly lost as the Red Purge heated up. Meanwhile, the quasi-conservative Ashida cabinet fell because of a colossal bribery scandal. Yoshida Shigeru, a genuine conservative, took over.

On June 30, 1949, Nugent told new education minister Takase Shotaro (in office from February 16, 1949 to May 6, 1950) at their regular meeting that the US government would give full maintenance scholarships to most qualified Japanese students for studying in the United States. Nugent said that the United States considered this expense as an investment in democracy. He emphasized that "the chosen students must be neither Communists nor members of communistic organizations."[74] This prerequisite for the coveted scholarships—the only ones available for going abroad at a time when MacArthur had completely isolated Japan from the rest of the world—excluded most politically active students.

DR. EELLS IN ACTION
The most controversial episode in the Red Purge of education was Dr. Walter C. Eells's nationwide lecture tour. In July 1949 he was sent out "to do a man's job" of battling communism on the campuses.

The idea came from Nugent, who sent a brief note to the Education Division on April 23, 1949. "It appears to me that at the inauguration of a new university," he said, "a stirring message on Academic Freedom" should be presented. Such a message should contrast "the western democracies with what goes on behind the Iron Curtain," which "would not have to be a la Dupell—it could be scholarly and sane." Nugent believed explicit examples of communist abuses of the people's basic rights would "hit Japanese students and scholars (all the intellectuals) right where they live." "God knows the intelligentisia (sic) need something like that just now."[75]

Eells's job was to explain at various universities the difference "between [the] political rights of all citizens in a democracy and fitness for the privilege of teaching in a university."[76] He tried to "show that Communist professors by joining the party [had] thereby surrendered their freedom to think independently" and hence were unfit to teach.[77] This stirring message was entitled "Academic Freedom and Communism," a full text of which Nugent read and approved prior to Eells's delivery.[78] "The first detailed presentation of this doctrine was made by the writer," Eells proudly stated, "in an address at the opening of the new Niigata University in July 1949, which caused much interest and comment in university circles and resulted in vigorous opposition and demands by Communist student groups in the universities for withdrawal of the doctrine."[79]

Eells's thinking, popular in the United States in the late 1940s and early 1950s, was actually an official insult to the Japanese professors and students. The Japanese Association of University Professors, alarmed by

Eells's speech, strongly defended the constitutional guarantee of individual conscience and freedom at its annual meeting on October 22, 1949.[80]

Eells interpreted the association's statement correctly when he complained that "the association was 'unable to see the justice of depriving a professor of his status merely because of his membership in a political party.'" CI & E, he said, "did not support the restrictive policy" of the association.

Conveniently for him, a few weeks prior to his speech at Niigata University the American Educational Policies Commission came up with "the stronger position" that "Communists, by virtue of their membership in that party, are thereby unfit to be teachers in the schools of the country."[81] CI & E diligently applied this stronger American position to Japanese education. In his speeches, Eells continually dropped names to give credibility to the American Educational Policies Commission. He told the Japanese audience that the commission members included "President Conant of Harvard University and President Eisenhower of Columbia University," and that President Truman approved the commission's report.[82] Furthermore, Sidney Hook, an eminent philosopher, had independently reached "the unequivocal conclusion" that communists were "unfit to teach in American public schools and colleges."[83]

Education Minister Takase parroted Eells's doctrine that the Communist teacher did not have "real freedom of thought and freedom of study," and was therefore "not acceptable for university education."[84] But Takase was forced by CI & E to retract his earlier statement that no one must be dismissed because of being Communist.[85] Eells was sensitive enough to realize the obvious dilemma: the Communist Party, as he complained, was legal in Japan and had elected "many members" to the Diet, while academic freedom was guaranteed by the Constitution.[86] But this neither stopped nor slowed down his crusade. Even D. M. Typer put aside his earlier scruples and joined Eells in urging that "intensive efforts at combating communism should be centered on the universities."[87] "The same doctrine of academic freedom," Eells said, "was restated, expanded, and defended in a series of university conferences carried out from November 1949 to May 1950."[88] During those six months Eells and the CI & E staff organized thirty two-day conferences throughout the nation.

The State Department, however, was worried that GHQ might be going too far. The Office of Northeast Asian Affairs asked the Office of Intelligence Research (OIR) to investigate the situation in Japan. On November 14, 1949, the OIR submitted a confidential report entitled "The Campaign Against Communist Teachers in Japan." The legal basis for the Red Purge, it stated, was "far from clear"; indeed, the Japanese officials themselves were "not confident that the current campaign [had] a well-founded legal basis." Not only the legality, but the purge itself, the OIR said, might well revive "the atmosphere of fear and uncertainty that increasingly directed presurrender Japanese scholarship into safe and sterile channels."[89]

The State Department sent MacArthur a telegram requesting full information so that it could meet the criticism it expected from the Far Eastern Commission. His reply, the State Department found, was "unsatisfactory," but the department could not and did not take action. As U. Alexis Johnson of Northeast Asian Affairs acknowledged, it was "a question of method rather than ends." After all, he said, "unquestionably serious Communist infiltration of schools" existed in Japan.[90] The Red Purge proceeded without interruption. Eells inspired profound dismay and disbelief in the university students and faculty, reminding them of the terrible days five years earlier. Hostile demonstrations followed Eells wherever he went. His speech, he lamented, "was often interrupted by boos and catcalls, by shouts of 'liar,' 'enemy of democracy,' and 'warmonger,' and was the object of frequent hostile attacks in circulars and handbills."[91]

A typical exchange between Eells and his audience took place at Hokkaido University on May 15, 1950.

> DR. EELLS: In communist nations even mathematics could not be true. [loud laughter]
> PROFESSOR MATSUURA [chief of Physical Science Department]:   Dr. Eells made an incoherent explanation today. [loud applause] I hope Dr. Eells will take a rest well this evening and discuss again tomorrow.[92]

Eells viewed the opposition, some of which was riotous, as the best evidence that "small, but well-organized and determined Communist minorities can thwart the will of the majority and can prevent and destroy the academic freedom which they profess to be defending in their universities."[93] His labors completed, Eells concluded that the fight against communism had "not yet been won," and that "eternal vigilance" would be necessary.[94]

Eells's and GHQ's missionary passion was that of a regime too insecure to let a minority exercise its right to question the majority. Their demand that this minority remain silent was the very same kind of demand that might have been made by an oppressive communist regime. A thoroughbred totalitarian government, which the Japanese people barely lived through, had repeatedly used the same argument and method as

Eells did for the sake of public order and tranquility. The people knew
such "order" was worthless if not downright frightening.

From Purge to Depurge

While Eells was campaigning against the Japanese
Communists, the Korean War broke out. An actual war encouraged him
to progressively greater efforts in behalf of what he called academic
freedom. MacArthur too was fighting desperate battles in Korea. Although
the probability of Japan succumbing to a Communist takeover was actually nil—the great majority of Japanese were and are both devoted to
capitalism and suspicious of Soviet Russia—the public fear of communism was fanned to hysteria and the Red Purge was intensified.

THE SECOND US EDUCATION MISSION
It was while the Korean War was going from bad to worse
for the United States that the Second United States Education Mission
to Japan (August 27 to September 22, 1950) came to support American
efforts in Tokyo.

President Nambara of Tokyo University as chairman of Japan Education Reform Council welcomed the Second US Mission. In his welcoming speech he warned the mission members about "the two immediate
and most serious dangers confronting us." "One is, needless to say," he
said, "communism. The other is a reaction to communism, the revival of
fascistic forces."[95]

The mission submitted a report to MacArthur. In it Japanese teachers and students were warned that

> faith in human nature, in the integrity and worthwhileness of individual
> men and women is the necessary basis for free government. Where it is
> absent fear rules supreme, and fear fashions for itself instruments of op-
> pression. It seeks to justify itself on the assumption that people cannot be
> trusted, that they are stupid and incapable of self-government. One of the
> greatest weapons against communism in the Far East is an enlightened
> electorate in Japan.[96]

Actually, if there was any place where fear ruled supreme and was fashioning instruments of oppression, it was in Tokyo, under the MacArthur
regime. Precisely because the regime believed people could not be trusted,
and were incapable of self-government, it instituted the Red Purge. On

the danger of reviving such "fascistic forces" the Second US Mission had nothing to say.

The Japan Education Reform Council, originally the Committee of Japanese Educators who had worked with the first mission, joined in the second mission's chorus. In September 1950 the Japan Council's report to the Japanese government stated: "Some teachers and students today are, without the slightest compunction, injuring the dignity of the teaching profession and disturbing the order of the campus by confounding political interest with political activities of ideological deviation."[97] This assessment had some validity. "Ideological deviation" was the euphemism for communism. The Japan Council, the think tank for the Ministry of Education, declared itself "determined to dispel this unfavorable situation as soon as possible and restore the dignity of the teaching profession as well as the order of the campus."[98]

DISSENT OVER THE RED PURGE

It must be stressed here that the Communist elements on university campuses were ferociously aggressive. Although they were definitely in the minority, they were the best-organized and hardest-working group in Japanese politics, and hence exerted a disproportionately powerful influence. They were articulate. But their vocabulary was doctrinal and their delivery a harangue. When combined, these tended to become monotonous. Nevertheless, their open criticism of the government and the occupation authorities appealed to a large segment of the students who were traditionally idealistic. A favorite tactic of the Communists was to shut down the campus, which naturally did not improve their relationship with the university administration. On June 1, 1949, Nambara suspended twenty Tokyo University students, as he put it, to teach them democratic principles. The students struck again. Nambara, who had lost favor with the Ministry of Education and CI & E because of his vocal opposition to the proposed Board of Trustees, regained some of his influence when he formally banned the student Communist group from the campus. Tokyo University received the largest portion of the nation's education budget, and this action pleased the government. Other universities soon followed Tokyo University. The conservative Japanese government was encouraged by GHQ's new approach to political liberties. Major businesses and industries declared they would not employ any Communists or their sympathizers. All of this reminded Japanese conservatives of the good old days.

Although the Japanese government and universities seemed to agree

on the need to suppress Communists, they by no means agreed on the
Red Purge. A dramatic break occurred in May 1950, before the Korean
War and during Eells's lecture tour. Prime Minister Yoshida and President Nambara of Tokyo University engaged in a sensational name-calling
match. Yoshida was known among the Japanese as "one-man" (i.e., bossy),
a nickname he fully deserved and that he bore with some pride. Nambara,
a political scientist, was critical of the sweeping Red Purge and frequently
said so. He also criticized Yoshida's drive to align Japan exclusively with
the American bloc. Nambara advocated a comprehensive peace treaty
with all former enemies (including the USSR and the People's Republic
of China) and neutrality for post-Occupation Japan. His stance was identical with that of the Japanese Communist Party.

Irritated, Prime Minister Yoshida interpreted Nambara's public
criticism as untimely support for the Communist cause and a serious
hindrance to his successful administration. At a closed meeting of Liberal
Party Diet members, Yoshida called Nambara "a sycophant scholar and
an opportunist." His statement was leaked to the press. It was Nambara's
turn to be irritated. He called Yoshida's tactic "the very same one" that
had been perfected by "the militarists and their henchmen since the days
of the Manchurian Incident." "[The tactic] amounts to downright slander
of learning and authoritarian suppression of scholars," Nambara continued. "He treated my opinion as an ivory-tower theory, the work of
some desk-bound scholar. But it is bureaucratic self-righteousness to declare that only high government officials can know anything about the
present international situation." Under Yoshida's leadership, he thundered, "Japan's democratic government will see nothing but crises."[99]

"I do not believe the people will listen to President Nambara's
counterblast," said Sato Eisaku, Yoshida's protégé, who was to become
prime minister in 1964 and enjoy the longest term of office in Japanese
history. Sato, who was to receive a Nobel Peace Prize in 1974 as architect
of Japan's nuclear policy, explained that while the government did of
course honor freedom of learning, it was "harmful for Japan" that a scholar
should take up the matter of the peace treaty, since it had "become a
political problem." It was not only harmful, Sato said, but "quite anti-
democratic to oppose political affairs from a scientific point of view." Such
an attitude was nothing more than a misuse of the protection afforded
to scholars by the government.[100] If the Japanese government could get
away with this kind of fancy footwork, the Red Purge could not fail to be a
resounding success. Eells's account says it all: "At the 1950 election of 403
members of prefectural and local boards of education, for which there were
49 Communist candidates . . . not a single one of them was elected."[101]

THE CONDUCT OF MINISTER AMANO

The Korean War quickly put an end to the theoretical debates over whether the peace treaty should be comprehensive or partial. A comprehensive peace treaty would have meant President Truman embracing Stalin and Mao in San Francisco—a utopian dream that Yoshida called "the obvious absurdity."[102] As Sebald reported to the State Department: "Korean conflict has emphasized futility of overall peace and neutrality theories strongly advocated by JCP [Japanese Communist Party]."[103]

The new era in Japan required a new minister of education. Amano Teiyu, a professor of philosophy for twenty years, whom Prime Minister Yoshida deeply respected, assumed the office on May 6, 1950 (he was to hold it until August 12, 1952). About this appointment Yoshida had written to MacArthur on April 9, 1950, "I should be much obliged if your approval is given."[104] On May 13 Minister Amano visited GS chief Whitney for advice. Whitney told him:

> Your primary duty is to prevent Japanese students from entering into politics and to bring stability to the current state of affairs. Although I do not think communism is a great threat, it is a fact that the Japanese Communist Party exploits the immature minds of students for its own causes. Student organizations frequently become a nurturing bed for the radical movement. I hope you handle the situation with a firm and stern attitude.[105]

On May 17 Amano visited Nugent. Amano deeply apologized for "the unfortunate incidents at Tohoku University and Hokkaido University," where students and faculty members had rioted against Eells's lectures on academic freedom. Nugent consoled him, saying, "I don't think it is your fault." At the same time he wanted to express what he called a "personal opinion" ("Please do not take it as my order to you"). If it was just an opinion, it was a strongly held one.

> (1) Although students pay lip service to freedom of speech, they deny the same freedom to others. They are just like gangsters. (2) These students are no different from Hitler's gang, who depended upon the Gestapo. They form a pack to destroy freedom of speech. They are trying to make Japan a totalitarian nation at war. (3) One of the great advances made by postwar Japanese education is in university freedom and autonomy. But this freedom, like all other freedoms, comes with responsibility. The universities owe a responsibility to the public, which supports them. The public makes no secret of its opposition to the Communists' gangster tactics. (4) Nobody questions the students' right and freedom to study political philosophies, but I feel sorry for those students who foolishly believe in communism. If, however, they have interfered with other students' freedom, I have a different feeling than pity. (5) I do not advise you on some definite course of

action. I only want to emphasize that the university must exercise the new freedom with more responsibility. Otherwise, the university loses this freedom and succumbs to communism or totalitarianism.[106]

"I heartily agree with everything you just said," Amano replied.[107]

After these encouraging meetings with Whitney and Nugent, Education Minister Amano declared that all Communist teachers should be dismissed with all possible speed. The Japanese Office of the Attorney General offered him a list of fifty-nine university professors to be purged.[108] On October 19, 1950, Amano submitted to Nugent the Ministry of Education's proposal for establishing committees throughout the nation to discover Communist teachers and their sympathizers. On October 24 Nugent responded through Arthur Loomis:

> It is not a wise policy to purge Communist teachers under a reason that they opposed the objectives of the occupation forces, because the Occupation is going to end with a peace treaty. You, then, would have no basis for purging them. . . . As elementary and secondary school pupils must be protected from the teaching of communism, I agree that the Communists from these schools have to be purged. Regarding Communist professors, I should agree with Minister Amano that they should not be purged simply because of being Communists. But, if they disturbed the university's autonomy by a strike or boycott, they deserve to be purged.[109]

Minister Amano became better known for advocating a revival of the "Japanese spirit"—an elusive quality in postwar Japan. His courage in gambling on it was remarkable. He reasoned that in prewar Japan the State had ruled supreme and the individual was subjugated; in postwar Japan "the individual had become everything and the State nothing." His remedy, therefore, was "to emphasize the importance of the middle way, and to teach people how difficult it is to actually keep to it." "I am completely in agreement with his view," Yoshida said later, in his memoirs, "and wanted him to reconstruct Japan's educational system along those lines."[110]

On February 7, 1951, Amano proposed a new national holiday, a "Cultural Day," on which the national anthem would be sung and "our flag hoisted."[111] The day was November 3, which happened to be the birthday of the Emperor Meiji, an old national holiday. He said in the Diet that this new Cultural Day would serve to nurture a "quiet patriotism" among the people. The Japanese press, which interpreted Amano's intention as one of rehabilitating the State as an object of devotion, summarily denounced his plan. His second proposal was more intriguing. On November 14, 1951, Amano came up with a code of Japanese ethics that was, as Yoshida viewed it, "a sort of moral minimum."[112] It was named "the National Code of Conduct." The government wanted the code because the Japanese people ever since the surrender had seemed far less respectful of authority and even downright dilatory in carrying out what the government told them to do. The press, reflecting the general public, dismissed it as a reactionary fit. Two weeks later Amano retracted his moral minimum. Japanese social fabric did not break down, however.

REALPOLITIK INTERVENES

Reactionary fit or no, the conservative Japanese leaders were convinced from the very beginning of the Occupation that capitalist America and communist Russia would eventually clash in internecine strife. This clash, they believed, was an historic inevitablity as well as an ideological necessity. When MacArthur sanctioned the Red Purge, they persuaded themselves that they had been vindicated for their unrelenting persecution of communism and socialism. Their belief in the eventual American-Soviet collision remained unshakable even while the two nations were at their most friendly. In February 1946, while Japanese enthusiasm for American-style democracy was at its height, "the Japanese special police, experts on the suppression of communism, [had] expressed confidence," Emmerson reported to Secretary of State Byrnes, that their services would "some day again be called for." Emmerson dismissed their opinion as "an exceedingly optimistic statement from a militarist's point of view, forecasting a Soviet-American war and the resurgence of his class." The Japanese special police, the cream of the reactionaries, had also prophesied with astonishing accuracy that "United States strategy will require Japan as a staging area for military operations against the Soviets and will therefore permit Japan to retain a reasonable industrial potential for such an eventuality."[113] The Korean War proved them perspicacious. Enormous procurement by the US military forces dramatically revitalized Japanese industry.

Robert A. Fearey, a conservative State Department officer, concurred with the prediction of eventual US-Soviet confrontation as early as April 1946. He warned Secretary Byrnes that the "preoccupation with the current programs of Japanese democratization and demilitarization" diverted American attention from "more important aspects of a realistically conceived United States security policy toward Japan."[114] The United States ought to build up the Japanese economy as quickly as possible "to prevent the possible alliance of Japan at some future date with a more powerful potential enemy of the United States."[115] "The prospect of lasting peace in the Pacific," Fearey argued, would be improved if the United States permitted Japan "to build up defensive fortifications and forces rather than to commit itself to remain disarmed indefinitely."[116] For re-building the Japanese armed forces, Fearey found a pool of proven talent in the prisons. "The occupation authorities and the Japanese govern-ment at a later stage in the occupation, say in a year or two" should lift the bar on those militarists and ultranationalists.[117] The Military Intelli-gence Division of the War Department concurred in its secret *Intelligence Review* (August 22, 1946) that the demobilized six million members of the Japanese armed forces comprised "the largest group of trained mili-tary personnel in the Far East." "They would add materially," the *Review* stated, "to the military potential of any Power that might undertake to mobilize them."[118]

Fearey's report was classified "secret" a day after its arrival at the State Department, while Emmerson's report was not. Emmerson con-veyed the public posture of American policy at the initial euphoric stage of the Occupation. Fearey mentioned the unmentionable, at a time when MacArthur was about to ensure that the Japanese constitution would be the most pacifist one in the world. But Japan's unilateral declaration in favor of eternal peace was a chimera. After the Korean War erupted, the time was suddenly ripe for realpolitik. But the Japan that MacArthur had isolated from the rest of the world had lost its feeling for this deadly art. Worse, diplomacy had become a field in which force rather than eloquence seemed to be the rule. Japan was too insecure to walk alone without a big stick. And so, while purging the Japanese Reds, the government with MacArthur's approval carried out a mass "depurge" of the formerly con-demned militarists and ultranationalists. The number of persons wel-comed back to society during September/October 1950 reached 13,340, and during June/October 1951, 359,530.[119] Yoshida expressed his deep appreciation for MacArthur's generous amnesty.[120]

12
The Peace Treaty

Japan, though not altogether displeased with American tutelage, nonetheless wanted to regain independence. Independence meant a peace treaty between Japan and its former enemies. The first peace treaty proposal was made confidentially by Secretary of State James F. Byrnes in February 1946 to President Truman. Nothing came of it. Byrnes's timing was simply too early.[1] It took a public statement by MacArthur to set the process of treaty making in motion. On March 19, 1947, during one of his rare press conferences MacArthur said that occupied Japan might soon become ready for a peace treaty, regain national sovereignty, and thereafter live a peaceful life. "Who is going to protect them [the Japanese]?" a correspondent asked him. MacArthur replied that one method would be to backtrack and permit a small military establishment. "But," he said, "the Japanese are relying upon the advanced spirituality of the world to protect them against undue aggression."[2]

The Debate Over Japanese Rearmament

The US government, especially the Department of Defense, did not share MacArthur's enthusiasm for a pacifist Japan, which it considered the most important nation, strategically and economically, in Asia. As late as December 1948, however, MacArthur was expressing his strong opposition to the Joint Chiefs of Staff, who had recommended a limited reactivation of Japanese armed forces. Underlying MacArthur's opposition was a top-secret policy debate between the Departments of State and Defense over the desirability of authorizing a Japanese military establishment in a peace treaty. A three-way debate took place between MacArthur and these two departments; none of them informed the Japanese government, which was merely, as US Military Intelligence Division put it, "the most expedient means for controlling the country and for carrying out the purposes of the occupation."[3]

On November 20, 1948, the Defense Department reasoned as follows in favor of Japanese armed forces:

1. Japan must be defended by armed forces, if necessary, to prevent its falling into the Soviet orbit.
2. If the peace treaty does not authorize Japanese armed forces, [the United States will have to retain in Japan] a disproportionately large share of US armed forces for the purpose of defending Japan. [However, the American public will demand, once a peace treaty is completed, that we] bring American boys back home and let the Japanese defend Japan.
3. [Training of a Japanese armed force will take time, so, a] postponement of their reactivation would only result in further delay which the United States cannot risk.
4. [Therefore, by reactivating Japanese armed forces the United States could withdraw some US forces from Japan] without basically altering our security position in the Pacific. [Also, Japanese military forces] would be a valuable and perhaps indispensable asset in the event of all-out war.[4]

On December 23, 1948, MacArthur replied:

1. Complete and guaranteed neutrality is the ideal post-treaty status for Japan. Eventual attainment of this goal should not be prejudiced by forcing on Japan during the Occupation a quasi-military alliance with the United States and a fundamental revision of the Japanese Constitution renouncing the "right of belligerency."
2. A peace treaty for Japan cannot possibly be consummated in the foreseeable future upon any basis other than complete disarmament and neutrality. Consideration of any alternate post-treaty status at this time appears premature, and inspired speculation by the press on the subject merely strengthens Communist propaganda and jeopardizes the strong moral position of the United States.
3. ... Establishment of any Japanese armed forces for other than police purposes would not only effectively prohibit the attain-

ment of the psychological unity essential to combat communism in the Orient but would jeopardize the attainment of economic stability in Japan.

4. ... Establishment of the inadequate armed forces visualized would, by forcing Japan into a quasi-military alliance with the United States and destroying the character and purpose of the Occupation, precipitate a situation vis-à-vis Soviet Russia which would demand a greater physical commitment of United States complementary forces than it has heretofore been found possible to maintain in the Far East. ...

5. While Japan should not be considered a military ally of the United States, her position vis-à-vis the United States economically and psychologically should be such that she will not fall into the orbit of Soviet domination.[5]

Accompanying MacArthur's reply was a detailed staff analysis of the military and psychological situation of Japan in relation to other Asian nations. His staff bluntly stated:

Experience with a "limited" German force after World War I (which led to unlimited rearmament), the well-known tendency of the United States to neglect military commitments in time of peace, the impracticability of establishing permanent controls short of complete disarmament, and the current bitterness mixed with envy with which these nations [i.e., the Western Pacific nations] view Japan would be insuperable obstacles to the establishment of completely friendly relations between Japan and other Western Pacific nations. ... Existence of the pool of experienced military personnel [of Japan] is a strategic asset in the event of hostilities. However, the existence of this pool is the very factor which necessitates maintenance of the guarantees of complete neutrality until such time as hostilities actually begin.[6]

The State Department, though fully agreeing with MacArthur and his staff, asked one of its top policy consultants, Philip Jessup, for his comment. "I agree vehemently with General MacArthur's view," he wrote back. "Any remilitarization of Japan would seem to me to have such adverse reactions through the Pacific area as to make this course unwise." He also thought that it would cause "violent repercussions in Europe where we know with what fear the Western European nations would regard the rearming of Germany."[7] Shortly after this the State Department, in the name of Secretary Acheson, presented to the Defense Department a top-secret memorandum entitled "Position of Department of State on Reactivation of Japanese Armed Forces"; dated November 16, 1949, it had been drafted by John Howard and concurred with by Philip Jessup. "For political reasons," the State Department said, "it is not feasible in the treaty of peace to authorize the reactivation of Japanese armed forces." The department presented six reasons:

1. The primary US concern with regard to Japanese security arrangements was "the prevention of the outbreak of war rather than [the] measure of military defense against actual armed attack by the Soviet Union." This could best be achieved "through the presence of US forces in Japan on behalf of the signatory powers and at Japan's request as evidence of US determination to regard an armed attack against Japan as provocation to an all-out war."

2. US aid and Japanese resources should be chiefly devoted to "the maintenance of a strong Japanese constabulary," on the one hand, and, on the other, to "the achievement of economic and social progress which in the long run will greatly influence the continued orientation of Japan toward the United States. This balance would be upset by the premature diversion of aid, efforts and resources to the maintenance of a Japanese military establishment."

3. The United States should not make a decision to rearm Japan without considering the Japanese people's desire "to continue or abandon their renunciation of war and armed forces in their Constitution." Otherwise, the Japanese would consider rearmament imposed upon them "for the purpose of promoting the strategic military interests of the United States." It was significant, the department continued, that to date no strong pressures had developed within Japan in favor of abandoning the Constitution.

4. Japan had to show "more adequate assurances than are now present" that it would "continue to be friendly, or at least not hostile, toward the United States." If it did become hostile, "any armed forces and war-supporting industry in Japan would, if made available for use against the United States, greatly augment the war potential of the Soviet Union and Communist China."

5. The reactivation of Japanese armed forces "would constitute a sharp break with Japan's renunciation of war and armed forces and with US occupation policies." This change of heart might "cast serious doubts among the Japanese concerning the sincerity of US purposes and the validity of the objectives of the Occupation, thereby weakening US influence and the influence of democratic principles in Japan, both of which are necessary to offset Communist influence in Japan."

6. The Allied Powers continued to "fear a renascent nationalistic and aggressive Japan." Japanese remilitarization would frighten them. Also, France would take it "as a precedent for the reactivation of Germany's armed forces." Hence, the United States should maintain its own military forces for Japanese security. This action had "the moral and psychological advantages," because the United States would be undertaking such an expensive and dangerous task on behalf of the United Nations, which was failing to take "full responsibility for the maintenance of peace and security with respect to Japan."[8]

The Defense Department and the Joint Chiefs of Staff accepted the arguments of MacArthur and the State Department. MacArthur was certain that he could defend Japan against the Soviet invasion. So, when he argued for Japan's neutrality, he implied neither a withdrawal of American forces from Japan nor the slightest reduction in them. Since his ideal of absolute neutrality could not be attained in the Communist-infested Orient, he considered a peace treaty with Japan "premature." In other words, he wanted to maintain the status quo under his supreme authority. "I firmly believe in the wisdom of our Constitution," Prime Minister Yoshida had said, "which renounces war and forswears all forms of armament." This wisdom, he emphasized, was "the best guaranty for our territorial integrity and independence."[9] These words are from his speech of September 4, 1949, which MacArthur had reviewed and approved on September 2.

AN ISLAND FORTRESS

While MacArthur and the State Department kept insisting on Japanese neutrality—or rather, on keeping Japan physically incapable of defending itself—Mao took over continental China, America's monopoly of the atomic bomb ended, and North Korea became a serious military threat. Indeed, MacArthur himself was warning Washington that North Korean attacks were imminent. Secretary of State Acheson, however, thought that "General MacArthur's intelligence was quite schizophrenic."[10] As the Soviet power bloc began to flex its military muscles, the Joint Chiefs of Staff who wanted to rearm Japan looked perspicacious.

On January 1, 1950, MacArthur, with the approval of the US government, declared that article 9 of the Japanese Constitution did not deny the inalienable right of self-defense. Japan, for its own sake no less than America's, was to become an island fortress, protected largely by its own martial reputation.

Prime Minister Yoshida, whose survival instinct in politics of any sort was superb, swiftly and secretly agreed with MacArthur's new interpretation. Secretly, because the Japanese people had been so well indoctrinated in MacArthur's brand of pacifism, that they would not have tolerated an overnight conversion to American military convenience on Yoshida's part. The State Department saw Yoshida's tactful maneuver for what it was: as Walton W. Butterworth, assistant secretary of state, said, "Mr. Yoshida had cleverly avoided commiting [sic] himself for or against [American military] bases—although he no doubt favored them."[11] At the same time the department began worrying about the Japanese people's growing desire to, in Secretary Acheson's words, "regain their freedom from the control of the military occupation and this feeling might well increase if the United States does nothing."[12] The department felt that the Soviet Union might capitalize on this Japanese feeling. If the Soviet Union first proposed a peace conference before the United States did, and if the United States rejected the Soviet proposal (which was very likely), what would the Japanese say about the well-publicized American promise of eventual self-government? A Soviet proposal, Acheson feared, "would catch the United States flat-footed." In fact, he felt that "the Soviet might propose a peace conference at any time."[13]

What Kind of a Treaty?

In September 1949 the Soviet Union exploded its first atomic bomb. The same month Secretary Acheson resumed talks on a Japanese peace treaty with the other Allied Powers, excluding the Soviets. Tracy S. Voorhees, Undersecretary of the Army, visited MacArthur in Tokyo during the workweek of December 5 to 9 to discuss the military aspects of a possible peace treaty. On December 15 he met Secretary Acheson and Undersecretary of State James E. Webb to report on his trip. He did not elaborate much on the substance of his conversation with MacArthur. Instead, he complained about leaks to the press concerning the nature of his mission. He blamed the State Department for the leaks.[14]

On April 24, 1950, a major conference took place between the Defense Department and the State Department. The Defense Department's position was: (1) a peace treaty should include the USSR and "the de facto government of China," that of Mao Tse-tung; (2) Such a treaty should also authorize the US forces to remain in Japan; (3) if the State Department could not arrange this with the USSR and Communist China, the peace treaty would be "premature."[15] The State Department countered by saying that the Defense Department's idea was "impossible" to accomplish. Secretary Acheson saw two immediate security problems regarding an independent Japan. One was "protection against the possible resurgence of Japanese aggression," which was "of particular concern to Australia and the Philippines." The other was "protection against Soviet-Communist aggression against a disarmed Japan."[16] He urged that the United States should proceed with a peace treaty immediately, so that the Soviet Union would have no chance of exploiting American inaction.

MacArthur, however, thought the State Department was offering the Soviet Union another excellent opportunity to abuse American prestige as well as decency by pushing prematurely for a Japanese peace treaty. The Joint Chiefs of Staff agreed with him, as they cited his argument during the conference with the State Department. General Hoyt S. Vandenberg, chief of staff, US Air Force, said that he received a clear impression from talking with MacArthur in Tokyo that "General MacArthur regarded a proposal for a peace conference as a propaganda move which would embarrass the USSR and improve US relations with the Japanese, rather than as a move which was connected with military considerations." Vandenberg, to make sure, asked MacArthur if he wanted the US government to proceed with peace negotiations. MacArthur appeared, he said, "not to desire the actual implementation of a proposal for a peace conference." Instead, MacArthur believed that the mere proposal would do the work, because the Soviet Union would surely refuse it "with consequent propaganda advantages to the United States."[17] General J. Lawton Collins, chief of staff, US Army, confirmed Vandenberg's views of MacArthur's opinion. Collins elaborated on MacArthur's lack of enthusiasm for a Japanese peace treaty. If one were concluded, MacArthur feared, "the size of US forces in Japan would be reduced to a mere token force." "This was disturbing to him," Collins said, "because US forces were even now so thin on Hokkaido [the northernmost island] that Soviet forces could easily land unopposed in many places and proceed inland a considerable distance before they would even make contact with US forces."[18] Collins believed that the Soviets might do just that.

Secretary Acheson countered reassuringly that the State Department was not proposing to reduce US forces in Japan. American security was the responsibility of the Defense Department, he said, and the State Department would assist as much as possible.[19] Assistant Secretary of State Butterworth, who had visited Tokyo from February 3 to 6, 1950, said that Japanese opinion did not appear to favor "the granting of military bases to the United States."[20] Secretary of Defense Johnson said that, if Butterworth's assessment was accurate, then he opposed a peace treaty even more strongly. The Japanese, if they did not accept US military bases, were not ready for a nonpunitive peace treaty.[21] Undersecretary of the Army Voorhees, who had been in Tokyo from August 29 to September 14 and again from December 5 to 9, 1949, saw a different picture in Japan. He was convinced that "almost all Japanese would welcome US forces and that they were concerned first about Japan's security and only secondly about a peace treaty."[22] Butterworth stressed in reply that the Japanese were worrying "whether or not US bases in Japan would act as a magnet to draw upon them the consequences of any military operations between the United States and the USSR."[23]

JAPAN ACCEPTS AMERICAN BASES
Secretary of Defense Johnson accompanied by General Omar N. Bradley, chairman of the Joint Chiefs of Staff, went to Tokyo and talked with MacArthur during the period June 17–23, 1950.[24] Two days after they left Japan, the Korean War broke out. The war termi-

nated all discussions. A Japanese peace treaty was no longer premature; it was urgent and, in fact, overdue. American military bases were paramount. The Japanese people too wanted them, as the price they had to pay for national security. They also thought the American military bases might well serve as a timely substitute for full Japanese rearmament. As the United States did not intend to encourage Japan to fully rearm, the American bases in Japan satisfied both nations.

"I authorize your government," MacArthur ordered Prime Minister Yoshida on July 8, 1950, "to take the necessary measures to establish a national police reserve of 75,000 men." He also ordered that the Maritime Safety Agency be expanded by an additional 8,000 men. These measures, MacArthur assured Yoshida, were for "the maintenance of internal security and order and the safeguard of Japan's coastline against unlawful immigration and smuggling."[25] On July 14 Yoshida in the Diet urged the need for national security. "To us," he said, "the battle of Korea is not a 'fire across the river.' It demonstrates how real and imminent is the menace of communism. We see before our own eyes the sinister arm of Red aggression reaching out for its hapless victim."[26]

The Korean War also ended all theoretical discussions in Japan over whether or not Japan should have a comprehensive peace treaty with all former enemies (including the USSR and Mao's China) or a partial peace treaty with the American power bloc nations. Prime Minister Yoshida, who had aligned himself exclusively with the United States, emerged as a leader of unmistakable foresight. Japanese leftists and Communists, who wanted to include the USSR and communist China in the treaty, suffered a decisive loss of public favor.

On January 9, 1951, Acheson and the new secretary of defense, George C. Marshall, recommended to President Truman that John Foster Dulles "be appointed by you as special representative of the president with the personal rank of ambassador" to carry on peace negotiations with the Japanese government "through and in cooperation with General MacArthur."[27] Acheson and Marshall drafted a letter to Dulles from the president, which he approved the next day. On January 10 Truman wrote to Dulles, informing him that he now was ambassador. Truman told him that the United States would "commit substantial armed force to the defense of the island chain of which Japan forms a part"; that it wanted Japan to "increasingly acquire the ability to defend itself" and that it was prepared to arrange mutual security treaties with other Pacific nations to resist attack by Japan, "if Japan should again become aggressive."[28] "You should have in mind," Truman stressed to Dulles, "our principal purpose in the proposed settlement is to secure the adherence of the Japanese nation to the free nations of the world and to assure that it will play its full part in resisting the further expansion of communist imperialism."[29]

Both the US and the Japanese governments moved swiftly to conclude both a peace treaty and a mutual security treaty, as their mutual enemies were clearly visible across the Sea of Japan. On January 25, 1951, Ambassador Dulles arrived at Tokyo to finalize the treaties. On February 12, 1951, a day after Dulles left Tokyo, Prime Minister Yoshida reported to the Diet. "What impressed me most," he said, "was the great good will of Americans." "I am convinced that the only way for Japan to work out her new destiny lies in the maintenance of close cooperation with all free, democratic nations—especially the United States." Then he got down to business. "The biggest issue involved in [the] Japanese peace settlement is that of the security of Japan, namely, the preservation of internal peace and order, and the expulsion of aggression from outside." The Dulles mission, he told the Diet, had conveyed America's willingness to provide the Japanese, if they wanted it, with "armed assistance against outside attack." Yoshida gladly accepted this offer and at the same time wished to respond in kind to American generosity, because "national self-respect would not permit us to rely entirely on another power for the defense of our own country while we did nothing ourselves for it."[30]

Truman Versus MacArthur

The Korean War confirmed MacArthur's worst suspicions about communism, of which he now developed a veritable phobia. He saw the shadow of communism behind every man and woman who could legally vote, and feared the shadow more than the substance. The infant Japanese democracy, his own foster child, was in danger, and he would do anything to protect it. The war became his private crusade against the forces of evil. His do-or-die attitude was evinced in a less-than-friendly exchange with Senator J. W. Fulbright at joint hearings before the Senate Committees on Armed Services and Foreign Relations on May 4, 1951.

> FULBRIGHT: Well, it seems to me, you do not fight communism with a gun. It is sort of like sin. We are all against sin, but you do not fight sin with anything tangible. Communism is an idea, but what really bothers us is when people start to shoot. . . .
> MACARTHUR: I think you do fight sin with every practical weapon, and I think we are fighting communism with very practical weapons.[31]

The sinful North Koreans were far better prepared for this war. Although the US government immediately responded to aid the crumbling South Korean forces, a cautious attitude pervaded the Truman administration. What was caution in Washington appeared to MacArthur as vacillation, a suicidal attitude in combat. Truman, on the other hand, was uncomfortable with MacArthur's immense prestige and arrogance and downright fearful of his visible eagerness to fight the Asian Communists regardless of national boundaries. On August 6, 1950, Truman sent W. Averell Harriman to Tokyo for a talk with MacArthur. "Tell him two things," Truman said to Harriman. "One, I'm going to do everything I can to give him what he wants in the way of support; and secondly, I want you to tell him that I don't want him to get us into a war with the Chinese Communists."[32] Harriman also relayed Truman's wish that MacArthur avoid giving the impression that the United States was backing Chiang Kai-shek in Formosa [Taiwan]. MacArthur replied that he did not agree with the president, but that he was a soldier and would obey orders.[33]

On August 24 a major flareup between Truman and MacArthur took place. For the first time, MacArthur was made to feel that Truman was the president and his superior in authority. On that day MacArthur sent a seven-page letter to be read at the Veterans of Foreign Wars National Encampment in Chicago on August 28. He sent it over the AP wires, which of course made it public. In it he emphasized the strategic importance of the Pacific Ocean, which, he said, had become "a vast moat to protect us as long as we hold it. . . . If we hold this line we may have peace; lose it, and war is inevitable." He then presented a lengthy analysis of how essential Taiwan was for American security. As if to defy the president's order to be cautious about backing Chiang Kai-shek, MacArthur said: "Nothing could be more fallacious than the threadbare argument by those who advocate appeasement and defeatism in the Pacific that if we defend Formosa we alienate continental Asia."[34]

Among the cabinet members Secretary Acheson was the first to learn about MacArthur's letter. He called Harriman, who took it to the president early on the following morning, August 25.[35] President Truman came into a meeting room where Secretary of State Acheson, Secretary of Defense Louis Johnson, all the chiefs of staff, and Harriman were discussing wholly different topics. Truman had the yellow AP wire dispatch in his hand. He had taken it off the ticker at the White House Press Club, which he was not supposed to do.

"The president told us to sit down," Acheson recalled,

and he was obviously very mad indeed. And he read this whole document through, from beginning to end. . . . and he said "I'm going to ask everyone in this room, individually, whether they had anything to do with this, whether they knew anything about it, whether they were connected in any way whatever with it." Well, by the time the president got through with that, it was a pretty thoroughly intimidated group; and he then turned to

Louis Johnson and said, "I want this letter withdrawn, and I want you to send an order to MacArthur to withdraw this letter, and that is an order from me. Do you understand that?" Louis said, "Yes, sir, I do." And the president said, "Go and do it. That's all." And that was the end of the meeting; everybody went out and disappeared very fast.[36]

Thirty minutes later Secretary of Defense Johnson called up Acheson and said that the president's order made no sense and that MacArthur's letter was already public on the AP ticker. "Louis," Acheson replied, "don't argue with me as to whether the president's order makes any sense or not. I heard him give it, and you accepted it; and whether it can be done or not, you'd better do it."[37] Johnson agonized and kept calling Acheson and Harriman. Acheson refused to talk with Johnson.

On August 27 Johnson called Acheson and said that MacArthur would withdraw the letter if the president really wanted that, but he did not understand what he had done wrong. MacArthur explained in his telegram to Johnson that his letter was merely restating what was clearly the policy of the US government, and hoped his explanation would change the situation. Johnson asked Acheson, "What shall I do?" "I suppose you'd better carry out the president's order," replied Acheson.[38] On August 28 MacArthur's letter was withdrawn. The press was surprised, and speculated that only the president could give MacArthur orders.[39]

On September 12 Secretary of Defense Johnson resigned. The same day MacArthur launched a brilliant amphibious landing at Inchon, and began chasing the North Korean troops towards the Chinese border. Truman, though pleased with MacArthur's military talent, worried about his anticommunist zeal. On October 15, 1950, Truman and MacArthur conferred on Wake Island. Truman publicly said that a "very complete unanimity of view" prevailed between them.

On October 20 US troops captured Pyongyang, the North Korean capital. On October 21 US parachute troops landed deep inside North Korea. Three days later Truman congratulated MacArthur: "The progress your forces under your command have made since we met at Wake continues to be most remarkable, and once again I offer you my hearty congratulations. The military operations in Korea under your command will have a most profound influence for peace in the world."[40]

ENTER CHINA, EXIT MAC ARTHUR

On October 28 Chinese army personnel were identified inside North Korea.

On October 30 MacArthur thanked the president for his kind letter; as they neared the Manchurian border, he said, enemy resistance had "somewhat stiffened," but he did not think that this represented "a strong defense in depth such as would materially retard the achievement of our border objective."[41] In fact, Truman himself did not think the Chinese would enter the war.[42] On November 24 MacArthur launched a major offensive to end the war. On November 27 massive Chinese armies crossed the border and stopped MacArthur's offensive cold. The next day he confessed that he now faced an entirely new war. US troops continued losing and Seoul, the South Korean capital, was about to fall into enemy hands.

On December 1 MacArthur publicly stated that the orders from the US government forbidding him to attack Chinese Communists in China was "an enormous handicap without precedent in military history." Unless the orders were lifted, he said, he could not win.

On December 6 the Joint Chiefs of Staff advised him to refrain from any more such statements or, if he had to speak, to clear his remarks first with the Department of Defense or the secretary of state. They also told him that the president wanted him to "exercise extreme caution" in his public remarks. MacArthur remained silent and fought fiercely to re-capture Seoul from the enemy. On December 29 the Joint Chiefs of Staff warned him that, according to their best estimates, the Chinese Communists had "the capability of forcing United Nations Forces out of Korea if they choose to exercise it."[43] Despite this, MacArthur successfully re-captured Seoul on March 7, 1951. The same day he said again publicly that a military stalemate would persist as long as the US government prohibited him from executing what he considered the best strategy—a massive attack on China.

On March 20 the Joint Chiefs told MacArthur that the US government was ready to discuss a truce with the enemy. Four days later they once again advised him that "any further statements" from him had to be "coordinated." The same day Truman told him that if Communist military leaders were to request an armistice in the field, he should "immediately report that fact to the Joint Chiefs of Staff for instruction." The same day, March 24, MacArthur, as if to defy the president's order, declared: "I stand ready at any time to confer in the field with the commander in chief of the enemy forces in an earnest effort to find any military means whereby the realization of the political objectives of the United Nations in Korea . . . might be accomplished without further bloodshed." The State Department announced that MacArthur's statement was "beyond his responsibility as a field commander."[44]

MacArthur's determination to win in Korea at any cost—he even suggested the use of atomic bombs—did not sit well with Truman. After MacArthur had criticized Truman in frequent public statements, almost calling him indecisive, Truman fired him, on April 11, 1951 (Tokyo time). The ostensible reason was his insubordination, but it was really his arrogance. Truman said he dismissed MacArthur to avoid World War III.

MacArthur's pride was badly hurt, not only by Truman's order for his dismissal but also by the way he learned about it. He revealed the latter on May 3, 1951, at the joint hearings before the Armed Services and Foreign Relations Committees. Senator Styles Bridges (R., New Hampshire) asked him: "How did you first receive word of your recall?"

> GENERAL MACARTHUR: I received it from my wife. One of my aides had
> heard the broadcast and instantly told her, and she informed
> me.
> SENATOR BRIDGES: You received it via the radio before you had any official
> notice?
> GENERAL MACARTHUR: Yes, sir.[45]

MacArthur received the official notice in a small brown envelope, with FLASH printed on it in red, that was handed to him by a senior aide, Colonel Sid Huff. The supreme commander made no comment. He was having lunch with his wife and with two visitors, Senator Warren G. Magnuson (D., Washington) and William Sterns of Northwest Airlines; the MacArthurs' thirteen-year-old son joined the party.[46]

The Japanese people were stunned by this dramatic display of civilian control. Who had dared to fire the majestic "Emperor of the Pacific"? Prime Minister Yoshida's letter to MacArthur of April 14, 1951, expressed the people's astonishment well: "Words fail me to tell you how shocked and how grieved I am at your precipitous departure from our shores."[47] After MacArthur had left amid the Japanese people's heartfelt farewells, a group of prominent Japanese leaders talked about establishing a "MacArthur Shrine." This interesting idea faded swiftly into oblivion (the Japanese had enough gods already); it was, in any case, contrary to MacArthur's own warnings against deifying human beings—warnings that he had persuaded even the Emperor Hirohito to take seriously. MacArthur's own countrymen have not been as restrained in their tributes. The impressive MacArthur Memorial at Norfolk, Virginia, treats visitors to a biographical movie in which a deep-voiced male narrator informs visitors that they are now in a "national shrine" of the United States.

Japan Joins the Free World

While MacArthur was fighting up and down the Korean Peninsula, the Japanese conservatives were exaggerating their fears of communism and loudly publicizing them to the Japanese people. The Japanese did not and still do not like communism; they have always associated it with its progenitors in the Soviet Union, a country they do not even secretly admire. But the conservatives who wished to revive Japanese nationalism in full force were not satisfied with the people's quiet rejection of communism. The Communists had to be hunted down incessantly, just as in the old days.

The Communists in Japan showed the habitual characteristics of an ethnic minority under persecution. They formed a secretive clique, developed a culture of their own, and remained intensely distrustful of the Establishment. They openly and vehemently talked about a violent revolution, as they thought they had nothing to lose but all to gain. Their antisocial attitude and behavior provided a further impetus for the government in power to crush them. It was a vicious circle.

The Japanese Communist Party became legal only in October 1945, and then only at MacArthur's discretion. Although the new Constitution of 1946 made all political parties legal, extraconstitutionally MacArthur's wishes ruled supreme. In 1949 he publicly wished the Japanese government to declare the Communists illegal. The government did not literally obey MacArthur, but through various arrangements succeeded in making the Communists feel miserable. In 1950 MacArthur banned the Communists from public life without declaring them unconstitutional. The Japanese government hailed his tact and wisdom.

While the Red Purge at its height resembled a witch hunt, former ultrapatriots were allowed to roam freely. The new Japan was coming increasingly to resemble the old. It was no coincidence that the Emperor confidentially informed Sebald, the US political adviser, of his sincere gratitude for the purge, and that he wished Japan could aid more American efforts to combat communism. However, a Japan that was still occupied could not too brashly interject itself into the affairs of independent nations. A peace treaty between Japan and its former enemies would make Japan independent. Thus a peace treaty that MacArthur had once thought only a propaganda gimmick to embarrass the Soviet Union became a matter of necessity.

The Korean War made the peace treaty urgent as well as necessary. Who provoked North Korea? Most Republican and some southern Democratic senators pointedly blamed Secretary of State Dean Acheson's speech of January 12, 1950, at the National Press Club; he had, they said, invited the North Koreans to attack. In the speech Acheson defined the so-called American defensive perimeter in the Pacific: "This defensive perimeter runs along the Aleutians to Japan and then goes to the Ryukyus [and] from the Ryukyus to the Philippine Islands."[48] Note that the Korean

Peninsula was not mentioned. But this definition of the perimeter was virtually a paraphrase of a statement by MacArthur less than a year before, on March 1, 1949, during a press interview in Tokyo.[49] Acheson was nonetheless criticized for offering South Korea to the Soviet bloc. Some senators were so outraged that they demanded his resignation; if he refused, they wanted Truman to fire him. Acheson called their invective "specious."[50] More plausible reasons for the attack, he argued in his 1969 memoir, were (1) the withdrawal of American combat forces from South Korea, (2) the defeat in the US Congress of an aid bill for South Korea [defeated in the House by one vote—193 to 192], and (3) "the increasing discussion of a peace treaty with Japan."[51] George Kennan, chief of the State Department's Policy Planning Staff, had appeared to concur when he said in Acheson's presence at Princeton in 1954 that he "felt morally certain that the origin of the Korean thing had to do with our move toward a unilateral treaty of peace in Japan." He added that the American initiative for the treaty might not have been the only reason for North Korea's attack.[52]

The peace treaty text was published in Japan on July 13, 1951. "On this joyful day," Prime Minister Yoshida wrote to MacArthur at the Waldorf Astoria in New York, "I desire to express the profound gratitude of myself and my government. . . . I only regret I cannot see and thank you in person."[53] On August 20 MacArthur sent Yoshida a five-page telegram. The peace treaty, he said, was "indeed a source of immense personal satisfaction." With this treaty, Japan would "take a firm and invincible stand with the free world to repel those evil forces of international communist tyranny which seek covertly or by force of arms to destroy freedom." The rest of the telegram was his lecture on the "sound political policies and principles of good government" that Yoshida had heard continually the past six years. "Continue faithful adherence" to them, he encouraged his best student.[54]

There was a suggestion to make MacArthur the official "master of ceremonies" of a sort at the San Francisco Peace Conference. But Acheson did not think it a good idea, and Truman agreed with him. Many Americans sent letters and telegrams to the White House protesting Truman's decision. The character of the protest may be judged from the following example. "Listen Harry, You stubborn Missouri mule, why can't you give old General MacArthur a place on the Japanese peace conference. He, more than anyone else is responsible for the affair. Harry, appoint him and we will love you. Harry, leave him out of it, and November 1952 will be tough. Sincerely yours."[55]

On September 8, 1951, Japan signed the San Francisco Peace Treaty. This promised Japan independence. The Soviet Union, Mao's

China (which officially did not even exist for the United States and Japan), and the Japanese Socialists, whom Prime Minister Yoshida had invited, did not come to San Francisco (the Japanese Communists were still underground). The same day Japan and the United States signed a mutual security treaty. The United States promised to defend Japan.

Japan did not recover Okinawa, where so many Japanese soldiers and civilians had perished in one of World War II's fiercest battles. Long before September 1951 the military importance of Okinawa was obvious to everyone: as Atcheson wrote to Truman on June 19, 1947: "Okinawa is of no economic value to Japan; on the contrary it was an economic liability. To us it is the western keystone of our military power vested in our air force island bases in the western Pacific."[56] Okinawa was one of the prices Japan had to pay for American defense services.

YOSHIDA'S APOLOGY

Two days after signing the peace treaty Prime Minister Yoshida, MacArthur's most faithful student, paid this tribute to his master:

> My heart and the hearts of all Japanese turn to you in boundless gratitude. For it is your firm and kindly hand that led us, a prostrate nation, on the road of recovery and reconstruction. It was you who propounded the principles for a fair and generous peace which we now have at long last. In the name of the Japanese government and people I send you our nation's heartfelt thanks.[57]

However, Yoshida bluntly told the new supreme commander for the Allied Powers, Lieutenant General Matthew B. Ridgway, to whom he felt he owed nothing, what he wanted from the United States. "I am aware of the American aversion to a political loan," he told Ridgway, "yet I feel it is of the greatest importance that America extend some financial aid to Japan at this time, not only as an economic measure to step up protection, but also as a political weapon to counter communism."[58]

With regard to the Japanese public's nagging suspicion that the successful Red Purge violated fundamental human rights, Yoshida tried hard to justify the part he had played. In his memoirs he wrote that

> the men concerned were not deprived of their employment because they were Communists, or because of their belief in certain ideas which the Government and public opinion did not share, but because the behavior of the Communists up to that time and during the purge period indicated that these men were potential menaces to the offices and industries employing them; so that in order to protect these from more trouble in the future, the government was justified in removing the men concerned.[59]

"The Constitution," he declared, "had to be safeguarded at the expense of the Communists."[60]

In so saying he hypocritically violated the spirit of the very document he was claiming to protect. The Japanese Constitution requires no human sacrifice of any political minorities; its life does not depend upon the death of freedom of conscience. The simple truth was that the frequently bombastic Japanese Communists had no chance of a successful revolution on this island of able capitalists. Perhaps, in the jeering slogans of Communist street demonstrations, Yoshida and MacArthur, both of whom possessed keen political hearing, could sense disturbing but accurate criticism of their own behavior in a land now governed by democracy.

Summary
and Conclusion

On August 6, 1945, the unsuspecting city of Hiroshima was blackened by the world's first atomic bomb. Two days later the Soviet Union declared war on a dying Japanese Empire. On August 9 Nagasaki succumbed to the second bomb. While Hiroshima and Nagasaki continued to smolder in the humid August night, imperial Japan surrendered without knowing its own fate.

On August 30, 1945, MacArthur landed unarmed on the training ground for kamikaze pilots, Atsugi Airfield, near Tokyo. The victor displayed his superior force by conspicuously concealing it; MacArthur carried no gun, not even a sword. The Japanese people, long expert in the art of self-presentation, appreciated the man's style.

President Truman appointed MacArthur as Supreme Commander for the Allied Powers (SCAP) and gave him vast, unprecedented discretionary power to rule Japan. MacArthur took all this power for granted; only the United States, he said, had defeated the Japanese Empire and no other Allied Power had the right to share the Occupation of Japan.

MacArthur's reluctance to share authority did not exempt the US government. While the State and War Departments frequently advised him, MacArthur took their advice as interfering with his efficient administration of occupied Japan. The US government could not do much to change his manner. MacArthur demonstrated his supreme authority when he told the US Senate in May 1951 that his orders to the Japanese people "were not subject to the controls of any higher authority." His words were the law of the land.

MacArthur Imposes Democracy

MacArthur's style of governance represented a calculated move by him to manipulate the logic of the Japanese mind. Believing as he did that the Japanese mind was thoroughly addicted to an autocratic order of authority, he stood majestically on the pinnacle of the Japanese society, which, he said, was four hundred years behind the West. The Japanese people and their government willingly acquiesced in Mac-Arthur's supremacy. This the occupying Americans did not expect. GHQ, nonetheless, explained the Japanese obedience as the natural result of MacArthur's "brilliant appraisal of the oriental mind." According to Mac-Arthur, however, this control was not difficult at all. "Measured by the standards of modern civilization," he informed the US senators, "they [the Japanese] would be like a boy of twelve compared with our development of forty-five years."

MORAL DISARMAMENT

As a precondition for the growth of democracy, Mac-Arthur ordered the Japanese government to search out all militarists and fanatic nationalists. The Japanese political, economic, and intellectual establishments were scrutinized, one level after another. All conspicuous imperial promoters of the war who had not yet committed suicide were immediately caught and, after the Tokyo Military Tribunal, hanged or imprisoned. The less obvious ones were eventually discovered and then purged from the public and private sectors. Millions of ordinary Japanese were screened, and those purged numbered between two and three hundred thousand. The people's disillusionment with their militaristic leaders—disillusionment that GHQ fanned—sustained the intensity of the nationwide purge. GHQ's term for this massive hounding of the undesirable Japanese militarists was "moral disarmament."

The process of moral disarmament extended into every sphere of Japanese life. For instance, GHQ believed that the *zaibatsu* (i.e., the family-centered monopolistic financial conglomerates) had supported the

Japanese militarists and with them instigated a series of imperialistic wars, and that they accordingly deserved to be disbanded outright. Mac-Arthur was convinced that, with the *zaibatsu* broken, oligopoly would end and a free economy would flourish. The State Department officially supported him, and together they vigorously disassembled the *zaibatsu* monopoly. Conservative Japanese leaders feared that the Japanese economy, already in shambles, would never recover from further demolitions. Their fear was shared by Japan's first Socialist prime minister, Katayama, who cautioned MacArthur to go slow in busting the *zaibatsu.* MacArthur sternly told him to mind his own business and carry out orders from GHQ. Some of the prominent policymakers in Washington also warned that further economic chaos in Japan would nurture the virus of communism.

MacArthur was aware of this threat, and moved to forestall it. Concurrently with the demolition of *zaibatsu,* he implemented a truly revolutionary principle of land reform: Those who tilled the land should own it. To MacArthur, the so-called absentee landlords appeared as callous exploiters of peasants. When the peasant became the farmer, MacArthur reasoned, the farmer would no longer listen to communist agitation. The absentee landlords had to swallow the bitter potion of democracy and practically give their land away to the peasants. The bitterness of the absentee landlords was aggravated when they, like everybody else living in cities, had to take jam-packed trains to rural areas to barter for foods with precious metals, jewels, or silk kimonos. MacArthur was right when he said that every farmer in Japan was now "a capitalist in his own right."

FREEDOM OF SPEECH AND THOUGHT

While food, shelter, and clothes preoccupied the Japanese people, MacArthur began to release an avalanche of democratic reforms. All thought-control laws and ordinances were to be abolished; no more "dangerous thoughts" as such were to exist in Japan. All political prisoners were to be released immediately. Most of them were hard-core Communists. Barely out of the prison gate, they blasted the prewar imperial government, not excluding the Emperor. Most Japanese found the public behavior of the Communists repulsive, but at the same time understood that the civil and political rights of every person, for the first time in the nation's history, could be exercised without fear of official intimidation. Political parties and labor unions mushroomed under GHQ's vigilant protection. America appeared to be truly the land of liberty, equality, and freedom. America became the ideal society that Japan should emulate.

Educational Reform

Japan's greatest resource is the intelligence of its people. It was this intelligence that made possible the remarkable prewar industrialization and modernization; it was also responsible for the equally remarkable postwar reconstruction and democratization. The Japanese people's insatiable appetite for education continually expands the range of what they can do. Indeed, school, or education, is viewed as essential to the life of Japanese society; the society cannot flourish unless education, too, is flourishing. One does not quit school, unless prepared to live with social ostracism. And Japanese pupils, from the first grade in primary school, clearly understand this ethos of learning.

Education played a crucial role in enhancing and fortifying militant Japanese totalitarianism; it was nurtured not only by the imperial government's physical oppression but also by the militants' effective mental conditioning of the Japanese people. Conversely, then, "reconditioning" or "reorienting" Japanese mores in favor of democracy called for another equally effective, systematic conditioning. MacArthur and the GHQ staff understood the immensity of their task: numerous significant reforms in the areas of politics and economics would not survive if Japan's future generations failed to comprehend and appreciate them.

The new Japanese education, MacArthur ordered, must teach and practice the sanctity and supremacy of the people and not of the state. The Emperor was just an individual like anyone else. This was truly a revolutionary concept for the Japanese people. The Civil Information and Education Section (CI & E), GHQ, which was the American supervisor of the Japanese Ministry of Education, rapidly issued directives to the Japanese government, for the most part to eliminate militaristic and nationalistic elements in teaching personnel and learning materials. The Ministry of Education did not hesitate to issue its own numerous reform directives to the nation's schools.

FROM IMPERIAL RESCRIPT
TO FUNDAMENTAL LAW

The new democracy was hard on the ancient regime and its faithful. With the 1889 Constitution abolished, the survival of another sacred document, the 1890 Imperial Rescript on Education, became precarious. The Japanese government feared that without the rescript's steadying influence the students would lack discipline, the teachers would lose authority, and, worst of all, future generations of Japanese would no longer respect the Emperor as their natural ruler.

The Japanese government tried desperately to salvage the rescript and revitalize it, and CI & E, though realizing that it was one of the underpinnings of Japanese totalitarianism, did not take swift action against it. The government took the American inaction as a timely opportunity. Japanese ministers of education, one after another, hailed the rescript's primary virtue of providing Japanese society with a model of vertical loyalty and horizontal harmony. Such loyalty and harmony, the education ministers declared, ought to remain the foundation of the new peace-loving Japanese nation and of education. Frequent public affirmation of the rescript's relevance to democracy by the Japanese officials alerted the Americans. The rescript's allegedly defective character, the Japanese said, resulted solely from the militarists' self-serving "misinterpretation" of it. The Americans, who had heard the same excuse made for the Meiji Imperial Constitution, now turned their critical attention to the rescript. A harsh consensus emerged from the American assessment: the 1890 Imperial Rescript was definitely unfit for education and had to go. In October 1946 the Ministry of Education so informed the nation through the press. To make sure the rescript remained on the shelf, the influential Government Section of GHQ pressured the Japanese Diet to pass a resolution that formally terminated the active life of the rescript in Japanese society.

The conservative Japanese government, under the Yoshida cabinet, suffered private despair, but did not give up hope of replacing the rescript with another similar document. When the rumor of the so-called Yoshida Rescript surfaced in mid-1949, the Americans reacted with fury. The rumor was killed and perhaps the real intention behind it as well. To fill the spiritual vacuum created by the death of the rescript, the Fundamental Law of Education was written by the Ministry of Education, closely supervised by CI & E. This law (effective March 1947) shared the same spirit as the new Constitution: that is, while the Constitution upheld popular sovereignty and accompanying human rights, the Fundamental Law of Education codified the responsibility of schools to inculcate the political knowledge necessary for democratic citizenship.

SECULARIZATION AND EVANGELISM

The American demolition of the Japanese ancient regime still continued. Japan's indigenous religion, Shinto, was stripped of public financial support. To the Americans, the origin of Shinto appeared too close to that of the Imperial Household. MacArthur contended that religion and the state must be separated. Shinto was banished from public universities; primary and secondary schools were prohibited from making organized tours to Shinto shrines. The Emperor declared that he was not sacred any more and that the Japanese people should abandon their racial superiority complex because there was no basis for it.

The American "moral disarmament" of the Japanese people left them devoid of spiritual support. MacArthur, with characteristic evangelical fervor, missed no opportunity to advocate Christianity as the religion of nonviolence and humanity. But his missionary work in pagan Japan was a decisive failure. The population of Japanese Christians (about one percent of the whole) hardly increased. Many Japanese accepted a free pocket Bible from the Americans, but they saw it as a cheap substitute for cigarette paper.

THE NEW TEXTBOOKS

The paper shortage was acute. Indeed, it was so critical that publication of new textbooks became doubtful. For instance, during the 1946–47 school year only a quarter of the paper actually needed was allocated for printing them—and only 40 percent of the allocation was delivered. This compelled the education minister to declare that students would learn Japanese history without textbooks. In the end, the Japanese government managed to reallocate some of the printing paper earmarked for newspapers.

More critical than the paper shortage was the content of textbooks. The Ministry of Education knew that the existing textbooks needed extensive revision to correspond to the new ideology of democracy. Soon after the surrender, the ministry ordered the schools to delete with black ink the militaristic and ethnocentric references in the textbooks. So extensive were the deletions that many sentences in the textbooks made no sense. CI & E solved this intractable problem by collecting all textbooks for pulping. It then ordered the Ministry of Education to carefully select Japanese authors to write new textbooks. The ministry submitted names of authors, whom CI & E screened. The approved authors then wrote textbook manuscripts, all of which CI & E assiduously revised. The Japanese history manuscript received CI & E's special care because—as GHQ well knew—the Japanese government considered Japanese history the basis of Japanese national identity. American sensitivity, therefore, stayed extraordinarily high to any positive assertions about Japan.

THE FIRST US EDUCATION MISSION:
ITS FAILURES AND ACHIEVEMENTS

Japanese schools were subjected to a cascade of American reforms. Especially confused were primary and secondary school teachers, who had had no experience in using the newly granted freedom of choice. With personal choice came personal responsibility for decision. Japanese teachers remained hesitant to act on their own initiative; in fact, they were afraid of doing so and of being punished later by the Ministry of Education or by GHQ. Most of them did nothing while they waited for even more directives from Tokyo. Their attitude was not exactly what GHQ and CI & E had expected. The Americans realized that the punitive phase of democratic reform had to end, and the constructive phase would have to begin with wide publicity to reduce the fear of the Japanese teachers. At MacArthur's invitation, the US Education Mission to Japan, composed of twenty-seven prominent American educators, arrived in early March 1946 to reconstruct Japanese education.

In welcoming the members of the US Mission, the Japanese education minister pleaded with them "not to deal with us simply from an American point of view" and not "to use Japan as a kind of laboratory in a rash attempt to experiment in it on some abstract ideals." His caution was timely but irrelevant. As one member said, "the Mission did not need to be reminded." Regardless of the Japanese wish, however, MacArthur did think of Japan as "the world's great laboratory for an experiment in the liberation of government from within." The mission's chairman, George Stoddard, concurred when he said, "we are here to help in a process of social evolution." No one dared to deviate from the general's wish. In less than a month the Education Mission wrote a report and submitted it to MacArthur. The report became the blueprint for postwar Japanese education.

Some of the mission's concrete proposals were to: (1) discontinue the use of imperial rescripts and the practice of obeisance before the Imperial Portraits in Japanese schools; (2) expand the years of compulsory schooling from six to nine to teach pupils basic human rights and individuality; (3) help teachers unionize for their own welfare; (4) institute local boards of education throughout the nation. All of these recommendations were carried out.

1. The Imperial Rescript on Education was abolished, and schools stopped conducting solemn ceremonies in front of the Imperial Portraits.
2. Expanding the years of compulsory schooling in the midst of Japan's financial shambles posed great difficulties. Many new school buildings had to be built, in addition to rebuilding and repairing those damaged by American fire bombs. Many classes were held under the open sky.
3. Japanese teachers had been organizing even before the mission's arrival. The two major unions that emerged were perpetually at loggerheads. GHQ and the Ministry of Education encouraged unionization. The Japan Teachers' Union (JTU) won popular support from the teachers. This union soon de-

veloped leftist tendencies, which the Ministry of Education and GHQ found repugnant. Political neutrality in the teaching profession became a heated political issue.
4. Establishment of local boards of education was, however, the most difficult task of all. The Ministry of Education resisted it; the Ministry of Home Affairs deplored it; Japanese public opinion did not fully understand it. Nonetheless, CI & E drafted a board of education bill. The Japanese Diet deliberated and passed it, and the Emperor promulgated it in the summer of 1948. The real difficulties began after that.

The election for school board members was set for October 5, 1948. The Military Government (MG, Eighth Army Headquarters) opposed teachers running for the school boards, because it feared that the leftist and Communist teachers would dominate the local school decision-making apparatus and because, besides teachers, only local bosses and wealthy members of the community were running. The MG proposed that the election be postponed. GHQ and CI & E replied that if MG's gloomy forecast, unlikely though it was, came true, then so be it: that was the price of democracy. Furthermore, MG was informed that the postponement would create Japanese misgivings about MacArthur's sincerity. All of the candidates, 1,530 of them, were screened and 8 were found unacceptable. The election was held as scheduled. No single political group dominated the scene. Decentralization was completed, and democratization of policy making began working, on paper. But decentralization was doomed from the start by the total lack of money everywhere. Local board members looked for policy and financial guidance to the Ministry of Education, which retained the real power of budget allocation. The Board of Education Law scattered power throughout Japan, but power migrated back to the center with the blessing of local board members. After the Occupation ended, the law was changed to abolish popular election of board members and to empower the Ministry of Education to appoint all of them.

Fifth, concerning Japanese higher education, the US Mission proposed a minimum reform. Minimum, because the mission fully understood that the imperial government had imposed too much control upon universities and had virtually incapacitated them. One of the most necessary reforms for the Japanese university system, the mission urged, was to break the cliquish monopoly of the imperial universities. To initiate this reform, the mission recommended that many more universities be established throughout the nation. Such proliferation did not please everybody. Many in the Japanese government were graduates of the imperial universities, who firmly believed that mass higher education would cause mass lowering of academic standards. There were good reasons for their anxiety in a nation that was on the brink of bankruptcy: few decent libraries anywhere, no construction funds for necessary buildings, and no adequate faculty pool to staff new universities. Imperial universities, in this miserable environment, looked even more attractive and without peer. Their prestige and general reputation for excellence climbed even higher—a development they took for granted. The academic pecking order was an accurate reflection of the social hierarchy. In organic harmony with the authoritarian order of society, the Japanese universities (led by the imperial universities) had perfected a most autocratic system of transmitting knowledge. Ironically, it was the universities that unfailingly championed democracy.

Academic Freedom and the Red Purge

The Education Mission advocated the primary importance of academic freedom. Japanese professors and students, who had often fought heroic battles against incessant government interference, understood that their intellectual integrity depended on freedom of inquiry. Their jubilation at their newfound freedom signaled the end of a quest long blocked by official insolence. The "dangerous thoughts" of imperial Japan—liberalism, Marxism, socialism, anarchism, and any ideas redolent of doubt about the sacredness of imperial sovereignty—became explosively popular on postwar campuses. Prewar prohibition triggered postwar fashion. Students and faculty openly employed communistic rhetoric; the louder they harangued, the more liberated they felt. Japanese academe was consumed by its determined pursuit for ever more freedom of speech and thought.

THE UNIVERSITIES RESIST
GOVERNMENT CONTROL

While GHQ and the Japanese government were encouraging the new academic culture of open speech, they were criticized by Japanese intellectuals in terms that owed much to the vocabulary of communism. Alarmed by this trend—the entire democratic world, they believed, was being threatened by international communist encroachment—they turned to regulate the campus activities. GHQ's first move was to empower prefectural governments with administrative authority over universities. All of the nation's universities fought back, arguing that a prefectural government had neither the administrative talent nor the financial resources to operate the universities, and that Japanese universities were not "local" as their American counterparts were. GHQ's second move was to install a board of trustees in each national university. This move was opposed even more vigorously by students and faculty. This time, however, GHQ and the Ministry of Education held firm and tried to push a bill through the Diet. In response, Japanese universities closed down throughout the nation, as students and faculty hit the streets with massive demonstrations. GHQ and the Ministry of Education could not change the belligerent mood on the campuses. Sensing defeat, the Ministry of Education with GHQ's consent withdrew the bill from the Diet. This successful opposition by the universities acting in unison preceded, if not precipitated, the Red Purge that removed liberals and Communists from the classrooms.

COMMUNIST INFLUENCE GROWS

Hunger and the fear of starvation were ever-present realities among the Japanese people at that time. When they had to scramble for the wherewithal to survive, democracy and human rights were mere words. The Japanese Communists, skillful orchestrators of public sentiment, voiced the people's grievances. The Communists were well aware that most of the public was against communism, as well as intensely hostile toward the Soviet Union. Accordingly, they pretended they were independent of Soviet command and succeeded in presenting themselves as opportunistic. Yet, when communism could penetrate the Japanese labor force so swiftly and effectively, GHQ naturally worried that Japanese teachers and students might have already succumbed to the same dangerous influence. The CI & E members advised MacArthur and the Japanese government that it ought to learn to stick up for itself or else communism, being more aggressive, would walk all over the tender young democracy.

THE EELLS MISSION

To remedy the situation, CI & E sent Walter Crosby Eells, a popular Stanford University professor who was assigned to CI & E's Higher Education Division, on a lecture tour of the entire Japanese university system. His first lecture in July 1949 at the new Niigata University caused an uproar among the Japanese academics. Eells said that Communist professors were unfit to teach because by joining the Communist Party they "surrendered their freedom to think independently." His provocative lectures were hotly opposed by university students and faculty at every campus he visited.

The Japanese Association of University Professors, alarmed by

Eells's way of defining academic freedom and political liberty, made a public statement that the new Japanese Constitution guaranteed the freedom of individual conscience. But Eells and other members of GHQ took the vigorous opposition of Japanese academics as undeniable proof that communism had penetrated still deeper into the hearts and minds of Japanese youth. And Eells, with the full support of GHQ, intensified his attack against all of the ideological suspects.

The State Department hinted at its reservations about GHQ's method of eliminating communistic elements from Japanese society, but it did not question the necessity for the Red Purge.

Peace and Rearmament

On January 1, 1950, MacArthur declared, with the US government's approval, that article 9 of the Japanese Constitution did not, after all, deny the inalienable right of self-defense. Japan must become an island fortress for its own survival as well as for American national security. Prime Minister Yoshida fully agreed with the general's revised interpretation of this most controversial article. It seems possible that the US government was expecting armed conflict to break out soon on the Korean Peninsula.

While the US government and MacArthur were talking about future Japanese rearmament, ordinary Japanese people were growing restless with the Occupation. Would it never end? Were those American promises of self-determination and democracy merely placebos? The State Department, sensing the Japanese mood, urged MacArthur to proceed with a peace treaty immediately. The Soviet Union, the department warned, might capitalize on American inaction and propose a peace treaty of its own. But MacArthur dismissed the idea; nothing of the sort would happen as long as he remained supreme commander for the Allied Powers in Tokyo. What was needed here, MacArthur advised Washington, was that the United States should merely propose a peace treaty without working for its conclusion. The Soviet Union, he argued, would surely refuse any American proposal, "with consequent propaganda advantages to the United States." For instance, the Japanese people would bitterly criticize the Soviets. A real peace treaty with Japan was still "premature," MacArthur informed Washington. That was as late as April 1950.

THE DEBATE OVER A PEACE TREATY

Because MacArthur publicly spoke about the desirability of an early peace treaty, both the Japanese people and Prime Minister

Yoshida truly believed that he was doing the best he could for Japanese independence. There was heated popular debate over whether a forthcoming peace treaty should be a partial or comprehensive one. A partial one would include only those former enemies of Japan that were friendly with the United States; a comprehensive one would include all former enemies, including Stalin and Mao. Prime Minister Yoshida, a dyed-in-the-wool conservative, openly disliked the Soviet Union and advocated an exclusive alliance with the United States; Japan, he added, might have to offer bases for American military forces as protection. Japanese Socialists, Communists, and their friends denounced Yoshida for prostituting Japan. Ordinary Japanese people wished to conclude a comprehensive peace treaty but suspected that the world beyond the seas was not as idealistic as they were. National debate continued in Japan as if the Japanese people could determine their own fate. And the Japanese Communists and their sympathizers kept up their vocal condemnations of "American imperialism."

In early May 1950 MacArthur made explicit his determination to silence the Communists. The Communist Party, he said, had assumed "the role of an avowed satellite of an international predatory force and a Japanese pawn of an alien power policy, imperialistic purpose and subversive propaganda." The prime minister could not have agreed more with his observation.

In late May 1950 the first clashes between American GIs and Communist demonstrators broke out in Tokyo. Five GIs received minor injuries (hostilities had been confined to fisticuffs). Eight Communists were arrested and swiftly brought to trial before an occupation court; they received unusually severe sentences. Prime Minister Yoshida said they deserved it; he was thinking, he told the Japanese public, that his government "might even have to consider outlawing the Communist Party."

THE DEBATE ENDS

Three weeks later, on June 25, 1950, the Korean War broke out. The Red Purge immediately became a crusade to save Japan from the barbarian at the gates. The Japanese government and GHQ did not worry about a few violations of human rights here and there; these were inconsequential in the light of the menace across the Sea of Japan. The Korean War terminated an elaborate discussion in Washington over the desirability of Japan's limited rearmament: MacArthur ordered Yoshida to establish a national police reserve of 75,000 men and to expand the Maritime Safety Agency by an additional 8,000 men. Thanks to the war, Japan was now well secured against conspirators of every description, whether foreign or domestic.

It was at this critical moment in Japanese history that the Second US Education Mission arrived at Tokyo to support the Red Purge. "One of the greatest weapons against communism in the Far East," the mission declared, "is an enlightened electorate in Japan." The Japanese people, frightened by the war that was even then raging between communism and capitalism, did not question the Red Purge, which forced 22,000 "undesirable" citizens from society into obscurity. The once-condemned militarists and ultranationalists emerged from the obscurity of past years. Three hundred and seventy thousand of them were welcomed back to the new society that could use their talents and thoughts.

The Korean War also brought to an end the national debate in Japan over whether there should be a comprehensive or a partial peace treaty. A peace treaty with the United States and its allies became a matter of urgency, so that an independent Japan could contribute voluntarily to the defense of democracy. Truman sent Dulles to Tokyo to finalize both a peace treaty and a mutual security treaty. Yoshida was grateful, and the Japanese people knew they had no other choice.

Conclusion

The bold American experiment with the Japanese future made the Japanese people intensely insecure—a natural reaction to their first and spectacular defeat in war, and to the humiliating foreign military control of their life. The Japanese government, dominated by conservative forces, resisted the American effort at reform, but only succeeded in strengthening it, since the uncompromising Americans proceeded to jam their reforms down the Japanese throat. The Japanese people had to swallow many alien ideas and practices. Much to their surprise, however, the people found these ideas and practices far from unpalatable; some of them, in fact, were downright appetizing. By the time the Americans left Japan in 1952, many of the reforms had already formed the basis of a new political culture. The Japanese psychology did not break down because of "American mass democracy" as the Japanese conservatives had feared. On the contrary, the Japanese people discovered democracy to be a pleasant, efficient, and even commercially profitable way of life.

VERTICAL CRAVINGS

In the light of the massive American attempt to democratize Japan, MacArthur's autocratic style was an obvious contradiction. Though annoying, the contradiction was not a serious matter: the Japanese people understood that MacArthur's manner was not exactly democratic; and the American reforms did after all succeed in changing the texture of Japanese political, social, and economic interaction. Despite the living contradiction at the helm of authority, this success was an epoch-making testimony to both the quality of American democratic ideals and the ability of the Japanese people to translate the ideals into practice.

There is, however, a serious contradiction at the heart of Japanese democracy—a contradiction not readily visible on first acquaintance with the stable and industrious Japanese society. By penetrating the surface of this society, one immediately encounters a powerful undercurrent of indigenous emotion that runs against the tide of democracy. The emotion is best described as a craving for the aesthetic simplicity of vertical loyalty. It is this Japanese emotion that MacArthur's autocracy, though camouflaged by democracy, unintentionally perpetuated.

THE SEARCH FOR AUTHENTICITY

The Japanese people have coped very well with the revolutionary changes in their life. But their capacity to assimilate hides a deep emotional malaise. Publicly the people are confident of their collective talent and resiliency. They have accomplished the "civilization and enlightenment" of democracy and reached the indisputable status of "rich nation." Indeed, they take great pride in their social harmony, political vitality, international amicability, and unprecedented prosperity. Precisely because of these difficult accomplishments, island Japan wants international recognition. Japan feels that the world does not seem to recognize anything else about it but the "Japanese economic miracle." Worse, even in the arena of international commercial competition Japan receives an ample amount of blame for being an "economic animal." Is this because Japan, a small, rich nation, does not maintain credible armed forces? Has Japan played a little too long and too well the role of a "humble, industrious, polite, peaceful nation," the role that powerful Allied nations once imposed upon the defeated empire?

Japan is retreating to an introspective mood: "What have we done to ourselves? What is Japan? What is it to be a 'Japanese'?" The Japanese people like to believe that they must have a hidden fountain of "uniquely Japanese traits" that are responsible for the extraordinary achievement of prewar and postwar Japan. But where can it be hidden? Somewhere deep in the labyrinth of Japanese democracy and prosperity? This late-twentieth-century search for the "true Japan" has a quality similar to the one imperial Japan launched in the late nineteenth century, in reaction against its excessive imitation of Western civilization, enlightenment, and technology. Imperial Japan found its identity in the realm of living myth.

The present groping for an authentic Japan is bound to head back into history. In Japan, "authenticity," like "wisdom," for some unknown reason, seems to exist not in the present but only in the past. The long history of Japan, still alive in the present, provides a vast depth and width for an imaginative mind to explore. Postwar Japan has found temporary solace in its memory of the early Meiji period, when a nation in upheaval produced numerous brilliant minds. For national glory, those minds pursued excellence unceasingly without thought of personal gain. In 1968 the Japanese government sponsored a national celebration of the Meiji Centennial.

The search for the authentic Japan continues to go back in time. The centuries of samurai warrior regimes, rich in idealized codes of honor, have always cast an irresistible spell upon the Japanese people, who wonder if their own code of behavior shamefully lacks some of the "true Japanese characteristics" such as self-discipline, simplicity, humility, and most critically, loyalty—the loyalty of the purest Japanese form that popular sovereignty and democracy were supposed to kill. Precisely because of their present hedonistic pursuit of material affluence, they search uneasily for a spiritual accommodation with the past. Their individualistic, almost egoistic, pursuit of "happiness," they fear, may have been undermining the collective interest and welfare. They fear that nationhood may become irrelevant; that Japanese history would be lost; that the intricacy and delicacy of Japanese social interaction, which took centuries of careful cultivation, would crumble beyond repair; and that Japan in future might be merely an aggregate of talented but amoral and opportunistic slaves of profit.

Various centuries-old manuscripts on the code of loyal warriors and on the lives of starkly disciplined artists and swordsmen have been resurrected and have attained the best-seller list. Also selling well are manuals on elaborate social manners and rituals. Perhaps, contemporary Japanese society has become too "free" to suit the Japanese taste for order, and too loose and informal for the Japanese sense of social decorum.

VOICES FROM THE PAST

In January 1972 an astonishing event happened. A soldier of the imperial army was discovered in the Guam jungles, where he had been hiding for twenty-eight years. He knew the war was over; but surrender was worse than death. The soldier was a living ghost. "I continue to survive," he told the reporters in Guam, "by believing in the Emperor and the Japanese spirit." He both frightened and delighted surviving members of the prewar generation of Japanese: frightened, as he reminded them of the misery and horror of the war and as he personified the blind loyalty that the imperial government so efficiently cultivated; delighted, as he embodied the "true loyalty" that the contemporary Japanese people passionately idealize although they have lost it. The conservative Japanese government, which had been decrying the moral decline of the people ever since the beginning of the US Occupation, did not fail to capitalize on this rare and historic discovery. The minister of public welfare among many prominent officials and citizens met him at Tokyo Airport and joined the chorus of praise for his patriotism.

One reporter asked the soldier in Tokyo, "What do you think about the war?" He replied: "The reason Japan lost is because we did not have adequate weapons. But we did have the spiritual strength. I have brought back safely with me a rifle the Emperor gave me. I would like to apologize most humbly to the Emperor for my insufficient servitude." (Every weapon in the Imperial Army and Navy was considered as the Emperor's.)

Japanese of the postwar generations were fascinated by his fugitive life in the jungles. To them his version of patriotism was anachronistic yet exuded a captivating romanticism. Indeed, the entire nation was transfixed by this reminder of the ageless, true Japanese spirit. In October 1972 two more imperial soldiers were discovered, this time in the Philippines, and engaged in shootouts with the Philippine army. One was shot to death and the other escaped into the jungle. A massive rescue hunt was organized by the Japanese government but he was not found. In February 1974 a Japanese free-lance reporter successfully contacted him, but he said, "I will surrender only on my superior's order." His superior, formerly a major in the imperial army, and the reporter met him again in March; and he now "surrendered." His return to Japan was the cue for frantic celebrations.[1]

A RETURN TO NATIONALISM
The present national bout of introspection has infused into the Japanese psyche a healthy dose of narcissism. It is a healthy reaction for an island nation that had been obsessed with the world beyond the oceans. Japanese neonationalism, though well camouflaged by gestures of internationalism, has already caused a change in the attitude of the Japanese people toward that most delicate of issues, "national self-defense." As the Japanese Constitution of 1946 declares, Japan renounces any and all "war potential." Yet Japan presently possesses a

large "Self-Defense Force." The world situation has changed considerably since the dreamy days of 1946, when the United Nations symbolized peace and humanity among the human race. The Soviet Union does not seem about to become friendly. Nor does the United States seem as dependable and steadfast as it used to; indeed, it appears to be downright callous about Japanese sensitivity. The most dramatic and brutal example of American insensitivity toward Japan was when President Nixon, without informing America's best ally in Asia, Japan, announced the recognition of Mao's China, the nation that the US government had been insisting to Japan was illegitimate, if not nonexistent. Taiwan, one of the most strategically located and loyal allies of the United States, was subsequently abandoned by none but the United States.

The Japanese people have clearly recognized that the only nation they can really depend on for their survival is Japan itself. Perhaps the postwar tradition of fanatical pacifism has become obsolete and dangerous for the third-richest nation in the world; Japan must assume, whether it likes or not, its due responsibility for its defense and the defense of its allies. Does this mean that Japan will go on building a massive military establishment, reminiscent of the mighty imperial armed forces? Would Japan even go nuclear? Why not? Although Japan, the only nation yet subjected to atomic attack, remains extremely nervous about anything nuclear, it is inevitable that Japan too will come to possess a nuclear arsenal. Otherwise, island Japan will not become a credible threat or pose a sufficient deterrent to any other nation, especially when all the major powers have their own huge stockpiles of ICBMs.

Japan of course has both the technological capability and the financial resources to launch construction of massive military forces. It is a matter of will and necessity. The necessity is obvious to the Japanese people in the light of American reluctance since Vietnam to get involved in other nations' defense. However, the will to fight a war—any war— does not prevail among the Japanese people today. The complete exhaustion in World War II and consequent misery have left them a nation of noncombatants. They have developed a strong aversion to physical confrontation. To help end the aversion, the Japanese Maritime Self-Defense Forces in February 1980 joined the naval forces of four other Pacific nations (the USA, Canada, Australia, and New Zealand), thus ending Japan's postwar taboo on collective defense operations. Protest in Japan was negligible.

The revolutionary contribution of the US Occupation has been absorbed and has become an integral part of Japanese society. "Postwar

Japan" has thus drawn to a close and a new era has begun. The new era brings to Japan both uncertainty about its future destiny and the memory of its glorious history. Among the many examples afforded by its past, Japan may well remember the catastrophic consequences of its own proclamation, in 1934, that war was "the father of creation and the mother of culture."

Notes

The following abbreviations are used in the notes:

CI & E   Civil Information and Education Section, General Headquarters (GHQ), Supreme Commander for the Allied Powers (SCAP), Tokyo

CIS   Civil Intelligence Section, US Army, Pacific, GHQ, Tokyo

FEC   Far Eastern Commission (in Washington, DC)

GHQ   General Headquarters

HI   Hoover Institution on War, Revolution and Peace (Stanford, California)

Kokken   Kokuritsu Kyoiku Kenkyu-jo [National Institute for Educational Research], Tokyo

MA   MacArthur Archives (Norfolk, Virginia)

NSC   National Security Council (Washington, DC)

OSS   Office of Strategic Services (Washington, DC)

POLAD   Office of the United States Political Adviser, Tokyo

RG   Record Group

R & A Report   Research and Analysis Report (by the Research and Analysis Branch of the Office of Strategic Services; later, of the Department of State)

SCAP   Supreme Commander for the Allied Powers (Douglas Mac-Arthur and/or his command post)

SCAPIN   SCAP instruction to the Japanese government

TL   Harry S. Truman Library (Independence, Missouri)
                MM File   Miscellaneous Material File
                NA File   Naval Aide File
                O File   Official File
                PS File   President's Secretary's File

USCSMJ   United States Cultural Science Mission to Japan

USEMJ   United States Education Mission to Japan

USNA   United States National Archives (Washington, DC)

WARCOS   War Department, Commander-in-Chief

Names of Japanese authors are given in Japanese order (surname first) when publications are in Japanese but in English order when they are in English.

A Personal Introduction

1. See *Mainichi Nenkan 1961*, pp. 133–39.

Introduction to Part I

1. Top-secret telegram, Admiral Edwards to Admiral Leahy's eyes only [William D. Leahy was chairman of the Joint Chiefs of Staff from July 1942 to March 1949], 9 August 1945, TL, NA File, "The Berlin Conference: Communications from the Map Room, August 3–7," box 6, folder 1. See also memorandum, Secretary of War Henry L. Stimson to the president, n.d., ibid.

2. Top-secret memorandum for the president, Stimson to President Truman, "Proposed Program of Japan" [June 1945 ?], Berlin Conference, TL, NA File, box 4, p. 7.

Chapter 1

1. For Fillmore's and Perry's letters, see Centre for East Asian Cultural Studies, *The Meiji Japan through Contemporary Sources* (Tokyo: The Centre, 1970), vol. 2, pp. 9–15.

2. The Bakufu told them, "Our accepting these letters delivered by the American ship in Uraga is just a political expedient" (ibid., p. 16). For some lengthy responses from those local officials, see pp. 17–35.

3. For full texts of all the treaties, see ibid., vol. 1, pp. 1–65. For a detailed description of the development of these treaties, see Kamikawa Hiromatsu, ed., *Japan-American Diplomatic Relations in the Meiji-Taisho Era*, trans. Kimura Michiko (Tokyo: Pan-Pacific Press, 1958), pp. 1–50.

4. For a full text of the Bakufu's letter of 20 August 1860 to the Imperial House, see Centre for East Asian Cultural Studies, *Meiji Japan*, vol. 2, pp. 41–47.

5. Ryusaku Tsunoda, William Theodore de Barry, and Donald Keene, *Sources of Japanese Tradition* (New York: Columbia University Press, 1964), vol. 2, p. 165.

6. Ikazaki Akio, *Daigaku no jiji no rekishi* [History of university autonomy] (Tokyo: Shin Nippon Shuppan-sha, 1965), p. 68.

7. See Kokken, *Nippon kindai kyoiku hyakunen-shi* (Tokyo: Kyoiku Kenkyu Shinkokai, 1974), vol. 1, *Kyoiku seisaku*, pp. 437–440.

8. Tsunoda et al., vol. 2, p. 137. For an original Japanese text, see Monbusho [Ministry of Education], *Gakusei hyakunen-shi* [A hundred-year history of the educational system], vol. 2 (Tokyo, 1972), p. 7 (hereafter cited as Monbusho, *GH*). This two-volume work (vol. 1, *Text*, 1141 pp. plus 30 pp. index, and vol. 2, *Source Material*, 710 pp.) is a prodigious compilation of Japanese educational documents since the 1868 Meiji Restoration. In fact, the work was a part of the Meiji Centennial that the government sponsored.

9. See Herbert Passin, *Society and Education in Japan* (New York: Teachers College, Columbia University, 1964), pp. 210–211. Passin quotes a much lengthier translation of the preamble from Kumaji Yoshida, "European and American Influence in Modern Japan," in Inazo Nitobe and Others, *Western Influence in Modern Japan* (Chicago: University of Chicago Press, 1931), pp. 34–35.

10. See Hiratsuka Masanori, *Nippon no kyoiku* [Education in Japan] (Tokyo: Nippon Kokusai Kyoiku Kyokai, 1966), pp. 9, 37; Monbusho, *Gakusei 70 nenshi* [Seventy-year history of school system] (Tokyo: Teikoku Chiho Gyosei Gakkai, 1942); and Herbert Passin, "Japan," in *Education and Political Development*, ed., James S. Coleman (Princeton, NJ: Princeton University Press, 1965), pp. 272–312.

11. Hiratsuka, *Nippon no kyoiku*, p. 9.

12. Tsunoda et al., vol. 2, p. 131.

13. For a fuller quotation of Ito's statement to the Emperor, see Passin, *Society and Education in Japan*, pp. 230–33.

14. For the full fourteen-article ordinance, see Monbusho, *GH*, vol. 2, p. 152.

15. See Tsunoda et al., vol. 2, p. 168.

16. For full translations of both laws, see Centre for East Asian Cultural Studies, *Meiji Japan*, vol. 2, pp. 30–42.

17. Nakayama Kenichi, *Gendai shakai to chianho* [Modern society and public peace laws] (Tokyo: Iwanami Shoten, 1970), pp. 45–56.

18. For Yamagata's full statement, see Centre for East Asian Cultural Studies, *Meiji Japan*, vol. 2, pp. 220–33.

19. For a full text, see ibid., pp. 235–41.

20. Japanese Imperial Government, Ministry of Education, *The Imperial Rescript on Education*, official translation (Tokyo, 1909).

21. Ikazaki, *Daigaku no jiji no rekishi*, p. 63.

22. See Doo Soo Suh, *The Struggle for Academic Freedom in Japanese Universities Before 1945* (Ph.D diss., Columbia University, 1952), pp. 168–89.

Chapter 2

1. Top-secret memorandum for the president, Cheston to the president, 31 May 1945, TL, MM File, box 15.

2. Top-secret memorandum for the president, Donovan to the president, 12 May 1945, ibid.

3. Top-secret memorandum for the president, Cheston, OSS, to the president, 31 May 1945, ibid., p. 1.

4. Top-secret memorandum for the president, Buxton, OSS, to the president, 4 June 1945, ibid., p. 1.

5. For a full text, see Government Section, Supreme Commander for the Allied Powers (SCAP), *Political Reorientation of Japan September 1945 to September 1948* (Wash-

ington, DC: US Government Printing Office, n.d. [1948 ?], vol. 2, p. 412 (hereafter the document—two volumes, consecutively paged—will be cited as SCAP, *Political Reorientation*). During the Yalta Conference James F. Byrnes, soon to become secretary of state, took shorthand notes of the discussion. On 24 April 1945 he gave the typed version to President Truman. See "The Crimean Conference: Minutes of Meetings prepared by James F. Byrnes," TL, NA File, box 7.

6. The third meeting, Kremlin, 8:00 P.M., 28 May 1945, in "Hopkins-Stalin Conference: Record of Conversations between Harry L. Hopkins and Marshal Stalin in Moscow, [26 May – 6 June 1945]," ibid.

7. Ibid.

8. Top-secret telegram, Hopkins to Truman, 30 May 1945, TL, NA File, box 7.

9. Top-secret memorandum for the president, Stimson to President Truman, "Proposed Program for Japan," n.d. [June 1945 ?], Berlin Conference, TL, NA File, box 4, pp. 1–7.

10. Winston Churchill suggested to Truman on 15 June 1945 that they "use the code word TERMINAL for the forthcoming Berlin conference." The code name "Terminal" was appropriate for this historic occasion, for the Berlin (Potsdam) Conference did formulate the final ultimatum of unconditional surrender for Japan. See top-secret telegram, Churchill to Truman, 15 June 1945, in "The Berlin Conference: Meetings of Heads of State," ibid., box 6. The same box contains extensive correspondence between the two men prior to the Potsdam Conference.

11. "Consultation on Problems Arising Directly from the Unconditional Surrender or Defeat of Japan and Procedure Relating Thereto," in "The Berlin Conference: Meetings of Heads of State," ibid., box 6, top-secret document 59. See the same for a State Department draft of the "Terms of Reference" for a proposed Far Eastern Advisory Commission, appendix A, unpaged.

12. "Military Government and Occupation of Japan—Unified or Zonal," ibid., top-secret document 60 unpaged.

13. Ibid., appendix, p. 1.

14. Ibid., p. 3.

15. Ibid.

16. See "The Berlin Conference: Communications from Map Room," TL, NA File, boxes 5 and 6.

17. US Department of War, Military Intelligence Division, "Japanese Jet-and-Rocket-Propulsion Development," *Intelligence Review* [secret] no. 27 (15 August 1946), TL, NA File, box 16, president's copy, p. 54.

18. See US Department of State, *Foreign Relations of the United States Diplomatic Papers: The Conference of Berlin 1945*, vol. 2, Department of State publication 7163 (Washington, DC: US Government Printing Office, 1960), pp. 1248–64, 1291–98.

19. See "Meetings of Heads of Government—Berlin—July 28, 1945, 10:30 P.M.," in "The Berlin Conference," TL, NA File, box 2, pp. 2–3.

20. Top-secret memorandum for the president, Donovan to the president, 16 July 1945, TL, MM File, box 15, pp. 1–2. The intermediary was Per Jacobson, a Swedish national and economic adviser to the Bank for International Settlement in Basel, Switzerland.

21. Ibid., pp. 3–4.

22. Top-secret memorandum for the president, Cheston to the president, 2 August 1945, TL, MM File, box 15, pp. 1–2.

23. See "Proclamation by the Heads of State, US—UK—[USSR]—CHINA," 1 July 1945, in "The Berlin Conference," TL, NA File, box 4. Also, see Stimson's revision of the text of the Potsdam Declaration, in top-secret memorandum for the president, 20 July 1945, ibid.

24. Secret telegram, Ayers to Ross, 27 July 1945, in "The Berlin Conference: Correspondence from Map Room, July 26–August 2, 1945," TL, NA File, folder 2.

25. Telegram, White House Map Room to Captain Vardaman, 28 July 1945, ibid.

26. For a full text, see SCAP, *Political Reorientation,* p. 413.

27. Telegram, White House Map Room to Captain Vardaman, 2 August 1945, in "The Berlin Conference: Correspondence from Map Room, July 26–August 2, 1945," TL, NA File, folder 2.

28. Top-secret memorandum for the president, Cheston to the president, 2 August 1945, pp. 3–4.

29. See "The Berlin Conference: Correspondence from Map Room," TL, NA File, boxes 5 and 6.

30. Top-secret letter, Stimson to the president, 31 July 1945, and enclosure, "Draft of 30 July 1945" [top secret], TL, PS File, box 199.

31. See ibid., final draft of 30 July 1945, p. 1.

32. Ibid., p. 4. Also, for a full text of Truman's statement, see *New York Times,* 7 August 1945, p. 4, col. 1.

33. The Pacific War Research Society, *Japan's Longest Day* (Tokyo: Kodansha International, 1968), p. 22. This book was originally published in Japanese as *Nihon no ichiban nagai hi* [Japan's longest day] (Tokyo: Bungei Shunju, 1965). The Soviet brutality in Manchuria became legendary. In mid-September 1945, William J. Donovan, director of the Office of Strategic Services (OSS), reported to President Truman that the Soviets were "indiscriminately killing Chinese and Japanese" and "carrying out a program of scientific looting." "Every piece of machinery," he reported, "is being removed and all stocks of merchandise in stores and warehouses are being taken away. Mukden presumably will be an empty city when they leave." See memorandum for the president, Donovan to the president, 17 September 1945, TL, MM File, box 15.

34. Telegram, Richard B. Russell to Truman, 7 August 1945, TL, RG-196, box 685.

35. Letter, Truman to Russell, 9 August 1945, TL, RG-196, box 685.

36. For various views on Truman's decision to use the atomic bomb, see Kenneth M. Glazier, Jr., "The Decision to Use Atomic Weapons Against Hiroshima and Nagasaki," *Public Policy* 18, no. 4 (summer 1970): 463–516; William Appleman Williams, *The Tragedy of American Diplomacy,* rev. ed. (Cleveland: World Publishing Co., 1962); P. M. S. Blackett, *Fear, War, and the Bomb* (New York: Whittlesey House, 1948); and Martin J. Sherwin, "The Atomic Bomb and the Origins of the Cold War: US Atomic-Energy Policy and Diplomacy," *American Historical Review* 78, no. 4 (October 1973): 945–68. Also, as a related issue, see Herbert F. York, "The Debate Over the Hydrogen Bomb," *Scientific American* 233, no. 4 (October 1975): 106–113.

37. Letter, Max Grassli, chargé d'affaires ad interim of Switzerland, to Secretary of State James F. Byrnes, 10 August 1945, in SCAP, *Political Reorientation,* p. 414.

38. See *Asahi Shimbun,* 10 August 1945, p. 1.

39. Letter, Byrnes to Grassli, 11 August 1945, in SCAP, *Political Reorientation,* p. 415. Also, see Byrnes, *Speaking Frankly* (New York: Harper and Brothers, 1947), p. 208.

40. For the text of the Japanese letter, see SCAP, *Political Reorientation*, p. 417.

41. Telegram, Truman to Churchill, 11 August 1945, in "Communications: Attlee to Truman, 1945–46," TL, NA File, box 6.

42. See Kyodo Tsushin-sha, ed., *Konoe nikki* [Konoe diary] (Tokyo: Kyodo Tsushin-sha, 1968), p. 156.

43. Secret memorandum for the president, Donovan, OSS, to the president, 13 September 1945, TL, MM File, box 15, p. 2.

44. Ibid., p. 3.

45. For full text, see SCAP, *Political Reorientation*, p. 416, pp. 419–420.

46. See top-secret appendix to "Military Government and Occupation of Japan Attitude Toward the Emperor," 3 July 1945, in "The Berlin Conference," TL, NA File, box 1, document 63, p. 1.

Chapter 3

1. For full texts of the radio exchange between MacArthur and Japanese General Headquarters concerning the surrender ceremonies, see *Department of State Bulletin* 12, no. 321 (12 August 1945): 257–60; also, for documents regarding American instructions to the Japanese government prior to MacArthur's arrival, see MA, RG-9, box 41.

2. Interview by the author of Arthur Coladarci at his office, Stanford University, 11 November 1977. Karl T. Compton, president of the Massachusetts Institute of Technology and a famous member of the Manhattan Project, encountered a similar case in September 1945: "On our first appearance they [children and young people] fled or were pulled out of sight by their mothers as if in terror for their lives." See letter, Compton to President Truman, 4 October 1945, TL, PS File, box 182, p. 5.

3. *Asahi Shimbun*, 31 August 1945, p. 1.

4. For the full text see SCAP, *Political Reorientation*, p. 427. It was prepared jointly by the Departments of State, War, and Navy, and approved by Truman on 6 September 1945.

5. William Sebald, *With MacArthur in Japan* (New York: W. W. Norton and Co., 1965), p. 103.

6. For the full text see SCAP, *Political Reorientation*, pp. 423–26. The document hereafter will be cited as *US Initial Policy*. As early as May 1944 the US government formulated *The Post-War Objectives of the United States in Regard to Japan*, which was the basis of the more elaborate *US Initial Policy*. See Department of State, *Postwar Foreign Policy Preparation 1939–1945*, General Foreign Policy Series no. 15 (Washington, DC: Division of Publication, Office of Public Affairs, 1950), pp. 591–92.

7. For the full text see SCAP, *Political Reorientation*, pp. 429–39. Hereafter it will be cited as *Basic Directive*.

8. For a description of how SWNCC came into existence, see Harold W. Moseley (State Department), Col. Charles W. McCarthy (War Department), and Com. Alvin F. Richardson (Navy Department), "The State-War-Navy Coordinating Committee," *Department of State Bulletin* 13, no. 333 (11 November 1945): 745–47.

9. Secret report, Bishop to George Atcheson, Jr., US political adviser, Tokyo, 31 December 1945, USNA 740.00119 Control (Japan)/1–746, p. 2. Atcheson forwarded it to Secretary of State Byrnes.

10. US Congress, Senate, *Military Situation in the Far East: Hearings before the Committee on Armed Services and the Committee on Foreign Relations*, 82d Cong., 1st sess., 3 May 1951, part 1, (Washington, DC: US Government Printing Office, 1951), p. 54 (hereafter cited as US Senate, *Military Situation*).

11. SCAP, *Political Reorientation*, p. 423.

12. Ibid., p. 738.

13. For instance, SCAPIN [SCAP Instruction] 211, *Contracts by Person in Japan With Foreign Concerns*, 30 December 1945, prohibited any person in Japan from entering into financial or commercial contracts without prior permission from GHQ. See also SCAPIN 1372, 2 December 1946.

14. See Douglas MacArthur, *Reminiscences* (New York: McGraw-Hill Book Co., 1964), p. 285. See also US Department of War, Military Intelligence Division, *Intelligence Review* [secret] no. 28 (22 August 1946), TL, NA File, box 17, p. 39.

15. Memorandum for the president, Edwin Locke, Jr., to the president, "Notes on the Current Situation in Japan Based on Talks With General of the Army Douglas MacArthur and Officers of His Staff, Tokyo, October 14–17, 1945," 19 October 1945, pp. 4–5. The memorandum was enclosed in a letter from Locke in Chunking, China, to Matthew Connelly, secretary to the president, 19 October 1945, TL, PS File, box 182.

16. Top-secret telegram, WARCOS [chief of staff, War Department] to MacArthur, 4 September 1945, MA, RG-9, box 146.

17. Top-secret telegram, WARCOS to MacArthur, 11 October 1945, ibid.

18. Top-secret telegram, MacArthur to WARCOS, 13 October 1945, ibid.

19. See "Agreement of Foreign Ministers at Moscow on Establishing Far Eastern Commission and Allied Council for Japan," SCAP, *Political Reorientation*, p. 421; for the membership of the two bodies, see ibid., pp. 421–22.

20. Top-secret telegram, WARCOS to MacArthur, 22 October 1945, MA, RG-9, box 146.

21. Top-secret telegram, MacArthur to WARCOS, 22 October 1945, ibid.

22. Top-secret telegram, Byrnes to MacArthur, 26 October 1945, ibid. See also top-secret telegram, Byrnes to MacArthur, 23 October 1945, ibid.; and top-secret telegram, George C. Marshall [chief of staff, War Department] to MacArthur, 23 October 1945, ibid.

23. SCAP, *Political Reorientation*, p. 422.

24. Ibid., p. 421.

25. *Department of State Bulletin* 14, no. 349 (10 March 1946): 378.

26. Confidential telegram, MacArthur to McCoy, 13 April 1946, "Far East Commission," MA, RG-9, p. 3.

27. Personal telegram, US War Department to MacArthur and General Hodge [in Korea], 4 December 1946, MA, RG-9, box 152.

28. Top-secret telegram, MacArthur to Draper, 26 December 1948, MA, RG-9, box 150. Draper visited MacArthur three times during the Occupation, on 18–27 September 1947, 20 March–2 April 1948, and 8–26 December 1949.

29. MacArthur, *Reminiscences*, p. 291.

30. Ibid., p. 293.

31. See "SCAP's Denial of Friction with FEC," SCAP, *Political Reorientation*, p. 751. See also FEC, *Activities of the Far Eastern Commission February 26, 1946–July 10,*

1947. Department of State Far Eastern Series no. 24 (Washington, DC: US Government Printing Office, 1947), pp. 10–11.

32. See "Comment on Far Eastern Commission Policy Decision," SCAP, *Political Reorientation*, p. 774.

33. US Department of War, Military Intelligence Division, "Trends," *Intelligence Review* no. 32 (19 September 1946), TL, NA File, box 17, president's copy, p. 1.

34. Top-secret report to the president from Clark M. Clifford, "American Relations with the Soviet Union," 24 September 1946, TL, PS File, box 15, p. 71.

35. CIA, *Review of the World Situation as It Relates to the Security of the United States* (hereafter cited as CIA, *Review*), CIA report no. 3, 17 December 1947, submitted to National Security Council meeting no. 4, 17 December 1947, ibid., box 203, copy 1, p. 8.

36. US Department of War, Military Intelligence Division, "Long-Range Detection of Atomic Explosions," *Intelligence Review* no. 37 (24 October 1946), TL, NA File, box 17, president's copy, p. 54.

37. Ibid.

38. Top-secret telegram, Churchill to Truman, 8 August 1945, in "Communications: Attlee to Truman, 1945–1946," TL, NA File, box 6.

39. See the responses from the cabinet members and prominent nuclear scientists in "National Security Council: Atomic," TL, PS File, box 199.

40. CIA, *Review*, CIA report no. 1, 26 September 1947, TL, PS File, box 203, copy 1; the quote is from the summary.

41. National Security Council, *A Report to the National Security Council by the Executive Secretary on the Position of the United States With Respect to Soviet-Directed World Communism*, 30 March 1948, submitted to NSC meeting no. 9, 2 April 1948, in "NSC," TL, PS File, box 203, p. 1 (hereafter cited as National Security Council, *World Communism*).

42. MacArthur, "Message to American People Concerning the Surrender," SCAP, *Political Reorientation*, p. 737.

43. MacArthur, "Statement First Anniversary of Surrender," 2 September 1946, ibid., p. 756.

44. Ibid.

45. MacArthur, "On Significance of 4th July," 4 July 1947, SCAP, *Political Reorientation*, p. 772.

46. US Senate, *Military Situation*, 5 May 1951, part 1, p. 310.

47. John K. Emmerson, "Political Factors in the Present Japanese Situation," 8 February 1946, USNA 740.00119 Control (Japan)/2-2546, p. 20. Emmerson wrote an informative memoir, *The Japanese Thread* (New York: Holt, Rinehart and Winston, 1978); see esp. pp. 249–80.

48. MacArthur, *Reminiscences*, pp. 283–84.

49. Ibid., pp. 282–83; see also his "Statement to the Japanese Government Concerning Required Reforms," 11 October 1945, SCAP, *Political Reorientation*, p. 741; and "Message to the Japanese People," 27 December 1945, ibid., p. 745.

50. MacArthur, "Statement First Anniversary of Surrender," p. 756.

51. MacArthur, "On Significance of 4th July," p. 772.

52. Ibid.

53. Ibid.
54. MacArthur, "New Year's Greeting to the Japanese People," 31 December 1946, SCAP, *Political Reorientation,* p. 761.
55. "Interview With Press Correspondents, Primarily Concerning Plan for United Nations Administration of Japan," 19 March 1947, ibid., p. 765.
56. MacArthur, "In Support of Appropriations for Occupation Purposes," 20 February 1947, ibid., p. 763.
57. MacArthur, "Second Anniversary of Surrender," 2 September 1947, ibid., p. 775.
58. Ibid.
59. MacArthur, "Statement First Anniversary of Surrender," SCAP, *Political Reorientation,* p. 756.
60. "Interview With Press Correspondents," ibid., p. 765.
61. MacArthur, "In Support of Appropriations," ibid., p. 763.
62. Ibid.
63. MacArthur, *Reminiscences,* p. 310.
64. Ibid., p. 311.
65. Arundel Del Re, memorandum, "Subject: Possibility of the Emperor Being Considered a War Criminal," n.d. [December 1945 ?] HI, Trainor Papers, box 45, p. 1.
66. Letter, Atcheson to Marshall, 17 March 1947, MA, RG-9, box 146.
67. Letter, Shujiro Iwasaki, president of International Club, to President Truman, 10 February 1948, USNA 894.43/2-1048; see also TL, O File 197, box 686.
68. Quoted in Richard H. Rovere and Arthur Schlesinger, Jr., *The MacArthur Controversy and American Foreign Policy* (New York: Farrar, Straus, and Giroux, 1965), p. 92.
69. Lawrence S. Witter, "MacArthur and the Missionaries: God and Man in Occupied Japan," *Pacific Historical Review* 40, no. 1 (February 1971): 97.
70. TL, Bunce Papers, box 1, p. 58.
71. William P. Woodard, *The Allied Occupation of Japan 1945–1952 and Japanese Religions* (Leiden, Netherlands: E. J. Brill, 1972), p. 245.
72. Memorandum, John W. Norviel to Office of Commander-in-Chief, GHQ, 13 September 1947, HI, Trainor Papers, box 37, pp. 1–2.
73. Letter, Nobuzo Samukawa to Norviel, 2 September 1947, ibid.
74. See Memorandum, Nugent, chief of CI & E, to commander-in-chief, 26 January 1948, in "History of the West," MA, RG-5, p. 1.
75. Letter, Benson to MacArthur, 14 January 1948, ibid.
76. Memorandum, Nugent to commander-in-chief, 26 January 1948, ibid., pp. 1–3.
77. Letter, MacArthur to Benson, 28 January 1948, ibid., p. 1.
78. Ibid., p. 2.
79. MacArthur, "In Support of Appropriations," p. 763.
80. See SCAP, *Political Reorientation,* p. 423.
81. "History points out the unmistakable lesson that military occupations serve their purpose at best only a limited time, after which a deterioration rapidly sets in—deterioration of the populace in an occupied country ... and deterioration of the occupying forces which in time assume a dominant power complex pointing to the

illusion of a master race." MacArthur, "In Support of Appropriation for Occupation Purposes," 20 February 1947, in SCAP, *Political Reorientation,* p. 764.

82. Rovere and Schlesinger, *The MacArthur Controversy,* p. 47.

83. Memorandum for the president, Edwin A. Locke, Jr., to the president, "Notes on the Current Situation in Japan Based on Talks with General of the Army Douglas MacArthur and Officers of His Staff, Tokyo, October 14–17, 1945," 19 October 1945, TL, PS File, box 182, p. 3; see enclosure to letter, Locke to Matthew Connelly, secretary to the president, 19 October 1945, ibid.

84. US Senate, *Military Situation,* 5 May 1951, part 1, p. 312.

85. Ibid., p. 311.

86. Top-secret letter, Bishop to secretary of state, "United States Policy Toward Japan," 13 February 1946, USNA 740.00119 Control (Japan)/2-1346, p. 1.

87. Memorandum, Howard Bell to Mark T. Orr, chief of the Education Division, Civil Information and Education Section, "Subject: Field Visit to Sapporo, Hokkaido, 17–24 September 1947," HI, Trainor Papers, box 37, p. 6.

88. Ibid., p. 5.

89. Ibid., pp. 5–6. Also, see Robert Fearey, "Reappraisal of United States Security Interests and Policies in Regard to Japan," 17 April 1946, first submitted to Atcheson and then to Byrnes, USNA 740.00119 Control (Japan)/4-2346, pp. 15–16. For the criminal deterioration of the occupation forces, see Tsukuda Jitsuo, "Yokohama kara no shogen" [Testimony from Yokohama], pp. 113–30; and ibid., "Senryoka no gunji saiban" [Military Court Under the Occupation], pp. 347–81; both in *Kyodo kenkyu: Nippon kenkyu* [Joint study: occupied Japan], ed., Shiso no Kagaku Kenkyukai (Tokyo: Tokuma Shoten, 1972).

90. Memorandum for the president, Charles A. Murphy to the president, 14 August 1950, TL, PS File, box 182.

91. Confidential report, Pendleton to President Truman, 9 August 1950, pp. 1–3. See enclosure to memorandum for the president, Murphy to the president, 14 August 1950, TL, PS File, box 182.

92. US Senate, *Military Situation,* 5 May 1951, part 1, pp. 310–11.

Chapter 4

1. SCAP, *Political Reorientation,* pp. 423, 424.

2. Ibid., pp. 431–32.

3. See US Department of War, Military Intelligence Division, *Intelligence Review* [secret] no. 48 (16 January 1947), TL, NA File, box 18, pp. 41–43.

4. Letter, Compton to the president, 4 October 1945, TL, PS File, box 182, pp. 2–3.

5. Top-secret telegram, Joint Chiefs of Staff to MacArthur, 31 October 1945, MA, RG-9, box 144.

6. Top-secret telegram, MacArthur to Joint Chiefs of Staff, 24 November 1945, ibid.

7. Top-secret telegram, Eisenhower to MacArthur, 28 November 1945, ibid.

8. Top-secret telegram, Hull to WARCOS [War Department, chief of staff] and to Richard K. Sutherland [chief of staff], SCAP, 3 December 1945, ibid.

9. Top-secret telegram, MacArthur to WARCOS, 3 December 1945, ibid.

10. Top-secret telegram, WARCOS to MacArthur, 4 December 1945, ibid.

11. Confidential telegram, secretary of war to MacArthur, 16 December 1945, ibid.

12. Secret telegram, Joint Chiefs of Staff to MacArthur, 15 December 1945, ibid.

13. Secret telegram, Marquat to Department of the Army, 18 April 1948, ibid.

14. Secret report, Bishop to Atcheson, who transmitted it to Byrnes, USNA 740.00119 Control (Japan)/1-746, pp. 2–3.

15. Letter, Bishop to Byrnes, 13 February 1946, USNA 740.00119 Control (Japan)/2-1346, p. 2.

16. Secret report, Bishop to Atcheson, USNA 740.00119 Control (Japan)/1-746, p. 3.

17. SCAP, *Political Reorientation,* p. 8.

18. Ibid., loc. cit.

19. Ibid., p. 413.

20. *Newsweek,* 24 September 1945, pp. 55–56.

21. SCAP, *Political Reorientation,* p. 424. The thoroughness of the purge was well documented in SCAP, *History of the Nonmilitary Activities of the Occupation of Japan, 1945–1951,* Monograph no. 7, "The Purge," USNA 65-4, RG 331; SCAP, *Political Reorientation,* pp. 479–564; and Hans H. Baerwald, *The Purge of Japanese Leaders Under the Occupation,* University of California Publications in Political Science, vol. 8 (Berkeley, Calif.: University of California Press, 1959).

22. See *Asahi Shimbun,* 4 December 1945, p. 1.

23. Top-secret appendix to "Military Government and Occupation of Japan Attitude Toward the Emperor," 3 July 1945, in "The Berlin Conference," TL, NA File, box 1, document 63, pp. 1–2.

24. John K. Emmerson, POLAD, "Memorandum of Conversation," 19 December 1945, pp. 1–2; to be seen as enclosure 2 in confidential letter, Atcheson to secretary of state, 26 December 1945, USNA 740.00119 Control (Japan)/12-2645. See also enclosure 1, confidential memorandum for the supreme commander and chief of staff, "Interview with Mr. Tokugawa Narihiro," from Atcheson, 19 December 1945, ibid.

25. Confidential letter, Atcheson to secretary of state, 26 December 1945, ibid.

26. Top-secret memorandum, Atcheson to MacArthur and chief of staff, 7 January 1946, to be seen as enclosure to letter, Atcheson to Byrnes, 8 January 1946, USNA 894.001 Hirohito/1-746, pp. 1–2.

27. Ibid., pp. 2–3.

28. Secret telegram, MacArthur to the War Department, 25 January 1946, USNA 894.001 Hirohito/1-2546, pp. 1–3. Arundel Del Re, an education adviser to the Civil Information and Education Section, GHQ, presented a similar view. See memorandum, "Possibility of the Emperor Being Considered a War Criminal," n.d. [December 1945 ?], HI, Trainor Papers, box 45.

29. Sebald succeeded Atcheson, who died in a plane crash off Pearl Harbor in August 1947. Sebald owed his promotion to MacArthur, who on 3 October 1948 recommended him to the State Department as "a most worthy successor to the late and beloved Ambassador George Atcheson." MacArthur liked Sebald because he "consistently demonstrated clear judgment, initiative, and the highest sense of responsibility." See telegram, MacArthur to Robert A. Lovett, undersecretary of state, 3 October 1948, MA, RG-10, box 151.

30. Sebald conveyed the result of his conversation with MacArthur in a personal and top-secret letter to his friend in the State Department, H. Merrell Benninghoff,

deputy director of the Office of Far Eastern Affairs. See personal and top-secret letter, Sebald to Benninghoff, 29 October 1948, USNA 894.001/10-2948.

31. US Department of War, Military Intelligence Division, *Intelligence Review* no. 31 (12 September 1946), TL, NA File, box 17, p. 46.

32. "Statement by General MacArthur on Election Results," 25 April 1946, SCAP, *Political Reorientation,* p. 719. This statement was prepared by Courtney Whitney, chief of the Government Section, as a memorandum, "Election Report," 22 April 1946; see MA, RG-5, box 80.

33. See US Department of War, Military Intelligence Division, *Intelligence Review* no. 9 (11 April 1946), TL, NA File, box 16, pp. 11–12. Also, see Takemae Eiji and Amakawa Akira, *Nihon senyro hishi* [Secret History of Occupied Japan], vol. 1 (Tokyo: Asahi Shimbun-sha, 1977), pp. 274–75.

34. "Statement by General MacArthur on Election Results," p. 719.

35. *Izvestiya,* 10 April 1946; see telegram, US Embassy in Moscow to Department of State and POLAD, SCAP, 12 April 1946, MA, RG-9, box 69.

36. Intra–State Department Memorandum, Emmerson, 12 April 1946, USNA 740.00119 Control (Japan)/4-1046, p. 2.

37. Letter, Yoshida to MacArthur, 15 May 1946, MA, RG-10, box 11.

38. Ibid.

39. US Department of War, Military Intelligence Division, "Significant Personalities," *Intelligence Review* [secret] no. 16 (29 May 1946), TL, NA File, box 16, president's copy, p. 61.

40. SCAP, *Political Reorientation,* p. 9.

41. Ibid. See also US Department of State, Research & Analysis Branch, R & A Report 3850, "Progress in Local Government Reform in Japan," 24 October 1947, USNA 097.3 Z1092.

42. US Department of State, Office of Intelligence Research (formerly Research & Analysis Branch), OIR Report 4518, "The Purge Problem and the Japanese Peace Treaty," 25 September 1947, USNA 097.3 Z1092, p. 16.

43. MacArthur, "On Selection of Tetsu Katayama as Prime Minister," 24 May 1947, in SCAP, *Political Reorientation,* p. 770.

44. Ibid.

45. Katayama, "Statement of the Prime Minister," 1 June 1947, MA, RG-10, VIP File, Katayama, 1947, pp. 1–2.

46. See *Asahi Shimbun,* 26 November 1947. CI & E's Public Opinion & Sociological Research Unit conducted a survey in Tokyo, where the public was the best-informed in Japan, on the Katayama White Paper on the Japanese economy. According to Herbert Passin, head of the unit, "a majority reported absolutely no knowledge of the White Paper." See Intra-section memorandum, Passin to chief of research and analysis, CI & E, 3 September 1947, HI, Trainor Papers, box 37.

47. Issued on 15 December 1945. For a full text see SCAP, *Political Reorientation,* pp. 467–69.

48. Secret report, Bishop to Atcheson, USNA 740.00119 Control (Japan)/1-746, p. 1.

49. See OIR report 4678, "The Democratic Liberal Party: A Resurgence of Conservative Forces in Japan," 15 August 1950, page v, USNA 097.3 Z1092.

50. See SCAPIN [SCAP Instruction] 1318, "Sponsorship and Support of Shinto by Neighborhood Associations," 6 November 1946.

51. US Eighth Army, Headquarters, "Funerals, Memorial Services, and Monuments for War Dead, Militarists and Ultranationalists," Operational Directive no. 21, 1 March 1947, USNA 894.413/3-1947.

52. SCAP, GHQ, Religions and Cultural Resources Division, Civil Information and Education Section, *Religions in Japan* (Tokyo: March 1948), TL, Bunce Papers, box 4, unpaged (excerpts from foreword). Bunce was chief of the Religions and Cultural Resources Division.

53. See ibid., box 1.

54. See appendix to "Political and Economic Objectives of Military Government in Japan," [top secret] 3 July 1945, in "The Berlin Conference," TL, NA File, document 61, pp. 1–2.

55. SCAP, *Political Reorientation*, pp. 433–34.

56. See appendix to "Political and Economic Objectives of Military Government in Japan," p. 2.

57. See SCAP, *Political Reorientation*, pp. 565–67; and, for related directives, ibid., pp. 567–74. Also, see US Department of State, Research & Analysis Branch, R & A Report 3378.2, "The Sumitomo Industrial Combine of Japan and Its Officers," 18 December 1945; and R & A Report 4573, "Deconcentration of Industry in Japan," 1 December 1947, both in USNA 097.3 Z1092. In January 1946 the US Mission on Japanese Combines, known as the Zaibatsu Mission, was sent to Japan to make recommendations to the War and State Departments. See US Department of State, *Report of the Mission on Japanese Combines*, Department of State Far Eastern Series 14 (Washington, DC: US Government Printing Office, 1946).

58. Secret report, Bishop to Atcheson, 31 December 1945, enclosure to letter, Atcheson to Byrnes, 7 January 1946, USNA 740.00119 Control (Japan)/1-746, p. 1.

59. Confidential letter, Atcheson to Truman, 5 November 1945, USNA 740.00119 Control (Japan)/11-2345, p. 4.

60. Matsuo Matsui, "A Report on a Trip to Tohoku," 8 December 1945, USNA 740.00119 Control (Japan)/12-1345, pp. 1–2. Smuggling of rice from Korea was so profitable that MacArthur had to take steps to eliminate it.

61. Letter, Compton to President Truman, 4 October 1945, TL, PS File, box 182, p. 1.

62. John K. Emmerson, "Political Factors in the Present Japanese Situation," 8 February 1946, USNA 740.00119 Control (Japan)/2-2546, p. 1.

63. MacArthur, *Reminiscences*, p. 306.

64. OSS, R & A Report 3831, "The Coming Food Crisis in Japan," 12 April 1946, p. i, USNA.

65. US Army, Pacific, GHQ, Civil Intelligence Section, "Trends: Japan—Korea—Philippines," (hereafter cited as CIS, "Trends") [secret] no. 30 (26 July 1946), MA, RG-4, box 39, p. 12.

66. Letter, Yoshida to MacArthur, 29 May 1946, MA, RG-10, VIP File, Yoshida, 1946.

67. See CIS, "Trends," no. 30, p. 12.

68. Ibid., no. 29 (16 July 1946), p. 3.

69. The Ministry of Education's directive of 28 August 1945; for a text, see SCAP, GHQ, Civil Information and Education Section (CI & E), *Education in the New Japan*, vol. 2 (Tokyo, 1948), p. 139 (hereafter cited as CI & E, *Education*).

70. For a text, see ibid., p. 148.

71. *Nippon Times,* 30 November 1945; quoted in POLAD, "Educational Affairs in Japan, November 9–December 1, 1945," USNA 894.42/12-1045, p. 1.

72. A personal note here. Skim milk at first tasted terrible, but soon I began to enjoy it. Through this lunch program I came to relish for the first time sweet strawberry jam, deliciously sour dried apple strips, and—our all-time favorite—roasted whole almonds, salted. The quantity I received at lunch time, for which I could barely wait, consisted of one cup of warm skim milk and two tiny dried apple strips or two almonds, or a tablespoonful of strawberry jam on a half loaf of bread. The half loaf was about six inches long, three inches wide, and two inches deep.

73. Karl C. Leebrick, POLAD, "Observations of Educational Institutions in Various Cities in Japan," 26 November 1945, USNA 894.42/12-546, p. 3.

74. POLAD, "Educational Affairs in Japan, December 1–31, 1945," USNA 740.00119 Control (Japan)/2-2046, p. 19. See also SCAP, *History of the Nonmilitary Activities of the Occupation of Japan, 1945–1951,* USNA 65-4, Monograph no. 31 "Education," pp. 119–23 (hereafter cited as SCAP, *Nonmilitary Activities: Education*).

75. See CIS, "Trends," no. 29 (16 July 1946), p. 24.

76. The letter was printed in the newspaper *Yomiuri–Hochi Shimbun,* Tokyo, 12 December 1945. The same teacher also wrote: "Formerly we bore our grievances silently because we were not permitted to complain, since doing so would invite charges of Bolshevism or degeneracy heaped upon us by the headmasters and educational authorities. . . . Needless to say we were forbidden to contribute articles to newspapers or magazines." See POLAD, "Educational Affairs in Japan, December 1–31, 1945," p. 20.

77. See CI & E, *Education,* vol. 2, pp. 205–6.

78. *Asahi Shimbun,* 21 December 1945; quoted in POLAD, "Educational Affairs in Japan, December 1–31, 1945," pp. 17–18.

79. Ibid., p. 19.

80. Emmerson, POLAD, "Memorandum of Conversation with Japanese University Students," 19 December 1945, USNA 740.00119 Control (Japan)/12-2245, p. 1.

81. SCAP, GHQ, CI & E, "Special Report: Student Expenses," 16 May 1946, HI, Trainor Papers, box 66, p. 1.

82. Masataka Sugi, "Economic Problems of Students in Japan of Post-War," June 1949, HI, Trainor Papers, box 68, p. 23.

83. Memorandum for the president, Edwin Locke, Jr., to President Truman, "Notes on the Current Situation in Japan Based on Talks With General of the Army Douglas MacArthur and Officers of His Staff, Tokyo, October 14–17, 1945," 19 October 1945, pp. 4–5. See chapter 3, note 15.

84. MacArthur, "Report of Japan's Food Situation for Herbert Hoover," 6 May 1946, SCAP, *Political Reorientation,* p. 749.

85. Quoted in personal telegram, Eisenhower [chief of staff, US Army] to MacArthur, 14 February 1947, MA, RG-9, box 144.

86. MacArthur, "Warning Against Mob Disorder or Violence," 20 May 1946, SCAP, *Political Reorientation,* p. 750.

87. Letter, Derevyanko to MacArthur, 21 May 1946, USNA 740.00119 Control (Japan)/6-1046.

88. Letter, Atcheson to Derevyanko, 22 May 1946, ibid. (stapled to the letter cited in note 87).

89. Secret letter, Atcheson to Byrnes, 10 September 1946, MA, RG-9, box 146. The total number of Soviet staff in Japan was not "more than 400" but 206 as of 1 April 1947. For the size and composition of other foreign government missions, see US Department of War, Military Intelligence Division, *Intelligence Review* [secret] no. 68 (5 June 1947), TL, NA File, box 19, pp. 48–55.

90. Telegram, Atcheson to Byrnes, 19 October 1945, MA, RG-9, box 146.

91. Letter, Atcheson to Byrnes, 10 June 1946, USNA 740.00119 Control (Japan)/6-1046, p. 1.

92. Telegram, top secret, WARCOS to MacArthur, 24 September 1945, MA, RG-9, box 43.

93. Memorandum for the supreme commander, "Report of G-2 Section on First Year's Occupation of Japan," 15 July 1946, MA, RG-5, box 80, p. 2. For crimes by occupation soldiers against Japanese civilians during the first year see CIS, "Trends," no. 30 (26 July 1946), esp. pp. 8–9, MA, RG-9, box 80.

94. MacArthur, "Statement Calling Off General Strike," 31 January 1947, in SCAP, *Political Reorientation,* p. 762. Also, see MacArthur, *Reminiscences,* p. 308.

95. MacArthur, "In Support of Appropriations for Occupation Purposes," SCAP, *Political Reorientation,* p. 764.

96. "Interview with Press Correspondents, Primarily Concerning Plan for United Nations Administration of Japan," ibid., p. 765.

97. Personal telegram, Eisenhower to MacArthur, 14 February 1947, MA, RG-9, box 144.

98. Telegram, MacArthur to Eisenhower and Petersen, 20 February 1947, ibid.

99. Telegram, Eisenhower to MacArthur, 21 February 1947, ibid.

100. Memorandum for the president, Locke to Truman, "Notes on the Current Situation in Japan," 19 October 1945, p. 2.

101. Personal and confidential letter, Atcheson to Truman, 19 June 1947, TL, PS File, box 182, p. 1.

102. Telegram, Department of the Army to MacArthur, 14 October 1947, MA, RG-9, box 152.

103. Memorandum, SCAP, GHQ, Public Health and Welfare Section, to MacArthur, 16 October 1947, ibid.

104. Telegram, MacArthur to Department of the Army, 17 October 1947, ibid.

105. Memorandum for the president, Locke to Truman, "Notes on the Current Situation in Japan," 19 October 1945, p. 3.

106. Ibid., pp. 5–6.

107. Ibid., p. 1.

108. Fearey, "Reappraisal of United States Security Interests and Policies in Regard to Japan," 17 April 1946, first submitted to Atcheson and then to Byrnes, USNA 740.00119 Control (Japan)/4-2346, p. 2.

109. US Department of War, Military Intelligence Division, *Intelligence Review* no. 28 (22 August 1946), TL, NA File, box 17, p. 46.

110. Secret office memorandum, Frank G. Wisner, deputy to the assistant secretary for occupied areas, to Secretary of State George C. Marshall, 19 November 1947, USNA 894.054/11-1947, pp. 2–3.

111. Letter, Katayama to MacArthur, 4 September 1947, MA, RG-10, VIP File, Katayama, 1947, pp. 1, 3.

112. Letter, MacArthur to Katayama, 10 September 1947, ibid., p. 1.

113. Letter, Kennan to Acheson, 26 May 1951, TL, Acheson Papers, box 66, p. 3.

114. Ibid., p. 2.

115. Ibid., p. 3.

116. "Acheson's Princeton Seminars," 13–14 February 1954, TL, Acheson Papers, box 76, pp. 1297–98.

117. Ibid., p. 1298.

118. Ibid., p. 1301.

119. Ibid.

120. Letter, Kennan to Acheson, 26 May 1951, p. 2.

121. Ibid., p. 1.

122. Top-secret memorandum, Department of the Army to MacArthur, 8 June 1948, MA, RG-9, Blue Binder Series, National Security Council, p. 5.

123. For a full text of the directive, see enclosure to secret office memorandum, Butterworth to Acheson, 25 January 1949, USNA 984.50/1-2549.

124. Letter, MacArthur to Yoshida, 19 December 1948, MA, RG-10, box 11. See also SCAP, *History of the Nonmilitary Activities of the Occupation of Japan, 1945–1951,* USNA 65-4, Monograph no. 28, "Labor and Agrarian Reforms—Development of the Trade Union," appendix 9.

125. Secret office memorandum, Butterworth to Acheson, 25 January 1949.

126. Ibid. Emphasis in the original.

127. Peter F. Magagna, "Memorandum: Discussion of ESS Comments on Magagna Silk Program of 20 March 1946," 26 March 1945, TL, File 197, box 686, p. 3. Magagna, silk adviser, was sent to Tokyo to report on the Japanese silk industry. He spent most of his time and energy fending off Marquat's interference.

128. Memorandum of conversation, subject: Japan, Acheson to the president, 26 January 1949, TL, box 64.

129. Secret office memorandum, Butterworth to Acheson, 25 January 1949.

130. Dodge's press statement; see Dodge Messages, n.d., MA, RG-9, p. 3.

131. Confidential office memorandum, Green to Bond, 2 May 1949, USNA 894.50/4-1249.

132. Ibid.

133. Ibid.

134. Telegram, MacArthur to Department of the Army, 2 May 1949, TL, PS File, Foreign Affairs, box 182. While Dodge was balancing the Japanese national budget, the Department of the Army and the Department of State discussed sending a US labor mission to Japan. Both MacArthur and Dodge, in separate telegrams, strongly advised against it, but Secretary Royall, especially, wanted it sent to start "a grass-roots" campaign "to combat communism." He suspected that communism dominated more than 60 percent of the Japanese labor movement. Max W. Bishop of the State Department's Division of North-East Asian Affairs concurred, saying, "I too had found far too much complacency [about communism] in SCAP Headquarters when I was out there." See secret office memorandum, Department of State, Bishop to Butterworth, 13 April 1949, USNA 894.504/4-1349, pp. 1–3.

135. Letter, Truman to secretary of defense, 10 June 1949, TL, PS File, box 182.

136. CIA, *Review,* 26 September 1947, TL, PS File, box 203, pp. 6–7.

137. Ibid., 10 March 1948.

138. Ibid., 8 April 1948, p. 8.
139. Telegram, Voorhees to MacArthur, 25 May 1949, MA, RG-9, box 144.
140. Quoted in telegram, Voorhees to MacArthur, 27 May 1949, ibid.
141. Ibid.
142. Personal telegram, MacArthur to Voorhees, 16 December 1949, MA, RG-9, box 112.
143. Personal telegram, Voorhees to MacArthur, 17 December 1949, ibid.
144. For a full text, see SCAP, *Political Reorientation*, pp. 575–76. Also, Department of State, see Research & Analysis Branch, R & A Report 3832, "Japanese Government Plans for Democratization of Agricultural Associations," 10 May 1946, USNA 097.3 Z1092.
145. US Senate, *Military Situation*, 5 May 1951, part 1, p. 313.
146. MacArthur, *Reminiscences*, p. 314.
147. Kazuo Kawai, *Japan's American Interlude* (Chicago: University of Chicago Press, 1960), p. 92. Kawai was editor of the *Nippon Times*.
148. Letter, Yoshida to MacArthur, 31 October 1946, SCAP, *Political Reorientation*, p. 497.
149. Letter, MacArthur to Yoshida, 1 November 1946, ibid., p. 498.
150. Shigeru Yoshida, *The Yoshida Memoirs*, trans. Kenichi Yoshida (London: Heinemann, 1961), p. 149 (hereafter cited as Yoshida, *Memoirs*).
151. Edwin O. Reischauer, *The United States and Japan*, 3rd ed. (New York: The Viking Press, 1967), pp. 245–46.
152. Mitoji Nishimoto, "Educational Change in Japan After the War," *Journal of Educational Sociology* 26 (1952):25.
153. Robert A. Fearey, "Reappraisal of United States Security Interests and Policies in Regard to Japan," 17 April 1946, USNA 740.00119 Control (Japan)/4-2346, pp. 16–17.
154. SCAP, *Political Reorientation*, p. 9.
155. Telegram, MacArthur to Draper, 23 January 1949, MA, RG-9, box 150.
156. MacArthur, *Reminiscences*, p. 298.
157. Yoshida, *Memoirs*, p. 159.
158. *Nippon Sangyo Keizai Shimbun*, 17 August 1945, quoted in OSS, Research and Analysis Branch, "Japanese Reaction to the Surrender," 27 August 1945, R & A Report 3231, USNA 097.3 Z1092, p. 3.
159. Bishop's report, 31 December 1945, USNA 740.00119 Control (Japan)/1-746, p. 1. Emphasis in the original.
160. Emmerson, "Political Factors in the Present Japanese Situation," pp. 6–7. See also confidential letter, Atcheson to President Truman, 5 November 1945, USNA 740.00119 Control (Japan)/11-2345, p. 1.
161. Confidential letter, Atcheson to President Truman, 5 November 1945, p. 1.
162. Emmerson, "Political Factors in the Present Japanese Situation," pp. 1–3.
163. Quoted in ibid., p. 2.

Chapter 5
1. SCAP, *Political Reorientation*, p. 413.
2. Ibid., p. 423.

3. Ibid., p. 424.

4. MacArthur, *Reminiscences*, p. 283.

5. Quoted in Office of Strategic Services, Research and Analysis Branch, "Prospect for Political Reform in Japan," 21 September 1945, R & A Report 3258, USNA 097.3 Z1092, p. 2.

6. Ibid.

7. Ibid.

8. Ibid., p. 2.

9. SCAP, *Political Reorientation*, p. 460.

10. SCAP, *History of the Nonmilitary Activities of the Occupation of Japan, 1945–1952*, Monograph no. 15, "Freedom of the Press," pp. 9–10, USNA (hereafter cited as SCAP, *Nonmilitary Activities: Freedom of the Press*).

11. For a full text of Hoover's statement, see William J. Coughlin, *Conquered Press: The MacArthur Era in Japanese Journalism* (Palo Alto, Calif.: Pacific Books, 1952), appendix B, pp. 148–49.

12. See SCAP, *Nonmilitary Activities: Freedom of the Press*, p. 11.

13. *Asahi Shimbun*, 17 September 1945, p. 1. Also, see SCAP, ibid., p. 11.

14. See SCAPIN 34, 18 September 1945. The *Asahi Shimbun* was suspended for 19 and 20 September.

15. See SCAP, *Nonmilitary Activities: Freedom of the Press*, p. 11.

16. Ibid., p. 12; see also Coughlin, *Conquered Press*, appendix C, pp. 149–50.

17. For the full text of the press release see CIS, "Trends," no. 29, 16 July 1946, MA, RG-4, box 39, p. 16.

18. See SCAPIN 43, 22 September 1945.

19. See SCAPIN 277, 13 November 1945.

20. See SCAPIN 28, 14 September 1945; also, SCAPIN 1166, 1222, 1283, 1323, and 1379—all related to either rejection or acceptance of the Japanese requests for use of the airwaves within Japan proper.

21. For the full text, see SCAP, *Political Reorientation*, p. 461; and SCAPIN 51.

22. SCAP, *Nonmilitary Activities: Freedom of the Press*, appendix 2.

23. MacArthur, *Reminiscences*, pp. 287–88.

24. John K. Emmerson, "Political Factors in the Present Japanese Situation," 8 February 1946, USNA 740.00119 Control (Japan)/2-2546, pp. 11–12.

25. For the full text see SCAP, *Political Reorientation*, p. 462.

26. *Asahi Shimbun*, 30 September 1945, p. 1.

27. See Matsuura Sozo, *Senryo-ka no genron dan-atsu* [Suppressed freedom of speech during the US Occupation of Japan] (Tokyo: Gendai Janarizuma Shuppan-sha, 1969), p. 28 (hereafter cited as Matsuura).

28. Emmerson, "Political Factors in the Present Japanese Situation," p. 6.

29. Letter, Atcheson to Byrnes, 10 October 1945, accompanying "Memorandum of Conversation with Dr. Yasaka Takagi, Tokyo Imperial University," USNA 740.00119 Control (Japan)/10-1045, p. 1.

30. For a full text, see SCAP, *Political Reorientation*, pp. 463–65.

31. *Asahi Shimbun*, 11 October 1945, p. 1.

32. See Matsuura, pp. 226–27.

33. See John K. Emmerson, *The Japanese Thread: A Life in the US Foreign Service* (New York: Holt, Rinehart and Winston, 1978), pp. 257–65.
34. "Memorandum of Conversation with Dr. Yasaka Takagi, Tokyo Imperial University," enclosure to letter, Atcheson to Byrnes, 10 October 1945.
35. See SCAPIN 119, 11 October 1945.
36. Emmerson, "Political Factors in the Present Japanese Situation," p. 6.
37. POLAD, "Educational Affairs in Japan, November 9–December 1, 1945," 10 December 1945, USNA 894.42/12-1045, p. 3. Dr. Karl C. Leebrick, an education adviser assigned to the Office of the US Political Adviser, submitted to Atcheson a monthly report on Japanese education.
38. US Army Forces, Pacific, GHQ, Public Relations Office, press release, "Jap Press Gets Ultimatum," 24 October 1945, HI, Trainor Papers, box 20.
39. See verbatim of Brown's briefing on public relations to the US Education Mission to Japan, 7 March 1946, HI, Trainor Papers, box 75.
40. See an analysis of the Yomiuri dispute, CIS, "Trends," no. 29, 16 July 1946, MA, RG-4, box 39, pp. 11–15.
41. Letter, Atcheson to Byrnes, 7 January 1946, USNA 894.911/1-845.
42. Letter, Atcheson to Byrnes, 9 December 1945, USNA 894.917/12-845.
43. See *New York Times,* 4 October 1945, p. 8, col. 3.
44. US Department of War, Military Intelligence Division, *Intelligence Review* no. 9 (11 April 1946), p. 19.
45. Confidential letter, Atcheson to Truman, 5 November 1945, USNA 740.00119 Control (Japan)/11-2345, pp. 2–3.
46. Bishop's report, 31 December 1945, USNA 740.00119 Control (Japan)/1-746, p. 1.
47. Coughlin, *Conquered Press,* p. 81.
48. Ibid.
49. US Department of War, Military Intelligence Division, *Intelligence Review* no. 9 (11 April 1946), p. 19.
50. SCAP, *Political Reorientation,* p. 466.
51. Emmerson, "Political Factors in the Present Japanese Situation," p. 11.
52. *Intelligence Review* no. 9 (11 April 1946), p. 19.
53. "Substance of Message from General MacArthur on the Subject of Japanese Constitutional Reform," n.d. [May 1946 ?], enclosure to letter, J. H. Hilldring, assistant secretary of state, to Major General Frank R. McCoy, chairman, FEC, USNA 740.00119 Control (Japan)/6-446, p. 6. Also, see *Intelligence Review* no. 28 (22 August 1946), TL, NA File, box 17, p. 44.
54. *Intelligence Review* no. 9 (11 April 1946), p. 62.
55. Emmerson, "Political Factors in the Present Japanese Situation," p. 12.
56. *Intelligence Review* no. 9 (11 April 1946), p. 62.
57. For a full text of his statement, see SCAP, *Political Reorientation,* p. 759.
58. Memorandum for the president, Edwin Locke, Jr., to the president, "Notes on the Current Situation in Japan Based on Talks With General of the Army Douglas MacArthur and Officers of His Staff, Tokyo, October 14–17, 1945," 19 October 1945, p. 4. The memorandum was enclosed in a letter from Locke in Chunking, China, to Matthew Connelly, secretary to the president, 19 October 1945, TL, PS File, box 182.

59. POLAD, memorandum of conversation, 25 November 1945, enclosure to letter, Atcheson to secretary of state, "Views on Liberal Party leader, Hatoyama Ichiro," 9 January 1946, USNA 740.00119 Control (Japan)/1-946, pp. 1–2.

60. Ibid., p. 3. The Military Intelligence Division of the Department of War stated that Hatoyama was "labeled 'liberal' before the war because he was not closely identified with militant aggression." For both Japanese and Americans the war was a convenient demarcation line between the "liberals" and the "conservatives." However, the line was soon to disintegrate. See *Intelligence Review* no. 9 (11 April 1946), p. 62.

61. Letter, Yoshida to MacArthur, 27 December 1946, MA, RG-10, VIP File, Yoshida, pp. 1–2. See also SCAP, *Political Reorientation,* p. 679.

62. Letter, MacArthur to Yoshida, 25 February 1947, MA, RG-10, VIP File, Yoshida, pp. 1–3. Also, see SCAP, *Political Reorientation,* p. 680.

63. Letter, Yoshida to MacArthur, 6 August 1949, enclosure to letter, Sebald to Secretary of State Acheson, USNA 894.105/9-349.

64. Letter, MacArthur to Yoshida, 8 August 1949, ibid.

65. SCAP, *Nonmilitary Activities: Freedom of the Press,* pp. 23–25; Matsuura, p. 35; Coughlin, *Conquered Press,* pp. 46–58; and Robert Jay Lifton, *Death in Life: Survivors of Hiroshima* (New York: Random House, 1967), pp. 328–29 (hereafter cited as Lifton). Lifton's *Death in Life* is a brilliant work on the psychological effects of the bomb among the Japanese people.

66. SCAP, *Nonmilitary Activities: Freedom of the Press,* p. 23.

67. For full texts of both laws, see The Centre for East Asian Cultural Studies, *Meiji Through Contemporary Sources,* vol. 3 (Tokyo: The Centre, 1972), pp. 30–42.

68. Quoted in Matsuura, pp. 52–54. For a detailed description of the articles censored, see ibid., pp. 54–72.

69. Nakayama Kenichi, *Gendai shakai to chianho* [Modern society and public peace laws] (Tokyo: Iwanami Shoten, 1970), p. 86.

70. Matsuura, p. 136.

71. Lifton, p. 327. Nevertheless, it seems doubtful that most Americans experienced such feelings. Almond cites a poll taken in September 1945 in which 43 percent of respondents said it was all right to drop the atomic bomb on one Japanese city at a time, while another 24 percent would have approved the indiscriminate use of atomic weapons against Japan; these findings, he adds, were roughly confirmed by a *Fortune* survey. See Gabriel A. Almond, *The American People and Foreign Policy* (New York: Harcourt, Brace and Co., 1950), pp. 112–13.

72. Ibid., p. 329.

73. See Matsuura, pp. 139–41; and Lifton, pp. 453–56.

74. R. H. Hillemkoetter, director of the CIA, "Atomic Energy Program of the USSR," 20 April 1949, TL, PS File, box 203.

75. See Matsuura, pp. 62–65.

76. For Circular no. 12, see Office of Strategic Services, Research and Analysis Branch, R & A Report 4246, "The Development of Media of Information in Japan Since the Surrender," 1 October 1947, USNA 097.3 Z1092, pp. 104–106.

77. SCAP, *Nonmilitary Activities: Freedom of the Press,* p. 34.

78. Matsuura, pp. 62–65.

79. See SCAPIN 947. The Religions Division and the Education Division, both in the

Civil Information and Education Section, coordinated who and what should be on Japanese currency and postage stamps. See intra-section memorandum, W. K. Bunce to Mark T. Orr, 17 June 1947, HI, Trainor Papers, box 37.

80. See SCAPIN 146. See also SCAPIN 287, "Elimination of Undemocratic Motion Pictures," 16 November 1945; SCAPIN 658, "Motion Picture Censorship," 28 January 1946; and SCAPIN 745, "Action Regarding Banned Japanese Motion Pictures," 18 February 1946. For a description of American control of Japanese movies, see SCAP, *History of the Nonmilitary Activities of the Occupation of Japan, 1945–1951,* USNA 65-4, Monograph no. 16, "Theater and Motion Picture."

81. Top-secret telegram, Department of the Army to MacArthur, 8 June 1948, MA, RG-9, Blue Binder Series, National Security Council, p. 6.

82. SCAP, *Nonmilitary Activities: Freedom of the Press,* pp. 23–25.

83. Matsuura, p. 75.

84. MacArthur ordered the Japanese government to assume control of distribution of newsprint in SCAPIN 195, "Elimination of Newspaper and Publishers' Association's Control Over Distribution of Paper," issued on 26 October 1945.

85. Matsuura, pp. 78–79.

86. Telegram, Byrnes to Atcheson, 8 June 1946, MA, RG-9, box 146.

87. Ibid.

88. Secret telegram, Atcheson to Byrnes, 10 June 1946, MA, RG-9, box 146.

89. Secret telegram, War Department to MacArthur, 19 October 1946, ibid., box 152.

90. Secret telegram, MacArthur to War Department, 22 October 1946, ibid.

91. Telegram, War Department to MacArthur, 28 November 1946, ibid.

92. Confidential telegram, MacArthur to War Department, 29 November 1946, ibid.

93. Confidential telegram, War Department to MacArthur, 9 December 1946, ibid.

94. See ibid.

95. Confidential telegram, MacArthur to War Department, 8 December 1946, ibid.

96. For instance, see Gayn's article in *Bungei Shunju* [a monthly magazine], January 1978, pp. 198–214.

97. Telegram, War Department to MacArthur, 1 November 1946, MA, RG-9, box 152.

98. Secret telegram, MacArthur to War Department, 2 November 1946, ibid.

99. Telegram, War Department to MacArthur, 4 December 1946, ibid.

100. Ibid.

101. Personal telegram, War Department to MacArthur and General Hodge, 4 December 1946, ibid.

102. Ibid.

103. Secret telegram, War Department to MacArthur, 9 December 1946, MA, RG-9, box 152.

104. Confidential telegram, MacArthur to War Department, 9 December 1946, ibid.

105. Telegram, War Department to MacArthur, 30 March 1947, ibid.

106. Secret telegram, MacArthur to War Department, 31 March 1947, ibid.

107. Secret telegram, Army Department to MacArthur, 12 April 1947, ibid.

108. Secret telegram, MacArthur to Army Department, 12 April 1947, ibid. On 15 January 1948 the War Department again asked MacArthur for his view on another press

tour of the Pacific. On 19 January he replied, "This Headquarters recommends against such a trip." His reasons were those familiar to the War Department, such as that his staff was too busy to be bothered by journalists. See Telegram, Army Department to MacArthur, 15 January 1948, ibid; and Telegram, MacArthur to Army Department, 19 January 1948, ibid.

109. Telegram, Army Department to MacArthur, 3 January 1948, ibid.

110. Telegram, MacArthur to Army Department, 6 January 1948, ibid.

111. Telegram, Army Department to MacArthur, 9 July 1948, ibid.

112. Telegram, MacArthur to Army Department, 10 July 1948, ibid.

113. Personal telegram, Royall to MacArthur, 23 July 1948, ibid.

114. Telegram, MacArthur to Royall, 23 July 1948, ibid.

115. See *Asahi Shimbun,* 2 May 1950, p. 2.

116. Quoted in confidential telegram, MacArthur to the Department of the Army, 2 May 1950, MA, RG-9, Blue Binder Series, Public Relations.

117. Ibid.

118. See *Asahi Shimbun,* 2 May 1950, p. 2.

119. Quoted in secret telegram, MacArthur to the Department of the Army, 18 May 1950, MA, RG-9, Blue Binder Series, Public Relations.

120. Ibid.

121. SCAP, *Political Reorientation,* p. 741.

122. See SCAP, *Nonmilitary Activities: Freedom of the Press,* appendix 4, for a full text of Japan's "Canons of Journalism."

Chapter 6

1. MacArthur, *Reminiscences,* p. 299.

2. SCAP, *Political Reorientation,* p. 90.

3. Ibid.

4. "Substance of Message from General MacArthur on the Subject of Japanese Constitutional Reform," n.d. [May 1946 ?], enclosure to letter, J. H. Hilldring, assistant secretary of state, to Major General Frank R. McCoy, chairman, FEC, USNA 740.00119 Control (Japan)/6-446, p. 1.

5. SCAP, *Political Reorientation,* p. 91.

6. Ibid.

7. Ibid.

8. Memorandum, Atcheson to MacArthur and chief of staff, "Japanese Opinion on the Revision of the Constitution," 23 October 1945, USNA 894.011/10-2445.

9. US Department of State, USNA 740.00119 Control (Japan)/11-245, p. 1.

10. Letter, Atcheson to Truman, 5 November 1945, p. 3.

11. Emmerson, *The Japanese Thread,* pp. 251–52.

12. Letter, Atcheson to Acheson, 7 November 1945, USNA 894.00119/11-745, pp. 1–2.

13. See SCAP, *History of the Nonmilitary Activities of the Occupation of Japan 1945–1951,* Monograph no. 8 "Constitutional Revision," USNA, pp. 32–33 (hereafter cited as SCAP, *Nonmilitary Activities: Constitutional Revision*).

14. See *Asahi Shimbun,* 7 December 1945, p. 1.

15. He left a death note. See Kyodo Tsushin-sha, ed., *Konoe Nikki* (Tokyo: Kyodo Tsushin-sha, 1968), p. 112.

16. See *Asahi Shimbun*, 17 December 1945, p. 1.
17. Yoshida, *Memoirs*, p. 129.
18. SCAP, *Political Reorientation*, p. 96.
19. Ibid., loc. cit.
20. Ibid., p. 97.
21. Ibid.
22. Top-secret memorandum, Atcheson to MacArthur and chief of staff, 7 January 1946, enclosure to letter, Atcheson to Byrnes, 8 January 1946, USNA 894.001 Hirohito/1-746, p. 2.
23. SCAP, *Political Reorientation*, p. 97.
24. Ibid.
25. Ibid.
26. MacArthur, *Reminiscences*, p. 300.
27. US Department of State, "Substance of Message from General MacArthur on the Subject of Japanese Constitution Reform," p. 1.
28. Ibid.
29. Top-secret memorandum, Atcheson to MacArthur and chief of staff, 7 January 1946, p. 2.
30. MacArthur, *Reminiscences*, p. 300.
31. SCAP, *Political Reorientation*, p. 99.
32. MacArthur, *Reminiscences*, p. 300.
33. SCAP, *Political Reorientation*, p. 98.
34. See ibid., pp. 605–21.
35. Ibid., pp. 99–101.
36. Yoshida, *Memoirs*, p. 132.
37. SCAP, *Political Reorientation*, p. 106.
38. Yoshida, *Memoirs*, p. 131.
39. See Office of Strategic Services, Research and Analysis Branch, "Prospect for Political Reform in Japan," R & A Report 3258, USNA 0973 Z1092, p. 2.
40. Yoshida, *Memoirs*, p. 139.
41. SCAP, *Political Reorientation*, p. 102.
42. See Robert Ward, "The Origins of the Present Japanese Constitution," *American Political Science Review* 50, no. 4 (Dec. 1956):991. Ward, to be sure, did not have the benefit of MacArthur's *Reminiscences*, Yoshida's *Memoirs*, or many State Department papers recently declassified.
43. SCAP, *Political Reorientation*, p. 102. The quote was MacArthur's own wording.
44. Yoshida, *Memoirs*, pp. 132–33. Government Section reported similarly about this meeting; see SCAP, *Political Reorientation*, p. 105.
45. SCAP, *Political Reorientation*, p. 105.
46. Ward similarly wrote: "If such a statement was made, one cannot refrain from wondering by virtue of what authority or prescience General Whitney could thus commit the still nonexistent FEC to the approval of a document it had never seen" ("The Origins of the Present Japanese Constitution," footnote 42, p. 998).
47. MacArthur, *Reminiscences*, p. 302.
48. SCAP, *Political Reorientation*, pp. 105–106.

49. Yoshida, *Memoirs,* pp. 133–34.

50. SCAP, *Political Reorientation,* p. 106. Yoshida had to concede that "General Mac-Arthur's headquarters was taking a far stiffer line in regard to the GHQ version than was expected by us, and there was little to be done about it" (*Memoirs,* p. 134).

51. Yoshida, *Memoirs,* p. 134.

52. SCAP, *Political Reorientation,* p. 106.

53. See SCAP, *Political Reorientation,* pp. 625–48, for these drafts and revisions.

54. Ward, "The Origins of the Present Japanese Constitution," p. 1002.

55. See *Asahi Shimbun,* 8 March 1946, p. 1.

56. Ibid., 7 March 1946, p. 1.

57. SCAP, *Political Reorientation,* p. 106; also, Yoshida, *Memoirs,* p. 135.

58. See *Asahi Shimbun,* 7 March 1946, p. 1.

59. Ibid., 8 March 1946, p. 1, quoted in SCAP, *Political Reorientation,* p. 109.

60. For a full text see *Asahi Shimbun,* 7 March 1946, p. 1. This imperial rescript was handed to Prime Minister Shidehara when he visited the Emperor on the night of 5 March.

61. See *Asahi Shimbun,* ibid.; also, SCAP, *Political Reorientation,* p. 109.

62. See enclosure no. 1 to letter, Atcheson to secretary of state, 26 June 1946, "General MacArthur's Statement on Submission of Draft Constitution to Japanese Diet," USNA 894.011/6-2646.

63. MacArthur, *Reminiscences,* p. 302.

64. Yoshida, *Memoirs,* p. 129.

65. For a full text, see SCAP, *Political Reorientation,* p. 682.

66. Ibid., p. 683.

67. MacArthur, *Reminiscences,* p. 299.

68. Quoted in SCAP, *Political Reorientation,* p. 93; the book was published on 3 November 1946, the same day the Emperor proclaimed the Constitution the law of the land. Also, see "Commentary of Minister of State Tokujiro Kanamori on the Constitution," Oct. 1946, appendix 6 in SCAP, *Nonmilitary Activities: Constitutional Reform.*

69. SCAP, *Political Reorientation,* p. 108.

70. Ward, "The Origins of the Present Japanese Constitution," p. 1000.

71. Letter, MacArthur to Yoshida, 6 February 1947, MA, RG-10, VIP File, Yoshida, 1947.

72. Letter, Yoshida to MacArthur, 23 April 1947, ibid.

73. Letter, MacArthur to Yoshida, 23 April 1947, ibid.

74. MacArthur, *Reminiscences,* pp. 302–303.

75. *Asahi Shimbun,* 8 March 1946, p. 1.

76. Yoshida, *Memoirs,* p. 137.

77. MacArthur, *Reminiscences,* p. 304.

78. Ibid.

79. *Intelligence Review* [secret] no. 9 (11 April 1946), p. 62.

80. For a fuller text of his statement, see Tsuji Kiyoaki, ed., *Shiryo: sengo nijunen-shi* [Materials: twenty-year history of postwar Japan], vol. 1, "Seiji" [Politics] (Tokyo: Nippon Hyoron-sha, 1966), p. 53.

81. Ibid. See also Yoshida, *Memoirs*, p. 140.

82. Letter, MacArthur to Yoshida, 8 July 1950, MA, RG-10, VIP File, Yoshida, 1950, p. 2. MacArthur ordered the US Eighth Army to train Japanese personnel. See top-secret memorandum, SCAP to Maj. Gen. W. P. Shepard, and to the Government Section, GHQ, 14 July 1950, MA, box CL-1; see also the enclosure to this memorandum, Staff Study, "Increase in Japanese Security Agencies." The Economic and Scientific Section. GHQ, estimated that the total cost for training the Japanese for six months would be 20 billion yen.

83. "The Address of the Prime Minister before the 8th Diet," 14 July 1950, MA, RG-10, VIP File, Yoshida, 1950, p. 3.

84. For a full text of the FEC's protest, see FEC, *Activities of the Far Eastern Commission, February 26, 1946–July 10, 1947,* Department of State Far Eastern Series 24, 1947, pp. 63–64.

85. Byrnes's 12 March 1946 press conference, quoted in intra-office memorandum, John C. Vincent to Byrnes, 16 April 1946, USNA 740.00119 Control (Japan)/4-1546, p. 1.

86. MacArthur, *Reminiscences,* p. 300.

87. For a full text, see FEC, *Activities of the Far Eastern Commission, February 26, 1946– July 10, 1947,* pp. 58–59. Also, see SCAP, *Political Reorientation,* p. 716.

88. See telegram, US Embassy in Moscow to MacArthur and State Department, 12 April 1946, MA, RG-9, box 69.

89. For MacArthur's reply, see FEC, *Activities of the Far Eastern Commission,* pp. 59–63. Also, see SCAP, *Political Reorientation,* pp. 717–18.

90. See memorandum, MacArthur to Whitney, chief of the Government Section, n.d., MA, RG-5, box 80. His memorandum was a response to the Government Section's "Election Report," 22 April 1946, USNA 097.3 Z1092.

91. Telegram, US Embassy in Moscow to MacArthur and POLAD, MA, RG-9, box 69. *Red Star* on 23 May 1946 carried a thirty-inch article attacking the draft constitution. See telegram, US Embassy in Moscow to MacArthur and POLAD, 27 May 1946, ibid.

92. For a full text, see *Department of State Bulletin* 14, no. 362 (9 June 1946):991–92.

93. Ibid.

94. Top-secret telegram, WARCOS to MacArthur, 13 October 1945, MA, RG-9, box 146.

95. Confidential and personal telegram, MacArthur to McCoy, 13 April 1946, MA, RG-9, Far Eastern Commission, pp. 1–6.

96. Memorandum, Vincent to Byrnes, 19 April 1946, USNA 740.00119 Control (Japan)/ 4-1546, pp. 1–2.

97. Memorandum, Vincent to Byrnes, 20 April 1946, ibid.

98. Ibid.

99. See enclosure to memorandum, Vincent to Byrnes, 20 April 1946. For McCoy's original draft and Vincent's edited version, see ibid.

100. See *Department of State Bulletin* 14, no. 362, (9 June 1946):991–92.

101. Secret letter, Atcheson to Hilldring, 21 June 1946, MA, RG-9, box 146.

102. See MacArthur's statement to Byrnes, "Substance of Message from General Mac-Arthur on the Subject of Japanese Constitutional Reform," pp. 4–5. His message was identical with his 13 April 1946 telegram to McCoy. Byrnes sent a copy of Mac-

Arthur's message to the FEC on 4 June 1946. MacArthur sent the same statement to the Joint Chiefs of Staff on 4 May 1946. See USNA CCS 383.21 Japan, section 10, box 120.

103. "Substance of Message from General MacArthur on the Subject of Japanese Constitutional Reform," p. 5.

104. Yoshida, *Memoirs*, p. 136.

105. MacArthur, *Reminiscences*, p. 293.

106. Top-secret office memorandum, Dunning to Bishop, 30 November 1948, USNA 894.011/11-3048, pp. 2–4.

107. Ward, "The Origins of the Present Japanese Constitution," p. 1010.

108. Quoted in *New York Times*, 3 October 1945, p. 10, col. 5.

109. See Kazuo Kawai, *Japan's American Interlude* (Chicago: University of Chicago Press, 1960), especially pp. 51–70.

110. Ibid., p. 58.

111. Ibid., p. 49.

112. Ibid., p. 58.

113. Ibid., loc. cit.

114. Ibid., p. 70.

115. Ibid., pp. 68–69.

116. Ibid., p. 55.

117. Yoshida, *Memoirs*, pp. 138–39.

118. SCAP, *Political Reorientation*, p. 88.

119. Ibid., p. 89.

120. Ibid., p. 745.

Introduction to Part II

1. Top-secret memorandum for the president, n.d. [June 1945 ?], in "The Berlin Conference," TL, NA File, box 4, p. 4.

2. SCAP, GHQ, CI & E, *Education in the New Japan*, vol. 1 (Tokyo: May 1948), p. 135; ibid., vol. 2, pp. 57–58. Volume 1 (text) summarizes the two-and-a-half years of educational reform under the Occupation. Vol. 2 lists the primary official American and Japanese documents. The sequel to these two volumes was ibid., *Post-War Development in Japanese Education*, 2 vols. (Tokyo: 1952).

3. Ibid.

4. Ibid.

5. Florence Powdermaker, MD, PH.D, visiting expert in the field of social reaction, submitted a report after her four-month stay in Japan. She recommended that the occupation authorities establish a "public opinion and sociological research division." See check list, Nugent, chief of CI & E, to C-in-C [Commander-in-Chief, i.e., MacArthur], 22 October 1948, MA, RG-5, box 106.

6. Kawai, *Japan's American Interlude*, p. 189.

7. Tamon Maeda, "The Direction of Postwar Education in Japan," *Japan Quarterly* 3 (1956):415–16.

8. Kenji Kaneko and Goro Iwamatsu, "Some Inside Stories of Monbusho," HI, Trainor Papers, box 38, pp. 1–9. This report was written while Tanaka Kotaro was Educa-

329 Notes to pages 144–152

tion Minister (22 May 1946–31 January 1947). Emphasis in the original.

9. Memorandum, Nugent to Education Division, n.d. [February 1947 ?], attached as cover note to the report cited in note 8.

10. POLAD, "Educational Affairs in Japan, February 1–28, 1946," 11 March 1946, USNA 740.00119 Control (Japan)/3-2746, p. 1.

Chapter 7

1. See *Asahi Shimbun*, 16 August 1945, p. 1; for the full text of his speech see ibid., 17 August 1945, p. 2. Also see US Department of State, Research and Analysis Branch, Interim Research and Intelligence, "Japanese Post-War Education Policies," 5 October 1945, no. 3266, USNA 097.3 Z1092, p. 1.

2. *Asahi Shimbun*, 19 August 1945, quoted in Suzuki Eiichi, *Kyoiku gyosei* [Educational administration] (Tokyo: Tokyo Daigaku Shuppan-kai, 1970), p. 160. Suzuki brilliantly analyzes postwar Japanese educational administration.

3. Research & Analysis Branch, "Japanese Post-War Education Policies," p. 1.

4. See Suzuki, *Kyoiku gyosei*, pp. 160–61.

5. Letter, Schieffelin to Dyke, 9 December 1945, HI, Trainor Papers, box 28; see ibid., "Proposed Showa Rescript on Education," in English and in the beautifully hand-written Japanese original.

6. For the directive, see SCAP, *Political Reorientation*, pp. 467–69.

7. "Emperor's Imperial Rescript Denying His Divinity," 1 January 1946, SCAP, *Political Reorientation*, p. 470.

8. SCAP, *Education in the New Japan*, vol. 2, pp. 157–58. The Japanese counterpart of these CI & E studies was Secretariat, Ministry of Education, *Shusen kyoiku jimu shori teiyo* [A handbook of postwar educational affairs], a four-volume compilation of every official document on Japanese education during the Occupation (Tokyo: The Ministry, 1945–50). Vol. 1 was published in November 1945 and vol. 4 in March 1950.

9. *Yomiuri Shimbun*, 10 January 1946; and *Mimpo* n.d., both quoted in POLAD, "Educational Affairs in Japan January 1–31, 1946," USNA 740.00119 Control (Japan)/3-1346, p. 3.

10. For a longer excerpt from Maeda's remarks, see Suzuki, *Kyoiku gyosei*, p. 161.

11. *Tokyo Shimbun*, 12 January 1946, quoted in POLAD, "Educational Affairs in Japan, January 1–31, 1946," p. 3.

12. Memorandum, George to Orr, 10 July 1946, HI, Trainor Papers, box 28. Before entering the Army, Orr was a newspaper reporter and editor in western North Carolina and also taught international relations at the University of Tampa, Florida. He was associate director of the Southern Council on International Relations, an affiliate of the Carnegie Endowment for International Peace with headquarters at the University of North Carolina.

13. Check sheet, "1890 Imperial Rescript on Education" and "Imperial Portraits," 12 July 1946, Religions Division to Education Division, HI, Trainor Papers, box 28.

14. Memorandum, Del Re to Orr, 15 July 1946, HI, Trainor Papers, box 28.

15. See memorandum, H. G. Henderson to Dyke, 16 October 1945; and memorandum, Major Farr to Lt. Col. Hawley, 9 November 1945; both in HI, Trainor Papers, box 46.

16. Memorandum, Wigglesworth to Orr, 17 July 1946, HI, Trainor Papers, box 28.

17. See US Department of War, Military Intelligence Division, "Significant Personalities," *Intelligence Review*, no. 16 (29 May 1946), TL, NA File, box 16, president's copy, pp. 61–62.

18. For a full text see Japan, Ministry of Education, *Monbu Jiho* [Ministry of education bulletin] no. 830 (10 July 1946), pp. 7–12; also, *Sengo Kyoiku Shiryo* section 1, item 8, Kokken.

19. Tanaka Kotaro, "Nippon kunshusei no goriteki kiso" [The rational foundation of Japanese monarchy], in ibid., *Kyoiku to seiji* [Education and politics] (Tokyo: Kogakusha, 1946), pp. 99–100.

20. Ibid., p. 110.

21. *Nippon Times*, 16 July 1946, HI, Trainor Papers, box 28.

22. Check sheet, "Diet Statement of Mr. Tanaka," Bunce to Orr, 18 July 1946, HI, Trainor Papers, box 28.

23. Memorandum, Donovan to Orr, 6 August 1946, HI, Trainor Papers, box 28, p. 1.

24. Ibid., pp. 1–2.

25. Ibid. *Ronin* literally means "a samurai warrior without a lord." The Forty-seven Ronin, whose lord was forced to commit suicide by another lord, planned for years to revenge. Their patient scheme worked. The Forty-seven are still the favorite Japanese example of true Japanese loyalty.

26. Ibid., p. 1.

27. Ibid., p. 3.

28. Ibid., p. 2; emphasis in the original.

29. Ibid., p. 3.

30. Ibid., p. 4; emphasis in the original.

31. Ibid., p. 4.

32. See CI & E, Education Division, routing slip, 9 August 1946, HI, Trainor Papers, box 28.

33. Memorandum, Trainor to Orr, n.d., ibid.; emphasis in the original.

34. Memorandum, Del Re to Orr, 15 August 1946, ibid.

35. For the two documents see ibid.

36. Memorandum, Del Re to Orr, 25 September 1946, ibid., pp. 1–2.

37. For a full text see SCAP, *Education in the New Japan*, vol. 2, p. 172; in Japanese, see "Kyoiku Chokugo no toriatsukai" [Handling of the imperial rescript on education], *Sengo Kyoiku Shiryo*, section 1, item 8; for the Education Division's draft, see HI, Trainor Papers, box 28.

38. Tanaka, "Kyoiku to Sekaikan" [Education and worldview], 1 March 1946 in Tanaka, *Kyoiku to Seiji*, pp. 116–17 and pp. 129–34.

39. Kaneko and Iwamatsu, "Some Inside Stories of Monbusho," p. 6.

40. Memorandum, Orr to Nugent, 24 June 1948, HI, Trainor Papers, box 28.

41. See, for a fuller (top-secret) verbatim, Japan, Ministry of Education, "Takase Daijin, Nugent Chusa kaidan yoshi" [Verbatim of the meeting between Minister Takasa and Lieutenant Colonel Nugent], 8 June 1949, *Sengo Kyoiku Shiryo*, section 1, item 39.

42. Letter, Tanaka to Doyle, 11 April 1950, TL, O File 197, box 686. Doyle forwarded Tanaka's letter to President Truman.

Chapter 8

1. US Department of State, Research & Analysis Branch, Interim Research and Intelligence, "Japanese Post-War Education Policies," 5 October 1945, no. 3266, USNA 097.3 Z1092.

2. Ibid.

3. For a full text of his statement, see SCAP, *Education in the New Japan*, vol. 2, pp. 140–43.

4. POLAD, "Educational Affairs in Japan, November 9–December 1, 1945," USNA 894.42/12-1045, p. 2.

5. For a full text see SCAP, *Education in the New Japan*, vol. 2, p. 166.

6. See Japan, *Ministry of Education's Digest*, 11 September 1945, HI Trainor Papers, box 41.

7. For a text see Monbusho [Ministry of Education], *Gakusei hyakunen-shi* [A hundred-year history of the educational system] vol. 2 (Tokyo, 1972), pp. 52–53.

8. Tamon Maeda, "The Direction of Postwar Education in Japan," *Japan Quarterly* 3 (1956):415.

9. Research & Analysis Branch, "Japanese Post-War Education Policies," p. 3.

10. Ibid., pp. 3–4.

11. See POLAD, "Digests of Japanese Ministry of Education Orders and Actions from August 25 through December 26, 1945," prepared by Lt. Col. Donald R. Nugent, USNA 740.00119 Control (Japan)/1-1246, n.p. Also, see Digest, Ministry of Education to CI & E, 3 October 1945, HI, Trainor Papers, box 41.

12. CI & E, "Concerning the Change in Constitution of Ministry of Education," 13 October 1945, HI, Trainor Papers, box 3.

13. Maeda, "The Direction of Postwar Education in Japan," p. 415.

14. For a full text, see SCAP, *Education in the New Japan*, vol. 2, pp. 26–28. Robert King Hall informed Chief Dyke that this directive was deliberately stated in broad terms "to permit considerable leeway in operational policies and techniques as the Occupation progresses and as special needs become apparent." See memorandum, Hall to Dyke, 21 October 1945, HI, Trainor Papers, box 20, p. 1.

15. *Jiji Press* [a news agency], 21 February 1946; quoted in POLAD, "Educational Affairs in Japan, February 1–28, 1946," p. 3.

16. The students kept a detailed diary of their fight. See Sanichi Shobo Henshubu, ed., *Shiryo sengo gakusei undo I, 1945–1949* [Sources: postwar student movement, vol. 1, 1945–1949], (Tokyo: Sanichi Shobo, 1968), pp. 3–12 (hereafter cited as Sanichi).

17. POLAD, "Educational Affairs in Japan, December 1–31, 1945," p. 11.

18. See *Asahi Shimbun*, 27 April 1946, and 24 May 1946. Also, see Sanichi, pp. 40–43.

19. *Nippon Newsreel*, 25 October 1945, quoted in Karl C. Leebrick, POLAD, "Japanese Student Organizations," 11 December 1945, enclosure to letter, Atcheson to Byrnes, 26 December 1945, USNA 740.00119 Control (Japan)/12-2645, p. 3.

20. *Tokyo Shimbun*, 27 November 1945, quoted in POLAD, ibid., loc. cit.

21. *Nippon Times*, 1 December 1945, quoted in POLAD, ibid., pp. 4–5.

22. *Asahi Shimbun*, 24 December 1945, quoted in POLAD, "Educational Affairs in Japan, December 1–31, 1945," p. 14.

23. See POLAD, ibid., p. 12.

24. Ibid.

25. POLAD, "Educational Affairs in Japan, November 9–December 1, 1945," p. 5. Also, see *Daigaku Shimbun,* 21 November 1945, in Sanichi, p. 25 and pp. 73–78.

26. POLAD, "Japanese Student Organizations," Leebrick to Atcheson, 11 December 1945, USNA 740.00119 Control (Japan)/12-2545, p. 4.

27. POLAD, "Memorandum of Conversation with Japanese University Students," by J. K. Emmerson, 19 December 1945, USNA 740.00119 Control (Japan)/12-2245, p. 5.

28. POLAD, "Japanese Student Organizations," p. 4.

29. US Department of State, Research & Analysis Branch, Interim Research and Intelligence, "Problems Involved in Japanese Educational Reforms," 26 October 1945, no. 3281, USNA 097.3 Z1092, pp. 1–2.

30. Ibid., p. 1.

31. POLAD, "Digests of Japanese Ministry of Education Orders and Actions from August 25 through December 26, 1945," unpaged.

32. See "List of Changes in Heads of Schools," HI, Trainor Papers, box 41.

33. POLAD, "Memorandum of Conversation with Japanese University Students," p. 3.

34. Hatoyama's intervention "became one of the reasons" for his purge. See SCAP, *History of the Nonmilitary Activities of the Occupation of Japan, 1945–1951,* Monograph no. 31, "Education," microfilm, USNA Record Group 331, p. 61 (hereafter cited as SCAP, *Nonmilitary Activities: Education*).

35. For a text of Maeda's speech see Digest, Ministry of Education to CI & E, 2 November 1945, HI, Trainor Papers, box 21.

36. See POLAD, "Educational Affairs in Japan, October 1–November 8, 1945," USNA 894.42/11-1045, p. 2.

37. *Asahi Shimbun,* 4 December 1945, p. 1. Also, see POLAD, "Educational Affairs in Japan, December 1–31, 1945," p. 3.

38. *Jiji Press,* quoted in POLAD, ibid., p. 6.

39. For the text see SCAP, *Education in the New Japan,* vol. 2, p. 155.

40. See ibid., p. 162.

41. See intra-division memorandum, Education Division, "The Investigation, Screening, and Certification of Teachers and Educational Officials," n.d. [late December 1945 ?], HI, Trainor Papers, box 43.

42. For a full text see SCAP, *Education in the New Japan,* vol. 2, pp. 29–30.

43. See "The Investigation, Screening, and Certification of Teachers and Educational Officials."

44. R. K. Hall, "Notes for the Record, 17 November 1945, Meeting With General Dyke, Lt. Col. Henderson, Lt. Hall, and Mr. T. Maeda," HI, Trainor Papers, box 43.

45. *Tokyo Shimbun* reported the ministry's purge criteria as early as 20 December 1945; see POLAD, "Educational Affairs in Japan, December 1–31, 1945," p. 8.

46. For the composition of the committees see SCAP, *Nonmilitary Activities: Education,* pp. 62–65.

47. SCAP, GHQ, CI & E, "Confidential Report of Civil Information and Education Section on Accomplishments of Second Year's Occupation of Japan, Together With a Brief Review of the First Year's Work," n.d. [late 1947 ?], HI, Trainor Papers, box 21, p. 3.

48. Ibid., p. 68.

49. POLAD, enclosure no. 1, "Address of Nambara Shigeru" [fully translated] in "Proposal to Create a Chair in Christianity at Tokyo Imperial University," USNA 740.00119 Control (Japan)/3-2647, p. 7.

50. Ibid., pp. 9–10.

51. Ibid., p. 16.

52. Letter, Bishop to Byrnes, 26 March 1946, USNA 740.00119 Control (Japan)/3-2646, p. 1. Earlier, on 25 February 1946, Bishop had sent to the secretary his own summary of the favorable press responses to the Nambara speech. See USNA 740.00119 Control (Japan)/2-2546.

53. Letter, Bishop to Byrnes, 26 March 1946, p. 1.

54. See enclosure, "Intellectual and Spiritual Reform of Japan: A Chair in Christianity for Tokyo Imperial University," ibid.

55. Ibid., pp. 1–2.

56. Ibid., p. 2.

57. Letter, Bishop to Byrnes, 26 March 1946; see enclosure no. 2, p. 6.

58. Ibid., enclosure no. 1, p. 2.

59. See USNA 894.42/11-2249.

60. Hidaka, "Greeting," 31 January 1948, HI, Trainor Papers, box 21, pp. 1–2.

61. See USNA 894.42/11-2249.

62. Letter, Grew to Butterworth, 21 November 1949, USNA 894.421/11-2149.

63. Ibid.

64. Letter, Butterworth to Grew, 22 November 1949, USNA 894.421/11-2249.

65. Letter, Jon C. Smith, vice-president, Japan International Christian University Foundation, to Acheson, 29 June 1949, USNA 894.4212/6-2949.

66. See William P. Woodard, *The Allied Occupation of Japan 1945–1952 and Japanese Religions*, p. 243.

67. See L. S. Witter, "MacArthur and the Missionaries: God and Man in Occupied Japan," p. 86.

68. The vice-minister of education issued this directive to prefectural governors; see SCAP, *Education in the New Japan*, vol. 2, pp. 144–45.

69. See intra-section memorandum, "Suspension of Teaching Morals, Japanese History, and Geography (Censorship of Textbooks)," CI & E, n.d. [January 1946 ?], HI, Trainor Papers, box 45.

70. Letter, Atcheson to Byrnes, 31 October 1945, USNA 740.00119 Control (Japan)/10-3145. A penciled scribble on the letter reads: "Letter Dr. Ford, American Historical Association, 3/2/46." Atcheson enclosed "The Scientific Study of Japanese History," a summary of the conversation with the Japanese historians written by John K. Emmerson and dated 22 October 1945.

71. Letter, Atcheson to Byrnes, 31 October 1945.

72. See intra-section memorandum, "Suspension of Teaching Morals, Japanese History, and Geography (Censorship of Textbooks)."

73. Ibid.

74. Memorandum, Ken Dyke to MacArthur, 13 December 1945, HI, Trainor Papers, box 43, pp. 3, 5.

75. Ibid., pp. 3–6. The "witch hunting" of undesirable textbooks was carried out through-

out the nation's school libraries. See CIS, "Trends," no. 29 (16 July 1946), MA, RG-4, box 39, p. 24.

76. Memorandum, Dyke to MacArthur, 13 December 1945, pp. 4–6. His memorandum contained six appendices. It included the CI & E–prepared draft directive to the Japanese government. This memorandum of Dyke's to MacArthur was dated 13 December 1945. MacArthur's Shinto abolition directive was ready but had not yet been issued to the Japanese government. The CI & E pondered which, in terms of maximum effectiveness, should be first, the textbook directive or the Shinto directive. Dyke decided on the Shinto directive, which MacArthur issued on 15 December 1945.

77. The middle school principals met with CI & E on 15 December 1945. Omura's letter was dated 17 December 1945. See intra-section memorandum, "Suspension of Teaching Morals, Japanese History, and Geography (Censorship of Textbooks)."

78. For a verbatim, see "Conference: Education for the Coming Elections," HI, Trainor Papers, box 40. The conference took place from 9:30 to 11:00 A.M. in the Radio Tokyo Building.

79. See appendix to the verbatim, ibid.

80. See intra-section memorandum, "Major Accomplishments in the Field of Text-books," 16 July 1946, CI & E, Education Division, HI, Trainor Papers, box 43.

81. For a text see SCAP, *Education in the New Japan*, vol. 2, pp. 36–39.

82. See digest, Ministry of Education to CI & E, 31 January 1946, HI, Trainor Papers, box 41.

83. See CI & E, "Textbooks and Curriculum," October 1946, perhaps part of a report of Education Division to SCAP, HI, Trainor Papers, box 43, p. 5. Also, see "Report of Conference [between Nugent and Vice-Minister of Education Yamazaki Kyosuke]," 25 June 1946, HI, Trainor Papers, box 40. Nugent told Yamazaki that the publishers were charging higher prices for textbooks and that they were taking more paper than necessary so that they could sell the excess paper on the black market.

84. CI & E, "Education," n.d. [January 1946 ?], HI, Trainor Papers, box 4.

85. SCAP, *Education in the New Japan*, vol. 1, p. 138.

86. Ibid., p. 239.

87. Ibid., p. 138.

88. POLAD, "Educational Affairs in Japan, December 1–31, 1945," USNA 740.00119 Control (Japan)/2-2046, p. 3.

89. See digest, Ministry of Education to CI & E, 8 November 1945, HI, Trainor Papers, box 41; see also SCAP, *Education in the New Japan*, vol. 1, pp. 243–44.

90. See SCAP, *Education in the New Japan*, vol. 1, p. 244.

91. R. K. Hall, "Summary: Education in Japan to 7 Nov., 45," 7 November 1945, HI, Trainor Papers, box 20, p. 8.

92. Ibid.

93. See intra-section memorandum, Education Division, CI & E, May 1946, HI, Trainor Papers, box 4.

94. See memorandum, S. Inada, head of the Section of Personnel of Minister's Secretaries, to Lt. Col. Harold G. Henderson, 28 November 1945, HI, Trainor Papers, box 4; and intra-section memorandum, Education Division, CI & E, May 1946, ibid. Also, see *Nippon Times*, 30 November 1945, quoted in POLAD, "Educational Affairs in Japan, November 9–December 1, 1945," p. 1.

335335335335 *Notes to pages 181–185*

95. Hall, "Summary: Education in Japan to 7 Nov., 45," p. 5.
96. See memorandum, Lt. Col. Farr to Lt. Col. Nugent, 17 February 1946, HI, Trainor Papers, box 4.
97. Ibid.
98. For instance, see "Report on Official Trip to Miye and Okayama Prefectures, August 1946," by Sekino Fusao, Education Ministry Secretary, Archives and Document Section, Minister's Secretariate, HI, Trainor Papers, box 4.
99. For instance, see memorandum, Howard Bell to Mark T. Orr, "Field Visit to Sapporo, Hokkaido, 17–24 September 1947," 24 September 1947, HI, Trainor Papers, box 37.
100. Memorandum, "Major Accomplishments in Field of Textbooks," Education Division, CI & E, 16 July 1946, HI, Trainor Papers, box 43.
101. Ibid.
102. SCAP, *Education in the New Japan*, vol. 1, p. 251.
103. SCAP, *Nonmilitary Activities: Education*, p. 148.
104. An entire manuscript of Japanese history for the teachers' colleges, written by Takeuchi Rizo, was translated into English. See HI, Trainor Papers, box 3.
105. SCAP, *Education in the New Japan*, vol. 1, p. 251.
106. For a text, see ibid., vol. 2, p. 47. For related documents, see R. Shishito, Bureau of Textbooks, Ministry of Education, "Proposed Examining Standard of English Textbooks," 15 April 1948, HI, Trainor Papers, box 4; and Shimojo Yasumaro, minister of education, "The Authorization Standard for Textbooks," submitted to CI & E, 12 January 1949, HI, Trainor Papers, box 1, 133 pp.
107. CI & E, "Textbooks and Curriculum," p. 6.
108. Ibid., p. 5.
109. Intra-section memorandum, "Preparation of Teacher's Manual," n.d. [January 1946 ?], HI, Trainor Papers, box 43.
110. Memorandum, Hall to Dyke, January 1946, HI, Trainor Papers, box 43, p. 3.
111. For a full text see SCAP, *Education in the New Japan*, vol. 2, p. 47. For a handwritten Japanese draft, see "Kokushi kyoiku no hoshin" [Principles of Japanese history education], n.d., *Sengo Kyoiku Shiryo*, section 2, item 36, Kokken.
112. Press release, Mark T. Orr, GHQ, 20 January 1947, HI, Trainor Papers, box 17, pp. 3–4.
113. POLAD, "Observation of Educational Institutions in Various Cities in Japan," 26 November 1945, USNA 894.42/12-546, p. 3. A Japanese adviser to CI & E similarly reported; see Hino Sei, "Kyoiku no uzu no nakade" [In a whirlpool of education], in *Kyodo kenkyu: Nippon senryo* [Joint study: occupied Japan], ed., Shiso no Kagaku Kenkyu-kai (Tokyo: Tokuma Shoten, 1972), pp. 415–32. Leebrick, as Atcheson briefed Secretary Byrnes, "visited Japan in 1924 at the invitation of the Japan-American Society and the Japanese government, for consultation on the bill for expatriation of Japanese and in the interest of formation of the Japanese Council of the Institute of Pacific Relations." See letter, Atcheson to Byrnes, 26 December 1945, 740.00119 Control (Japan)/12-2645.
114. See appendix of POLAD, "Educational Affairs in Japan, January 1–31, 1946."
115. POLAD, "Observation of Educational Institutions in Various Cities in Japan," p. 3.
116. POLAD, "Educational Affairs in Japan, October 1–November 8, 1945," p. 3.

117. SCAP, *Political Reorientation,* p. 363.
118. Ibid., p. 364.
119. Ibid.
120. Ibid., p. 365. Originally J. W. Gaddis, policy and programs officer, CI & E, drafted a detailed plan for political reeducation. See memorandum, Gaddis to Nugent, 10 November 1947, HI, Trainor Papers, box 45.
121. POLAD, "Educational Affairs in Japan, December 1–31, 1945," pp. 9–10.
122. See J. F. Sullivan, political affairs information officer, CI & E, "Plan for Coordinated Political Information—Education Program," n.d. [November 1947 ?], HI, Trainor Papers, box 45.
123. SCAP, *Education in the New Japan,* vol. 1, p. 247.
124. Memorandum, Gaddis to Nugent, 10 November 1947, HI, Trainor Papers, box 45, p. 2.
125. Memorandum, Bell to Orr, 21 April 1947, HI, Trainor Papers, box 45, pp. 1–2. Emphasis in the original.
126. Memorandum, Gaddis to Nugent, 10 November 1947, p. 4.

Chapter 9
1. Interview of Stoddard by the author, 8 March 1978, at his residence in New York City.
2. Interview of Hilgard by the author, 21 November 1977, at his office at Stanford University, California.
3. For MacArthur's full statement, see *Report of the United States Education Mission to Japan* (Tokyo, 30 March 1946), n.p. (hereafter cited as USEMJ, *Report*).
4. Carroll Atkinson, "Japanese Education is Getting Revised—à la American!," *School and Society* 64, no. 1651 (17 August 1946):115.
5. I. L. Kandel, "The Revision of Japanese Education," *School and Society* 64, no. 1652 (24 August 1946):134.
6. USEMJ, *Report,* "Introduction," n.p.
7. *Department of State Bulletin* 14, no. 348 (3 March 1946):345.
8. Letter, Chapman to MacClellan, 16 October 1945, USNA 740.00119 Control (Japan)/10-3145.
9. Letter, MacClellan to Byrnes, 31 October 1945, USNA 740.00119 Control (Japan)/10-3145.
10. See Hall, "Summary: Education in Japan to 7 Nov., 45," 7 November 1945, HI, Trainor Papers, box 20, p. 11.
11. Telegram, MacArthur to War Department, 4 January 1946, USNA 894.42A/1-1446.
12. Letter, Royall to Byrnes, 14 January 1946, USNA 894.42A/1-1446.
13. Letter, Acheson to Royall, 19 January 1946, USNA 894.42A/1-1446.
14. Office memorandum, Vincent to Benton, 15 January 1946, USNA 894.42A/1-1446.
15. Ibid.
16. See *Department of State Bulletin* 14, no. 348:345.
17. Interview with George D. Stoddard by the author, 8 March 1978, in New York.
18. See *Department of State Bulletin* 14, no. 348:345–46. Also present were Gordon T. Bowles and Paul P. Stewart of the Office of International Information and Cultural

Affairs of the State Department, and Col. John N. Andrews as military liaison from Selective Service.

19. For a full text of the directive, see SCAP, *Education in the New Japan*, vol. 2, pp. 40–42. For Japanese documents on establishing the committee, see *Sengo Kyoiku Shiryo*, section 3, item 8, Kokken. The three-way Steering Committee, which involved the Ministry of Education, CI & E's Education Division, and the Japan Education Reform Council, met weekly to coordinate policy making. See, for related documents, HI, Trainor Papers, boxes 22, 30, and 40; see also Japan, Ministry of Education, *Monbu Jiho*, no. 827, pp. 16–20.

20. See the verbatim of the briefing, 7 March 1946, HI, Trainor Papers, box 75.

21. See POLAD, "Educational Affairs in Japan, February 1–28, 1946," p. 1. Chairman Stoddard in his covering letter to MacArthur praised "your excellent staff." See USEMJ, *Report*, unpaged.

22. See memorandum, Lt. Col. Edward H. Farr, acting chief of Education Division, to all officers of the same division, 15 February 1946 [Farr advised them to prepare their lectures for the mission], HI, Trainor Papers, box 75. For the texts of their lectures, see ibid.

23. See "Beikoku Kyoiku Shisetsudan ni kyoryoku subeki Nihon-gawa Kyoiku Iinkai no Hokokusho," *Sengo Kyoiku Shiryo*, section 3, item 12, Kokken. As an example of American-Japanese committee discussion see "Digest of Discussions of Committee IV," 9–13 March 1946 [on higher education], HI, Trainor Papers, box 21; and memorandum for the record, Robert King Hall, meeting with Dr. Nambara and Dr. Takagi of Tokyo Imperial University at Radio Tokyo Building, 25 March 1946, ibid., box 40.

24. See "Tentative Schedule of US Education Mission," *Sengo Kyoiku Shiryo*, section 3, item 11, Kokken, unpaged.

25. See verbatim of the 7 March 1946 public relations briefing, HI, Trainor Papers, box 75. Also, see ibid. for Nugent's 7 March speech of welcome to the mission.

26. See Japan, Ministry of Education, "Beikoku Kyoiku Shisetsudan raicho ni yosuru keihi," n.d. [February 1946], *Sengo Kyoiku Shiryo*, section 3, item 7, Kokken.

27. Abe's speech was released to the public the same day: see HI, Trainor Papers, box 75. Also, see for a portion of translated Abe's speech *School and Society* 64, no. 1649:73–75. For a full text in Japanese, see *Monbu Jiho* 1946, no. 827:1–6. Also, in his farewell speech to the Ministry of Education officials on 22 May 1946, he told them: "Although you must be worrying about your own life under the present circumstances, you must never forget Japan and the Japanese people." He said that such an attitude was the true meaning of patriotism. See *Monbu Jiho* 1946, no. 830:1–4.

28. MacArthur, *Reminiscences*, p. 282.

29. Stoddard, "Response to Japanese Minister of Education," 8 March 1946, HI, Trainor Papers, box 75.

30. I. L. Kandel, "The Revision of Japanese Education," p. 134.

31. Letter, Compton to MacArthur, 29 April 1946, enclosure to letter, Compton to Benton, 1 May 1946, USNA 894.42A/5-146.

32. Newspaper article, see enclosure to letter, Woodward to Benton, 8 April 1946, USNA, Diplomatic Section, no file number.

33. USEMJ, *Report*, p. 2.

34. Ibid. Emphasis in original.

35. Ibid.

36. Ibid., p. 3.

37. Ibid., p. 2.

38. Ibid., p. 5.

39. Ibid., p. 6.

40. Ibid.

41. Ibid.

42. Ibid., p. 8.

43. Ibid.

44. See memorandum, Helen Heffernan and Vivian Edmiston to chief, Education Division, n.d. [mid-1946 ?], HI, Trainor Papers, box 17.

45. USEMJ, *Report,* p. 8. Emphasis in the original.

46. Ibid., pp. 7–8.

47. Ibid., p. 9.

48. Ibid., p. 9.

49. This directive was issued by the vice-minister of education, but the author was the minister of education. For a text see SCAP, *Education in the New Japan,* vol. 2, p. 163.

50. Ibid., p. 9.

51. Ibid., p. 10.

52. Ibid.

53. Report of conference, Trainor with Sekiguchi, 12 November 1946, HI, Trainor Papers, box 26, pp. 1–3.

54. Report of conference, Trainor with Sekiguchi, 18 November 1946, ibid., pp. 1–2.

55. Record of conference, Trainor with Sekiguchi, 21 November 1946, ibid., pp. 1–2.

56. Record of conference, Trainor with Sekiguchi, 29 November 1946, ibid., p. 1.

57. Record of conference, Trainor with Sekiguchi, 2 December 1946, ibid., pp. 1–2.

58. See CI & E, *Teachers' Unions: A Year of Demands and Results, December 1945–December 1946,* A Special Report, 8 January 1947, HI, Trainor Papers, box 13; see also CI & E, *A History of Teachers' Unions in Japan,* 25 March 1948, ibid.

59. See CI & E, "Report of Conference" [with the Ministry of Education], 25 June 1946, HI, Trainor Papers, box 40.

60. Japan, Ministry of Education, *A Tentative Suggested Course of Study, General,* HI, Trainor Papers, box 4, p. 2.

61. See memorandum, Orr to Nugent, 10 April 1947, HI, Trainor Papers, box 4. President Nambara of Tokyo University told the staff of the US political adviser that "the most dangerous and ill-considered activity" came from elementary school teachers, who exerted "undue influence." See POLAD, confidential memorandum of conversation with Nambara, 27 December 1947, p. 2, enclosure no. 1 to letter, Sebald to secretary of state, 20 January 1948, USNA 894.4121/1-2048.

62. USEMJ, *Report,* p. 14.

63. Ibid., n.p.

64. Interview with Stoddard by the author, 8 March 1978.

65. Hall, "The Exclusive Use of Katakana as Official Written Language," enclosure to

letter, John H. Hilldring to Eugene H. Dooman, 3 July 1945, USNA 894.402/7-345, p. 1. Hall's memorandum was typewritten, single-spaced, and five-page.

66. Hall, ibid., pp. 2–5.

67. Letter, Hilldring to Dooman, 3 July 1945, USNA 894.402/7-345.

68. Letter, Dooman to Hilldring, 6 July 1945, USNA 894.402/7-345.

69. See intra-section memorandum, Education Division, CI & E, n.d. [Sept.–Oct. 1945 ?], HI, Trainor Papers, box 43.

70. For a full text of Hall's speech see Hall, "Language Revision," 13 March 1946, HI, Trainor Papers, box 75.

71. For Ando's speech see Hall, "Language Revision," HI, Trainor Papers, box 75, pp. 18–27. The quote is from p. 20.

72. Ibid., p. 26.

73. USEMJ, *Report,* p. 14.

74. Hall, "The Exclusive Use of Katakana as Official Written Japanese," p. 1.

75. USEMJ, *Report,* p. 14.

76. Ibid.

77. Ibid., p. 15.

78. Ibid., p. 16.

79. Ibid., loc. cit.

80. Ibid., p. 14.

81. Memorandum, Benton to Byrnes, 19 April 1946, USNA 740.00119 Control (Japan)/ 4-1946, p. 1.

82. Letter, Compton to Benton, 1 May 1946, USNA 894.42A/5-146.

83. G. B. Sansom, "Education in Japan," *Pacific Affairs* 19 (1946):413–15.

84. Letter, Hilldring to Atcheson, 19 November 1946, USNA 894.402/11-1946, pp. 1–2.

85. Letter, Atcheson to Hilldring, 14 December 1946, USNA 894.402/12-1446, pp. 1-2. The Ministry of Education, for the sake of simplifying the written language, established the National Language Research Institute (Kokuritsu Kokugo Kenkyu-jo) on 20 December 1948, and the Japanese Language Council (Kokugo Shingi-kai) on 17 April 1950.

86. R. K. Hall, *Education for a New Japan* (New Haven, Conn.: Yale University Press, 1949), pp. 400–401.

87. See "Romaji Kyoiku Kyogikai kankei shiryo," *Sengo Kyoiku Shiryo,* section 2, item 27, Kokken. Also, see SCAP, GHQ, CI & E, Education Division, *Post-War Development in Japanese Education,* vol. 1 (Tokyo: April 1952), pp. 103–107. Vol. 2 is a compilation of educational laws and regulations in addition to numerous statistical data. The two volumes were an extension of *Education in the New Japan,* published in 1948.

88. See the speech of the vice-minister of education at the second general meeting of the Romaji Education Committee, 22 October 1946, ibid.

89. See memorandum, Mark Orr, chief of Education Division, to Nugent, chief of CI & E, 10 April 1947, HI, Trainor Papers, box 4.

90. SCAP, GHQ, CI & E, Education Division, *The Development and Present Status of Romaji in Japan,* December 1950, HI, Trainor Papers, box 19, p. 15.

91. For instance, see a report of *Romaji Chosakai Tsuzurikata ni Kansuru Shusa Iinkai* [Romaji Research Council's Subcommittee on Romaji Writing Styles], *Sengo Kyoiku Shiryo,* section 2, item 40, Kokken. Also, see HI, Trainor Papers, box 47, for related documents on Romaji education.

92. Memorandum, Secondary Education Branch to Arthur K. Loomis, chief of Education Division, CI & E, 9 June 1949, HI, Trainor Papers, box 22, p. 1.

93. Memorandum, Nugent to Arthur K. Loomis, 15 July 1949, HI, Trainor Papers, box 22, p. 1.

94. Memorandum, Monta R. Osborne to Loomis, 9 June 1949, HI, Trainor Papers, box 22, p. 2.

95. Bundo Keichi, "Important Items for Calligraphy in the Elementary School," n.d. [March–April 1949], HI, Trainor Papers, box 22, pp. 1–2.

96. Letter, Bundo to Loomis, 15 April 1949, HI, Trainor Papers, box 22, p. 1.

97. Ibid.

98. Ibid.

99. Memorandum, Pauline Jeidy to Loomis, 6 June 1949, HI, Trainor Papers, box 22, pp. 1–2.

100. Memorandum, Osborn to Loomis, 9 June 1949, HI, Trainor Papers, box 22, p. 2.

101. Memorandum, Nugent to Loomis, 15 July 1949, HI, Trainor Papers, box 22, pp. 1–2.

102. Memorandum, Nugent to Loomis, 12 September 1949, HI, Trainor Papers, box 19, p. 17.

103. CI & E, Education Division, *The Development and Present Status of Romaji in Japan,* December 1950, HI, Trainor Papers, box 19, p. 17.

104. Ibid., p. 18.

105. Memorandum, Nugent to Loomis, 15 July 1949, HI, Trainor Papers, box 22.

106. See Takemae Eiji, "Sengo demokurashi to eigokaiwa," in Shiso no Kagaku Kenkyukai, *Kyodo kenkyu: Nippon senryo* [Joint study: occupied Japan] (Tokyo: Tokuma Shoten, 1972), pp. 131–46.

107. USEMJ, *Report,* p. 19.

108. Ibid., p. 17.

109. Ibid.

110. Ibid., p. 19.

111. Ibid.

112. Ibid.

113. Ibid., p. 20.

114. Memorandum, Nugent to MacArthur, "Proposed Indorsement to Letter from Commander General, Eighth Army," 21 September 1948, HI, Trainor Papers, box 16, p. 1.

115. Report of conference, Orr with Naito, 27 August 1946, HI, Trainor Papers, box 40, p. 1.

116. Memorandum, Trainor to Orr, 15 March 1947, HI, Trainor Papers, box 4.

117. Ibid.

118. See Loomis's proposal, "Suggestions for Redrafting the Bill for City and Prefectural Boards of Education," n.d., [Nov.–Dec.], HI, Trainor Papers, box 16.

119. Memorandum, Secondary Education Unit to Loomis, 3 January 1948, HI, Trainor Papers, box 16, p. 10.

120. Memorandum, Nugent to MacArthur, 21 September 1948, p. 1.

121. Intra-section memorandum, Orr to Nugent, "Conference With Mr. Morito," 29 June 1948, HI, Trainor Papers, box 16, p. 1.

122. Memorandum for the record, Orr to Nugent, "Conference With GS on Election of Local School Boards," 4 September 1948, HI, Trainor Papers, box 16, p. 1.

123. Memorandum, Nugent to MacArthur, 21 September 1948, p. 1.

124. Letter, Satterwhite to CI & E, 23 August 1948, HI, Trainor Papers, box 16, p. 1.

125. Memorandum for the record, Orr, "Information from Osaka Prefecture," 2 September 1948, HI, Trainor Papers, box 16.

126. Ibid.

127. See Japan, Ministry of Education, Acceptability Inquiry Board, "Board of Education Screening," 17 September 1948, HI, Trainor Papers, box 16.

128. Memorandum for the record, Orr to Nugent, 4 September 1948, pp. 2–3.

129. See a draft of reply to Ryder, enclosure tab C to memorandum, Nugent to MacArthur, 21 September 1948, HI, Trainor Papers, box 16.

130. Intra-section memorandum, Herbert Passin to Orr, 13 September 1948, HI, Trainor Papers, box 16, pp. 1–2.

131. Memorandum for the record, Orr, conference with Tanaka and Kora, 9 September 1948, HI, Trainor Papers, box 34.

132. Memorandum for the record, Orr, "Conference With Mr. Morito [Minister of Education] Relative to Election of School Boards," 14 September 1948, HI, Trainor Papers, box 16, p. 1.

133. Ibid.

134. R. B. Finn, "Problems in Japan's Educational Reform," 25 July 1949, submitted to William J. Sebald, US political adviser, enclosure to letter, Sebald to Dean G. Acheson, secretary of state, 27 July 1949, USNA 894.42/7-2649, p. 1.

135. See Media analysis, CI & E, Analysis & Research Division, *Political Analysis*, no. 212 (7 October 1948), HI, Trainor Papers, box 16.

136. Finn, "Problems in Japan's Educational Reform," p. 4. For a complete list of board of education members throughout Japan, see Japan, Monbusho [Ministry of Education], *Kyoiku iinkai geppo* [Monthly Report of the Board of Education] 1, no. 1 (July 1949):2–18.

137. Ibid., p. 6.

138. Memorandum, Osborne to Trainor, n.d. [late 1949 ?], HI, Trainor Papers, box 4.

139. Memorandum, Nugent to Loomis, 12 September 1949, HI, Trainor Papers, box 19, p. 1. Also, see memorandum, Loomis to Nugent, 2 September 1949, ibid.

140. Finn, "Problems in Japan's Educational Reform," p. 3.

141. Ibid., p. 9.

142. The Ministry of Education Establishment Law, promulgated on 31 May 1949, was another decentralization attempt on the part of CI & E. This law, however, gave the ministry the power of budget preparation.

143. A verbatim of the talk between the Tokyo Military Government team and the Tokyo School Board, 8 December 1948, HI, Trainor Papers, box 16, pp. 1–4.

144. Memorandum, Nugent to Orr, n.d. [December 1948 ?], HI, Trainor Papers, box 16.

145. Memorandum for the record, Trainor, conference with JTU representatives, 15 July 1948, HI, Trainor Papers, box 34.

146. See intra-section routing slip, 12 October 1948, HI, Trainor Papers, box 34.

147. Intra-section memorandum, Orr to Nugent, "Conference with Mr. Morito," 29 June 1948, pp. 1–2.

148. Memorandum for the record, Orr, "Conference with GS on Election of Local School Boards," 4 September 1948, HI, Trainor Papers, box 16, p. 3.

149. See Japan, Ministry of Education, "Main Points of the Law for the Establishment of the Ministry of Education, Science and Culture," 27 March 1948, HI, Trainor Papers, box 41. It was Education Minister Morito's idea; see his speech at Tokyo Forum, 17 October 1947, HI, Trainor Papers, box 21.

150. Memorandum for the record, Orr, 4 September 1948, p. 3. The Ministry of Education was well aware of the Government Section's wish. Resigning Education Minister Morito visited Mark T. Orr and said he was gravely concerned about GS's remarks. See Memorandum for the Record, Orr, 21 October 1948, HI, Trainor Papers, box 40, p. 1.

151. USEMJ, *Report*, p. 35.

152. SCAP, *Political Reorientation*, xxxi.

153. "Note on Conversation With Dr. T. Ueda of the Tokyo University of Commerce," n.d. [perhaps soon after the Occupation began or late 1945], HI, Trainor Papers, box 46, p. 1.

154. USEMJ, *Report*, p. 35.

155. For a detailed description, see SCAP, *Education in the New Japan*, vol. 1, pp. 267–68; see also SCAP, *Post-War Developments in Japanese Education*, vol. 1, pp. 319–20. The Ministry of Education had no jurisdiction over this association.

156. For instance, see Eells's speech, "University Accreditation in Japan," to the Tokyo Bar Association on 25 July 1947, HI, Trainor Papers, box 27.

157. See SCAP, *Education in the New Japan*, vol. 1, pp. 268–70; ibid., vol. 2, pp. 103–104. The Ministry of Education supervised the University Chartering Committee.

158. For the text of the law, see SCAP, *Post-War Developments in Japanese Education*, vol. 2, pp. 129–47. The quotes are, respectively, articles 58 and 59.

159. For the text of this law, see ibid., vol. 2, pp. 59–84.

160. Finn, "Problems in Japan's Educational Reform," pp. 2–3.

161. Monbusho [Ministry of Education], *Gakusei Hyakunen-shi* [A hundred-year history of the educational system], vol. 2, (Tokyo, 1972), pp. 239, 256.

162. Ibid., p. 256. On 7 April 1949 Education Minister Takase visited Col. Nugent, chief of CI & E, and said that he would like to present legislation for the establishment of junior colleges. They met again on 11 April to discuss the subject. See Monbusho, "Nugent-shi to no kaidan yoshi—juniya kareji ni kansuru ken" [Verbatim of the conference with Mr. Nugent concerning junior college], *Sengo Kyoiku Shiryo*, section 1, item 39, Kokken.

163. Maeda, "The Direction of Postwar Education in Japan," pp. 418–19.

164. USEMJ, *Report*, p. 35.

165. Ibid., p. 37.

166. Ibid., loc. cit.

167. Ibid., pp. 37–38.
168. For a full text of the association's charter, see SCAP, *Education in the New Japan,* vol. 2, pp. 290–92.
169. See SCAP, *Post-War Developments in Japanese Education,* vol. 1, p. 331.
170. USEMJ, *Report,* p. 39.
171. Ibid., p. 40.
172. Ibid., p. 39.
173. Ibid.
174. SCAP, *Education in the New Japan,* vol. 1, p. 25. Also, see CI & E, Religions and Cultural Resources Division, "War Damage to National Treasures and Important Art Objects," n.d., TL, Bunce Papers, boxes 1 and 2.
175. See Nambara's ecstatic speech on 8 March 1947, in letter, Nambara to Nugent, 11 March 1947, HI, Trainor Papers, box 42.
176. See MacArthur's press release, 22 February 1948, MA, RG-5, box 106. For the report of the Library Mission, see Department of State Publication 3200, Far Eastern Series 27, 1948. In November 1950 the Japanese Ministry of Education submitted to CI & E a "List of Foreign Publication (Back Numbers) Desired by Universities in Japan," which ran to sixty-one pages of legal paper. See HI, Trainor Papers, box 4.

Chapter 10
1. Memorandum, Eells to Orr, 12 January 1948, HI, Trainor Papers, box 27.
2. Eells, "Suggested Plan for Publicly Controlled Universities in Japan," n.d. [12 January 1948 ?], enclosed with the foregoing.
3. Memorandum, Trainor to Orr, 21 January 1948, HI, Trainor Papers, box 27, p. 1.
4. Ibid., loc. cit.
5. Ibid., p. 2.
6. Ibid.
7. Ibid.
8. Memorandum, Eells to Orr, 26 January 1948, HI, Trainor Papers, box 27, p. 1.
9. Finn, "Problems in Japan's Educational Reform," pp. 10–11.
10. See Kaigo Tokiomi and Terasaki Masao, *Daigaku kyoiku* [University education] (Tokyo: Tokyo Daigaku Shuppan-kai, 1969), pp. 587–88.
11. POLAD, confidential memorandum of conversation with Nambara, 27 December 1947, p. 2. Nambara believed this decentralization plan was instigated not by CI & E but by the Government Section. He was wrong.
12. See Eells's second draft, 5 June 1948, HI, Trainor Papers, box 27.
13. Letter, Nambara to Orr, 15 July 1948, ibid.
14. See "On the Proposal to Establish Boards of Trustees in National Universities—A Composite Statement of the Opinions," n.d., ibid.
15. Finn, "Problems in Japan's Educational Reform," p. 5.
16. Ibid., p. 13.
17. Ibid., p. 5.
18. See Kaigo and Terasaki, *Daigaku kyoiku,* pp. 588–609.

19. For a fuller statement of Sebald, see SCAP, *Education in the New Japan*, vol. 2, pp. 16–23. Quotes are from p. 22.

20. Ibid., p. 19.

21. Memorandum, Orr to Nugent, 12 February 1947, HI, Trainor Papers, box 16, p. 1.

22. Memorandum, Orr to Nugent, 17 February 1947, ibid., p. 1.

23. Japan, Ministry of Education, "Takase daijin to ESS Chief Marquat to no kaidan yoshi" [Verbatim of the conference between Minister Takase and ESS Chief Marquat], secret verbatim, 7 April 1949, *Sengo Kyoiku Shiryo*, section 1, item 39, Kokken.

24. Finn, "Problems in Japan's Educational Reform," p. 16.

25. See Japan, Ministry of Education, *Bricks Without Straw*; vol. 1, *Description*, vol. 2, *Photographs*; 15 September 1950, HI, Trainor Papers, box 1. See also ibid., *The Condition of School in the Local Districts Suffering from the Shortage of School-Rooms*, two vols., n.d., HI, Trainor Papers, box 2.

26. Letter, Carr to Patterson, 19 March 1946, USNA, Diplomatic Section, no document number.

27. *Report of the US Education Mission to Germany*, Department of State Publication 2664, European Series 16 (Washington, DC: US Government Printing Office, 1946), p. 1 (hereafter cited as USEMG, *Report*).

28. USEMJ, *Report*, p. 8.

29. USEMG, *Report*, p. 1.

30. For a full text, see FEC, *Activities of the Far Eastern Commission, February 26, 1946–July 10, 1947*, pp. 94–97.

31. For a full text of the press release, see SCAP, *Education in the New Japan*, vol. 2, pp. 13–15.

32. University of Washington, Institute of International Affairs, *Report of the United States Cultural Science Mission to Japan* [January 1949] (Seattle, Wash.: The Institute, August 1949), p. 1 (hereafter cited as USCSMJ, *Report*).

33. Check list, Nugent to C-in-C [MacArthur], 11 February 1949, MA, RG-5, box 106.

34. USCSMJ, *Report*, p. 66.

35. Ibid.

36. Japan, Ministry of Education, *Guide to New Education in Japan*, vol. 1, part A, *Fundamental Problems of the Establishment of New Japan* (Tokyo, 21 May 1946). Vol. 1 dealt with the theory and aims of the new education, while vol. 2 described more specific teaching materials and techniques. Only vol. 1 will be discussed here. Hereafter it will be cited as *Guide*. For a full Japanese text, see Igasaki Akio and Yoshihara Koichiro, *Sengo kyoiku no genten 1* [Original materials of postwar education], (Tokyo: Gendaishi Shuppan Kai, 1975), pp. 39–159.

37. See Monbusho, *Gakusei Hyakunen-shi*, vol. 1, pp. 688–89.

38. See Japan, Ministry of Education Publication List, 1945–1949, HI, Trainor Papers, box 4.

39. *Guide*, unpaged.

40. Ibid.

41. Ibid., p. 9.

42. Ibid.

43. Ibid., p. 3.

44. Ibid.

45. Ibid., p. 4.
46. Ibid.
47. As the mission itself graciously noted. See USEMJ, *Report,* p. 8.
48. *Guide,* p. 4.
49. Ibid., pp. 4–5.
50. Ibid., p. 5.
51. Ibid., p. 6.
52. Ibid.
53. Ibid., p. 7.
54. Ibid., pp. 6–7.
55. Ibid., p. 7.
56. Ibid., p. 8.
57. Ibid., pp. 51–52.
58. Ibid., p. 52.
59. Ibid., p. 56.
60. Ibid., p. 64.
61. Ibid., pp. 19–20.
62. Tanaka, "Kyoiku to Sekaikan," 1 March 1946, in Tanaka, *Kyoiku to seiji,* p. 112.
63. See a newspaper article enclosed in letter, Woodward to Benton, 8 April 1946, USNA Diplomatic Section, no document number.
64. Letter, Helen I. Kennedy to the Emperor, 10 April 1946, USNA 894.0017/7-1146.
65. Telegram, commander-in-chief, Pacific, to Stoddard, 6 August 1946, USNA 894.001/8-1046.
66. Letter, Stoddard to Benton, 10 August 1946, USNA 894.001/8-1046, pp. 1–2; also, see letter, Stoddard to Vining, 10 August 1946, USNA 894.001/8-1046.
67. Letter, Benton to Stoddard, 20 August 1946, USNA 894.001/8-1046.
68. Secret office memorandum, Butterworth to Secretary of State Acheson, 17 February 1949, USNA 894.001/2-1749.
69. Personal and secret letter, Butterworth to Sebald, 17 February 1949, USNA 894.0111/2-1749, pp. 1–2.
70. For an excellent biographical study of Mori Arinori, see Ivan Parker Hall, *Mori Arinori* (Cambridge, Mass.: Harvard University Press, 1973).
71. Letter, Counts to Benton, 9 May 1946, USNA 894.42A/5-946.
72. See a newspaper article enclosed in letter, Woodward to Benton, 8 April 1946, USNA Diplomatic Section, no document number.
73. Letter, Counts to the author, 24 May 1974.

Chapter 11
1. See TL, PS File, Foreign Affairs, box 182.
2. Kawai, *Japan's American Interlude,* p. 211.
3. Walter Crosby Eells, *Communism in Education in Asia, Africa and the Far Pacific* (Washington, DC: American Council on Education, 1954), p. 2 (hereafter cited as Eells, *Communism in Education*).
4. Yoshida, *Memoirs,* pp. 232–33.

5. *The New York Times*, 20 March 1947.

6. Letter, Tsarapkin to Acheson, 31 March 1947, USNA 894.002/3-3147.

7. Letter, Acheson to Tsarapkin, 10 May 1947, USNA 894.002/3-3147.

8. MacArthur's letter was released to the press on 23 July 1948 at Ashida's request. For a full text see enclosure to letter, Sebald to Secretary of State Marshall, 24 July 1948, USNA 894.017/7-2448.

9. Yoshida, *Memoirs*, pp. 232–33. For related documents see letter and enclosure, Sebald to Acheson, 10 August 1948, USNA 894.017/8-1048; and office memorandum, State Department, USNA 894.504/10-1848. For the State Department's internal discussion on the Japanese labor situation, see USNA, Confidential File, RG-59, boxes 924 and 934.

10. Coughlin, *Conquered Press*, p. 104.

11. Ibid., pp. 104–106. Matsuura gives his personal account of how the Red Purge was carried out in journalism: see Matsuura, pp. 221–44.

12. John Gunther, *The Riddle of MacArthur* (New York: Harper and Brothers, 1951), p. 159; Yoshida, *Memoirs*, pp. 234–35.

13. SCAP, *History of the Nonmilitary Activities of the Occupation 1945–1951*, USNA 65-4, monograph no. 11, "Development of Political Parties," pp. 64–65 (hereafter cited as SCAP, *Nonmilitary Activities: Political Parties*).

14. See Coughlin, *Conquered Press*, pp. 106–107; and Robert Fearey, *The Occupation of Japan, Second Phase: 1948–1950* (New York: Macmillan Co., 1950), p. 206.

15. For Yoshida's statement, see MA, RG-10, box 11.

16. Yoshida's speech of 4 September 1949, MA, RG-5, box 106.

17. Ibid.

18. Yoshida, *Memoirs*, p. 235.

19. Ibid.

20. C. A. Willoughby, Military Intelligence Section, GHQ, "Special Report: The Soviet Fraction in the Japan Communist Party," (secret), 25 October 1947, MA, RG-6. The quote is from Willoughby's brief to MacArthur (capitals in the original).

21. Ibid., "Special Report: The Japan Communist Party and the Cominform," (secret), 1 July 1948, MA, RG-6. The quote is from Willoughby's brief to MacArthur, which was dated 6 July 1948.

22. Yoshida, *Memoirs*, pp. 233–34.

23. Quoted in Fearey, *Occupation of Japan*, p. 206. See *Asahi Shimbun*, 3 May 1950, p. 1, for a full text in Japanese.

24. Yoshida, *Memoirs*, p. 233, 236.

25. Gunther, *Riddle of MacArthur*, p. 162.

26. SCAP, *Nonmilitary Activities: Political Parties*, p. 145.

27. Gunther, *Riddle of MacArthur*, p. 162.

28. Yoshida, "Statement of the Prime Minister," 4 June 1950, MA, RG-10, VIP File, Yoshida, 1950.

29. SCAP, *History of the Nonmilitary Activities of the Occupation 1945–1951*, USNA 65-4, monograph no. 7, "The Purge," p. 71 (hereafter cited as SCAP, *Nonmilitary Activities: The Purge*).

30. Letter, MacArthur to Yoshida, 6 June 1950, MA, RG-10, VIP File, Yoshida, 1950, pp. 1–2. Also, see SCAP, *Nonmilitary Activities: The Purge,* pp. 274–75.

31. *Yomiuri Shimbun,* 7 June 1950; see HI, Trainor Papers, box 17.

32. Yoshida, *Memoirs,* p. 238.

33. *Yomiuri Shimbun,* 7 June 1950.

34. Letter, MacArthur to Yoshida, 7 June 1950, MA, RG-10, VIP File, Yoshida, 1950, pp. 1–2. Also, see SCAP, *Nonmilitary Activities: The Purge,* p. 276.

35. *Akahata,* 7 June 1950; for the translation, see HI, Trainor Papers, box 17.

36. For top-secret policy discussion memoranda of the US government see Papers of Dean Acheson, TL, box 65.

37. Letter, MacArthur to Yoshida, 26 June 1950, MA, RG-10, VIP File, Yoshida, 1950.

38. Secret telegram, Sebald to the State Department, 6 July 1950, MA, RG-9, box 83.

39. Yoshida, *Memoirs,* p. 241.

40. Secret telegram, Sebald to the State Department, 19 July 1950, MA, RG-9, box 83.

41. Quoted in Eells, *Communism in Education,* pp. 23–24; the data came from Floyd Shacklock, *Which Way Japan* (New York: Friendship Press, 1949).

42. Eells, "Activities of Education Division Countering Communism," a draft, n.d. [1951 ?], HI, Trainor Papers, box 45, p. 2.

43. Check list, Nugent to Col. Bunker in the Office of Commander-in-Chief, 30 December 1948, MA, RG-5, box 106.

44. Memorandum, Bell to Orr, 21 April 1947, HI, Trainor Papers, box 45, p. 2.

45. Memorandum, Bell to Orr, 13 April 1948, ibid., box 45.

46. Memorandum, Bell to Orr, 16 July 1948, ibid., p. 1.

47. Ibid., loc. cit.

48. Ibid., p. 2.

49. Check list, Nugent to Col. Lawrence Bunker [MacArthur's aide], 30 December 1948, MA, RG-5, box 106.

50. Check list, Whitney, Government Section, to Nugent, CI & E, 16 August 1948, HI, Trainor Papers, box 45.

51. The *Primer of Democracy* was in two volumes. Vol. 2 was published on 26 August 1949.

52. *Stars and Stripes,* 8 January 1949, p. 2.

53. Check list, Nugent to Whitney, 11 February 1949, HI, Trainor Papers, box 45. Also, see check list, Nugent to MacArthur, 11 February 1949, MA, RG-5, box 106.

54. See check list, Whitney to Nugent, 11 February 1949.

55. See check list, Whitney to Nugent, 24 March 1949.

56. Eells, *Communism in Education,* p. 24.

57. *Intelligence Review* (secret) no. 28 (22 August 1946), TL, NA File, box 17, p. 41.

58. Eells, "Activities of Education Division Countering Communism," p. 2. See GHQ, Civil Intelligence Section, "Special Report: Jap Repatriates from Soviet Territory—Communist Indoctrination," (secret) 2 February 1949, MA, RG-6, box 78.

59. Memorandum, O'Donovan to chief, Religions and Cultural Resources, n.d. (perhaps late 1948 or early 1949), HI, Trainor Papers, box 45.

60. Check list, Nugent to Office of C-in-C, 17 February 1949, MA, RG-5, box 106. For another critical article in *The Missionary Bulletin* (October–December 1948) by J. Roggendorf, S. J., see ibid.

61. Memorandum, Bell to Loomis, 24 March 1949, "Catholic Advisor's Review of *Primer*," HI, Trainor Papers, box 45.

62. Memorandum, Bell to Orr, 21 October 1948, HI, Trainor Papers, box 45, p. 1.

63. Memorandum, Orr to Nugent, 26 October 1948, HI, Trainor Papers, box 45.

64. See intra-section memorandum, CI & E, 18 August 1949, HI, Trainor Papers, box 64.

65. Memorandum, Orr to Nugent, 26 October 1948, HI, Trainor Papers, box 45.

66. SCAP, *Political Reorientation*, p. 770.

67. Memorandum, Orr to Nugent, 29 June 1948, HI, Trainor Papers, box 16, pp.1–2.

68. SCAP, *Nonmilitary Activities: Education*, p. 224.

69. Captain Paul T. Dupell, civil education officer, Tokyo Military Government, was perhaps the most active one: he tried to intimidate the candidates who were members of the Japan Teachers' Union. The union complained about him to the Education Division. See memorandum for the record, Joseph Trainor, meeting with representatives of Japan Teachers' Union, 7 September 1948, HI, Trainor Papers, box 34. See also Kanazawa Kaichi, *Aru shogakko kocho no kaiso* [Recollection of one elementary school principal] (Tokyo: Iwanami Shoten, 1967), especially pp. 66–68.

70. See Hatsu Gaku, no. 468, translated in *CI & E Bulletin*, supplement 1, HI, Trainor Papers, box 17, pp. 1–21.

71. For a full text of Dupell's speech, see news release, 4 February 1949, HI, Trainor Papers, box 17, pp. 1–7. On 10 May 1949 Military Government education officers and fifty Japanese educational leaders met at Nikko to formulate a policy against communism in the schools. The policy was entitled "Political Activities in the Educational Program." See memorandum, Eells to Loomis, 20 May 1949, and the policy document in both English and Japanese, HI, Trainor Papers, box 17.

72. Memorandum, Typer to Orr, Loomis, Trainor, 7 February 1949, HI, Trainor Papers, box 45, pp. 1–2.

73. Memorandum, Loomis to Orr, 24 February 1949, HI, Trainor Papers, box 45.

74. See, for a top-secret verbatim of their meeting, *Sengo Kyoiku Shiryo*, section 1, item 39, Kokken.

75. Memorandum, Nugent to the Education Division, 23 April 1949, HI, Trainor Papers, box 45.

76. Eells, *Communism in Education*, p. 24. Emphasis in the original.

77. Ibid., p. 29.

78. Memorandum, Eells and Typer to Loomis, 2 September 1949, HI, Trainor Papers, box 17, p. 1.

79. Eells, *Communism in Education*, p. 29. For a text of his speech, see *CI & E Bulletin*, 3 August 1949, pp. 9–12, HI, Trainor Papers, box 17; and Kaigo and Terasaki, *Daigaku kyoiku*, pp. 50–55 (in Japanese translation).

80. For a full text of the association's statement see Kaigo and Terasaki, *Daigaku kyoiku*, p. 56. In 1949 Nambara, president of Tokyo University, made a public statement affirming academic freedom. See, for a text, Shigeru Nambara, "Freedom of Learning and Responsibilities of a University Professor," 17 October 1949, HI, Trainor Papers, box 27.

81. Eells, *Communism in Education*, p. 29.

82. See *CI & E Bulletin*, 3 August 1949, p. 9.

83. Eells's speech at Hosei University, Tokyo, 29 October 1949. See, for an excerpt from the speech, enclosure, p. 2, in Eells, "Activities of Education Division Countering Communism."

84. Quoted in Eells, *Communism in Education*, pp. 28–29.

85. See Suzuki Eiichi, *Kyoiku gyosei* [Educational administration] (Tokyo: Tokyo Daigaku Shuppankai, 1970), pp. 80–85.

86. Eells, *Communism in Education*, p. 29.

87. Memorandum, Eells and Typer to Loomis, 2 September 1949, HI, Trainor Papers, box 17, p. 1.

88. Eells, "Activities of Education Division Countering Communism," p. 4; see also ibid., *Communism in Education*, p. 30.

89. US Department of State, Office of Intelligence Research, "The Campaign Against Communist Teachers in Japan," OIR Report no. 5087, 14 November 1948, pp. i–ii.

90. Confidential office memorandum, Marshal Green to U. Alexis Johnson, 23 November 1949, and Green's comment on the same memorandum, USNA 894.42/11-2349. President Nambara of Tokyo University was invited to attend the National Conference on Occupied Areas in Washington, DC, in December 1949. As Nambara had "expressed some pretty strong views against the dismissals" of Communist professors, the State Department met him for a discussion (see ibid.). For Nambara's speech on Japanese education at the National Conference on Occupied Areas, see Nambara, "The Ideals of Educational Reforms in Japan," 10 December 1949, HI, Trainor Papers, box 21. See also Nambara Shigeru, *Nippon to Amerika* [Japan and America] (Tokyo: Nissho Insatsu Kabushiki Kaisha, 1950).

91. Eells, "Activities of Education Division Countering Communism," p. 6.

92. See, for a verbatim of a round-table conference held before an audience of 2,000 students and faculty, *Akahata*, 24 May 1950, HI, Trainor Papers, box 17.

93. Eells, "Activities of Education Division Countering Communism," p. 6. See also ibid., *Communism in Education*, pp. 32–33.

94. Eells, "Activities of Education Division Countering Communism," p. 12.

95. Nambara, "Futatabi Beikoku Kyoiku Shisetsudan o mukaete" [Again welcoming the US Education Mission], *Sengo Kyoiku Shiryo*, section 3, item 19, n.d., p. 9. For a welcoming speech of Education Minister Amano, see *Sengo Kyoiku Shiryo*, section 3, item 18, Kokken.

96. *Report of the Second United States Education Mission to Japan* (Tokyo, 1950), pp. 11–12. The five members of the Second Mission had all participated in the First Mission: namely, H. Benjamin, G. W. Diemer, F. G. Hochwalt, P. A. Wanamaker, and W. E. Givens (chairman). See HI, Trainor Papers, box 75, for documents related to the Second Mission.

97. Japan Education Reform Council, *Education Reform in Japan: The Present Status and the Problems Involved* (Tokyo, 1950), p. 191.

98. Ibid.

99. *Asahi Shimbun*, 7 May 1950.

100. Ibid.

101. Eells, *Communism in Education*, p. 24.

102. "The Address of the Prime Minister Before the 8th Diet," 14 July 1950, MA, RG-10, VIP File, Yoshida, 1950, p. 3.
103. Secret telegram, Sebald to State Department, 19 July 1950, MA, RG-9, box 83.
104. Letter, Yoshida to MacArthur, 9 April 1950, MA, RG-10, box 11. His letter was handwritten.
105. For a secret verbatim of their conversation, see Japan, Ministry of Education, "Amano daijin, Whitney kyokucho sonota to kaidan no ken," 13 May 1950, *Sengo Kyoiku Shiryo*, section 1, item 40. *Sengo Kyoiku Shiryo* is in Japanese. For instance, this secret verbatim was recorded in Japanese, although Whitney did not speak it. The author has therefore retranslated statements by English-speaking participants from Japanese to English.
106. For a secret verbatim of their conversation, see ibid., "Amano daijin, Nugent kyokucho kaidan" [Conference between Minister Amano and Chief Nugent], 17 May 1950, *Sengo Kyoiku Shiryo*, section 1, item 40, Kokken.
107. Ibid.
108. See "List of Professors to be Purged," published in *Seinen Shimbun*, 26 September 1950, HI, Trainor Papers, box 17.
109. Top-secret memorandum, vice-minister to Minister Amano, "Kyoin no tekkaku shinsa no ken" [Concerning teachers' suitability], 24 October 1950, *Sengo Kyoiku Shiryo*, section 4, item 28.
110. Yoshida, *Memoirs*, p. 173.
111. Ibid.
112. Ibid.
113. John K. Emmerson, "Political Factors in the Present Japanese Situation," 8 February 1946, USNA 740.00119 Control (Japan)/2-2546, pp. 3–4.
114. Robert A. Fearey, "Reappraisal of United States Security Interests and Policies in Regard to Japan," 23 April 1946, USNA 740.00119 Control (Japan)/4-2346, p. 1.
115. Ibid., loc. cit.
116. Ibid., p. 20.
117. Ibid., p. 19.
118. *Intelligence Review* (secret) no. 28 (22 August 1946), TL, NA File, box 17, p. 41.
119. See SCAP, *Nonmilitary Activities: The Purge*, pp. 122, 127.
120. See letter, Yoshida to MacArthur, 28 December 1949; and letter, Yoshida to MacArthur, 12 October 1949; both in MA, RG-10, box 11.

Chapter 12

1. See top-secret memorandum for the president, "Subject: Peace Treaty Regarding Japan," 27 February 1946, TL, PS File, box 182.
2. SCAP, *Political Reorientation*, pp. 765-66.
3. *Intelligence Review* (secret) no. 14 (16 May 1946), TL, NA File, box 16, p. 38. The use of the Japanese administrative machinery was decided before the Occupation. See, for the State Department's recommendation to President Truman, "Political Economic Objectives of Military Government in Japan," 3 July 1945 (top secret), in "The Berlin Conference," TL, NA File, box 1, appendix to document 61, p. 1.
4. See top-secret office memorandum, Walton W. Butterworth and John Howard to Secretary of State Acheson, 15 November 1949, USNA 894.20/11-1549, p. 2.
5. Top-secret memorandum, Paul J. Mueller, major general, General Staff Corps, chief

of staff (for the commander-in-chief, MacArthur), to Joint Chiefs of Staff, 23 December 1948, TL, PS File, box 182, pp. 1–2.

6. See "Staff Analysis of Plans and Operations Division Study 'Limited Military Armament for Japan'," n.d. [December 1948 ?], enclosure to top-secret memorandum, Mueller to Joint Chiefs of Staff, 23 December 1948, ibid., pp. 3–4.

7. Top-secret letter, Jessup to John Howard, 14 November 1949, USNA 894.20/11-1449, p. 1.

8. Top-secret memorandum, "Position of Department of State on Reactivation of Japanese Armed Forces," 16 November 1946, enclosure to top-secret office memorandum, Butterworth and Howard to Acheson, 15 November 1949, pp. 1–3.

9. Yoshida, the speech of 4 September 1949, MA, RG-9, box 11.

10. See Acheson's Princeton Seminars, 13–14 February 1954, TL, Papers of Dean Acheson, box 76, p. 1188.

11. US Department of State, top-secret memorandum of conversation, "Subject: Japanese Peace Treaty," 24 April 1950, TL, Acheson Papers, box 65, p. 3.

12. Ibid., p. 2.

13. Ibid., p. 4.

14. US Department of State, top-secret memorandum of conversation, "Subject: Japanese Peace Treaty," 15 December 1949, TL, Acheson Papers, box 64, pp. 1–2. Philip Jessup and W. Butterworth were also present.

15. US Department of State, top-secret memorandum of conversation, "Subject: Japanese Peace Treaty," 24 April 1950, TL, Acheson Papers, box 65, p. 1.

16. Ibid., p. 2.

17. Ibid., p. 3.

18. Ibid.

19. Ibid., p. 4.

20. Ibid., p. 5.

21. Ibid., p. 6.

22. Ibid.

23. Ibid.

24. Ibid., p. 3.

25. Letter, MacArthur to Yoshida, 8 July 1950, MA, RG-10, VIP File, Yoshida, 1950, p. 2.

26. "The Address of the Prime Minister Before the 8th Diet," 14 July 1950, MA, RG-10, VIP File, Yoshida, 1950, p. 3.

27. Top-secret memorandum for the president, Acheson and Marshall to the president, 9 January 1951, TL, PS File, box 182.

28. Top-secret letter, Truman to Dulles, 10 January 1950, TL, PS File, box 182, pp. 1–2.

29. Ibid., p. 2.

30. "Report of Prime Minister Shigeru Yoshida to the Diet on the Japanese-American Conversations," 12 February 1951, MA, RG-10, VIP File, Yoshida, 1951, pp. 1–3. A copy of his speech was first submitted to MacArthur for review and comment.

31. US Senate, *Military Situation*, part 1, 4 May 1951, p. 143.

32. See Acheson's Princeton Seminars, 13–14 February 1954, TL, p. 1292.

33. Ibid.

34. Ibid., p. 1294–95.
35. Ibid., p. 1295.
36. Ibid., p. 1296.
37. Ibid., p. 1297.
38. Ibid.
39. See *New York Times*, 28 August 1950, p. 1, col. 6, and p. 3, col. 2.
40. Letter, Truman to MacArthur, 24 October 1950, MA, RG-10, VIP File, Harry Truman.
41. Letter, MacArthur to Truman, 30 October 1950, ibid.
42. Top-secret memorandum by Secretary Acheson, "Meeting with the President, Subject: President's Proposed Trip to Hawaii," 9 October 1950, TL, Acheson Papers, box 65. Truman went to Wake instead of Hawaii.
43. Top-secret telegram, Joint Chiefs of Staff to MacArthur, 29 December 1950, MA, RG-9, box 112.
44. For a more detailed chronology with full texts of pertinent documents see US Senate, *Military Situation*, 17 August 1951, part 5, pp. 3571–72, and appendix.
45. Ibid., 3 May 1951, part 1, p. 26.
46. *New York Times*, 11 April 1951, pp. 1, 8.
47. Letter, Yoshida to MacArthur, 14 April 1951, MA, RG-1, box 10.
48. Dean Acheson, *Present At The Creation: My Years in the State Department* (New York: W. W. Norton and Co., 1969), p. 357. For the full text of his speech see *Department of State Bulletin* 22 (23 January 1950):111–18; and for related articles see *New York Times*, 13 January 1950, pp. 1–2.
49. Acheson, ibid.
50. Ibid., p. 358.
51. Ibid.
52. See Acheson's Princeton Seminars, 14 March 1954, TL, Acheson Papers, box 76, p. 1386.
53. Letter, Yoshida to MacArthur, 13 July 1951; see also letter, Yoshida to MacArthur, 7 August 1951; both in MA, RG-10, VIP File, Yoshida, 1951.
54. Telegram, MacArthur to Yoshida, 20 August 1951, ibid.
55. Letter, Robert G. MacKendrick, Pennsylvania, to Truman, 27 August 1951, TL, RG-197, box 687.
56. Personal and confidential letter, Atcheson to the president, 19 June 1947, TL, PS File, box 182, pp. 4–5.
57. Telegram, Yoshida to MacArthur, 10 September 1951, MA, RG-10, VIP File, Yoshida, 1951.
58. Memorandum for the president, Ridgway to the president, 22 May 1952, TL, PS File, box 182. Yoshida said this two days before Ridgway left Japan for the United States for good.
59. Yoshida, *Memoirs*, p. 241.
60. Ibid., p. 232.

Summary and Conclusion
1. See *Mainichi Nenkan 1975*, p. 338; *Jiji Nenkan 1975*, pp. 176–77.

Selected Bibliography

A Comment on the Archival Materials and the News Media Sources

For the past several years the US government has been declassifying fascinating documents of the 1940s and early 50s with remarkable thoroughness. Without this admirable policy of declassification this book could not have been written. Voluminous State Department papers at the US National Archives (Washington, DC) provided me with valuable insight into the highest foreign policy-making machinery of the US government. The State Department papers also contain the frequent dispatches of the Office of United States Political Adviser (POLAD, political adviser to MacArthur) from Tokyo. The POLAD dispatches conveyed detailed, gripping information directly to the White House and secretary of state. Rich archival materials at the Harry S. Truman Library (Independence, Missouri) have rarely been utilized until now, partly because security classification was removed only recently and partly because students of the US Occupation neglected to visit there. The Truman Library holds a massive, exciting collection that includes President Truman's papers, the President's Secretary's File, the Naval Aide File, Dean Acheson's papers, other cabinet members' letters and memoranda, the

OSS reports "For the Eyes of the President Only," and the CIA's assessments of the world situation. Many boxes and files at the MacArthur Archives (Norfolk, Virginia) are filled with an abundance of precious primary documents. MacArthur's lively telegram correspondence with the Department of Army and Joint Chiefs of Staff reveals his administration of occupied Japan in the most intimate detail. The Hoover Institution on War, Revolution and Peace (Stanford, California) has the scarcely used papers of Joseph C. Trainor, who served in the Civil Information and Education (CI & E) Section of SCAP–GHQ. He collected, it appears, every letter, memorandum, and report that crossed his desk, and his collection is, to put it mildly, vast. *Sengo Kyoiku Shiryo* (Postwar Education Materials) at Kokuritsu Kyoiku Kenkyu-jo (National Institute for Educational Research, Tokyo) is a careful compilation of rare original Japanese documents on the educational reforms during the Occupation. The documents include, for instance, top-secret verbatims of conversations between the Japanese minister of education and the CI & E chief on various controversial subjects. By interweaving Trainor's papers and those Japanese documents I have tried to show how the most revolutionary reforms Japan had ever experienced became a drama of two cultures struggling for supremacy.

In addition to the archival materials, the following news media publications proved to be excellent, often invaluable, sources of pertinent information: *Akahata* (Red Flag, the daily newspaper published by the Japanese Communist Party), *Asahi Nenkan* (Asahi Yearbook), *Asahi Shimbun* (a national daily newspaper), *Mainichi Nenkan* (Mainichi Yearbook), *Jiji Nenkan* (Jiji Yearbook), and *Monbu Jiho* (Ministry of Education Bulletin).

This bibliography is limited primarily to sources cited in the notes. Not all individual titles of archival documents and reports are given here. Such archival materials will be found listed under the name of the city where the archive is located, e.g., materials in the US National Archives are listed under "Washington, DC." Official publications are listed under the name of the country in question, e.g., Japanese government publications under "Japan." One US government report, the original of which I could not trace, has been listed under "University of Washington," which issued a reprint.

Akahata (Red Flag), 1928–. Tokyo: Japanese Communist Party, Central Committee, Bureau of Publication. A daily newspaper.

Asahi Nenkan (Asahi Yearbook), 1925–. Tokyo: Asahi Shimbun-sha. Annual.

Asahi Shimbun (Asahi Newspaper), 1888–. Tokyo: Asahi Shimbun-sha. A daily newspaper.

ATKINSON, CARROLL. "Japanese Education Is Getting Revised—à la America!" *School and Society,* 17 August 1946, pp. 115–16.

BEARSLEY, W. G. *The Meiji Restoration.* Stanford, Calif.: Stanford University Press, 1972.

BAERWARD, HANS H. *The Purge of Japanese Leaders Under the Occupation.* University of California Publications in Political Science, vol. 8. Berkeley, Calif.: University of California Press, 1959.

BLACKETT, P.M.S. *Fear, War, and the Bomb.* New York: Whittlesey House, 1948.

BUTOW, ROBERT J. C. *Tojo and the Coming of War.* Stanford, Calif.: Stanford University Press, 1972. First published by Princeton University Press in 1961.

BYRNES, JAMES F. *Speaking Frankly.* New York: Harper and Brothers, 1947.

CENTRE FOR EAST ASIAN CULTURAL STUDIES. *The Meiji Japan Through Contemporary Sources.* 3 vols. Tokyo: The Centre, 1969–72.

COUGHLIN, WILLIAM J. *Conquered Press: The MacArthur Era in Japanese Journalism.* Palo Alto, Calif.: Pacific Books, 1952.

Domei Jiji Nenkan (Domei Jiji Yearbook), 1919–44, 1947–. Tokyo: Jiji Tsushinsha.

DORE, RONALD. *Education in Tokugawa Japan.* Berkeley, Calif.: University of California Press, 1965.

EELLS, WALTER CROSBY. *Communism in Education in Asia, Africa and the Far Pacific.* Washington, DC: American Council on Education, 1954.

EMMERSON, JOHN K. *The Japanese Thread: A Life in the US Foreign Service.* New York: Holt, Rinehart and Winston, 1978.

FEAREY, ROBERT A. *The Occupation of Japan, Second Phase: 1948–1950.* New York: Macmillan Co., 1950.

GLAZIER, KENNETH M., JR. "The Decision to Use Atomic Weapons Against Hiroshima and Nagasaki." *Public Policy* 18, no. 4 (summer 1970): 463–516.

GUNTHER, JOHN. *The Riddle of MacArthur.* New York: Harper and Brothers, 1951.

HALL, IVAN PARKER. *Mori Arinori.* Cambridge, Mass.: Harvard University Press, 1973.

HALL, JOHN W. AND JANSEN, MARIUS B. *Studies in the Institutional History of Early Modern Japan.* Princeton, NJ: Princeton University Press, 1968.

HALL, ROBERT KING. *Education for a New Japan.* New Haven, Conn.: Yale University Press, 1949.

HAROOTUNIAN, HARRY D. *Toward Restoration: The Growth of Political Consciousness in Tokugawa Japan.* Berkeley, Calif.: University of California Press, 1970.

HOSHINO YASUSABURO. *Sengo Nippon no kyoiku to kenpo* [Postwar Japanese education and constitution]. Tokyo: Shin Hyoron, 1971.

IKAZAKI AKIO. *Daigaku no jiji no rekishi* [History of university autonomy]. Tokyo: Shin Nippon Shuppan-sha, 1965.

—— AND YOSHIHARA KOICHIRO. *Sengo kyoiku no genten* [Original materials of postwar education]. Vol. 1. Tokyo: Gendaishi Shuppan-kai, 1975.

INDEPENDENCE, MISSOURI. Harry S. Truman Library. Naval Aide File, President's Secretary's File, Miscellaneous Material File, Papers of Dean Acheson, 1945–52.

JANSEN, MARIUS B. (ed.). *Changing Japanese Attitudes Toward Modernization.* Princeton, NJ: Princeton University Press, 1965.

JAPAN. The Japan Education Reform Council. *Education Reform in Japan: The Present Status and the Problems Involved.* Tokyo: The Council, 1950.

——. Monbusho [Ministry of Education]. *Gakusei hayakunen-shi* [A hundred-year history of the educational system]. 2 vols. Tokyo, 1972.

——. *Nihon ni okeru kyoiku kaikaku no shinten* [Progress of educational reforms in Japan]. Tokyo, August 1950. This is the Ministry of Education's report to the Second US Education Mission.

——. ——. Secretariat. *Shusen kyoiku jimu shori teiyo* [Handbooks of postwar educational affairs]. 4 vols. Tokyo: Ministry of Education, 1945–50.

Japan Biographical Encyclopedia and Who's Who, 1964–65. 3d ed. Tokyo: The Rengo Press, 1965.

KAIGO TOKIOMI AND TERASAKI MASAO. *Daigaku kyoiku* [University education]. Tokyo: Tokyo Daigaku Shuppankai, 1969.

KANAZAWA KAICHI. *Aru shogakko kocho no kaiso* [Recollection of one elementary school principal]. Tokyo: Iwanami Shoten, 1967.

KANDEL, I. L. "The Revision of Japanese Education." *School and Society*, 24 August 1946, p. 134.

KAWAI, KAZUO. *Japan's American Interlude.* Chicago: University of Chicago Press, 1960.

KYODO TSUSHIN-SHA, ed. *Konoe nikki* [Konoe diary]. Tokyo: Kyodo Tsushin-sha, 1968.

LEWE VAN ADUARD, E. J. *Japan from Surrender to Peace.* New York: Frederick A. Praeger, 1954.

LIFTON, ROBERT. *Death in Life: Survivors of Hiroshima.* New York: Random House, 1967.

MACARTHUR, DOUGLAS. *Reminiscences.* New York: McGraw-Hill, 1964.

MAEDA TAMON. "The Direction of Postwar Education in Japan." *Japan Quarterly* 3 (1956):414–25.

Mainichi Nenkan (Mainichi Yearbook), 1920–. Osaka: Mainici Shimbun-sha.

MARUYAMA, MASAO. *Thought and Behavior in Modern Japan.* Edited by Ivan Morris. London: Oxford University Press, 1963.

MATSUURA SOZO. *Senryo-ka no genron dan-atsu* [Suppressed freedom of speech during the US Occupation of Japan]. Tokyo: Gendai Janarizuma Shuppansha, 1969.

Monbu Jiho (Ministry of Education Bulletin), 1920–. Tokyo: Ministry of Education.

NAKAYAMA KENICHI. *Gendai shakai to chianho* [Modern society and public peace laws]. Tokyo: Iwanami Shoten, 1970.

NAMBARA SHIGERU. *Nippon to Amerika* [Japan and America]. Tokyo: Nissho Insatsu Kabushiki Kaisha, 1950.

NISHIMOTO MITOJI. "Educational Change in Japan After the War." *Journal of Educational Sociology* 26 (1952):16–26.

NORFOLK, VIRGINIA. MacArthur Memorial, MacArthur Archives, 1945–52, Record Groups 4, 5, 6, 9, 10, 25.

PACIFIC WAR RESEARCH SOCIETY. *Japan's Longest Day.* Tokyo: Kodansha International, 1968. Originally published in Japanese as *Nihon no ichiban nagai hi.* Tokyo: Bungei Shunju, 1965.

PYLE, KENNETH B. *The New Generation in Meiji Japan: Problems of Cultural Identity 1885–1895.* Stanford, Calif.: Stanford University Press, 1969.

REISCHAUER, EDWIN O. *The United States and Japan.* 3rd ed. New York: Viking Press, 1967.

ROVERE, RICHARD H., AND SCHLESINGER, ARTHUR, JR. *The MacArthur Controversy and American Foreign Policy.* New York: Farrar, Straus, and Giroux, 1965.

SANICHI SHOBO HENSHUBU, ed. *Shiryo sengo gakusei undo I, 1945–1949* [Materials: postwar student movement]. Tokyo: Sanichi Shobo, 1968.

SHERWIN, MARTIN J. "The Atomic Bomb and the Origins of the Cold War: US Atomic-Energy Policy and Diplomacy." *American Historical Review* 78, no. 4 (October 1973):945–68.

SHISO NO KAGAKU KENKYU-KAI, ed. *Kyodo kenkyu: Nippon senryo* [Joint study: occupied Japan]. Tokyo: Tokuma Shoten, 1972.

STANFORD, CALIF. Hoover Institution on War, Revolution and Peace. Joseph Trainor Papers, 1945–52.

STIMSON, HENRY L., AND BUNDY, McGEORGE. *On Active Service in Peace and War.* New York: Harper and Brothers, 1947.

SUPREME COMMANDER FOR THE ALLIED POWERS (SCAP), GHQ. *History of the Non-military Activities of the Occupation of Japan 1945–1951.* Fifty-five monographs, twelve not yet declassified, on different areas of activity.

———. Civil Information and Education Section (CI & E). *CI & E Bulletin.* 1949–50.

———. ———. *Education in the New Japan.* 2 vols. Tokyo, 1948.

———. ———. *Post-War Developments in Japanese Education.* 2 vols. Tokyo, 1952.

———. ———. Religions and Cultural Resources Division. *Religions in Japan.* Tokyo, March 1948.

———. Government Section. *Political Reorientation of Japan September 1945 to September 1948.* 2 vols.

SUZUKI EIICHI. *Kyoiku gyosei* [Educational administration]. Tokyo: Tokyo Daigaku Shuppankai, 1970.

TAKEMAE EIJI AND AMAKAWA AKIRA. *Nihon senryo hishi* [Secret history of occupied Japan]. 2 vols. Tokyo: Asahi Shimbun-sha, 1977.

TAKEMORI KAZUO. *Taisho demokurashi no shi no nakade* [In the middle of the death of Taisho democracy]. Tokyo: Jiji Tsushin-sha, 1976.

TANAKA KOTARO. *Kyoiku to seiji* [Education and politics]. Tokyo: Kogakusha, 1946.

TOKUTAKE TOSHIO. *Kawariyuku kyokasho* [The changing contents of textbooks]. Tokyo: Shin Nippon Shuppan-sha, 1967.

TOKYO. Kokuritsu Kyoiku Kenkyu-jo, *Sengo Kyoiku Shiryo* [Postwar Education Materials], 1945–52.

TSUJI KIYOAKI, ed. *Shiryo: Sengo Nijunen-shi* [Materials: twenty-year history of postwar Japan]., Vol. 1, *Seiji* [Politics]. Tokyo: Nippon Hyron-sha, 1966.

UCHIDA KENZO. *Sengo Nippon no hoshu seiji* [Postwar Japanese conservative politics]. Tokyo: Iwanami Shoten, 1972. Originally published in 1969.

UNITED STATES. US Army. GHQ, Civil Intelligence Section. "Trends: Japan–Korea–Philippines." Secret biweekly report, 1945–50.

———. Central Intelligence Agency. *Review of the World Situation as It Relates to the Security of the United States.* 1947–.

———. Congress. Senate. *Military Situation in the Far East: Hearings Before the Committee on Armed Services and the Committee on Foreign Relations.* 82d Cong., 1st sess., 1951. Washington, DC: US Government Printing Office, 1951.

———. Department of State. *Activities of the Far Eastern Commission February 26, 1946–July 10, 1947.* Far Eastern Series 24 (1947).

———. ———. *Department of State Bulletin,* 1939–.

———. ———. *Foreign Relations of the United States Diplomatic Papers: The Conference of Berlin 1945.* 2 vols. Department of State Publication 7163 (1960).

———. ———. *Occupation of Japan: Policy and Progress.* Far Eastern Series 17 (1946).

———. ———. *Postwar Foreign Policy Preparation 1939–1945.* Department of State Publication 3580, General Foreign Policy Series 15 (1950).

———. ———. *Report of the Mission on Japanese Combines.* Far Eastern Series 14 (1946).

———. ———. *Report of Research and Analysis Branch,* 1945–52. The State Department took over the Research and Analysis Branch from the Office of Strategic Services when the latter was disbanded in September 1945.

———. ———. *Report of the United States Education Mission to Germany.* Department of State Publication 2664, European Series 16, (1946). Washington, DC: US Government Printing Office, 1946.

———. ———. *Report of the [First] United States Education Mission to Japan.* Department of State Publication 2579, Far Eastern Series 11 (1946). Washington, DC: US Government Printing Office, 1946.

————. Department of War (*after July 1947,* Department of the Army). Military Intelligence Division. *Intelligence Review.* 1945–.

————. Adjutant General's Corps. *Report of the Second United States Education Mission to Japan.* Washington, DC: US Government Printing Office, 1950.

————. National Security Council. *A Report to the National Security Council by the Executive Secretary on the Position of the United States With Respect to Soviet-Directed World Communism.* 30 March 1948.

UNIVERSITY OF WASHINGTON. Institute of International Affairs. *Report of the United States Cultural Science Mission to Japan* [Jan. 1949]. Seattle, Wash.: The Institute, Aug. 1949.

WARD, ROBERT. "The Origins of the Present Japanese Constitution." *American Political Science Review* 50, no. 4 (December 1956):980–1010.

————. "Reflections on the Allied Occupation and Planned Political Change in Japan." In *Political Development in Modern Japan,* edited by Robert Ward. Princeton, NJ: Princeton University Press, 1973. First published in 1969.

WASHINGTON, DC. US National Archives, Department of State Papers, 1945–51, including Papers of the Office of the US Political Adviser, (POLAD).

————. ————. POLAD. *Educational Affairs in Japan.* Monthly report, 1945–51.

WILLIAMS, WILLIAM APPLEMAN. *The Tragedy of American Diplomacy.* Rev. ed. Cleveland: World Publishing Co., 1962.

WITTER, LAWRENCE S. "MacArthur and the Missionaries: God and Man in Occupied Japan." *Pacific Historical Review* 40, no. 1 (February 1971):77–98.

WOODARD, WILLIAM P. *The Allied Occupation of Japan 1945–1952 and Japanese Religions.* Leiden, Netherlands: E. J. Brill, 1972.

YORK, HERBERT F. "The Debate over the Hydrogen Bomb." *Scientific American,* October 1975, pp. 106–13.

YAMADA FUTARO. *Senchu-ha fusen nikki* [A diary of a noncombatant war-generation man]. Tokyo: Kodan-sha, 1973. Vivid depiction of Tokyo in the last months of the war.

YOSHIDA SHIGERU. *The Yoshida Memoirs.* Translated by Kenichi Yoshida. London: Heinemann, 1961.

Index

About the Author

Toshio Nishi is a research fellow at the Hoover Institution. From 1977 to 1991, he was a postdoctoral fellow at Hoover Institution and the first recipient of the Paul and Jean Hanna Endowment Fellowship.

From 1991 to the present, Nishi has been a distinguished guest professor at Reitaku University in Japan. Nishi worked from 1968 to 1971 for J. Walter Thompson Company in New York and Tokyo as the first Japanese account representative. From 1985 to 1991, Nishi was a foreign correspondent for *NHK Journal*, a radio program on Japan's largest media system.

Nishi has written extensively on the U.S. military occupation of defeated Japan and contemporary Japan and Asia. His representative book in English is *Unconditional Democracy: Education and Politics in Occupied Japan, 1945–1952* (Hoover Institution Press, 1982; reissued in 2003).

His books in Japanese are: *Nichibei Konryokusen* (Battle over Japan's soul, Tokyo: Chuo Koron-shinsha, July 2003, 2nd printing), *Kuniyaburete MacArthur* (The invasion of MacArthur, Tokyo: Chuo Koron-shinsha, 1996, 6th printing, best-seller), *Fukoku Jakumin: Nippon*

(Wealthy nation, weak people: Japan, Reitaku University Press, 1996, 5th printing, best-seller), and *MacArthur no Hanzai* (The "crime" of MacArthur, Tokyo: Otemachi Books, 1983).

Nishi is working on several manuscripts: *Japan's Last Stand in the 21st Century* (in English), *Hearts of the Empire* (fiction in English), and an article entitled "Holy Ghost, Divine Greed, Slow Massacre: The Europeans in the 16th-Century Japan."

Nishi has been one of the most sought-after speakers on Japan's national speech circuit. He has been a member of the Board of Regents of Executive Forum of Japan since 2000. From 1997 to 1999, Nishi was a commentator for TV Tokyo. Nishi is chairman of the editorial board for *Kokkai News* (a news magazine on politics, Japan's oldest monthly magazine, running sixty-three consecutive years since 1940) and its monthly columnist.

Nishi has been awarded many scholarships and grants. From 1977 to 1985 he received a postdoctoral fellowship from the Hoover Institution. In 1977 he also received the prestigious Harry S. Truman Scholarship from the Harry S. Truman Library Institute in Missouri.

After earning a BA in literature from Kwansei Gakuin University in Japan in 1964, Nishi received his MA in Communications in 1968 and his Ph.D. in political studies of education in 1976 from the University of Washington at Seattle.

* * *

His hobbies: Fencing (1964 All Japan Intercollegiate Saber Champion; could not make the Olympic Team for Tokyo Olympics), orchid growing, survival camping (mauled by a giant moray eel on the Island of Kauai, but after numerous stitches, survived), cruising on California's beautiful back roads, and reading occasionally.